Facebook® Marketing

ALL-IN-ONE

FOR

DUMMIES®

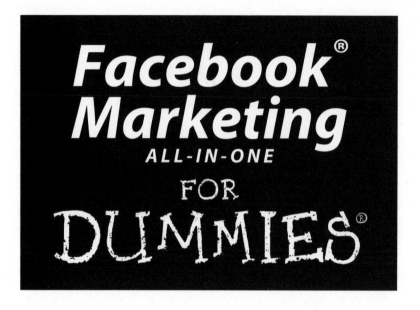

by Amy Porterfield, Phyllis Khare, and Andrea Vahl

WILEY

Wiley Publishing, Inc.

Facebook® Marketing All-in-One For Dummies®

Published by
Wiley Publishing, Inc.
111 River Street
Hoboken, NJ 07030-5774

www.wiley.com

Copyright © 2011 by Wiley Publishing, Inc., Indianapolis, Indiana

Published by Wiley Publishing, Inc., Indianapolis, Indiana

Published simultaneously in Canada

WILEY

About the Authors

Amy Porterfield: With a foundation in traditional marketing and content development, Amy has taken the social media world by storm and has mastered the art of engagement and online communities. She has worked in the marketing and event arena with Harley-Davidson Motorcycles as well as for six years with Peak Performance Coach and Entrepreneur Anthony Robbins. She has also had the opportunity to work with top real estate moguls, celebrity chefs, travel industry executives, Fortune 500 companies, and industry leader entrepreneurs. Amy is a regular contributor for the online magazine Social Media Examiner and helped build and grow its thriving Facebook Page that is now well beyond 45,000 Fans. She also manages Internet product launches for the online heavy-hitter Traffic Geyser. Amy is also the creator of the online program "The Simple Social Media Formula," a four-week online program designed to help entrepreneurs and small business owners create a social media strategy that's customized to fit their unique needs, goals, and style of doing business.

Phyllis Khare: Phyllis Khare is a marketing strategist and social media marketing trainer for businesses all over the country. She combines her almost 30 years of educational performance experience and her award-winning curriculum design with her deep research and application of social media into memorable social media marketing training programs. Phyllis is also the Social Media Director and a writer for iPhone Life magazine (www.iphonelife.com), which is a hard-copy and digital magazine for iPhone (iPad, iPod Touch) enthusiasts. Her regular column, *The Social Media Report,* is seen by more than 100,000 readers of the magazine. She is an innovative marketing consultant to artists, writers, and entrepreneurs all over the country, using advanced learning techniques to find the right mix of social media for their individual needs. You can learn more about her Socially Congruent Consulting at http://about.me/phylliskhare.

Andrea Vahl: Andrea Vahl is a social media coach, strategist, and speaker who consults with small and medium-sized businesses all over the world. She uses her improv comedy skills to blog as Grandma Mary, Social Media Edutainer. Learning social media is way more fun with Grandma Mary. You can learn more about Andrea and Grandma at www.AndreaVahl.com. Andrea is also the Facebook Community Manager for Social Media Examiner.

Dedication

This book is dedicated to my husband, Hobie. You're just crazy enough to think I can do anything, and that makes me the luckiest girl ever.

–Amy Porterfield

To my husband, Ron, my biggest fan, for always being there with words of appreciation and encouragement. I couldn't do this without you.

–Phyllis Khare

To my parents, Marilyn and Carl Sodergren, who taught me everything I know about being social, and to my wonderful family Steve, Devin, and Henry, who so generously supported me through this project.

–Andrea Vahl

Authors' Acknowledgments

I want to acknowledge my family (a.k.a. my cheerleaders). My husband, Hobie, my mom, Beverly, and my sister, Tracie — these three have given me the courage to go after everything I've ever wanted. And thank you to my dad, JB, for teaching me the work ethic needed to get the job done. I must also acknowledge my friend Gina. Her commitment to seeing me succeed surprises me daily. We must have been business partners in another lifetime (or maybe that's in the works in just a few years?!). I also want to acknowledge my two amazing co-authors, Phyllis Khare and Andrea Vahl. As a real testament to networking, this book opportunity came to me because I sat next to Andrea at a networking dinner. Two years later, she recommended me to Wiley Publishing, and the rest is history. As for Phyllis, she was the voice of reason throughout this whole process, and her insight and knowledge were invaluable from day one. In addition, a big acknowledgement to both Amy Fandrei and Susan Christophersen of Wiley Publishing. I know you both worked many late nights to see this book to completion, and not one minute of that hard work went unnoticed. I was lucky to work with you two lovely ladies. And last, I want to thank Facebook for changing, updating, tweaking, and fully revamping your platform almost weekly — it made for a very interesting editing process, to say the least!

–Amy Porterfield

I want to acknowledge my husband, Ron, my daughter, Celestial, and her husband Wes, and my son, Ron, for reminding me to stay the course and to keep my eye on the finish line! I want to also acknowledge the person who set this ball in motion, Ellen Finkelstein, who has published more than 28 books and revisions, for seeing the potential in me enough to suggest me to an editor at Wiley. I also want to thank her for being there for all sorts of Skype calls and urgent requests for mental and emotional support! You are the best. Along those lines of mental and emotional support, I have to deeply thank my two co-authors Amy Porterfield and Andrea Vahl. I consider you friends (and drinking buddies) for life! I want to thank the many Facebook Page owners (too many to count) who have graciously contributed to my understanding of how Facebook works by helping me navigate the almost daily changes of the Facebook environment for businesses. You are the true social pioneers! And finally, I want to thank Amy Fandrei and Susan Christophersen for their tireless attention to making this All-in-One get finished! Their dedication made the sometimes arduous process of editing an ever-moving target (Facebook) wonderful!

–Phyllis Khare

Publisher's Acknowledgments

We're proud of this book; please send us your comments at http://dummies.custhelp.com. For other comments, please contact our Customer Care Department within the U.S. at 877-762-2974, outside the U.S. at 317-572-3993, or fax 317-572-4002.

Some of the people who helped bring this book to market include the following:

Acquisitions and Editorial

Project Editor: Susan Christophersen

Acquisitions Editor: Amy Fandrei

Development Editors: Colleen Totz Diamond, Linda Morris, Melanie Nelson, Kathy Simpson, Susan Christophersen

Copy Editors: Teresa Artman, John Edwards, Susan Christophersen

Technical Editor: Michelle Oxman

Editorial Manager: Jodi Jensen

Editorial Assistant: Amanda Graham

Sr. Editorial Assistant: Cherie Case

Cartoons: Rich Tennant (www.the5thwave.com)

Composition Services

Project Coordinator: Sheree Montgomery

Layout and Graphics: Joyce Haughey, Corrie Socolovitch, Kim Tabor

Proofreaders: Melissa Cossell, BIM Indexing & Proofreading Services

Indexer: Rebecca Salerno

Publishing and Editorial for Technology Dummies

    Richard Swadley, Vice President and Executive Group Publisher

    Andy Cummings, Vice President and Publisher

    Mary Bednarek, Executive Acquisitions Director

    Mary C. Corder, Editorial Director

Publishing for Consumer Dummies

    Kathy Nebenhaus, Vice President and Executive Publisher

Composition Services

    Debbie Stailey, Director of Composition Services

Contents at a Glance

Table of Contents

Introduction

*O*ne thing we know for sure from writing this book is that Facebook loves change. The folks at Facebook love to change things up, tweak their platform, upgrade their programs, and above all, innovate each chance they get. This is great for all of us looking to use Facebook to grow our business, but not so great when writing a "how things work" book with Facebook marketing as the topic. On Facebook, how things work one day might not be how things work the next! The good news is that we were able to stay on top of all the changes and pack this book with the latest and greatest in Facebook marketing strategies.

With that said, Facebook's unwavering dedication to innovation is exactly why it is the social networking powerhouse it is today. With Facebook's constant growth and massive influence, it's obvious that Facebook's not just a flash-in-the-pan phenomenon. These days, you can't surf the Web, listen to the radio, watch TV, or even flip through a magazine without hearing or seeing something about Facebook.

Facebook represents a huge opportunity for your business. If you're in business of any kind, you absolutely should consider Facebook a key player in your marketing strategy. With more than 600 million active users, your ideal audience is highly likely to be spending time on Facebook. You have a huge opportunity to capture the attention and build relationships with the people who could potentially become your most loyal customers. When you are fully leveraging the power of Facebook, you can build an engaging Facebook presence, attract and engage quality customers, and quickly grow your business.

Whether you're a complete newbie on Facebook or looking to take your Facebook marketing to a new level, this book is for you. There are many roles you can play on Facebook, and this book will give you the tools to help you decide how Facebook will fit into your overall marketing plan.

You may decide that you want to use Facebook as a mini-hub, an extension of your own Web site where your Fans first go to get to know, like, and trust you. After you've created a solid relationship with your Fans, you can then encourage them to visit your Web site to learn more about what you have to offer. Or you might want to use Facebook as a robust customer service portal, a place where you answer client questions, help troubleshoot product challenges, and become the go-to source for all your clients' needs. Your opportunities are endless, and this book will help you understand which opportunities are right for your business.

How This Book is Organized

Facebook Marketing All-in-One For Dummies is divided into nine minibooks that will take you from understanding why Facebook is important for your business marketing strategy all the way through advanced marketing tactics and measurement.

Each minibook is designed to be a complete stand-alone guide to help you master the subject covered within. So you can read this book cover to cover or pick and choose the areas that interest you and dive right in. Here is a description of each minibook so that you can determine which ones will help you the most.

Book 1: Joining the Facebook Marketing Revolution

You might be wondering how Facebook can benefit your business. How do you get started and, more important, why? This minibook guides you to understand the potential that Facebook holds for any business and how to reap the rewards of a well-crafted Facebook marketing plan.

We lead you through the basics of searching and finding your audience on Facebook, defining your goals, and putting the measurement tools in place to monitor your return on your investment.

Book II: Claiming Your Presence on Facebook

Plant your flag and set up your Facebook Page in this minibook. Book II walks you through the setup process, including selecting a Page type and naming your Page, so that your business can start connecting with the 500 million people out there. You also get a complete tour so that you know how to add photos, edit your Page, and understand how to navigate all aspects of your Page.

Book III: Adding the Basics to Your Facebook Page

Find out all the different ways to post content to your Page including videos, links, and photos. You also learn how to add a custom iFrame Welcome Page to invite your visitors to Like your Page. You discover several different methods to add custom pages so that your Facebook Page is branded and stands out.

If you have a blog, you can automatically import the blog posts to help save you time. Connect your YouTube, LinkedIn, and Twitter accounts for a richer experience for your community.

Book IV: Building, Engaging, Retaining, and Selling to Your Community

Start out by building visibility to your Page through your existing customers and then find creative ways to connect to new Facebook users. This minibook gives you plenty of ways to engage your customers and basic rules for participating in the conversation in a meaningful way. You also find out how to expand your e-commerce and bring it onto your Facebook Page with apps and by building your own store.

Book V: Understanding Facebook Applications

Explore the world of Facebook applications and find out how they can integrate with your Page and make it a better place for your community. Look at the best existing applications to add and learn about creating your own branded application that can maybe even create a new stream of income for you.

Book VI: Making Facebook Come Alive with Events and Contests

In this minibook you learn the ins and outs of creating and marketing your Event. And if your Facebook Page needs a little fun, consider a contest to engage and grow your community. Learn about the different types of contests, how to follow Facebook's contest rules, and what applications can help you run your contest. Make sure you are getting the most out of your contest efforts with promotional strategies and results analysis.

Book VII: Advanced Marketing Tactics

Get ready for Facebook 201 in this minibook. Here, you learn how to create the ultimate "Facebook Experience" for your audience, including how to grow your Page, build social proof, and use the viral nature of Facebook to your advantage.

You find out how to use the Facebook social plugins to bring the Facebook experience to your own Web site. Also learn how to create real-time events on your Facebook Page by creating a live streaming video experience — one that will allow you to connect with your community in a much bigger way. This minibook also covers how to tap into mobile marketing with Facbeook Places and Facebook Deals.

Book VIII: Facebook Advertising

Looking to create a Facebook ad campaign? If so, this is the minibook for you. Find out how to design your campaign, allocate a budget, and split-test your ads so that you get the most bang for your buck. You also learn how to write a click-worthy ad that targets your specific client. Then dive into the report section to find out how well your ad performed.

Book IX: Measuring, Monitoring, and Analyzing

Here we bring it all home with the analysis of your Page data. Make sure you're measuring your efforts and setting realistic targets for your Facebook Page. Explore and understand the Facebook Insights section that will track your progress and compare the third-party measurement tools to see what is right for your business.

Conventions Used in This Book

We use a few specific conventions in this text for ease of comprehension. When we tell you type something (in a box or a field, for example), we put it in **bold.** When we provide a URL or refer to text that you see on-screen, we put it in a typeface that `looks like this.`

Icons Used in This Book

All through the book, special icons appear in the margin to point draw your attention to particular bits and pieces of information. The following descriptions demystify these graphics:

This icon signifies a trick to use or other bit of helpful information that you might find especially useful.

When you see this icon, try to hang on to what we tell you; it's important to keep in mind.

You want to pay especially close attention on the rare occasions when you see this icon.

We use this one sparingly; it indicates information that's safe to skip over but that you might find interesting.

Book I

Joining the Facebook Marketing Revolution

The 5th Wave · By Rich Tennant

"I hope you're doing something online. A group like yours shouldn't just be playing street corners."

Contents at a Glance

Chapter 1: Exploring Facebook Marketing

In This Chapter

✔ **Discovering Facebook's marketing potential**

✔ **Understanding the basics of Facebook marketing**

✔ **Looking at four key Facebook marketing strategies**

✔ **Mastering the art of Facebook engagement**

✔ **Examining Facebook's global market opportunities**

✔ **Seeing the benefits of selling from the Facebook platform**

*F*acebook is the most powerful social network on the planet. With more than 600 million active users, Facebook presents a unique opportunity to connect with and educate your ideal audience in a way that your Web site and your blog can't even come close to matching.

The reach of the Facebook platform has grown exponentially in the past few years and will only continue to get bigger. In fact, the number of marketers who say that Facebook is "critical" or "important" to their business has increased by 83 percent in just the last two years. Today, almost anyone or any company can find a following on Facebook. From big brands such as Starbucks to small, lesser-known mom-and-pop shops, Facebook's platform can turn a business into a living, breathing, one-to-one online marketing machine. Facebook is changing the game, and there's no better time than the present to jump on board.

In this chapter, we cover why Facebook should become a key marketing tool to help you grow your business. Specifically, we look at Facebook's massive marketing potential, its expansive ability to reach your ideal audience, and the core strategies you can implement today to seamlessly add Facebook to your marketing program.

Seeing the Business Potential of Facebook

We have good news and bad news for you when it comes to Facebook marketing. The bad news first: Facebook marketing isn't free. Sure, it doesn't cost actual dollars to get set up with a presence on Facebook, but it is sure to cost you both time and effort — two hot commodities that most business owners have very little of these days. You have to account for the time and energy it takes to plan your strategy, set it up, get yourself trained, execute your plan, build your relationships, and take care of your new customers after you start seeing your efforts pay off — all of which all goes to show that a lot of time and effort must go into creating a successful Facebook marketing plan, and your time and effort are anything but free. But here's the good news: This book was designed to help you streamline your Facebook marketing efforts and eliminate the guesswork that often goes into figuring out anything that's new and somewhat complex.

Facebook marketing can help you create exposure and awareness for your business, increase sales, collect market data, enhance your customer's experience, and increase your position as an authority in your field. However, before you can start to see real results, you first must determine why you're on Facebook.

If you take the time to ponder the following questions, you'll gradually begin to create a road map to Facebook marketing success:

✦ **Why do you want to use Facebook to market your business?** More specifically, what do you hope to gain from your use of Facebook, and how will it help your business?

✦ **Who is your ideal audience?** Get specific here. Who are you talking to? What are the demographics, needs, wants and desires of the person who will buy your products, programs or services?

✦ **What do you want your ideal audience to do via your efforts on Facebook?** In other words, what feelings, actions, or behaviors do you want your audience to experience?

You are not in the Facebook marketing business!

Remember this very important fact: You are *not* in the business of Facebook marketing. Your job is not to become an expert or master of Facebook. As you navigate this book, remember that your job is to be an expert at your business — and Facebook is a tool that you will use to do just that. Take the pressure off yourself to master Facebook marketing. This will make all the difference as you master the strategies outlined throughout these pages.

When you're clear about *why* you're on Facebook, you're better able to design a strategy that best fits your business needs. We explore many potential strategies through the course of this book, but for now — in the name of helping you better understand how you can use Facebook to market your business — here's a list of just a few of the opportunities that are at your fingertips when you embrace Facebook marketing:

✦ **Set up special promotions inside Facebook and offer special deals exclusively to your Facebook community.** For example, you could create a coupon that your visitors can print and bring into your store for a special discount.

✦ **Offer Q&A sessions in real time.** Your visitors can post questions about your niche, product, or service, and then you and your team can offer great advice and information to your Facebook community.

✦ **Highlight your Facebook Fans by offering a Member of the Month award.** You could choose and highlight one Fan who shows exemplary participation in your Facebook community. People love to be acknowledged, and Facebook is a fantastic platform to recognize your best clients and prospects.

✦ **Highlight your own employees with an Employee of the Month feature on your Facebook Page.** Profile someone who's making a difference at the company. You can include photos and video to make it even more entertaining and interesting to your audience.

✦ **Sell your products and services directly inside of Facebook.** Include a button that links your Fans to an electronic shopping cart to enable them to buy "in the moment." There are many opportunities to promote and sell your products and services on Facebook.

The preceding list is just a glimpse of what you can do inside of Facebook's powerful walls. Many more opportunities await you — but you'll have to read a few more of our minibooks to get acquainted with them.

Reaping the benefits for business-to-consumer companies

When it comes to business-to-consumer (B2C) companies, one of the greatest advantages of Facebook marketing is the ability to engage one-on-one with your ideal clients. By asking questions, encouraging conversations, and creating personal engagement with your customers and prospects, you can build relationships in a way that wasn't possible before social networking took the marketing world by storm.

Although we all know that consumer brands with big marketing budgets can attract millions of followers on Facebook, there is still room for the littler guys.

Here's a thought experiment: Rather than feel frustrated because your company can't compete with big-brand giants on Facebook, turn the success of those companies into an opportunity for you to model the best and learn from them. Here are four key strategies that the big B2C companies have adopted in their Facebook marketing strategies to help them stand out from the rest:

✦ **Acknowledge your fans.** The B2C giants on Facebook do a fantastic job of spotlighting their Fans. When Fans feel appreciated, they'll continue to engage with your Page. One great example of this is from Oreo, as shown in Figure 1-1.

Figure 1-1:
Oreo can "wow" its audience by creating unique experiences.

Oreo knows a thing or two about standing out. Its fun World's Fan of the Week campaign encourages fans to post photos for a chance to claim the coveted Fan of the Week spot. Oreo's Facebook Page has more than 9 million Fans, so those folks must be doing something right!

✦ **Know your audience.** When you get clear on who you're communicating with on Facebook, you're better able to create experiences around your audience's interest and likes. An example of a B2C company in tune with its audience is the team behind the Red Bull Facebook Page. This is evidenced in that Page's custom apps and unique content throughout the Page.

Red Bull knows what its audience will respond to best, and Red Bull delivers: for example, a series of online games for Fans, aptly called the Procrastination Station. The games are geared toward sports and high-impact competitions, as shown in Figure 1-2.

Figure 1-2:
Red Bull keeps it fun with its Procrastination Station on Facebook.

Going viral

When a video, article, or other piece of content goes *viral*, it means people are continually sharing that content through their online networks. For example, someone might post a funny video on YouTube. People start to pass it along to their friends by e-mailing the link, posting it on their Facebook Page, and tweeting about it. If a massive amount of people begin to share the video, it will spread to others like wildfire, therefore becoming what many call a viral sensation.

✦ **Mix up your media.** Facebook strategies that infuse a variety of media, including photos and video, often draw a bigger crowd. One example of this is Old Spice's use of video in an (in)famous Facebook campaign.

Old Spice was able to grab the attention of Facebook users with its Old Spice Guy videos, as shown in Figure 1-3. These videos showed a topless guy responding to Fans' silly and often hilarious questions and were quickly a viral sensation. When the two-day campaign ended, the Old Spice YouTube Channel had almost 8 million views and 616,000 Fans on Facebook. That's impressive!

✦ **Have fun.** Face it — most people log on to Facebook to have fun and connect with friends. Interacting with brands and businesses is not the #1 reason why people get on Facebook each day. That doesn't mean, however, that these users aren't a captive audience! The key is to infuse fun into your Facebook activity when appropriate.

Figure 1-3: Got a question for the Old Spice Guy?

Coca-Cola secured its spot at the top of many best-of-the-best Facebook Page lists with its fun, innovative promotions and playful, interactive features. For example, Coke's Summer Snapshot contest encouraged Fans to take photos of themselves holding their special Summer Coca-Cola cans. Figure 1-4 shows an example of a Fan photo. Notice how others can vote on the photos — which, of course, allows everyone to get in on the fun.

Photos are viewed more than anything else on Facebook. They go viral quickly because when a Fan posts a photo, that photo is sent to the news feeds of all of their friends. Hundreds of thousands of potential new Fans will see these photos.

When reviewing these four strategies illustrated by some well-known B2C companies, remember that you, too, can create these experiences for little or no cost. Again, model the best that's out there, and make the strategies work for your own business.

Figure 1-4:
A Fan photo serves as part of Coca-Cola's summer campaign on Facebook.

Reaping the benefits for business-to-business companies

We know that Facebook marketing works well for B2C business, but if you're a business-to-business (B2B) company, you might be wondering whether Facebook makes sense for your business. In short, the answer is yes! In fact, 41 percent of B2B companies have reported acquiring a customer through Facebook.

Not only can B2B companies incorporate the four key strategies mentioned in the previous section, but B2B companies also have a unique advantage over B2C when it comes to Facebook marketing: Facebook's platform is designed to support *exactly what* B2B companies need to be successful in attracting clients and securing sales.

To better explain this idea, here are three key factors that make B2B a perfect fit for Facebook marketing:

✦ **B2B has a smaller potential customer base.** This means that B2B companies don't have to constantly focus on growing their followers to hundreds of thousands, but instead can put the majority of their focus on nurturing the relationships they already have. Facebook is a platform that thrives on one-to-one relationships.

✦ **Buying decisions in B2B heavily rely on word of mouth and reputation.** Businesses looking to make a huge buying decision often want to know what their peers are doing and how they feel about a product or service. Facebook's open network allows people to see whom their peers are interacting with and what they are talking about at any given time, therefore making it easy to find out what others think about a product or service.

✦ **B2B has a higher average price point than most B2C businesses.** When the price of the product or service is considered high, the client is likely to seek out information and content to support buying decisions. On Facebook, content is king. The more a company can generate high-value content, the more likely it will attract the ideal client base and become a Facebook success story.

For B2B companies, connection, knowledge sharing, and reputation management are key ingredients to success. Facebook's unique platform can help optimize these key strategies.

Developing genuine relationships with customers and prospects

No matter whether your business is B2B or B2C, it all really comes down to one person talking to another. No one wants to interact with a faceless brand, business, or logo. We all want to buy from a friend — someone we trust and feel comfortable engaging with regularly.

Facebook allows us to move beyond the obstacles of tradition marketing (very one-sided) and instead communicate with our clients and prospects on a one-on-one level by putting a name to a face, making the entire exchange more human.

Creating one-to-one customer engagement

Engagement is crucial in mastering Facebook marketing. If you build rapport and can get your Facebook community talking, your efforts will go a long way.

It's one thing to broadcast a special promotion on Facebook, but it's an entirely different experience to ask your Fans a question related to your products and services and receive 50 responses from people telling you exactly how they feel about what you're selling. In many cases, this real-time engagement can be priceless! In Figure 1-5, the popular online shoe and clothing retailer, Zappos. com, asks its audience about winter fashion preferences.

Figure 1-5:
Ask
(a question),
and ye shall
receive.

Zappos.com How would you describe your fall/Winter Fashion? Sweaterrific, Hoodie-ful, Jeggings galore?

Fall/Winter Fashion Trends
www.zappos.com
Free shipping BOTH ways, 365-day return policy, 24/7 customer service. Millions of men's shoes, women's shoes, girl's shoes, boy's shoes, handbags, men's clothing, women's clothing, Uggs, Nike shoes!

One very successful Facebook marketing strategy is to ask your followers interesting questions. It's human nature that most of us enjoy talking about our likes and interests; therefore, encourage sharing by asking your Fans to express *their* thoughts about their likes and interests. It's a great way to increase Fan engagement.

Being able to provide prompt customer service

Before the days of social networking, a phone call, an e-mail, or a hand-written letter were just about your only options when it came to reaching out to your clients. Today, you can send a Tweet or a Facebook post to inform your customers of new features, benefits, or changes to your products or services. Social media allows you to get the word out quickly, making it easier for you to keep your customers informed and satisfied.

If you optimize your Facebook marketing experience, you can provide your customers a superior customer experience — a much richer experience than you've ever been able to offer before. Not only can you create a social media experience where you are keeping your customers informed, but you can also give them an opportunity to reach out to you as well.

Imagine this: You sell shoes. A client orders a pair of your shoes online and receives them in the mail. When the shoes arrive, they're the wrong pair. That client logs on to Facebook and posts this message:

> I just received my much anticipated pair of red stilettos in the mail . . . too bad the company messed up and sent me sneakers instead! I'm frustrated!

At first glance, you might think that a post like that would hurt your business. However, on social sites like Facebook and Twitter, you can turn a potentially bad post into an opportunity to gain a customer for life.

Imagine that you respond within just five minutes with this post:

> Julie, we are so sorry that you received the wrong pair of shoes! We are shipping your red stilettos overnight, and make sure to look for the 50% off coupon we included on your box as well. Two pairs of shoes are always better than one!

Here's what's great: The opportunity for real-time problem solving is powerful. You not only just saved a sale and made Julie a happy customer but also let anyone watching on Facebook see that you care about your clients and will go above and beyond to make them happy. This type of experience wasn't possible before social media came on the scene.

You can find out more about online tools that will help you monitor who is talking about you online in Book IX, Chapter 3. These tools will help you stay in the know and in tune with your customers.

In addition to proactively monitoring Facebook for customer service issues, many robust tools exist that you can use to create a virtual service desk directly inside Facebook. For example, Livescribe has incorporated a support desk directly into its Facebook Page. As you can see in Figure 1-6, you can ask the folks at Livescribe a question, share an idea, report a problem, or even give praise directly from that Facebook Page.

Customers commonly use social media sites to post questions or complaints. If you provide a designated place for support, you're likely to keep your customers happy and turn them into repeat buyers!

What's even more important is that others can see these posts. Fans and potential buyers can then go to this tab to get answers or see what others are saying about the products. It's another great way to educate fans about your products and services. In addition, this tool can cut down service calls when executed correctly, saving your company time and money.

Figure 1-6:
Check out the Livescribe Facebook support desk.

Previewing new products and services and opening a portal for consumer purchasing

Facebook's expansion into the e-commerce sector might forever change the way we shop. In the past, creating an e-commerce Web site took a lot of money and even more time. Today, Facebook's platform — interwoven with third-party apps — has allowed millions of businesses to showcase their products and services and sell them online. (To find out more about how third-party apps can be a part of your Facebook marketing strategy, check out Book V.)

When it comes to the kinds of shopping interfaces you can create on Facebook, you have two options:

✦ **A storefront:** Here's where potential buyers come to browse products. When users want to buy, they click the Buy button and are then taken to a separate, e-commerce–equipped Web site to finalize the purchase. Currently, this is the most popular interface; however, we'll likely see the second interface option (see next bullet) catch up soon.

✦ **A fully functioning store:** Your second interface option involves creating a full-blown store where shoppers can browse and purchase without leaving the Facebook environment.

One example of such a fully functioning store is Threadless, a company that sells custom t-shirts. Threadless has created a buying experience within Facebook where you can not only buy directly from that Facebook Page but also post comments about the t-shirts for all your friends to see, as shown in Figure 1-7.

When Facebook users post about products they love, the users' friends naturally want to know more. This curiosity creates viral exposure for your products and services.

Figure 1-7:
Threadless allows visitors to post comments directly inside the Facebook e-commerce platform.

Facebook offers an extremely valuable opportunity to showcase your products and services and create a new portal to sell your goods.

Using Facebook with the Global Market

Few would argue with the fact that social media, and Facebook specifically, are growing at a staggering pace. It's important to note that social media is not just exploding in the U.S. Online users in Australia, Japan, and Italy all show even stronger adoption of social media than Americans do. And those in China, Denmark, and Sweden are said to be adopting social media at the same usage rates as Americans. To give you a glimpse of the magnitude of Facebook's global reach, here are some statistics provided by Facebook as of November, 2010:

✦ More than 600 million active users are on Facebook.

✦ People spend more than 700 billion minutes per month on Facebook.

✦ One-half of Facebook's active users log on to Facebook in any given day.

✦ People interact with more than 900 million objects (Pages, Groups, Events, and community Pages).

✦ More than 150 million people engage with Facebook on external Web sites every month.

✦ More than 200 million active users access Facebook through their mobile devices, and people who use Facebook on their mobile devices are twice as active on Facebook as nonmobile users.

✦ Young adults continue to be the heaviest Facebook users; however, their growth is not nearly as rapid as those 50 years old and older. This group is the fastest-growing demographic on Facebook today.

✦ From 2008 to 2009, Facebook's international audience grew from 34 million people to 95 million. Today, this number is coming up on 400 million, and there are more than 100 translations available on the site.

✦ Although the U.S. is the largest country on Facebook, Indonesia is Facebook's second largest market, with more than 45 million of its 200 million people online. The United Kingdom and Turkey are in the third and fourth spots.

With more than 70 percent of Facebook users being outside of the United States, it's essential to understand Facebook's place in the global markets. Facebook breaks down barriers and makes introducing your products and services to international audiences easier. Here are some opportunities you can explore to extend your brand's footprints into more global markets:

✦ **Use Facebook advertising to reach international audiences.** You can target 25 different countries with one Facebook Ad or you can target one country at a time and drill down into specific cities within the country. You can also create multiple ads and target numerous cities in the countries you want to target with your ads. The more localized you make your ads, the better chances you'll have at reaching your ideal audience.

✦ **Translate your content:** With the rise of international markets on Facebook today, it's wise to consider translating your content on Facebook. In fact, English only accounts for 31% of language use online. Facebook has its own crowd-source Translation product, Facebook Internationalization. Over 300,000 users have helped translate the site through the translations application.

✦ In many countries, the majority of people do not have access to computers with Internet access. However, mobile devices are increasingly making it possible for Facebook to reach more people. As mentioned, more than 200 million Facebook users access the site via their mobile device. For example, Facebook's Indonesia executive, Chamath Palihapitiya, reported that nearly every Indonesian Facebook user is accessing the platform via his or her mobile phone. That's a pretty astounding stat, to say the least!

Chinese social media is more relevant than Facebook's social platform

If your company is targeting international business, you absolutely must know what's going on in other countries. Facebook is by far the largest social network in the United States, although this isn't necessarily the case in other parts of the world. This fact is most evident when you take a look at China.

China has more than 300 million Internet users, but Facebook and Google aren't in the top user sites. The social networking market is dominated by "Chinese social media," which consists of social networking, discussion forums, blogs, and instant messaging, all of which have been running long before the rise of Facebook. Also, China's social networks rely more on micropayments and the sale of virtual goods, unlike the model in the United States.

To further examine the differences in Chinese social networks versus those in the United States, you can read about social media marketing on the Web site Dragon Tail at `http://www.dragontrail.com`.

Understanding Facebook Marketing Basics

Facebook offers you a way to supercharge your existing marketing efforts by giving you a platform to grow your audience, create deeper connections, and create new experiences to foster loyal client relationships. The magic of Facebook is found in Facebook Pages, which are like a digital storefront, where you can highlight your best programs, products, and services to interact with an interested audience.

A large portion of this book is dedicated to creating and optimizing your Facebook Page. Before we get into all the how-to's and strategies, though, we thought we'd point out a few of the more important details you need to know to get off on the right foot.

Marketing on your Page, not your profile

Although you'll soon find out all you'll ever need to know about the differences between a Facebook profile and a Facebook Page, for the purposes of starting things off, here's a quick rundown:

✦ **When you sign up for Facebook, you create a Facebook profile.**

   A Facebook personal profile is meant to be all about you. It highlights who you are and what you're about, acting as a platform for you to connect with your friends and family.

✦ **Promoting your business, brand, or any other entity other than a person via a profile goes against Facebook's Terms of Service.**

✦ **A Facebook Page is designed to highlight your business, and its purpose is to allow businesses to communicate with their customers and Fans.**

   Those who follow your Facebook Page expect to see promotions and conversations about your programs and services, so it's perfectly acceptable to promote your business on a Facebook Page.

For a more comprehensive understanding of profiles and Pages, check out Book II, Chapter 1.

Developing your Page to be a hub of activity

Your Facebook Page can serve as a meeting place for people who share similar interests and values. Involve your customers in your conversations by asking them questions and encouraging them to share their thoughts.

One way you can create a hub of activity is by encouraging your Fans to use your Facebook community as a platform to connect with other like-minded individuals.

For example, you can become the go-to source in your industry, making your Page the hub of your industries latest news and happenings. By delivering valuable content via your Facebook Page, you're setting up your company as the authority, a trusted advisor.

One great example of a company using Facebook to position itself as the go-to source for an industry is 360i, a major player in the field of social media marketing. (See Figure 1-8.)

Figure 1-8:
360i
Facebook
engagement
activity.

During the course of this book, you'll have the opportunity to familiarize yourself with many strategies that can help you create a unique hub of activity — including a whole slew of strategies found in Book VII.

Understanding privacy issues

After you set up your Facebook Profile, you have a number of privacy options to choose from to determine just how much or how little of your Facebook self you want to share.

Here's how to find your privacy settings:

1. **Point your browser to** www.facebook.com **and log in to your account.**

2. **In the upper right of your screen, click Account, and then choose Privacy Settings from the drop-down menu that appears.**

   On the Privacy Settings page, you can see all your options for setting your privacy controls on Facebook, as shown in Figure 1-9.

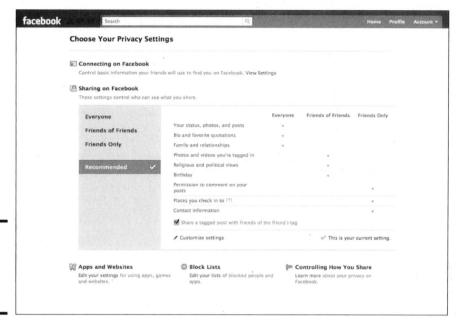

Figure 1-9:
Privacy
Settings
page on
Facebook.

Facebook's privacy settings allow you to control exactly who sees what within your Facebook Profile. The challenge is that the privacy settings are extremely detailed, and Facebook changes or upgrades them often. But don't worry: When Facebook does make changes, it always notifies users, thereby keeping everyone informed. To be honest, we (the authors) think that all the privacy options can get overwhelming. To help you navigate through the layers of privacy options, we identify the most important options and give you some guidance for the best course of action for each setting.

When you first log in to the privacy settings area on Facebook, you're taken to a main dashboard that Facebook calls the "Master Switch" (see Figure 1-9). This dashboard gives you the option to set all your settings via one click. Facebook gives you four main levels of group settings: Everyone, Friends of Friends, Friends Only, and Recommended. You can also dive deeper into the settings and customize specific sections of your Profile, and we suggest that you do just that. To better understand your level of privacy options, here are the four main levels of group settings:

✦ **Everyone:** This setting includes users not on your Friends list

✦ **Friends of Friends:** This setting filters out anyone who is not connected to you via a mutual Friend

✦ **Friends Only:** This setting includes only those you have accepted as friends

✦ **Recommended:** This setting was designed by Facebook to encourage social interaction while still maintaining privacy. When you select this setting, you will be sharing some of your Profile to everyone while filtering out more personal information to Friends of Friends or Friends only.

You also have the option to click the Customize Settings link, which takes you to a Page that lets you limit access to individual sections of your Profile within that main setting. For example, you can choose Everyone for one section of your Profile and choose Friends of Friends for another section.

There are five main areas you want to pay close attention to in the privacy setting area:

✦ **Connecting on Facebook:** This setting allows you to set how much information you want to share with people on Facebook and identifies the different ways people can search for you inside Facebook. You can decide whether you want everyone on Facebook to have access to some of your personal information, including where you went to school and your home town. Allowing others to access this information will make it easier for them to locate and connect with you on Facebook. Here you will also decide who can request to add you as a Friend or send you a message. We suggest that you let everyone search for you and request to be added as a Friend. You will still get to decide whether you want to add people, so the control stays in your court. (*Note:* If you get too strict with these settings, people might not be able to find you, including those you truly want to connect with!)

✦ **Sharing On Facebook:** You use this setting to decide what you want to share and with whom. Specifically, you can choose who sees your photos you're in and the videos you're linked to as well as who can respond to your comments. Also, here you decide who can see your religious and political affiliations and your birthday and contact information. Depending on how you want to use Facebook, we suggest that you spend some time here to make sure that the information you consider to be private stays private.

✦ You have the option to click the Customize Settings link to then be able to give different groups access to specific areas. This means that your choice doesn't have to be all or nothing, so you can, for example, let everyone see your hometown but only Friends see your photos.

✦ **Checking Into Places:** We discuss Facebook Places in detail in Book VII, Chapter 4. For the moment, you just need to know that your Friends can check you into a location via Facebook Places and tell everyone online your location at any time. We suggest that you disable this setting to keep your location private, unless you choose to share it.

✦ **Instant Personalization:** This setting allows Facebook to give third-party Web sites (those outside the Facebook platform) your personal information so that those Web sites can personalize your experience on their site. For example, when you Like a post on your favorite blog site, Facebook puts it on your Wall for you and your Friends to see. Facebook also instantly sends this information to outside sites such as Yelp or Bing. We suggest that you disable this setting to keep your online activity more private.

✦ **Public Search:** This setting allows search engines to preview your data on your Facebook Profile. For example, when people search for you on Google, they might get a preview of your public Profile. You might be sharing information that you don't want to share with strangers. To avoid that scenario, turn this option off.

To learn more about your privacy settings on Facebook, go to `http://www.facebook.com/privacy/explanation.php`.

You can change your privacy settings at any time. Experiment with the settings, and when you feel you need to tighten them or, conversely, loosen the constraints, it's easy to log in to Facebook and make these changes.

Although it's true that you first need a Facebook profile in place before you can create a Business Page, there's no way for others to see the connection between your new Page and your existing Profile Uless you tell them, of course. Only you know the connection, and you can keep it that way for eternity if you like. People who choose to connect with you on your Page won't be able to access any information from your personal Facebook Profile.

Keeping things professional but personal

Facebook allows you the opportunity to give a face and personality to your company. Sure, many of us use Facebook in our day-to-day business (as previously mentioned), but the vast majority of Facebookers are there to engage with their friends and have fun. And no matter how serious your product or service might be, you always have room for a little levity.

People want to know *you,* not your brand. Be careful about using jargon in your posts and coming across as too "corporate" because this is often seen as inauthentic on social networking sites. Talk to your Facebook community as though they were your friends, not potential clients. The more real you come across on Facebook, the more your Fans will want to engage with you and your business.

Chapter 2: Creating Your Facebook Marketing Plan

In This Chapter

✔ Researching and targeting your ideal audience on Facebook

✔ Finding new connections using Facebook Search

✔ Understanding the core rules for a successful Facebook Page

✔ Creating a Facebook team that will help grow your community

✔ Measuring the success of your Facebook investment

*F*acebook has changed the game of marketing for everyone. In the past, people interested in your products or services would read a brochure, visit your brick-and-mortar shop, or maybe watch a commercial to find out the information they needed before making a buying decision. Today, people go to Google or search popular social networks for answers to their questions instead. That's why you need an online presence, in real-time, to answer their questions when they seek you out. After all, if you make customers wait, they can be knocking on your competitor's virtual door with a click of a button. With that in mind, it's essential that you create a solid, well thought-out Facebook marketing plan that defines your goals and maps your online strategies.

By the end of this chapter, you'll be able to start putting your Facebook marketing plan to work. Begin by defining your target audience and finding that audience inside the virtual walls of Facebook.

Defining Your Ideal Audience on Facebook

With more than 600 million active users as of this writing, more likely than not, your brand will find an audience on Facebook. The key here is finding out where they are and what they do while inside this thriving social network.

The first step in creating a Facebook marketing plan involves identifying your *brand*. You want to determine who you are and who your customers are. Ask yourself what's unique about your product or service and what about your product or service attracts buyers. Are you a life coach who teaches people how to find their true passion? Are you a yoga teacher who lives a green lifestyle and sells organic specialty soaps online? In a nutshell, who are you, and what do you do? After you get clear about your brand, you can identify your ideal audience.

Identifying the demographics of your ideal audience before you start

Before you begin marketing on Facebook, you want to compile all the information you already have regarding the demographics of your ideal audience. Commonly used demographics include gender, race, age, location, income, and education. If you haven't done this research, one way to approach it is to survey your existing customers. Ask them questions to find out their specific demographics to help you better understand who is buying your products or services.

To help survey your audience, you can use inexpensive (and often free) online tools to make the process easy and anonymous for your audience. Two great sites to explore are Polldaddy (`www.polldaddy.com`) and SurveyMonkey (`www.surveymonkey.com`).

With this information in hand, using the tips and techniques I highlight in this chapter, you can research similar Facebook users to find potential customers to target inside of Facebook. The more information you collect before you start to market on Facebook, the more success you'll have finding new potential clients. As you dig deeper into Facebook marketing in this chapter, we show you precisely how to use your existing information to find your ideal audience on Facebook.

Understanding the psychographics of your ideal audience

The more you understand your target audience, the more equipped you are to keep the attention of your existing audience and attract new clients, as well.

In addition to demographics, you'll also want to identify your ideal audience's *psychographics*. Don't let the word scare you; it's pretty easy to do, we promise.

Psychographics are attributes often related to personality, values, attitudes, or interests. Figuring out what a person likes or dislikes, or even favorite hobbies, can be priceless information as you market your products or services.

One way to figure out the psychographics of your ideal audience is to simply ask them. Use your social media networks to post engaging, thought-provoking questions to learn more about your audience. Ask them about their interests, hobbies, and needs. People love to talk about themselves, and if they trust you, they'll often reveal even more than you initially asked.

As mentioned earlier, online surveys are another great way to learn more about your ideal audience. Offering prizes or giveaways in exchange for information is a great strategy to get people to participate in your surveys. Remember, the more you know, the smarter you can be in your overall marketing activity.

Figure out what your customers want to know from you. What information do you have that they want? If you cast too wide a net, you're likely to come up short in the end. Make sure to stay focused on the people who matter most.

You'll also want to find out where your audience spends time while on Facebook. What Facebook Pages do they interact with often? Who do they follow? What do they post on their own Facebook Profiles? This information will tell you a lot about your Facebook audience. (In Book IX, we walk you through how to use the Facebook tracking tool, Insights, as well as third-party monitoring tools. Understanding these tools will help you monitor your ideal audience's activity and interactions on Facebook.)

After you know what your business is about, what you are selling, and who your audience is, you want to spend a little time on your tone. In other words, you want to talk to your Facebook audience in a manner that they're familiar with.

Always stay conversational, but try to use words and phrases that they use in their everyday conversations. For example, if your audience is 14-year-old boys who love to skateboard, you would talk to them much differently than if your audience were new moms looking to connect with other moms. When you know your audience's lingo and style of communication, you can quickly become part of the community.

Finding Your Ideal Audience inside Facebook

One of the biggest benefits of marketing on Facebook is that you have access to the information that Facebook users add to their personal Profile. Depending on users' Profile privacy settings, you may be able to see their date of birth, marital status, hometown, current location, political views, religious views, employment details, hobbies, bio, and so much more. In the past, with traditional marketing, people would pay big bucks for this type of information, but now it's free to you — and at your fingertips.

A great tool you can use to help locate your ideal audience on Facebook is Facebook Search. This tool allows you to enter keywords into a search field, and the people, Groups, and Pages that are using your keyword(s) will show up in a list. Facebook Search is an ideal tool for anyone looking to connect with people who share interests or similar views.

When you do a search using Facebook Search, you can find information that users add to their Info tab and post in their status updates as well as information about the Groups and Pages users interact with. It is a very powerful tool, to say the least.

Here's how to use Facebook Search:

1. **Go to** www.facebook.com/search.

In the search field enter the keyword or phrase you want to search for inside Facebook. In the left column, the default for search is All Results. Make sure that it is highlighted. To check out an example of the Facebook search page, see Figure 2-1.

2. **Enter the keyword or phrase you want to search for; then click Search.**

The results for your keyword or keyword phrase will populate into different sections on Facebook. You can explore the following sections by clicking the links in the left column:

- People
- Pages
- Groups
- Applications
- Events
- Web Results
- Posts by Friends
- Posts by Everyone

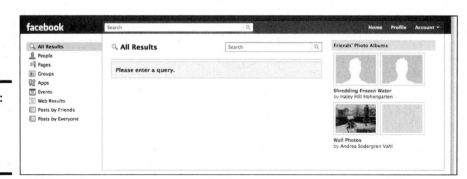

Figure 2-1:
The
Facebook
search
page.

For the purposes of finding your audience on Facebook, we suggest spending your time researching People, Pages, Groups, and Events.

After you click a specific category, the search results for that keyword show up in one stream. For example, I searched for the word *sushi* and then chose the category, *Pages,* as shown in Figure 2-2.

Figure 2-2: Click a category of your choice to see results for your keyword.

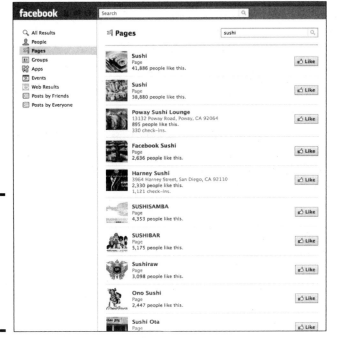

How to filter Facebook search results

After you complete your search inquiry, you might be thinking, "Great! But now what do I do with all this info?" Here are a few strategies for putting that info to use in going after your ideal audience on Facebook:

✦ **Send a Friend request.** Identify the Facebook users you want to target, and Friend them on Facebook. Make sure to include a short note when you send the Friend request to make the connection more personal, as shown in Figure 2-3.

✦ **Ask them to become a Fan.** Invite your targeted users to become a Fan of your Page. You can do this by sending them an e-mail inside Facebook, adding the link to your Facebook Page, and requesting that they check out your Page and click the Like button to join your community.

Figure 2-3:
Attach a
personal
note to
a Friend
request.

✦ **Join the Groups that count the most.** The best strategy is to join active Facebook Groups related to your brand or niche and become part of that community. After joining, consistently post helpful tips that will eventually connect people back to your Facebook Page, as shown in Figure 2-4.

Figure 2-4:
Post
comments
to a
Facebook
Group
devoted to
your niche.

Using Community Page search for keywords

Facebook Community Pages are a great place to find your ideal audience on Facebook as well. In Book II, Chapter 1, you get to find out all about Facebook Community Pages, but in a nutshell, Community Pages were designed to be set up around generic, non-business topics or ideas and are monitored and run by the Community connected to it. They are similar to Facebook Pages because they allow you to connect with others interested in the same experiences and topics as you.

For the sake of identifying your ideal audience, Community Pages are a good place to find out who is talking about things related to your brand.

Just imagine that you search for a keyword like "cooking" and saw the Community Page in your search results associated with this Web address: www.facebook.com/pages/Cooking/113970468613229. If you scroll down this page, you see what your Friends or everyone else on Facebook are saying with regard to the keyword cooking.

If you click Related Posts in the left column of the page (as shown in Figure 2-5), the page refreshes so that you can see just what your Friends and others on Facebook are saying about that keyword.

Figure 2-5:
View related
posts on a
Community
Page.

Then, you can use the posts from others to figure out what questions and concerns people are posting about your keyword and use that valuable information in your own posts.

In addition, when you post using that keyword on your Page or on your Profile, it could end up on the Community Page for that keyword, depending on how you have set up your Profile privacy settings. If people are searching for your keyword or if they're viewing that specific Community Page, they may see your post and might decide to explore what you are all about.

Therefore, as you can see, the Community Page can help you research what people are talking about and also help you recruit potential Likers who find you interacting with the Community Page. Pretty powerful stuff.

To find Community Pages that relate to your brand, do a Facebook search as explained earlier, but choose Pages, Posts by Friends, or Posts by Everyone to find out what people are posting about as it relates to your brand.

Using Facebook Ads to research your ideal audience

Even if you don't plan to use Facebook Ads as part of your overall Facebook marketing plan, you can still benefit from the Facebook Ads platform to find out to what degree your target audience is on Facebook.

Here's how you can access this valuable information:

1. **Go to your Facebook Profile, scroll down to the bottom of the page and click the Advertising link in the footer of the page.**

2. **Click the Create an Ad button in the upper-right corner.**

3. **Ignore the first step, and for Step 2, "Targeting," enter the location of your target audience in the text fields of the Location section.**

   You skip the first step, "Designing Your Ad," because you're not using this tool to actually create an ad.

   In the Location section, first enter a country. Then get more specific by choosing states, provinces, or cities. You want to drill down as much as possible to get a good representation of your ideal client on Facebook.

   You can enter multiple cities in the same location field.

4. **If you want to indicate a specific age or an age range, or specify male/female, do so in the Demographics section.**

5. **In the Likes and Interests section, enter a keyword that describes your audience.**

   After you type in a keyword, a drop-down menu appears, as shown in Figure 2-6. From that drop-down menu, you can choose the keywords that Facebook identifies as best choices based on your initial keyword. After you choose the keyword, you can then be even more specific by selecting subcategories of your keyword.

   For example, say you choose "cycling" as your keyword because you know your target audience consists of avid cyclists who will likely mention cycling in their Profiles. After you choose this keyword, you then get to see options to drill-down even more. You can then click any of the boxes that also relate to your target audience and thereby drill down on your target audience even more.

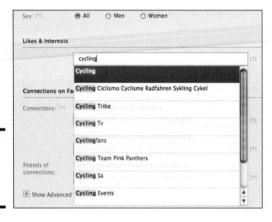

Figure 2-6:
Search by
Likes &
Interests.

After you enter the appropriate information for location and demographics, a number to the right of the screen shows you how many people on Facebook match your ideal target audience criteria, as shown in Figure 2-7. If you have that nugget of information, you know whether your target audience is on Facebook.

Figure 2-7:
Check out
how many
people meet
your ideal
audience
criteria.

Identifying the Core Goals of Your Facebook Marketing Plan

With Facebook growing by the minute, there's no question that Facebook must be a part of your marketing mix. However, these days it's not enough to sign up for a Facebook account, put up a Facebook Page and hope that potential readers find you. Unfortunately, the *Field of Dreams* model of "Build it, and they will come" doesn't apply.

Book II is dedicated to teaching you everything you need to know about the importance of a Facebook Page and how to strategically set up your Page. However, to set up your Facebook marketing foundation, it's essential to create a Facebook marketing plan or strategy. Think of your strategy as a road map — the directions you need to create a thriving, active, loyal community on Facebook.

The strategy behind a Facebook marketing plan doesn't need to be complicated, but it does need to be carefully thought out. When it comes to growing your brand on Facebook business owners and marketers commonly get stuck, often because they overcomplicate things. The goal of this section is to help you create a Facebook marketing plan without going absolutely crazy in the process.

Defining your Facebook marketing goals

As you think about crafting your Facebook marketing plan, understand what Facebook can do for your business. Consider these six Facebook marketing goals as you craft your new plan:

+ Increasing overall exposure

+ Building brand awareness

+ Creating a loyal, engaged community

+ Listening to your clients' needs, interests, and feedback

+ Monitoring what people are saying about your brand

+ Driving action (often in the form of sales of your products or services)

These six core goals will help you shape the specific outcomes you want to achieve from your Facebook marketing plan. We touch on each of these core goals below as you get a chance to explore what makes a successful Facebook marketing plan.

Deciding on a social media budget

You've likely heard that social media marketing is free. Well, we're sorry to break it to you here, but that's not exactly the case. It can be free, but there are some areas where we encourage you to consider spending a little money to take your campaign to a professional level. Here are three areas where you should consider spending a little money:

+ **Branding:** We suggest that you hire a designer to create the look and feel for all your social media profiles. They should all be consistent across channels and match your branding as much as possible. With everything you need being easily assessable online these days, finding a designer for this task is affordable and quick. Sites like www.freelance.com and www.tweetpages.com are great resources to find designers to create your social media profiles. In Book III, Chapter 2, we show you how to use iFrames to brand your Facebook Page.

+ **Social media consulting:** We often suggest that entrepreneurs and businesses that are new in the social media arena spend a little money educating themselves. Although we don't suggest that you run out and hire someone to take over your social media activity, we do suggest that you consult with a social media expert for a review of your social media strategy to gain feedback and insight on your new plan.

+ **Facebook Ads:** The third area where you might want to consider budgeting for is Facebook Ads — which leads us right into the next section.

Before you hire a social media consultant

If you decide to hire a social media consultant to review your social media marketing plan, treat the experience as if you're hiring a new employee. Ask for references, and do your due diligence to make sure that you're hiring a skilled, experienced consultant who has achieved real results for other clients. One way to start your search for a social media consultant is to search in Facebook by going to `www.facebook.com/search` and typing in these keywords: "social media consultant" "social media marketing" and "social media marketer."

Deciding whether a Facebook Ads campaign is right for you

Consider experimenting with Facebook Ads, even if you only plan to test them for a limited time with a small budget. You might be pleasantly surprised on the effectiveness of this advertising channel because Facebook Ads allow you to promote your business, get more Likers for your Facebook Page, and drive more leads to build up your sales funnel.

The reason why Facebook Ads are so popular is because the targeting is like no other advertising vehicle available today. You can target by sex, age, race, location, and interests — and even by who is or who isn't a Liker of a specific Facebook Page. It's an impressive tool worth checking out, for sure.

We spend an entire minibook (Book VIII, to be exact) exploring Facebook Ads in greater depth. To get a quick taste of how Facebook advertising works, check out the Facebook description at `www.facebook.com/advertising`. And don't forget this companion, *Facebook Advertising For Dummies*.

After you establish your core goals for you Facebook marketing plan, you can focus on creating a successful Facebook Page.

Rules for Successful Facebook Pages

One of the most important questions to ask as you create your Facebook marketing plan is, "What do you want to achieve with your Facebook Page and overall marketing on Facebook?"

To help you sort through the many layers of Facebook marketing, there are nine core rules to consider as you create your Facebook Page.

+ Give your Page a human touch.

+ Create fresh content.

+ Cultivate engagement with two-way dialog.

+ Create consistent calls to action.

+ Make word-of-mouth advocacy easy.

+ Encourage Fan-to-Fan conversations.

+ Focus on smart branding.

+ Be deliberate and manage expectations.

+ Monitor, measure, and track.

Dive in to explore each of the nine core rules for a successful Facebook Page.

Rule #1: Give your page a human touch

To give your Page a human touch, highlight the team behind your Facebook Page. Your Fans don't want to connect with your brand or product — they want to connect with you. As you have likely heard numerous times, social media is about transparency and authenticity. People want to know that they are communicating with the real you; that's why first names and photos are the norm on Facebook.

Brands that allow their Page administrators to have real conversations with their Fans are much more likely to have active, engaging Pages. Here are a few key strategies to give your Facebook Page a human touch:

+ **Address your Fans by their first names and craft your posts in the first-person singular voice.**

+ **Use a conversational tone in your posts.**

+ **Encourage your Page administrators to add their name at the end of their posts, as shown in Figure 2-8.**

+ **If you have multiple admins, add your Page administrators' photos and bios on a custom tab, as shown in Figure 2-9.** This allows your Fans to get to know the people that are representing your Page.

You can also do this if you only have one person posting to your Page. For example, Axe does a great job of spotlighting its Community Manager, as shown in Figure 2-10.

Don't make your Page another static Web site. Give it a human touch by encouraging your admin team members to be themselves, communicate with your Fans as though they were talking to their friends, and give each post that spark of personality.

Figure 2-8:
Have Page
admins add
their names
to their
posts.

Figure 2-9:
A Facebook
Page Tab that
spotlights
the Page
admini-
strators.

Rule #2: Create fresh content

To get the most reach from your content, make sure that your content educates, entertains, and empowers your Fans. This will pique their interest and
keep them coming back for more.

Also, publish everything you have, in as many places as possible. What this
means is that you want to get your content online, and you want it to be
seen by as many potential prospects as possible.

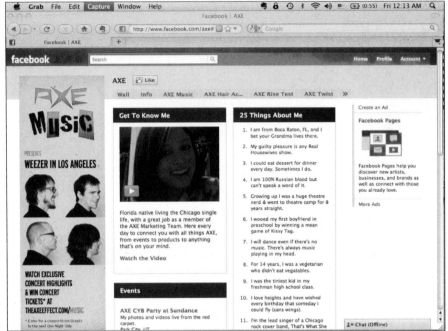

Figure 2-10: Axe spotlights its Community Manager on its Facebook Page.

You can also monitor what others are publishing. If you see something that would be valuable to your audience — and is not in direct competition with your business — publish that content (and make sure to give them credit for it!). Third-party publishing is a great way to continue to add value to your Fans without your having to be the one who is creating all the content.

To help you create content consistently, we suggest that you create an editorial calendar. It might sound daunting, but it's actually very simple. Here's how you do it:

1. **Create a six-month digital calendar.**

   You can do this in Word or you can find digital calendars online. One of our favorite digital calendar sites is www.calendarsthatwork.com.

2. **Decide how often you want to create content and in what form.**

   Consider creating blog posts, video posts, articles, reports, podcasts, or any other form of media you know your audience will like. Mix it up and deliver your content in many different formats to attract a wider reach of ideal clients.

3. **Brainstorm content ideas related to your brand or niche.**

   Again, think of what interests your clients the most. (*Hint:* Check out your competition's content. This will help you decide what might be best for your audience.)

4. **Create a calendar of content.**

   Choose the specific dates you plan to post and list the topic of the content and the type of delivery. For example, add the following in the June 18 box: Blog post and Facebook update on "How to Create a Facebook Page" — it's as easy as that!

TIP

Stay diligent with your content calendar. After you create it, stick with it. The more disciplined you are sticking to your content calendar, the more traction you will see with your audience.

Rule #3: Cultivate engagement with two-way dialogs

In a nutshell, engagement is about getting your Fans to take action, meaning post on your Page, comment on your posts, click the Like button next to your posts and share your content. A well-executed engagement strategy takes time and effort. More than anything, engagement is really about showing up daily and taking a genuine interest in the likes, interests, and opinions of your Fans.

The rule for engagement is to make it about your Fans and not about you. Remember that people love to talk about themselves, so craft your posts and questions around them, and you're sure to see some great conversations begin to surface on your Page. Check out Figure 2-11 for an example of a question that's about the user — not about a brand.

Figure 2-11:
Make your
posts less
promotional
and more
inclined
to engage
people.

REMEMBER

A massive Fan base left disengaged is a recipe for disaster! Take action and start talking with your Fans regularly.

Rule #4: Create consistent calls to action

To move your Fans to action, you need to give them a reason to take action. Discounts or specials are a great way to reward your clients. You're basically saying, "Hey, I really appreciate you being a Fan. Thanks for coming on over. I want to do something special for you now."

You can give out discount codes or even create a special tab using iFrames (see Book III, Chapter 2) and allow your Fans to print the coupons.

You want to keep your Fans happy and get them to take action. Everybody loves a discount or a special, so think of ways you can incorporate these into your Facebook marketing plan.

Another way you can encourage Fans to take action is ask them to sign up for your online newsletter or sign up for a giveaway. This is considered an *opt-in strategy,* and with iFrames, you can easily create an opt-in box (see Figure 2-14) where you collect names and e-mails of your Fans. Again, check out Book III, Chapter 2 for more details about iFrames.

Rule #5: Make word-of-mouth advocacy easy

It's a fact that customers trust their friends and other customers more than they trust a brand. Think of it this way: If you were going to buy a new pair of running shoes, who would you listen to the most: your good friend who is an avid runner and just purchased a pair, or the makers of the shoe who are posting a promotion about them on their Facebook Page? It's human nature to gravitate toward the person you have a relationship with. That is precisely why word-of-mouth advocacy is essential.

To encourage word of mouth advocacy, you want to make it easy for your Fans to talk about you. Here are a few suggestions:

✦ **Ask a Fan to Like a post or Share a post.** When you post a link to a new article on your Facebook Page, add a line at the end of the post that says, "If you like this article, please click the link to share it with your friends!" Keep it light and conversational, and your Fans will be happy to oblige.

✦ **Do something that encourages self-expression.** People love to talk about themselves and share their thoughts, feelings, and feedback. Create an experience where they'll want to share your content with their friends. This is how the viral experience is created. To do this, you can create a poll on your Page or run a contest that gets your audience excited to engage with you. We mention testing polls earlier in this chapter. (To find out more about contests on Facebook, check out Book VI, Chapter 2.)

Rule # 6: Encourage Fan-to-Fan conversations

The key here is to enhance your Fans' experience by creating a community that encourages peer-to-peer communication among your Fans. Here are a few key strategies you can use to get Fans talking to each other:

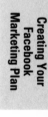

✦ **Showcase Fans.** Create a Member of the Month campaign directly on your Facebook Page, as shown in Figure 2-12. When Fans get recognized, they will tell their Friends — and that encourages even more Fan-to-Fan interaction.

Figure 2-12:
This
Member of
the Month
campaign
spotlights
members.

✦ **Recognize top contributors.** When you have someone on your Page who likes to answer questions from Fans, or who often offers tips or suggestions, take advantage of it. Ask the Fan to be an ambassador of your Page and encourage him to help out when appropriate. Give your biggest advocates specific guidelines and responsibilities and reward them with perks; their involvement will free up time for you to concentrate on other ways to grow your Page.

Rule #7: Focus on smart branding

One way to understand the power of a Facebook Page is to look at it as a mini-site of your own Web site. Some of the most successful Facebook Pages act as an extension of the brand and are essentially mini–Web sites inside Facebook. Smart branding allows you to create a bridge from Facebook to your Web site. The key is to create a Page that sparks familiarity with your brand when your existing customers visit your Page.

Here are two examples of Facebook Pages (one of which is shown in Figure 2-13) that do a great job of mirroring their Web site branding. Check them out to see branding done right.

Figure 2-13: Smart branding via Social Media Examiner.

Social Media Examiner

Web site: www.socialmediaexaminer.com/

Facebook Page: www.facebook.com/smexaminer

Red Bull

Web site: www.redbull.com/

Facebook Page: www.facebook.com/redbull

You can't expect that consumers on Facebook will find you easily and automatically. Facebook users don't typically search actively for a brand's Facebook Page; instead, most users will stumble upon a Page, either through a Friend or from a hub, such as your Web site. Branding your Page allows you to make your Page dynamic (stand out above the rest) and viral (increasing the number of people who will see it).

Rule #8: Be deliberate and manage expectations

Before anything else, you first need to decide why you want to have a presence on Facebook. What is your overall vision for your Page? Often, your vision for Facebook will be aligned with your overall company vision.

For example, if you own a high-end clothing store for women, your company vision might be to offer the highest fashion and the best quality clothing in your area to make women feel great about how they look. And on Facebook, your vision for your store might be to create a community for women who love high fashion and give them a place to talk about clothes and share ideas with each other. Your Facebook Page can become the hub for fashion-minded women (and the best place for you to engage with your ideal audience on Facebook).

A clear vision does two things: First, it allows you and your team to clearly understand why you are on Facebook. When you understand the "why," your actions are deliberate and have purpose. Also, when you have a clear vision, you can communicate this to your Facebook Fans, and they then know how to interact with your Page.

Your vision is only as strong as the individual or team behind it. It's up to you to spread the word. The good news is that after you have a solid Fan base, your Fans will help spread your message and virally attract new followers. It's up to you to "sell" your vision to get others to pay attention.

Rule #9: Monitor, measure, and track

Although it may not sound like a fun task, it's essential that you monitor, measure, and track your Facebook activity. In Book IX, we explore in depth the various ways for you to do this, but for the sake of your Facebook marketing plan, you want to make sure you have surefire methods in place that enable you to consistently track your Facebook marketing progress.

The great thing about social media marketing is that it's not set in stone. In the past, you'd have to print a marketing brochure for thousands (if not hundreds of thousands) of dollars and then cross your fingers that it worked — because if it flopped, you had to wait until that brochure ran out and then spend a handful of money to test something new.

Figure 2-14: Add an opt-in box on a Facebook Page.

On Facebook and other social sites, most of the time, tweaking a marketing campaign is as easy as a click of a button. That's a huge advantage to marketing online.

The key here is to be diligent in testing what's working and instantly tweaking what's not. When you get into this habit, you can see progress much faster than you ever did with traditional marketing endeavors.

To wrap up this section on the nine core rules of your Facebook marketing Page, remember this: There's a lot of noise on the Web about the dos and don'ts of social media marketing, and it tends to be overwhelming. These rules are meant to simplify your process.

If you add a bunch of extra components to the rules, you're less likely to see the results you want — or worse, you're likely to get overwhelmed and not take action. In short, ignore the chatter, and stick to the plan.

Creating a Facebook Page is fairly simple, but growing its momentum and getting it to thrive takes time, dedication, and some planning. Don't expect to create a Page and then see a massive following instantaneously. Create valuable content, encourage Fans to share your Page with their friends, and tell people about it. With time and patience, your Page will grow.

Setting up the Resources and Manpower for Your Facebook Marketing Plan

After you nail down what goes into your Facebook marketing plan, you'll want to explore what resources and manpower you have at your disposal. If you're an entrepreneur or a small business, you probably don't have a large team. The good news is that you don't need hundreds of thousands of Fans to be successful. By following the nine core rules of a Facebook Page we describe — and keeping it simple — you can grow your Page to the level you need with only a few hands on deck. Take a look at the people and resources needed to put your Facebook marketing plan to work.

Identifying your existing resources and manpower

First, do an internal assessment to identify your resources and manpower. For entrepreneurs and small business owners, the essential players for your Page are at least two Page administrators (assign one admin the Community Manager role), one Community Manager, and a designer and programmer to help with your branding. If you have the funds, we also suggest you put some money toward a few sessions with a social media strategy consultant to review your existing plan.

Integrating your social media strategies

Along with your Facebook marketing plan, you'll also likely want to consider other social media initiatives. Perhaps you'll want to include Twitter into your social media mix or create a YouTube channel as part of your social media outreach plan.

To get the most momentum for your social media marketing plan, don't separate your social media marketing efforts. One person, or one solid team, should oversee all social media efforts. It's important to have a strong synergy between all social media sites; therefore, you want the person managing your Facebook Page to also know firsthand what is taking place on your Twitter account, YouTube channel, and any other social site.

For larger businesses, if you have a marketing team, we suggest integrating your Facebook marketing plan into your existing marketing initiatives. Your Facebook marketing plan should not be a standalone Facebook marketing tool, but instead be closely integrated into your overall marketing plan. Sit down with your exiting marketing team and go through the six Facebook marketing goals and nine core rules of a successful Facebook Page to see how they align with the programs and initiatives you already have in place.

Deciding in-house or outsourced

After you decide to create a Facebook marketing plan, you have to decide who's going to run it. There are multiple options to consider for your social media management and support.

Option 1: Hire an agency (or consultant) to manage your Facebook Page

As with most things, this option has both pros and cons. We offer both sides for your consideration.

Pros:

+ **You gain access to social media expertise and knowledge.** This is especially helpful if your knowledge is limited.

+ **An agency or consultant can save you a tremendous amount of time.** If you're not consistently listening to your Fans and interacting with them regularly, your Fans will quickly lose interest in your Page. It might be a smart move for you to hire someone to take on this important task.

✦ **Social media experts tend to be "in the know" with the latest trends.** Because social media changes quickly, it's important to stay on the cutting edge and be the first to adopt new strategies or tools as they prove promising. An agency or consultant can advise you on the latest and greatest in social media marketing to keep you current and ahead of the pack.

✦ **You get expert advice on your social media content strategy.** One of the most important pieces of your Facebook marketing strategy is the content you post on your social networks. An agency or consultant can help you create a content plan to align with your overall marketing plan.

✦ **An agency or expert has access to monitoring and tracking tools and technology that you might not.** This is important because an agency can quickly see what is working and what needs to be tweaked, allowing your campaign to be monitored in real-time.

Cons:

✦ **An agency won't know your products or services like you do.** If you're not careful, an agency might end up "representing" you or your brand in ways that don't particularly inspire confidence. Potential customers often ask questions about a product or service via a company's Facebook Page. Ask yourself this question: If an agency or consultant were managing your Page, would they be able to give the prospects accurate information?

Incorrect information could cost you a new client — or worse, backlash from your Facebook Fans. One solution to help with this is to make sure that your agency or consultant has direct access to the appropriate people inside your company who can give them real-time support when needed.

✦ **An agency doesn't understand your brand like you do.** Successful brands have a specific voice, and it's critical that this voice be consistent throughout all your marketing initiatives. With that said, it's paramount that your agency or consultant understands your brand voice and is clear on your brand personality and positioning. This will allow a seamless transition between your company's communication style and the agency's communication on your behalf.

✦ **An agency doesn't intimately know your company culture and is unaware of the "behind the scenes" activities.** One of the most important aspects of Facebook marketing is the transparency factor. Your Fans want to know your company and brand at an intimate level — that's what makes social media networking so attractive to consumers.

Only you and those who work with you intimately know what your company stands for and what its values are. This is a difficult thing to explain to someone from the outside who isn't experiencing it firsthand.

Some of the most popular brands on Facebook allow their Fans to get a glimpse of their company culture and what goes on behind the scenes. Zappos is a great example of this: www.facebook.com/zappos.

An agency or consultant isn't a part of your culture and won't be able to communicate the special benefits of your culture to your Fans, if they are not educated in advance. It will take some dedication on your part to make sure they understand your company and culture.

✦ If you or someone on your team isn't directly managing your Facebook Page, you won't see what's happening on a day-to-day basis. This means you lose a little control over what is taking place on your Page.

One solution for this is to ask your agency or consultant to report back to you on a regular basis to inform you on what is taking place on your Page and to let you know about any challenges and what was done to take care of them.

If you do decide to hire an agency or consultant, make sure you discuss what's expected; the procedures you want them to adhere to at all times; and the rules, guidelines, and any specifics to follow in case of a crisis situation on any of your social networking sites.

Option #2: You manage your Facebook marketing plan

Most mid- to small-sized businesses manage their Facebook marketing plan in-house. Overall, there are multiple benefits to this strategy. If you're managing your strategy in-house, you can essentially eliminate all the cons discussed previously concerning outsourcing to an agency.

Option #3: The hybrid model

If you're new in the social media arena (as are the majority of people), consider hiring support to some degree. One solution we suggest is the "hybrid model." In essence, you hire an agency or consultant to help build your social media marketing strategy (including your Facebook marketing plan), and that agency or consultant can also support the launch of the strategy in the early stages. After things are off the ground and running smoothly (it may take about six months to get going), you and your team take over long-term. Not only do you benefit from the consultants' expertise and experience, but you also can work in a certain amount of training so that you and your team are well equipped to take it over after the contract ends.

Defining Your Admin Team

One of the most important roles for your Facebook Page is the administrator or administrator team. You can have just one admin for your Page; however, we suggest that you assign multiple admins to help support your Facebook Page activity.

In the world of Facebook, any admins of your Page can do the following:

✦ **Post status updates on your Wall as the Page's identity.** This means that when you're an admin of a Page, you will automatically be posting on the Page as that Page's identity. However, you can change your settings and post as your personal Profile. To post on your Facebook Page as your own personal Profile, you need to deselect a setting for your Page that's found in Your Settings (We show you how to deselect this setting in Book II, Chapter 3.)

✦ **Add admins or delete admins.** Any admin of the Page can add or delete admins. Due to this function, it is essential that you can trust all admins of your Page to act respectfully and with integrity.

✦ **Edit the Page.** All admins can edit the Page. This means that admins can add photos and videos, change out the Profile image, remove posts, and add new tabs.

There is no way to limit the admin's access and functionality on your Page. This means that when you add an admin, it's all or nothing. Make sure to choose your admins wisely!

Adding an admin

To add an admin to your Facebook Page, you first have to be an admin of your Page. Only admins can add other admins. Here's how you do it:

1. **Log in to Facebook and go to your Facebook Page.**

2. **Click the Edit Page button, located in the upper-right corner.**

You will be taken to your Page dashboard.

3. **Click the Manage Admins Link in the left column.**

If you already have multiple admins, you see your current admins images and names pop up. You also see a field to enter the name or e-mail address of the person you want to add as an admin, as shown in Figure 2-15.

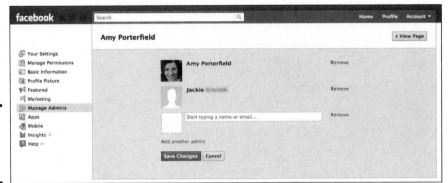

Figure 2-15:
Add a new
admin to
your Page.

4. **Type in the name or e-mail address of each person you want to add as an admin.**

   As you type the name, a drop-down menu appears. Click the correct name and his or her Profile image and full name populates instantly.

   If you want to add more admins to your Page, they must already be a Friend of your Profile or a Fan of your Page. If they are not either, you can add them as an admin by typing in the e-mail address they use to login to Facebook. When you enter an e-mail address, that person receives an e-mail from Facebook saying that he or she was just made an admin of your Page.

5. **Click Save Changes, and if you want to add more admins, click the Add Another Admin link, located above the Save Changes button.**

Deleting an admin

To delete an admin, follow these simple instructions:

1. **Log in to Facebook and go to your Facebook Page.**

2. **Click the Edit Page button in the upper-right corner.**

   You will be taken to your Page dashboard.

3. **Click the Manage Admins link in the left column.**

   If you already have multiple admins, you see your current admins images and names pop up.

4. **Click the Remove link next to the admin's name and then click Save Changes.**

   When you remove an admin, that person is automatically removed from your admin list. The admin will not receive notification that he has been removed as an admin.

Just as you are able to remove other admins of your page, you can also remove yourself as an admin. However, we don't recommend this. If you remove yourself as an admin of your Page, you lose all access to your Page, and you can no longer act as the owner of the Page. This means that you can't edit the Page, you can no longer post on behalf of the Page, and you can't access the Facebook Page dashboard. Therefore, always keep yourself as one of the administrators of your Facebook Page.

The benefits of assigning multiple admins

Having a few admins is a smart strategy because your admins can divide and conquer. With multiple admins, you can assign roles and responsibilities that are aligned with the admins skills and strengths and your Page will be more consistently managed with multiple people watching over the day-to-day activity.

Make sure to assign each admin clear tasks to avoid overlap or confusion on your page. Create a set of rules and guidelines for your Page to make sure everyone is clear of the Page expectations for admins.

Choosing the right Community Manager

A *Community Manager* is an admin of your Page who is ultimately responsible for managing the Page and making sure that it runs smoothly. In many ways, this admin also manages the other admins that you have assigned to the Page. Also, the Community Manager should be well aware of your Facebook marketing plan and executing that plan on a daily basis on your Page.

When looking for the right Community Manager for your Page, you want to make sure that person's personality is a good fit for your audience. Here are six personality traits of a superstar Community Manager:

✦ Natural communicator

✦ Problem solver

✦ Enjoys people

✦ Good listener

✦ Professional

✦ Positive attitude and enthusiastic

In addition to these traits, also consider your ideal audience. Make sure that your Community Manager will easily connect with your Fans.

And although personality traits are important for a Community Manager, keep in mind that these necessary skills any successful Community Manager must possess:

✦ Solid understanding of social networking

✦ Social media savvy

✦ Infallibly committed to helping people in social channels

✦ Ability to multitask and think quickly

✦ Understands online marketing

✦ Ability to grasp how social media activity aligns with business goals

To help you make the right decision, here are some important questions you want to ask before you decide who will ultimately manage your Facebook Page:

✦ Does this person show the ability to be social online?

✦ Does this person show a genuine interest in connecting with our clients?

✦ Can I trust this person to be professional and respectful at all times?

✦ Do people naturally gravitate toward this person?

✦ Will this person actively contribute to new ideas to grow the Page and make it better each day?

A Community Manager will be interacting with your Fans daily. It's paramount that you take the time to choose this person wisely. More often than not, the person you end up choosing is already on your internal team because he knows your brand and your clients better than someone from the outside. Of course, this isn't always possible. If you do need to hire an outside source, make sure you train that person well and monitor his activity closely.

Coordinating posts and strategies

It's important to not only assign clear guidelines and rules for your Community Manager, but also for your multiple admins as well. In order for your admins to stay on task, and not duplicate efforts, give them clear direction. That way your Page will be updated regularly, your Fans will be supported and your admins will not be confused as to their posting responsibilities. Here are some guidelines to consider as you coordinate posts and strategies:

✦ **Decide how you want your admins to post on your Page.** Here are some questions you want to ask about your status updates and posts on your Wall:

• How often will you post updates to your Page?

• What will you post about?

• Will you include links in your posts to direct Fans to content outside of Facebook?

- Will you use third-party content like posts from your favorite blog sites and videos from YouTube to add value?

- Will you mix up the media and use video, audio, photos?

✦ **Determine a communication strategy.** There's a fine balance between policing or controlling your Page and allowing your Fans to interact with each other and come to their own conclusions with questions or feedback you might ask from your posts. Decide how your admins should manage this important balance. The goal is to not be too controlling, as you might stop conversations that will develop freely, but to monitor your Page to make sure there is no inappropriate behavior or posted content that could damage your reputation.

✦ **Assign roles and document them.** One admin might be responsible for posting one third-party article a day, and another admin might be assigned the task of uploading company videos throughout the week. Other tasks might include posting questions, uploading company photos to a photo album, monitoring and responding to all Fan posts, or posting on Fan Pages to increase overall engagement. Whatever the task, make sure your admins are clear on their duties so there is no confusion as you get going.

✦ **Create internal guidelines.** Every Facebook Page should have a "dos and don'ts" list associated with it that your internal team will use as a guide. Make it very clear what's allowed and what you won't tolerate on your Page. Include what can and cannot be discussed, including company-related content and personal content. Decide how often you will promote your programs and services and what acceptable promotion looks like. Think about your company, your mission, and your goals to carefully craft your guidelines around all three. The time spent here will save you a lot of headache in the future!

Considering a Social Media Manager

A Social Media Manager differs from a Community Manager in that the Social Media Manager is responsible for all social media channels as well as the overall social media marketing strategy. In addition, a Social Media Manager must interact regularly with your internal marketing team (if you have one).

The size of your organization, your overall budget, and your access to resources will be major deciding factors when deciding whether a Social Media Manager is right for your business.

A Social Media Manager will possess similar personality traits and skill sets as a Community Manager. See the section, "Choosing the right Community Manager," previously in this chapter, to review the necessary traits and skills to better grasp what is needed here.

In addition, the Social Media Manager must know your company, brand, products, and services well and also have a strong background in traditional marketing as well as a strong grasp of new media marketing trends. In a nutshell, a Social Media Manager is a higher-level position than a Community Manager and has many more responsibilities. Whereas you might be able to add the Community Manager roles to an existing employee's plate, the role of a Social Media Manager is a more robust role that is more time consuming and requires more experience and a higher-level skill set.

We suggest that you start small and first identify and test a dedicated Community Manager for your Facebook Page and a social media consultant or agency for just a few months to get you up and running. From there, review your activity and then decide whether a Social Media Manager would add value and growth to your overall plan. Just as you would with a Community Manager and admins of your Facebook Page, if you do decide to hire a Social Media Manager, make sure to create clear roles, responsibilities, and guidelines for this new position.

Measuring Your Return on Investment (ROI)

Because we are still in the early days of social media marketing, measuring return on investment is, in a word, tough. There is still much debate on what you can and cannot measure today because in many ways, social media is seen as a soft marketing vehicle, meaning that concrete data on its effectiveness is still debatable by most marketers.

With that in mind, you want to first think about your marketing goals and what you plan to accomplish via your new Facebook marketing plan. If you start from there, you're sure to identify areas you can measure to track your results.

Defining success

To define success, it's essential to have a solid Facebook marketing plan. You have to know what success looks like before you start. It might include getting people to interact and leave comments on your Facebook Page, encouraging your Facebook Fans to check out your Web site, and/or selling your products and services on your Facebook Page. It comes down to aligning your social media metrics with metrics your company is already comfortable with. In Book IX, we drill into the specific areas you'll want to track and analyze to make sure your Facebook marketing plan is working for you.

Measuring brand ROI

The best way to think about measuring brand ROI is to consider how recognizable your brand is to your target audience. It really comes down to how often your Fans are engaging with your Page. Beyond the number of Likers you have, it's more important to consider how often your Fans are responding to your questions or engaging with your posts. It's also important to track how many times your Fans are clicking your links and responding with comments to your posts.

In addition, you want to consider how well your existing customer can identify with your brand on Facebook. Is your Facebook branding consistent with your Web site, products, and or services? You want to create a bridge from Facebook to your main hub. You do this with consistent branding.

Measuring financial ROI

The best way to measure financial ROI for your Facebook marketing plan is to set benchmarks. This means that you want to clearly document what you're working toward in terms of sales and how you can use Facebook as part of this strategy. You also want to decide whether your goal is to sell directly from your Page or to use your Page as a channel to funnel interested prospects to a sales page after you have built their trust and offered them immense value. Measuring your financial ROI comes down to your sales strategy for your Page.

If your goal is to sell your products or services from your Facebook Page, you need to identify benchmarks for this process. Look at how many people you manage to attract to your Page daily, track which tabs they click, and how long they stay on your Page overall. All this can be done by using Facebook Insights and third-party monitoring tools. In Book IX, we walk you through how to use Facebook Insights and third-party monitoring tools to help you better understand how to track your financial ROI for your Facebook marketing initiatives.

Book II

Claiming Your Presence on Facebook

The 5th Wave   By Rich Tennant

"These are the parts of our life that aren't on Facebook."

Contents at a Glance

Chapter 1: Understanding the Different Types of Facebook Pages

In This Chapter

✔ Familiarizing yourself with Facebook's Page options

✔ Addressing privacy concerns

✔ Understanding why you need a personal Profile to have a business Page on Facebook

*F*acebook offers many different types of Pages to encourage community and networking. To create the biggest buzz around your product, service, or business, you need to be aware of Facebook's Page options and the pros and cons of each. This chapter explains those options so that you can decide which type of Page best fits your needs.

We cover personal Profiles, business Pages, Places Pages, Group Pages, Community Pages, and a limited business account. Although each of these page choices has merit, it's almost always best to create a business Page for your product, service, or business (and we explain why in this chapter).

If you already have a personal Profile on Facebook, you know how easy it is to create an account. You may think it's a snap to set up your own business Page, too, and get it in your head to just skip this chapter. We have one word for you, though: Don't! You need to know about some interesting intricacies to this whole profile/business Page thing that you might otherwise miss along the way.

One of the most important things we discuss in this chapter is who can and cannot create a certain kind of Page. We go into detail as we discuss each type of Facebook Page, but the gist is this: You must be an authorized representative of an organization in order to create a business Page for it. If you aren't the authorized representative and want to create a space where fans of a certain topic or figure can share their thoughts and opinions, Facebook suggests that you create a Group Page for them.

Reviewing Facebook Page Types

The two types of Pages most likely to interest you are personal Profiles and business Pages. That's because those are the two types of Pages that you use to establish a marketing hub for your business on Facebook.

The other Pages that you come across on Facebook can supplement your Facebook marketing efforts. The next few sections offer a brief review of each one and tell why you should avoid or embrace them. Everyone's needs are a little different, and you might find that one of the options listed here is a good fit for your particular endeavor on Facebook.

There is a type of account called the Facebook "business account." A *business account* is created just to be able to open a business Page and run ads. It is very limited in that you will not be able to Like, Share, or Comment (all important aspects of a social environment) anywhere on Facebook with this type of account. That said, at the end of this chapter we have included steps on how to open this type of account. All the authors of this book recommend that you start with a personal Profile and then open a business Page.

Personal Profile

More than 600 million people use Facebook as a social space to keep up with friends, share photos and links, and share great stuff they find online. It is a space where people can connect after not being in touch for a long time, or find people they would like to get to know better. It is a place for social interaction.

In Book I, we discuss the history and development of Facebook and its impact around the world. It's where the social party is right now! It's time to join the party by creating a personal account and using Facebook as a social and commerce environment.

Facebook likes us to keep these two uses, social and commerce, separate, but there is a reason to create a personal account, even if the only reason you're joining Facebook is to promote your business.

By creating a personal account and starting to be Friends with your friends and existing customers, you reconnect and create a lively space for interaction. As you build your business Page on Facebook, you will be able to go back to these Friends and invite them to join you on your business Page. If you don't have this initial personal connection, the only way to invite people to your Page is through paid Facebook ads, e-mail, or by phone.

A personal account on Facebook is easy to open. One of the largest-growing demographics of people joining are people over the age of 35, so if that describes you, and you have never enjoyed a social space, it might feel a bit strange at first, but you'll catch on. Then you'll see how easy it is to engage and develop social connections for your business.

We feel that a Facebook personal Profile is a vital first step.

If you don't already have a personal Profile set up on Facebook, run (don't walk) to `http://facebook.com` and set up an account. Facebook makes it super easy. Right from the home page, enter your

Book II
Chapter 1

✦ First and last name

✦ E-mail address (and then again as confirmation)

✦ Password

✦ Sex

✦ Birthday

Facebook requires all users to provide their real date of birth to encourage authenticity and provide only age-appropriate access to content. You will be able to hide this information from your connections (people who Like your business Page) if you want, and its use is governed by the Facebook Privacy Policy.

After entering the necessary personal information, click the Sign Up button. You now have a Facebook personal account. Figure 1-1 shows what your Profile might look like.

If you want a thorough description of opening a personal account, check out *Facebook For Dummies,* Third Edition, by Leah Pearlman and Carolyn Abram (Wiley), or wander over to the Facebook business Page for this Dummies title at `www.facebook.com/facebookfordummies` and post questions on their Page.

You might be tempted to click the link under the account creation fields that says, *Create a Page for a Celebrity, Band, or Business.* Don't click it! This creates what Facebook calls a *business account.* A business account has limited functionality and is for people who don't already have a Facebook personal Profile and want to use Facebook only to administer a business Page and run ad campaigns.

Figure 1-1:
A personal
Profile.

When you create a business account, you won't be able to interact on Facebook in a normal way. It is very limiting. According to Facebook, you won't be able to Share other posts, Like Pages, or comment. You won't be able to view personal Profiles and, worst of all, business accounts can't be found in a search. There might be rare situations where this type of account is needed, and for such cases we have put the instructions on how to open a business account at the end of this chapter.

Some people worry that visitors will see the connection between their personal Profile and the business Page they create, so they make a bogus personal Profile before they open their business Page. We don't recommend doing this, either. Besides, Facebook frowns on creating fake accounts. By "frowns on," we mean that Facebook might delete *all* your Facebook accounts if it discovers that you've been creating fake Profiles. Don't risk the wrath of Facebook by setting up a bogus account!

Be assured that people who choose to connect to your business Page won't be able to see that you are the Page owner or Admin (administrator), nor will they have access to your personal account, unless you change your Page settings to list you publicly as an Admin of the Page.

It's all very clear from Facebook's side: You may create business Pages only to represent real organizations of which you are an authorized representative. No pretending to be someone you're not. In other words, even if you intended all along for the account you created to be just a great joke, Facebook lacks a sense of humor in that regard.

It's important to note that it is against Facebook policy to create a personal Profile to promote your business. Facebook offers many options for businesses, but personal Profiles aren't among them. So, in other words, you can't create a personal Profile that uses the name of the business — as in O'Grady's for the first name and Cleaners for the last name. The same holds for creating a personal Profile with your real name, but using the account only to promote your business.

If you do create a personal Profile for your business, Facebook can (and will) delete all of your accounts, and they will not be reinstated. In case you've made the mistake of creating a personal Profile as your business Page, we explain how to change it in the next chapter.

Facebook recently opened a service to let you migrate your personal profile into a "business account" Page, sometimes called a business profile. We discuss the business account at the end of this chapter. In general, the authors of this book do not recommend doing this migration. If you already have a personal account with a lot of Friends who are in fact business connections, or if your personal account has been functioning as a business, you might want to explore this option. If it is available you will be able to access it here: `www.facebook.com/pages/create.php?migrate`, but please read the last section in this chapter, "Creating a limited business account," before you make a decision.

Whew! All that just to explain how important it is to create a real personal Profile!

Now that you have a real personal Profile and you've started the process of finding old and new friends on Facebook, you can move on to explore a business Page.

Business Page

A business Page provides wonderful opportunities for marketing and promoting your business. It doesn't matter whether you're talking about a brick-and-mortar business or a virtual consulting firm based out of your car. This is the Page that can help your business grow, as we cover in Book I and throughout this entire book.

Facebook has deliberately tried to make business Pages as broad and useful as possible. You can create a business page for a

✦ Local Business or Place

✦ Company, Organization, or Institution

✦ Brand or Product

✦ Artist, Band, or Public Figure

✦ Entertainment

✦ Cause or Topic

In Chapter 2 of this minibook, we explain each of these options (and how to choose the one that's right for you) in more detail. We also give you the steps for creating your business Page on Facebook.

As we note in the previous section about personal Profiles, you can't have a personal Profile as your business presence on Facebook. Creating a personal Profile and then creating a Facebook business Page makes sense for most businesses because of the many features of both. The following table shows you a brief comparison between a personal Profile and business Page.

Personal Profile	*Business Page*
Limited to 5,000 Friends	Unlimited connections or Likes
Cannot use applications	Can install multiple applications
Not searchable outside Facebook	Fully searchable outside Facebook

These business Page features are an integral part of why you should use a business Page as your product, service, or company hub on Facebook.

Although you may want to keep your personal Profile private and connect with only certain people, you'll likely want as many people as possible to connect with your business on Facebook. The way to do that is via a Facebook business Page, which has no limits on the number of fans (that is, Likes) you can have, and lets you install *applications*, as well.

Applications (commonly referred to as apps) are so useful to business pages! You can install apps for contact forms, newsletter sign-ups, live video chats, and so much more. Depending on which apps you install, you can use these apps to improve your fans' interaction with your page and streamline your Facebook administrative duties. We tell you all about Facebook applications and give you our top suggestions for apps in Book V and throughout this book. We give you a little peek at what you can expect your business Page to resemble in Figure 1-2.

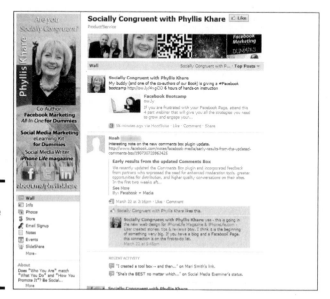

Figure 1-2: An example of a Facebook business Page.

Places Page

A Places Page ties the computer Facebook experience with the mobile Facebook experience. Places is an effort by Facebook to create a community experience with your Facebook Friends while you're out and about. Places is Facebook's answer to other geolocation applications like foursquare and Gowalla. Places allows your fans to use their smartphone through `http://touch.facebook.com` to check in to your bricks-and-mortar store or restaurant when they visit. This check-in then shows up in their News Feed so that their Friends will see it. Considering that the average Facebook user has 130 Friends, that's a lot of extra promotion for you! Figure 1-3 shows what a Places Page on a mobile phone may look like when someone checks in.

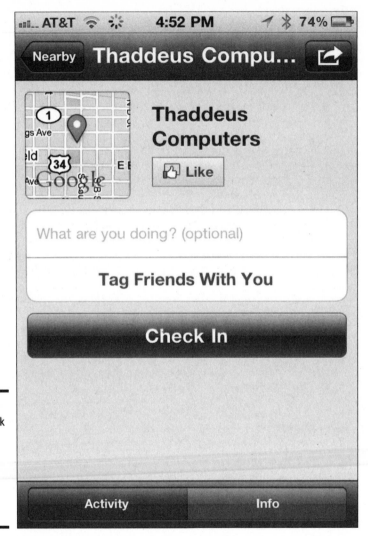

Figure 1-3:
A Facebook
Places
Check-in
Page has
just a
few Page
elements.

Places Pages can be created by anyone at any time. When user check in via their smartphone, by using `http://touch.facebook.com`, or `http://m.facebook.com` the place the user is checking into doesn't have a Places Page, he or she can create one. As a business owner, you can surely see why you'd want to retain control over your Places Page rather than leave that control to the masses. You have two options:

✦ If your business doesn't have a Places Page, you can create one and claim it as your official Places Page.

✦ If a Places Page is already created for your business, don't worry! You can still claim the Places Page as the official representative and obtain control of the page.

✦ After you have claimed your Places Page, you can offer Deals to people who check in.

We explain how to figure out whether your business has a Places Page already created or whether you need to create one, and how to create Deals in Book VII, Chapter 4.

After you've determined whether you have a Places Page, it's a good idea to *claim* your Facebook Places page so that you have control over how that page is administered. When you claim your Places Page (again, see Book VII, Chapter 4), you're just confirming with Facebook that you're the owner of the company or authorized representative acting on behalf of the company.

After you've claimed your Places Page, you'll have the opportunity to merge your Places Page with your business Page on Facebook. If you decide to merge your business and Places Pages, a good process would be to create your business Page first and then go and claim or create your Places Page.

You need to know that even though a merged Page retains everything from your business Page (photos, posts, events, video, ads) and will now contain a map and check- ins from Places, you won't be able to set a landing page — everyone will go straight to your Page Info link, which might not provide the best first impression for new visitors. You therefore need to consider whether it's in your company's best interest to have one merged Page or two separate Pages.

A merged Page will look a lot like Figure 1-4. Notice the number of "Checkins" and Friend Activity link on the left navigation menu. The Info link on a merged Page contains a map.

Group Page

A group Page is not officially a business-type Page. A group Page can, however, be used to supplement a business's Page. You have three options when it comes to creating a group Page:

Figure 1-4:
This is how
a merged
Places and
business
Page looks.

✦ **Closed group Pages:** This type is the default. The members are *public* (meaning that they're visible to the Facebook community), but the content is private. You will see the updates to this type of Page in your News Feed, but there will be a small locked icon indicating that this post is private, and only you can see it in your Feed.

✦ **Open group Pages:** The members and content are public. Anything you post inside this group Page will show up on your Wall as well as on your Friends' News Feeds.

✦ **Secret group Pages:** The members and content are private. The only ones who can see anything posted on a secret group Page are the members of this group. Group members will see these posts in their News Feeds but with a little lock icon next to it.

Most group Pages look the same but simply have different privacy settings. Figure 1-5 shows what a group Page looks like to members.

Although a group Page isn't considered an official business Page, it can offer some wonderful benefits to your business when used in conjunction with your business Page. To see what we mean, consider the following business uses for a group Page:

Figure 1-5:
A Facebook group Page is a great way to collaborate on projects or discuss specific topics.

✦ **You can create a closed group page for the members of a collaborative project.** The members of this type of group are public as a way to create a bit of mystery or buzz about an upcoming event for those who see the group listing in Facebook Search, but discussions between members are private.

✦ **You can create an open group Page for training.** A really cool idea is to create an open group Page for coaching or training sessions. On the day and time of the event, everyone could go the group Page, ask questions in the group chat box, and the organizer could post answers in the post box. By doing this in an open group format, it could be found in Facebook Group Search at `www.facebook.com/search.php?type=groups`, and in the Group Directory at `www.facebook.com/directory/groups`. What a wonderful and innovative way to advertise your expertise.

Several DIY courses and e-books are available, such as Darren Rowses's *Build a Better Blog in 31 Days* and Kelby Carr's *Mom Blog SEO in 30 Days* (published by Carr Creations LLC). A group would be a great place to meet up and go through the materials with others doing the same exercises.

✦ **You can create a secret group Page for your staff.** With a secret group Page in place, your staff can post updates, links, videos, events, and documents that only those staff members in the group can see. They can have a group chat, where everyone can type text in the chat box all at the same time. A Facebook group chat in the morning before work starts would be a fun way to start the day.

Community Page

Community Pages are a type of Facebook Page dedicated to a single cause or topic. Facebook automatically generates them from the fields people fill out in their personal Profile. These community Pages should not be confused with the Cause or Community business Page options that individuals can create.

This section explains the generic Facebook-generated community Page, and we explain the Cause or Community option for a business Page in Chapter 2 of this minibook. We know it's confusing, but these are two separate types of Pages. Figures 1-6 and 1-7 show how these pages are different.

Generic, Facebook-created community Pages are commonly disregarded because they lack the information and functionality of a business Page. They don't make good business hubs for several reasons:

✦ **No one owns a community Page.** You cannot administer or impose your business culture on a generic community Page because it does not belong to you.

✦ **You cannot post regularly to a generic community Page.** These pages will pull in articles you or your Friends post about a topic, but no one can contribute information directly to a community Page. The only way to have any post show up on a community page is to use the keyword that is the Page's title. For example; use 'beach' in a post, and it will show up on the community Page for "Beach." In fact, as you can see in Figure 1-8, community Pages do not have a traditional Wall, they have an Info page as the landing page.

✦ **You can't install applications on a community Page.** As we've stated previously, applications can be an important part of your marketing strategies because they add functionality and customization to your business Page.

✦ **Updates to community Pages do not appear in the News Feed.** Although a community Page has a Like button at the top (just as a business Page does), these pages don't generate News Feed stories, so you won't see anything from a community Page show up in your personal News Feed (and neither will your customers and fans). If you click the Like button, though, that Page will now show up in your personal Profile under Likes and Interests on your Info tab.

Figure 1-6:
A generic, Facebook-generated Community Page.

Figure 1-7:
A Community business Page has all the functions of a business Page.

So how do you know whether you're looking at a generic, Facebook-generated community Page? There are several ways. Please refer to Figure 1-8 as we explain each.

✦ The left navigation bar is limited to three options: Info, Related Posts, and Wikipedia. If no Wikipedia information is available, that navigation option doesn't appear. There is no traditional Wall tab. On the other hand, a business Pages will have at least six navigation options (possibly more), including a traditional Wall tab.

✦ Most pages will display a related Wikipedia article if one is available. You may also see posts by your Friends or the global Facebook community that contain the keyword of the community Page (for example, if the community Page is for "beach," any articles posted by your Friends with the word *beach* will show up here).

✦ Many community Pages display a generic image as the profile image, whereas others display an image related to the topic. Depending on the type of community Page, you may see a gray square with a white silhouette of a specific image (such as a briefcase, a student in a mortar board, or something similar to a molecule) or a logo or image from a business, school, topic, and so on.

Figure 1-8:
Facebook Community Pages have three distinguishing features.

We encourage you to search your keywords related to your particular business to see whether Facebook has created community Pages for them. When you find a community Page related to your keyword(s), you can get an idea of how people are interacting with those words and topics and use that information to influence what you post on your business Page.

Creating a limited business account

If you prefer not to use Facebook as a regular social user with a personal Profile, you can create a *business account*. A business account has limited functionality and is for people who do not already have a Facebook personal Profile and want to use Facebook only to administer a business Page and run ad campaigns.

When you create a business account, you will not be able to interact on Facebook normally. It is very limiting. You will not be able to Share other posts, Like Pages, or comment. You will not be able to view personal Profiles and worst of all, business accounts can't be found in a search.

If you still feel to create this type of account, follow these steps:

1. **Go to** http://facebook.com.

2. **At the bottom of the personal profile form, click the Create a Page for a Celebrity, Band, or Business link.**

3. **Click to choose the type of business Page you'd like to create.**

4. **Complete the requested Page information.**

   You will need to type in the Page name and, depending on the Page type you choose, you may need to add the physical location.

5. **Select the check box next to I Agree to Facebook Pages Terms.**

6. **Click the Get Started button.**

   A Security Check pop-up window appears.

7. **Type in the words you see.**

8. **Click the Submit button.**

   You're now on the interface to continue developing your new business account Facebook Page.

Business accounts are only for individuals who do not currently have a personal Profile. If you already have a personal Profile, you should log in to Facebook with that account and create your business page (refer to Chapter 2 of this minibook to see how to create a business Page connected to your personal Profile).

Your business account is now live and your browser opens your new business Page so that you can finish setting it up. Now, any time you log in to Facebook, you won't see a personal Profile News Feed as most users do; instead, you'll see the admin panel for your Page (shown in Figure 1-9).

Remember, this is not the type of account we recommend you open on Facebook, but is an option. If you use this type of account and try to interact on Facebook (by trying to comment on another post), you will get an error message dialog box asking you to open a personal account to be able to complete the action.

Figure 1-9:
Logging in with a business account on Facebook takes you to the admin panel of your business account Page.

Chapter 2: Creating Your Business Page

In This Chapter

✔ Choosing your Page name and type

✔ Going through the steps to publish your new business Page

✔ Modifying Page settings to match your needs

✔ Sharing your business Page with customers

This chapter is all about creating your business presence on Facebook by opening a Facebook Page. We always think it's a good idea to read through instructions before building something new, and we suggest that here, too. Choosing your Page type and category might be very clear-cut for you, or maybe not. Reading and exploring how it works can be an interesting first step.

One way that we enjoy exploring how other people have done it is by going to www.facebook.com/pages. Notice the names of Pages; sort by the types at the top of the Page; hover your cursor over a linked Page name and look at the little box that pops up with the type and category under the title. For example, if you hover over the Starbucks name, the box says "Food/beverages." You can learn a lot by seeing how other have created their Pages.

In this chapter, we take you through the steps to create your Facebook business Page, and then we show you how to let people know that your Page is open for business.

Things to Consider Before You Start

Creating your Facebook business Page is an important process, and we want you to be as wide awake as possible while going through it. Some of the selections you make will determine many future functions, such as the navigation links on your Page as well as the promotional information fields on your Info page that you'll surely want to use in your marketing plan. In particular, you want to carefully consider what to name your Page and which type of business Page to create.

The name you give to your business Page is extremely important because it becomes the title of your Page. When a customer, Fan, or Friend searches for your business Page on Facebook, it's this name/title that will enable them to find you. Because naming your Page is so important, we'd like you to mull over a few things. Here are a few naming dos and don'ts to consider before you create your business Page:

Page names

+ Must use proper, grammatically correct capitalization

+ Must have logical, correct punctuation

+ Need to include your name, if you're branding yourself

+ Need to include your business keywords, if you're branding your niche or product

Page names cannot use the following:

+ Excessive capitalization or all capitals

+ Symbols such as ! or ® or TM (but you can use a hyphen)

+ Repeated and unnecessary punctuation

+ Abusive terms

+ The word *Facebook* or any variation of it

Facebook wants you to create concise page names without long tag lines after the name. You have up to 75 character spaces for your Page name, and we encourage you keep things short and sweet. All the businesses we know that created long page names eventually wanted to shorten them. For example, we created a Page with a very long tagline: iPhoneLife Magazine & iPhoneLife.com — *User created stories, tips & reviews.* Facebook approved it, but now that we want to change it, we can't because we have more than 100 Likes or what Facebook calls *Connections.* Connections are the people who have clicked the Like button for your Page.

Facebook doesn't want you to use superfluous descriptions or unnecessary qualifiers such as the word *official* in a Page name. Campaign names and regional or demographic qualifiers, though, are acceptable. For example, Nike Football Spain is just fine.

Stay clear of generic terms for your Page name, too. If you name a Page using a generic reference to the category; like "Jewelry" instead of "Sparkle's Jewelry Store" you may have your administrative rights removed and the Page will become an uneditable Facebook-generated Community Page.

Facebook might make exceptions to this generic rule if your organization, business, celebrity, or band name is known to the public with a generic word. If you think that's the case, you need to provide proof with newspaper publications. And to present your proof, you need a Facebook Form to request that an exception to the generic rule be made in your case. You can find that form at

```
www.facebook.com/help/contact.php?show_form=create_page_s
```

If you want to convince Facebook to let you create a Page with a generic name, you have to provide three sources that reference your proposed name, and those sources can't be your own press releases. They have to be three completely different articles in three different publications.

Choosing the right type of business Page

Facebook offers six different types of Facebook Pages so that you can choose the one that best first with your product, service, brand, or business. When you go to `www.facebook.com/pages/create.php`, you see the business Page options, as shown in Figure 2-1.

We know you're probably wondering which type you should use for your own business Page. To help you, the following bullets give you the skinny on what each Page type offers and when you should choose a particular Page type over another.

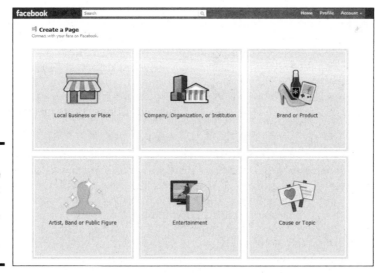

Figure 2-1:
Choose one of these six options to create your business Page.

✦ **Local Business or Place:** This Page type is for brick-and-mortar businesses. Choose this type only if you truly have a local, open-to-the-public type of business.

When you click the Local Business of Place option, you see a drop-down menu with 38 category choices! You can choose one of these categories to create a Page, or if none of the categories fits your business, you can choose Local Business and go from there. The Info page for this type of business Page is very detailed, with editing fields for hours of operation, parking options, and price ranges.

✦ **Company, Organization, or Institution:** This Page type is for a company that isn't necessarily open to the public like a local business would be. Many of the categories in the drop-down are the same as the local type, but the resulting Info page will not have the same detailed interface to fill in for prices, parking, and so on.

If you have multiple stores in the same city, you will need to sit down and decide on a company policy about Facebook Pages. Some questions to ask are; Do you or your store managers want to manage one Page or a Page for each store? Starbucks runs one company Page, and Aveda has a custom link that helps you find a local store. Obviously, these are large corporations, but there are other companies that give the managers the option to open a Page, as long as they adhere to company social media policies.

✦ **Brand or Product:** If you have an actual, physical product you sell, this is the Page type to consider. There are many categories that are offered up by Facebook; cars, clothing, computers, pet supplies, and a generic product/service category.

✦ **Artist, Band or Public Figure:** Obviously, if you are a band or artist this is the one to choose, but this Page type also includes politicians, business people, chefs, dancers, and actors. You might think the actor category would be under Entertainment, but it isn't! Notice, you would use this type for your Band, but if you are only promoting your CD on Facebook, you can use the Entertainment type with the category of Album.

Just keep in mind, you must be the official, recognized and authorized representative of whatever type and category of Page you create on Facebook.

✦ **Entertainment:** If you have a TV show, or a magazine, or creating a Page just for your music CD, select this Page type. There are close to 30 different categories listed here. I'm still trying to figure out why Library is listed as a category under Entertainment. Is your library entertaining?

✦ **Cause or Community:** If you have been on Facebook for awhile, don't confuse this type of Page with the Causes application. Also, don't confuse it with a Facebook-generated Community Page, as outlined in the previous Chapter that is created out of a person's Likes in their personal account info. If you are new to Facebook, and are creating a Page for a non-profit or community organization, you can consider this type of Page, as in the beginning it functions just a like all Facebook business Pages, except that, if you garner thousands of people who Like this type of Page, Facebook could decide to take away your admin rights and let it self-run as a Facebook adopted Community Page.

Every Page type has an Info section. Also, many categories have specific fields in that Info section that are used when someone *Shares* your Page with their friends. Anyone can Share your Page using a Share link on the bottom left side of your Page. Most Page categories will use the Company Overview text to populate the Share invitation. Clicking that Share link auto-populate a post that will go on your personal account Wall that will be seen in the news feed, or you can decide to Share it as a Facebook Message instead. You can add personal text with this Share post. We go into detail on how to do all that in minibook IV, Chapter 1

One of the authors of this Book recently changed her Page type from Brand or Product to Artist/Band/Public Figure with a category of Business Person. It seemed to fit her a little better, even though she's also a teacher, author, and entertainer — other category choices for this Page type. Which brings up the point that you can adjust this Page type and category setting in the future if you need to. The interface is a bit different and can be accessed right from the top of your Page. The steps to change your Page type and category can be found at the very end of this chapter and in Chapter 3 of this minibook.

Setting Up Your New Business Page

Goodness. Finally. Time to set up a new business Page on Facebook!

Are you ready? Read through these steps first before you attempt to create your business Page.

1. **Log into your personal Facebook account.**

2. **Go to** http://facebook.com/pages/create.php.

Doing so brings up a wall with six Page types, as shown in Figure 2-2. If you need to, take the time to click each Page type and click the drop-down category list. Look for a category that matches your business.

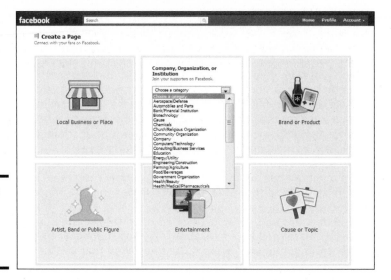

Figure 2-2:
Find a
category
for your
business.

3. **Select the type of Page to create.**

   New options will now be available to fill in.

4. **Select the category of Page you want.**

   The category you choose determines the types of Info fields for your Page. All types, except Cause or Community, ask you to select a category for your Page. The reason to find the best category is that the category determines what details are shown on your business Page's Info link. For example, a Book category will display an Info link with fields for your ISBN, a Café category will give you fields for hours and types of credit cards you take.

5. **Type in the requested information.**

   Depending on which business Page type you choose, you see different text fields to fill in. The Name field will end up being the title of the Page. Each of the six types call the Name field something different: Local business calls it Business or Place, Company calls it Company Name, Brand or Product calls it Brand or Product, Artist or Band calls it Name, Entertainment calls it Name, and Cause or Community calls it Cause or Community.

   Facebook likes (insists upon) first letters being capitalized for Page names. You will need to fill out all fields to be able to create your Page.

Take the time to think through this whole naming business. Better yet, read the earlier section called Naming your Page. You'll be able to change a Page name only up until the point at which you have 100 people who Like your Page. After that point, you're stuck with it. So think it through.

6. **Select the I agree to Facebook Pages Terms check box.**

   You must be the official representative of this person, business, band, or product to create this Page. If you are not, you are in violation of Facebook Terms and Services, and Facebook can (and will) remove your page and not reinstate it.

7. **Click the Get Started button.**

   You created a Facebook Page!

A very boring Page is what you see as soon as you click the Get Started button. This page, shown in Figure 2-3, is the interface for modifying your new Facebook Page to suit your business.

When you create a new Page, Facebook defaults it as published! Yikes! You might want to change this, as you don't even have your Page image uploaded yet, or have your Info link filled in completely! To unpublish your Page to the public, so you can continue to work on it privately, look for the Edit page button on the top right side on the Page and follow these steps:

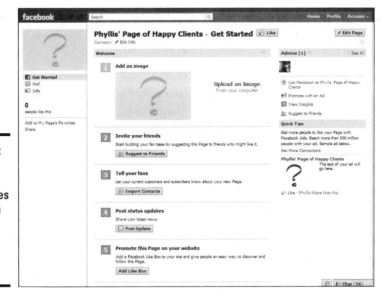

Figure 2-3: The Get Started Page guides you as you customize your business Page.

1. **Click the Edit Page button.**

   This is located in the top right corner of your new Page.

2. **Click the Manage Permissions link on the left navigation menu.**

3. **Click to select the top check box, Page Visibility (see Figure 2-4) so that only Admins can see this Page!**

   This effectively un-publishes your new Page, hiding it from everyone except Page Admins.

4. **Click Save.**

   Your business Page is now visible only to you and any other admins. After you have decked out your Page with an image, detailed info, photos, and other fun things, you can publish the Page for all to see by coming back to this Page and deselecting this Page Visibility check box.

To see what a finished Local Business Page might look like for a food establishment, check out the Facebook business Page for one of our favorite restaurants, Seasons 52, at www.facebook.com/seasons52. Figure 2-5 shows the Info tab for Season 52 in all its glory, as all that information about credit cards and parking are the defining difference in selecting the Local Business or Places page type and a food services category.

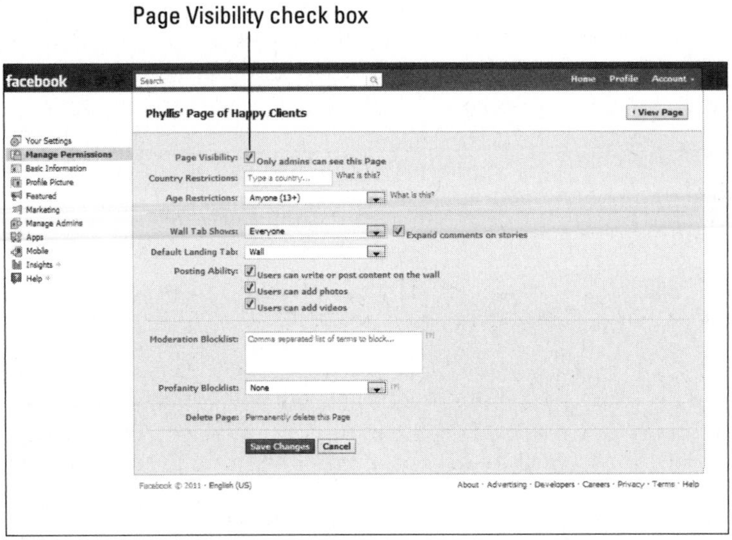

Page Visibility check box

Figure 2-4: Click this Page Visibility check box to hide it from the public.

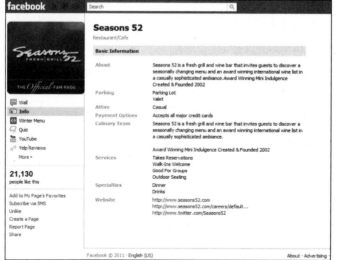

Figure 2-5:
Check out
this Info tab,
full of vital
information
for a
local food
business.

A well-done business Page

Seasons 52 has a really nice Facebook Page with a type of Local Business and category of Restaurant/Cafe. Even though this is Season 52's corporate account (not an individual local restaurant), it has decided to go with the Local type so that it could have a fuller Info link that includes parking, payment, and service information that all sites share. Season 52 has a nice interaction going on the Wall, and it has added several apps. It has a custom link called "Quiz" a Yelp app to add customer reviews, and a YouTube app for its instructional videos. This business Page is really well done, so while you're there looking at the Info link, explore the other Page links as well. We talk about adding apps to your Page in Book V and various other places throughout this book.

Using the Getting Started Page

The Getting Started page, shown in Figure 2-3, is what you see as soon as your create a new Facebook Page. Only you and anyone you designate as an admin will be able to see this particular interface. The Getting Started page is Facebook's step-by-step process to help you develop your business Page.

You have six steps to go through, as follows:

1. Add an image

2. Invite your Friends

3. Tell your Fans

4. Post status updates

5. Promote this Page on your Web site

6. Set up your mobile phone

In the following sections, we walk you through each of these steps. Try not to skip ahead because these steps are important to form your new Page! As you complete a step, it disappears and the next step moves up.

If, by chance, you opened a *business account* instead of a personal Profile then a business Page, your Getting Started page will have only five steps, as you will not be able to access any Friends (since a business account is not connected to a personal Profile on Facebook).

Add an image

You know all about pictures saying a thousand words and such, right? You need to an image to your Page — no ifs, ands, or buts about it.

One graphic design artist (Fluent Design `www.facebook.com/getfluentdesign`) says this about your Facebook image:

"The graphic image on your Facebook page is also a key ingredient to getting visitors to stay on your page longer. If you have an attractive and easy-to-read image that promotes your product or service you will have a higher rate of conversion as opposed to graphics that are just ok and don't get the message across in a clear and effective manner."

If you are branding yourself, it's a good idea to feature your face in this image, to help connect the human element into the rest of the Page that contains text and links. Adding this human element can make people feel more connected to you and what you are trying to sell.

If you are branding your company, make sure your logo or product image is on this image.

Whichever way you choose, the image finds a new home in the top-left position on your Page, as shown in Figure 2-6. We highly suggest that you create a custom image to upload that contains your logo, contact information, your photo (if branding yourself), or a combination of these things. The image size can be up to 180 x 540 pixels. The space you get for a Page image is quite a bit larger than a personal Profile picture and can really make a statement on your Page.

Depending on your business, you might want a shorter image so that the navigation links are higher up on the Page. If those links, or extra links you might add (apps such as videos, SlideShare, Livestream, custom pages, and others), aren't going to be used, a longer image is better. You can always change out your Page image later.

**Book II
Chapter 2**

Creating Your
Business Page

Figure 2-6:
This Profile
image
incorporates
product
images
and team
member
photos.

To upload an image from your hard drive to your Facebook Page:

1. **Click the Upload an Image link on the Get Started Tab.**

Refer to Figure 2-7.

2. **Click the Browse button in the Image dialog box that appears, and then find the image (4MB max) you want to upload on your computer.**

As soon as you double-click the image file you want to upload, Facebook starts the upload process. After the file is uploaded, you will be back on the Getting Started page.

You might want to check the *thumbnail* that Facebook generates for this image. A thumbnail is a smaller version of your original image. In the world of Facebook, thumbnail images show up next to every status update or comment you make as your Page (more on that in Chapter 3). As you can imagine, your thumbnail will be a key component in branding your business Page.

Follow these steps to adjust the thumbnail image:

1. **Click the Edit Page button.**

You find this button on the top-right corner of your Page.

2. **Click the Profile Picture link in the left navigation menu.**

This is where you will be able to change your Profile image from now on (after going through the Getting Started page). You will also be able to snap a picture from your webcam to use as a Profile image, adjust your thumbnail, and unhide and photos you have hidden from the top of your Page (we go through those steps more thoroughly in upcoming Chapter 3).

3. **Click the Edit Thumbnail link under your image.**

Doing so pulls up the Edit Thumbnail dialog box, as shown in Figure 2-8.

4. **Drag the thumbnail image around until it looks good as a thumbnail.**

5. **Click Save.**

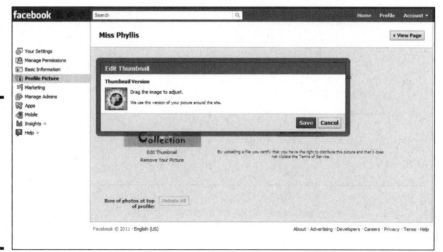

**Book II
Chapter 2**

Creating Your
Business Page

Figure 2-8:
This is the
dialog box
where
you can
adjust your
thumbnail
to look just
right.

Invite your Friends

The next step on the Getting Started Page is inviting your Friends. We suggest customizing your Page as much as possible (with posts, photos, apps) before sharing it, but if you feel your Page is ready, inviting your Facebook Friends is the next step.

When you click the Suggest to Friends button, a new dialog box appears in which you can select your personal Facebook Friends to invite them to Like your Page. To select a Friend, just click that person's picture. Continue clicking until you have selected everyone you want to share your Page with. Click the Send Recommendations button. Your Friends will get a generic-looking invitation delivered to their Messages inbox.

If you want to do this step later, you can find the Suggest to Friends link on the right side Admin area of your Page. Both have the same steps.

If you opened a business account, instead of a personal account to start your business Page, you will not see this step at all.

Tell your Fans

Your contacts outside Facebook might be a gold mine of people who would benefit from your Page. With the help of the Tell Your Fans dialog box, you can import the contact info for all the folks you know into a space where you can invite them to your Page.

To import your contacts, click the Import Contacts link. Doing so brings up a new Tell Your Fans dialog box, as shown in Figure 2-9.

The Tell Your Fans dialog box contains two options:

✦ Upload a Contact File

✦ Find Your Web Email Contacts

The idea here is that you can either upload a contacts file you put together yourself or you can have Facebook search though your Hotmail, Gmail, or Yahoo! address book to find people for you to contact who are already on Facebook.

To help you create a contact file to upload, Facebook has created instructions specific to whichever mail system you use. Click the *How to Create a Contact File* link and select the system you use from the list. In addition to the list shown in the dialog box, Facebook supports the following types of contact files: comma-separated values (.csv); vCards (.vcf); tab-delimited text (.txt); and LDAP (Data Interchange Format; .ldif).

If you want Facebook to search through your address book contacts directly, you need to type your e-mail address and password into the text boxes provided and click the Find Contacts button.

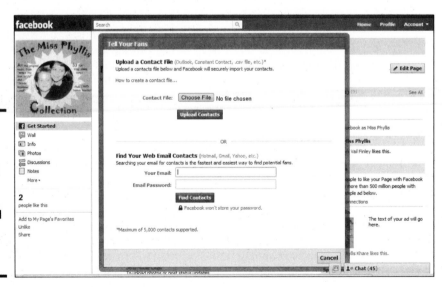

Figure 2-9:
You can import your e-mail contacts to tell your Friends and contacts about your new Page.

Then you can select the people you want to invite to your Page. The pre-view, as shown in Figure 2-10 shows how the invitation will look to those whose e-mail address matches a personal Facebook account already, as you can see at the top, and how it would look if sent to someone's e-mail that is not associated with a Facebook account on the bottom.

For users already on Facebook, this invitation will show up on the right side of their News Feed on Facebook as an invitation from your Page. If they do not have a Facebook account, they will get an e-mail suggesting that they join Facebook so that they can Like your Page.

A kind of obscure place that Facebook puts Page invitations is here `www.facebook.com/pages`. No one knows to go there, but Facebook has a very nice section on the right side called Page Invites with all the invitations that have been sent to you. Currently, it is the best place to go to see those invitations. Spread the word.

Post status updates

Posting a few interesting status updates to populate your Wall encourages people to stick around once they find your business on Facebook. We suggest informational posts about the purpose of your Page, its history, and some introductory posts about you or your business. You should also include one post with a link to either your Web site or e-commerce site.

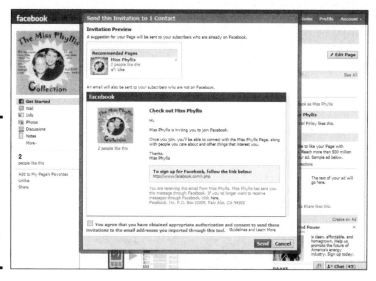

Figure 2-10:
Facebook
will send a
message to
your e-mail
contacts
and invite
them to Like
your Page.

When you click the Post Status Update button on the Get Started Page, you are taken straight to your Page's Wall to create a post. You have the option to create a simple text post or one with a link, video, or photo. Those instructions on how to post is discussed thoroughly in minibook III.

Promote this Page on your Web site

One of the best ways to have people connect with your business on Facebook is to place a Like box on your Web site or blog. Facebook thinks so highly of it, they have placed this process on the Getting Started page.

If you want to preview the process, click the Add Like Box button. You are taken to the Like Box page on the Facebook Developers site. From here you can customize a Facebook Like *box (a box that can be placed on your website's sidebar)*. After you tweak the Like Box's design to your heart's content, you'll be given code to place on your Web site or blog.

The complete description and instructions on how to do that are in minibook VII, Chapter 2, where all the Facebook social plugins (Activity Feed, Comments, Facepile, Like Box, Like Button, Live Stream, Login Button, and Recommendations) are explained.

To be clear; there are *social plugins* and there are *badges*. Badges contains links to take people back to your Page, whereas a social plugin allows you to click the Like button for a Page without leaving the website on which the box is placed. There are four types of badges that can also be created for your website. Two of them work with your Page; the Like badge and the Page badge. You can find the interface to create them here: www.facebook.com/badges/. We don't recommend using badges. They're not as helpful in gaining more Likes — they don't contain a built-in Like button as Like *boxes* do.

Set up your mobile phone

Facebook understands that you aren't always at your desk or computer when you need to post an update to your business Page. If you're on the go and need to share something with your Fans, you can use your smartphone, and in this section we show you how.

Under Set Up Your Mobile Phone, you find two links:

✦ **Send Mobile Email:** This option gives you the information you need to upload photos or post updates from your mobile e-mail account.

✦ **Send Text Messages:** This option allows you to set up a way to post status updates through a text message.

First, take care of the mobile e-mail business. To set up your mobile e-mail so that you can send status updates remotely, follow these steps:

1. **Click the Send Mobile Email link.**

   A dialog box appears with an e-mail address, as shown in Figure 2-11. You can use this e-mail address to send a photo or status update to your Page. This is a secret e-mail address just for your Page.

   You can select the Refresh Your Upload Email link to get a different address to use, but you can use this refresh option only a few times.

2. **Click the Send the Upload Email Link to Me Now link.**

   You will get an e-mail to the address you used to set up your Facebook account, with your Facebook Page's e-mail address. Save this to your contacts for easy access.

3. **Click Okay.**

   If you didn't write down that address, don't worry. We show you where you can find it again. (Hint: You find it through the Navigation menu, which we tell you about in the next chapter.)

When you use this e-mail address to send a status update to your business Page, the e-mail subject line will be used as the caption of your photo or video (if you're including one of those items). If you're just writing a text update, the subject line will *be* the status update, so don't bother writing anything in the body of the e-mail because it won't show up anywhere.

Book II
Chapter 2

Creating Your
Business Page

Figure 2-11: You can generate an e-mail address to send updates to your Page.

If you'd like to send status updates to your Facebook business Page, follow these steps to set that up:

1. **Click the Send Text Messages link.**

   The Activate Facebook Texts (Step 1 of 2) dialog box appears.

2. **Select your Country and Mobile Carrier from the drop-down menus.**

3. **Click the Next button.**

Follow the instructions specific to your carrier to connect your mobile phone and your Page. Now you can create a text message on your mobile phone and have it post directly to your Page.

If you have a smartphone with a Facebook app, it's probably easier to just open the app and post a status update inside the app than to text message your Page, but try them both out to find the best system for you. If you have an administrative team that will be posting to your Page, make sure that team gets the mobile e-mail address, too.

That's it for the Getting Started tab. If all goes well, it will now disappear so that you can continue to develop your new Page. If not, no worry, as it is only seen by admins of the Page.

Managing Missteps

You might discover that you've made a mistake when you were creating your business Page. Maybe you created your personal Profile for your business instead of a business Page. Or maybe you created the wrong kind of business Page and want to change that. Or maybe you created a personal Profile in your name, but most of your Friends are there because of the business you promote from this account. You can almost always fix your issue, but the sooner you realize and can correct your mistake, the better. It's always easier to change a Page when you have fewer connections.

Businesses as personal Profiles

A misconception that users have is that it's perfectly okay to create a personal Profile using a business name, or to use your real name and only promote your business. This is completely against Facebook rules. If you committed that misstep, don't worry: it's fixable, and we tell you how shortly. We hope that you haven't developed an extensive group of Friends yet, though, because you'll need to ask all of them to move over to a real business Page and then Like it.

It's a bit like the separation of church and state. Facebook requires a separation of your personal life and your business affairs. Facebook doesn't want you to run a business from your personal Profile. In fact, Facebook states quite clearly in its Statement of Rights and Responsibilities, "You will not use your personal Profile for your own commercial gain (such as selling your status update to an advertiser)."

Sorting out or deleting a personal Profile set up as a business

If you created a personal Profile with your business name or created a personal account with your name but only promoted your business, your first step to making things all better is to build your new, honest-to-goodness "Official Business Page" and then add a status message to the original personal Profile you created for the business of the change. The new status update should give your Friends the correct URL to the new business Page and explain that you have created a new business Page in order to conform to Facebook guidelines. Tell them that you hope they'll join you over there and Like the Page.

Book II Chapter 2

Creating Your Business Page

If you created this personal Profile in the business name, you can also tell them that you'll be deactivating the current Profile page and explain what they can find at the new business Page (for example, coupons, special deals, updates, and so on). You will likely need to post this status update several times before people start migrating over. We suggest setting a deadline for moving to the new business Page so that your connections will know exactly when you'll deactivate the business name Profile page.

If you created a personal Profile in your real name, but only promoted your business from there, you can keep the original personal Profile and use it as your personal account, but ask people who became Friends with you because of the business to move to the new business Page.

Status updates alone may not be enough. Some people have even gone so far as to create an image that contains the URL of their business Page and use it as the Profile image to remind people to click over to the new business Page. It will take some time to move everyone over to the new business Page, and you may lose some of your connections, but you must make the switch. This is necessary not only to conform to Facebook guidelines but also to gain the functionality of business Pages.

Here's a sample of a post that someone wrote asking her Friends to move over to her business Page:

Hi everyone, I have a new Page for my new CD of contemporary lullabies, "Midnight Lullaby." This project has been a long time coming, and I'm hoping you can check it out and click the Like button. Here's the link: `www.facebook.com/ladylullabymusic`. There are many things I plan to add to this new Page, but for right now please Like it, and I'll keep you posted from there. This new Page is where I will be spending my time on Facebook, so if you want to connect with me, please do it from there.

Thank you!

Jane (Jane Roman Pitt) `www.facebook.com/midnightlullabyCD`

She decided to keep her original personal Profile, because it was her name, but moved all her posts about her business to her new Page. She had already created a vanity URL for her personal Profile with her CD's name which could not be modified.

If you created a personal Profile with the business name, when your move date arrives, you need to deactivate this personal Profile account associated with your business. To deactivate that account, follow these steps:

1. **Log in to Facebook with the e-mail you used to create the personal account for your business.**

2. **Click the Account link in the top-right corner of your Page.**

3. **Choose Account Settings from the menu.**

4. **Scroll to the bottom of the Page and click the Deactivate Account link.**

   A Deactivate Account page appears, asking whether you're sure you want to deactivate your account.

5. **Complete the form on this page.**

6. **Click the Confirm button to deactivate this account.**

Now that you've deactivated your personal account with the business name, sign in to Facebook with your new personal account and go to your new official business Page and start interacting with your connections! Welcome them to your new space and encourage them to interact with you.

Changing your business Page type or name

Sometimes people make a business Page and realize they've made a mistake. Maybe they chose the wrong type of business Page or they want to change the name of the Page or the category that is associated with the Page. You can change the category or type of Page at any time, but you can change a business Page's name only if you have fewer than 100 people who Like the page. To make those types of changes, follow these steps:

1. **Log in to Facebook**.

2. **Go to** www.facebook.com/pages.

Look on the top-right of the page for the following three links: My Pages, Pages I Admin, and Create Page.

3. **Click the Pages I Admin link**.

A new page appears, listing all the Pages you admin.

4. **Find the name of the Page you want to edit and click the Edit Page link underneath it.**

You are now in the editing area for your Page, with a navigation menu on the left side.

5. **On this navigation menu, click the Basic Information link (as shown in Figure 2-12).**

This is where you can edit the type (or group), category, and name of your business Page. At the top of the Page, you can see two drop-down menus, and you can take any of the following actions to make desired changes:

- To change the type of business Page, click the first drop-down menu and make your choice.

- To change the category of your business Page, click the second drop-down menu and make your choice.

- To change your business Page name, click inside the Name text box, delete the existing name, and then retype the new name. We encourage you to review the "Name your Page" section in Chapter 2 of this minibook before changing your business Page's name. The new name will appear as the title of your Page, but will not change your vanity URL (see Chapter 3 of this minibook) if you have already created it.

6. **Click the Save Changes button.**

If you have more than 100 Likes, but must change your business Page name, you need to delete the original Page and start from scratch. We sincerely discourage you from doing this because you will lose all of your Likes (connections) and will have to recreate your community from scratch. Changing your name after you have more than 100 Likes is confusing for your audience, and it will be hard to woo them back. However, if you must delete your Page, follow these steps:

Book II
Chapter 2

Creating Your
Business Page

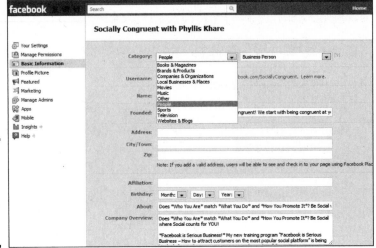

Figure 2-12:
Change or
modify a
Page Group,
Category, or
Name here.

1. **Log in to Facebook.**

2. **Go to** `http://www.facebook.com/pages.`

   Look on the top-right of the page for following the three links: My Pages, Pages I Admin, and Create Page.

3. **Click the Pages I Admin link.**

   A new page appears, listing all the Pages you admin.

4. **Find the name of the Page you want to edit and click the Edit Page link underneath.**

   You are now in the editing area for your Page with a navigation menu on the left side.

5. **Select Manage Permissions from this navigation menu.**

6. **Click the Permanently Delete This Page link (just above the Save Changes button).**

   A Confirmation dialog box appears, asking whether you really, *really* want to do this. After all, this is a permanent deletion.

   Any admin can delete a Page that he or she administers. Please delete with caution, because you absolutely cannot reinstate a removed Page.

7. **Click Delete.**

   Your Page is now history.

Chapter 3: Administering Your Facebook Business Page

In This Chapter

✔ Interacting with Facebook as your personal Profile or as your Page

✔ Understanding what other people see when they visit your Page

✔ Learning how to use your Page Editing dashboard

*N*ow that you are a Page admin, Facebook has granted you an additional permission: You can view Facebook as yourself (that is, through your personal Profile) or as your Page (that is, through your business Page). This particular administrative perk can be a little confusing at first, but by the end of this chapter, you'll completely understand how and when to use this option.

As admin of your Facebook business Page, you need to maintain it. An important part of maintenance is simply understanding how your Page looks to visitors and fans, what you can customize and control, and what Page elements are visible only to you as the admin and when you view your Page "as" your Page. This chapter explains the elements of your business Page and then shows you how to use your administrative dashboard to control some of those aspects.

Viewing Facebook as your Page

Now that you have a Facebook business Page, you have two separate Profiles with Facebook: your personal Profile and your Page Profile. Each profile allows you to view Facebook, post status updates, and comment on other posts. But, depending on which profile you're using, you'll either show up as your personal Profile (you) or your Page Profile (your business).

In addition, each Profile has its own News Feed:

✦ **Your personal Profile News Feed:** Based on your Friends' status updates and the business Pages you've Liked as your personal Profile.

✦ **Your Page Profile News Feed:** Based solely on the Pages you've Liked as your Page (which we explain in a minute).

In this section, we explain how and when you may want to use each of your Profile options. Before we do, though, it may be helpful to see each of these Profile options in action. We start by changing your Profile view from Personal Profile to Page Profile. To do that, follow these steps:

1. **Log in to Facebook as you normally do.**

2. **Click the Account link in the top-right corner of the page.**

3. **Click the Use Facebook as Page link.**

   This is where you go to toggle between your personal and Page Profiles. If you are an admin of several pages, you need to select the correct Page after clicking the Use as Page link by clicking the Switch button next to it.

After you click the Switch button, you are brought directly to that Page. You are now viewing your Page "as" your Page, not as your personal account with admin privileges of the Page. This is an important point to understand, and you might need to switch back and forth from your personal Profile to your Page Profile to see the differences.

There are a couple of things you will be able to see now as your Page that you can't see when viewing your Page as a personal account admin. We go over them in detail in a moment, but in a nutshell, in the top-left corner of your Page, there are two icons (Likes and Notifications) rather than the three personal Profile icons (Friend Requests, Messages, Notifications) that you see when viewing your Page as a personal Profile admin.

Also, your Page Profile News Feed is based solely on the Pages you've Liked as your Page. To see that News Feed, click the link on the top-right of the Page called Home. This functions just the same as your personal Profile News Feed, except that it's filled with posts by other Facebook Pages that you (as your Page) have Liked. If you haven't Liked any Pages yet as your Page, you won't have anything in this News Feed.

To switch back to your personal Profile, follow these steps:

1. **Click the Account link in the top-right corner of the page.**

2. **Click the Use Facebook as. . . *your personal account name* link.**

   This is where you go to toggle between your personal and Page Profiles.

3. **Alternatively, if you are on your Page, you can click the Use Facebook as. . . link in the admin box on the right-side of your Page.**

   This link is available only if you are on your Page. If you're somewhere else on Facebook, using the Account link to switch back to your personal Profile is the way to go.

Now that you've had a chance to see your different Profile options and are comfortable switching back and forth, we have a few tips for you:

✦ If you are viewing Facebook with your Page Profile and you go to another business Page you admin, you won't be able to do any admin stuff (editing, posting as that Page, etc.) until you switch back to your personal Profile first.

✦ You can't post as your Page on anyone's personal Facebook Profile, but you can post as your Page on another Page.

✦ Try not to be too spammy by posting as your Page all the time! Yes, it's a great way to promote your Page, but remember that this is a social network and not a place to go dropping your name everywhere!

Liking other Pages as your Page

If you have been on Facebook a while, maybe you've already Liked your favorite business Pages as yourself (that is, your personal Profile). If so, you know that when you Like a Page, any status updates or shared content for that Page makes its way into your News Feed. Liking a Page is one more way to keep up with the brands you enjoy.

Why would you want to Like another Page as your Page? Well, when you Like another business Page using your business Profile, you can then interact on that other business Page as your Page.

For example, say you have a business Page on Facebook called Socially Congruent and your Friend has a business Page called Fluent Design. If you want to comment on his business Page as Socially Congruent rather than as yourself, I need to Like his Page while using Facebook as Socially Congruent; otherwise, there is no way to leave a comment unless I switch back to my personal Profile. There will be no Comment link available for me (as my Page) until I Like the Page as my Page. Commenting as your business Page instead of yourself is one way to promote your own business Page and increase its visibility in new communities.

Also imagine that you're viewing Fluent Design as your Page and you prefer to comment as your personal Profile instead. You need to switch back to your personal Profile first (click the Account link and toggle back to your personal Profile). When you switch back, you will be deposited on your personal Profile News Feed instead of the Page you were just viewing! You'll need to navigate back to that Page and then leave your comment as your personal Profile.

Follow these steps to Like a Page with your Page Profile:

Book II
Chapter 3

Administering
Your Facebook
Business Page

1. **Switch to your business Page Profile, as noted previously.**

2. **Navigate to a Page you want to Like.**

   We encourage you to spend some time developing a strategy around which Pages you want to have associated with your own business Page. When choosing which Pages to Like, it's a good idea to choose Pages that you think will fit with your audience's expectations. For example, maybe Liking the NFL Page would seem incongruous with your Doll Factory Page and wouldn't mesh well with your established community. On the other hand, that same community may appreciate a link to another business Page about restoring antique dolls.

3. **Click the Like button at the top of the Page.**

   Note that this is the same process you use when you Like a Page as your personal Profile.

4. **Post a comment.**

   Pages don't receive a notification when a Page Likes their Page, so it's nice to leave a comment as your Page to say hello. They will, however, be able to see that you've Liked their Page as a Page when they look through their Likers and filter for Pages (more on that coming up). Note that when you leave your comment, the posting name and thumbnail image are that of your Page Profile, not your personal Profile.

When one business Page Likes another business Page, that Like does not count toward the total number of Likes. For example, say that Blogging Basics 101 has 800 Likes. If the Simply Amusing Designs Page decides to Like Blogging Basics 101, the total number of Likes on Blogging Basics 101 stays at 800 instead of increasing to 801. That way, the Likes on a Page aren't artificially inflated by being Liked by both the personal and business Profiles owned by the same person.

Using a strategy of Liking certain Pages as your Page will give you a curated News Stream for you to view (as your Page). It's a bit like creating a list of the businesses you want to keep up with. The Home News Feed for your Page Profile can become a great place to view what other pages are doing for marketing on Facebook, too.

Setting posting preferences for your Page

By default, your Facebook business Page settings are such that when you are on your own business Page, any post you make appears to be from your Page (in other words, the Page image thumbnail and name will be what people will see for those posts). But you can change this default setting and post as yourself (your personal Profile) on your own Page, too.

For example, your Page might be for your magazine, but you want to post as yourself — the publisher — for a particular reply or comment to a post. You would need to adjust your settings as noted to do that. Businesses have to decide how they want their admins to post and comment on the Page. Some have decided to "sign" their posts with their real name, and some have decided to switch back and forth from Page Profile to personal Profile, depending on what they are posting on the Page.

To change your default settings, follow these steps:

1. **Click the Edit Page button on the top-right of your Facebook business Page.**

   Your administrative dashboard appears.

2. **Click the Your Settings link on the left sidebar.**

3. **Click to deselect the Posting Preferences box.**

   Now when you post or make a comment on your own Facebook business Page, that comment will have your personal Profile thumbnail image and your real name.

Viewing Notifications and Likes for your Page

Being able to go through your *Notifications* — all types of interaction on your Page, and *Likes* — everyone who has Liked your Page, are two important tasks you will want to do on a regular basis. You can consider it a mini analytics system in which you can do a quick check on the state of your Page. The full analytics system, Facebook Insights, will be an important part of your tasks as a Page owner, too. We dive deeply into that system in Book IX. In the meantime, you can get a quick view of the Notifications and Likes.

When you view your Page using your personal Profile (admin), you can see a View Notifications link in the admin section (top-right) of the Page. If you have any new activity on your Page since you last checked, a number will also be there in parentheses. Clicking that link will bring up a page with all the activity on your Page for the last week, as you can see in Figure 3-1.

You can see who has Liked, commented on a Post, or posted to your Page's Wall. If you put your cursor over a Page name, a small info box will come up with a direct link to that Page, its Page image and a quick link to Like that Page. It also shows the number of people that have Liked that Page.

If you put your cursor over a personal Profile name, you can see the Profile image and a direct link to the Profile. If several people did the same activity (Liked a post), Facebook combines them and says, *7 other Friends* . . . . When you hover over that number, a list will come up with all the Profile's Friend's names.

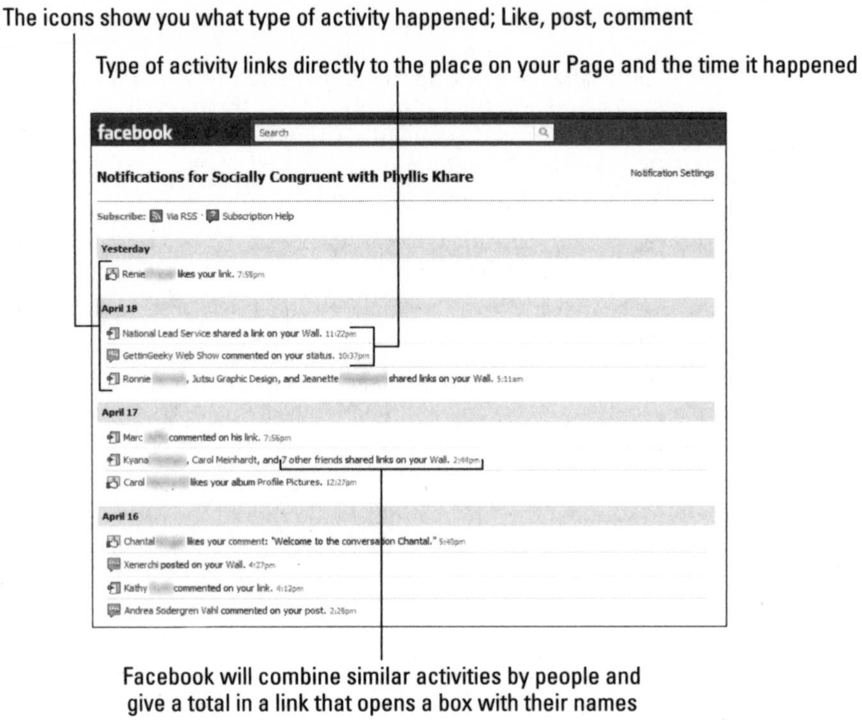

The icons show you what type of activity happened; Like, post, comment

Type of activity links directly to the place on your Page and the time it happened

Figure 3-1:
The Notifications link in your admin section pulls up a list of recent activity.

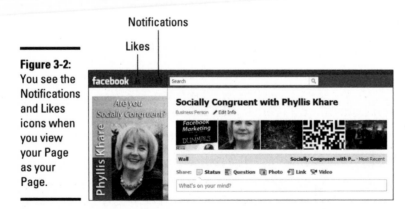

Facebook will combine similar activities by people and give a total in a link that opens a box with their names

Currently, you still need to switch over to viewing your Page as your Page Profile to see Likes. When you switch over to viewing your Page as your Page Profile, you'll see two icons at the top left of the page, next to the Facebook logo, as shown in Figure 3-2.

Notifications

Likes

Figure 3-2:
You see the Notifications and Likes icons when you view your Page as your Page.

These icons are the following:

✦ **Notifications:** Clicking this icon provides a history of your business Page's activity, including who liked a post, commented on a post, and so on. It also tells you when someone commented on a Page that you (as your Page) commented on. If you click the See All Notifications link it will pull up the page we just discussed above.

✦ **Likes:** Clicking this icon shows you a list of who has recently Liked your Page. Click the See All link and a drop-down is available. You can see who has Liked your Page by People, other Pages, admins, and banned.

Check your new Likes on a regular basis, and welcome new people to your Page by posting their first names or tag their business Pages (all about tagging in Book IV, Chapter 3). Sort the new Likes by Page, then go and Like those Pages as your Page and leave a comment.

Now you know how to roam around Facebook as your Page and how to check a few analytics (Notifications and Likes) as your Page — a view from the inside, so to speak. Next up is a look from the outside — how a visitor sees your Page.

Understanding How Other People See Your Page

We think it is a good idea to look at some fully functioning Pages as an overview to see how business Pages look to the public. The best place to start is back at the www.facebook.com/pages site. Click any of the Pages listed and note these Page features:

✦ Photo strip

✦ Mutual connections

✦ Left-side navigation

✦ Bio box

✦ Likes (number of personal Profiles that have Liked the Page)

✦ Business Pages the Page has Liked (as their Page, not their Profile; we explain this more thoroughly in a bit)

✦ Wall view toggle

✦ Bottom links

Figure 3-3 has call-outs for each item on the list above so that you can see how they appear on a business Page. This section of the chapter explains each element.

About

Navigation links

Photo strip

Mutual connections

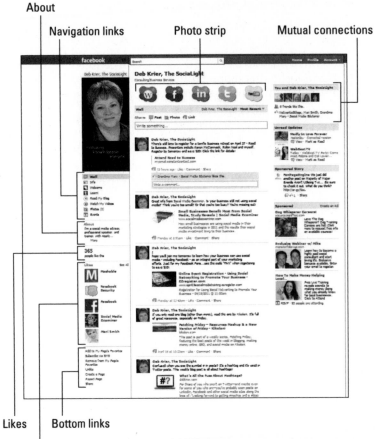

Figure 3-3:
A business
Page as
seen by the
public.

Likes

Bottom links

Pages the page has liked and possibly featured

Photo Strip

The photos seen at the top of every business Page in the photo strip are the
five most recent photos any Page admin (not anyone else) has posted to
the Page Wall or uploaded to the Page's photo albums. The order of these
photos changes each time the Page is refreshed (a personal Profile photo
strip, on the other hand, does not have the random reordering feature).

The photo strip offers a tremendous marketing opportunity here, which we
discuss in great detail in Book IV, Chapter 1. But as a quick preview to that
Chapter, think how great it would be try the following (remember that you
can have text and links as captions to photos):

✦ Each photo is of a different product you offer

✦ Each photo could be a smiling face of the admins of the Page (if one a magazine Page; one for customer service, one for billing questions, one for advertising, one for the publisher, and so on)

✦ Each photo highlights your expertise; icons for Twitter, Facebook, LinkedIn, YouTube and VYou (www.vyou.com)

If you don't want a particular picture to show up in the photo strip, you can mouse over the picture and click the X. Clicking the X removes the picture only from the photo strip; it does not delete the picture from your Page's photo albums. As you remove one picture, another takes its place (unless you don't have any more photos uploaded).

If you accidentally remove too many images, or remove the wrong one, you can reset the photo strip, and all the photos you removed will be put back in (even the ones you meant to remove). Now you have to start over!

To reset the photo bar, go to your business Page and then follow these steps:

1. **Click the Edit Page button.**

2. **Select Profile Picture from the left navigation menu.**

3. **Click the Unhide All button at the bottom of this page, as shown in Figure 3-4.**

Now you can go back to Xing out the photos you don't want to show in the photo strip.

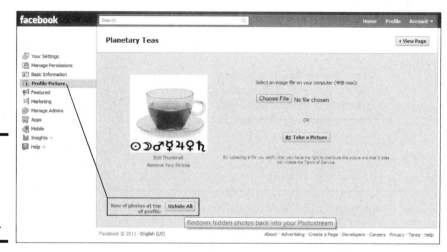

Figure 3-4:
Click the
Unhide All
button to
reset the
photo strip.

Mutual connections

Facebook has a section on the top-right of personal Profiles that shows friendship connections. If you are viewing Facebook with your personal Profile and go to someone's personal Profile you can see which Friends you have in common, which photos have you and that Friend tagged in common, and Pages you both have Liked.

Facebook has created a similar space for Pages. When you visit any Facebook Page, you will see in that top-right corner a similar space for seeing which of your personal Profile Friends have Liked that Page, too. You see this only if you are viewing Pages as your personal Profile. If you switch over to viewing Facebook as your Page, that section disappears.

Left-side navigation

If you have a brand-new Page, and haven't added any apps or custom landing pages yet (more on that soon), your visitors will only see three links on the left navigation menu: Wall, Info, and Photos. You will want to add links to the side navigation as you develop your Page, and we show you how to do that starting in the next chapter. You might want to add your e-commerce page, newsletter sign-up page, custom landing page, YouTube videos, and many more things.

Your visitors will see links to these things on your Page and be able to click through all of them. You'll learn in the next chapter how to add links, work with these links, arrange them, hide or delete some them, and so on.

If you have more than seven links, visitors to your site will be able to expand or contract the list by toggling a More and Less link at the bottom of the list.

We have seen Pages with more than 27 links in this left navigation menu, so there are a lot of links you can add to your Page!

There is one link in this menu (on your own Page) that only you as an admin of your Page see. It is under the Wall link and it's called Hidden Posts. When you click it, you will see any posts that Facebook considers spam, or contains words you designated to be blocked (you will learn how to block words in the upcoming Manage Permissions section later in this Chapter).

The Bio Box

Under the left-side navigation links is a little section called the *Bio box*. This Bio box contains some of the words you put in the field marked Company Overview in the Basic Information section. To adjust the text that shows up here, click the Edit Page button and then click Basic Information and change the text in the Company Overview field.

Facebook collapses the text so that only approximately 75 characters show with a More link to expand out to about 250 characters. Any Web address you put here, even if it contains the `http://` part, won't be hyperlinked in this space, but you can type it out for people to copy.

Notice what is appealing here, as you are looking at other Pages. Some Pages have used the space for giving a quick understanding of the Page and a call to action. Here are a few good examples:

✦ *Gettin' Geeky is a place where technology isn't so scary! It's a place where we can learn together and not feel intimidated to ask questions, post challenges and discover ways to use technology to build our businesses!*

✦ *This page is for the fans of all things iPhone, iPad and iPod touch and our award-winning magazine – iPhone Life –Go to http://iphonelife.com*

✦ *Learn the truth about your beauty with Carol Tuttle's Beauty Profiling System. The only system that can help you express your unique natural beauty no matter your age, weight, or figure. Share this page by clicking on the Share button below!*

Number of Page Likes

Currently, Facebook only puts a number here with the text @@*people like this* underneath it. It is a public number for all to see. It is the number of people who have clicked the Like button at the top of the Page. This number doesn't include business Pages that have Liked the Page, only personal Profiles who have done so.

You can't hide this number, or move its location on the left sidebar. If you are the admin of the Page the text below the number that says *people like this* will be hyperlinked. Click it and the interface to view everyone who has Liked the page will come up. You can then click the See All link and then, as noted previously, you can click the drop-down to see who has Liked your Page by People, other Pages, admins, and banned.

As you build the number of people who click the Like button you will find more interaction on your Page. You will also have better EdgeRank (more about that in Book IV, Chapter 2) and hopefully a growing revenue or branding awareness, or the main goal you decided on developing back in Book I, Chapter 2.

Some Facebook consultants say a good time to start running contests is when you reach more than 1,000 Likes, as you should have more entries, but you know your niche better than anyone. When you have reached a milestone number, do something special for your Page community. Some Pages celebrate that number at 100, 500, 1000, 2000, and so on. Think of something special for each one. If you decide to give something away, make sure you follow Facebook's guidelines for sweepstakes and contests. You can find all the info about that in Book VI, Chapter 2.

Currently, the Like list is chronological; newest to oldest. I say currently, because this feature has been known to change back and forth in the last few weeks.

Business Pages Liked

Under the left navigation links is a section called Likes. Here, you and your visitors can see other Pages that your business Page has Liked, as shown in Figure 3-5. This section shows only up to five other Pages at one time. Every time anyone refreshes your Page, the Pages listed will be in a different order.

You will need to decide whether you want your visitors to see these Pages or not. Some businesses like to associate themselves with certain Pages to add to their reputation; others don't want to show anything that will take someone off their Page. So, you will need to make a decision about this.

These are not the Pages you have liked as your personal Profile. Pages you Like as yourself (that is, as your personal Profile) are listed on your personal Profile's Info page.

All the instructions on how to Like Pages as your Page in order to place them in this section, how to remove them, or Feature them are located further along in this chapter under *Featured*.

Figure 3-5:
These are other business Pages the Page has Liked.

Wall view toggle

Your visitors can toggle what they see on your Page. They do that with a set of links at the top-right of the Page Wall. Facebook currently defaults a visitor to the Top Post view which uses an algorithm to rank posts by an engagement formula called *EdgeRank*. Again, we talk a lot about EdgeRank in Book IV, Chapter 2, and how much Facebook loves to arrange things according to Likes and comments and other engagements, but a visitor has the option to click the drop-down and toggle the view to Most Recent, which will sort all the posts in chronological order.

Visitors can also sort the posts they see by only what the Page itself has posted. They do that by clicking the name of the Page next to the drop down links.

Currently, it's a matter of educating people to know to click the drop-down list and selecting Most Recent if they want to see the posts in order.

Book II
Chapter 3

Administering
Your Facebook
Business Page

Figure 3-6:
Toggle the
Wall view
between
Posts by
Page, Top
Posts or
Most Recent.

Bottom links

At the bottom of the left column on all Facebook Pages, there are a collection of links. What regular visitors see on your Page and what you (and anyone who is an admin of any Facebook Page) see will be different. And if you are viewing your Page, as your Page, there will be only one link showing @@Share!

✦ **Add to My Page's Favorites:** this link is seen only by admins of any Facebook Page. It is a quick link to add a Page to your Favorites and by-passing Liking the Page. In other words, you can add a Page to your Favorites List and even Feature it — all without ever clicking the Like button for the Page. We're not sure why this is so, but just so you know, clicking this bottom link doesn't mean you have Liked the Page.

✦ **Subscribe via SMS**: This link is not seen by you on any Page where you are an admin. For users to subscribe to get all posts delivered to them via SMS, they need to activate their phone with Facebook Mobile. If they click this link and haven't activated their phone, an interface will come up and take them through the process to do that first. Some people will subscribe by SMS to competitors Pages, so they know when the Page posts or someone makes comments. They use this information to make posts to their own Page or to go and comment. Use wisely.

✦ **Remove from My Page's Favorites**: This link is seen only by admins of any Facebook Page. This is a quick link to remove a Page from your Page's Favorites. Clicking this link will also remove the Page from your Featured Pages, if it was there, too. This is not the same as Unliking a Page.

✦ **Unlike/Like:** if you have already Liked the Page you are viewing, you will see Unlike here. If you haven't Liked it yet, you will see Like.

✦ **Create a Page:** This is a quick link to start the process to create a new Facebook Page.

✦ **Report Page:** You can report any Page that you feel is breaking Facebook rules. And others can report your Page if they feel it is breaking Facebook rules. When you click this link, you bring up a dialog box that takes you through the process of reporting the Page. We discuss this a bit more in the next chapter.

✦ **Share:** This is, by far, the most important link in the left column. This is the link you want visitors to your Page to click! Doing so brings up an auto-populated post that posts on their Wall for all their Friends to see. We talk about this in detail in Book IV, Chapter 1. Go ahead and click the link on any Page to see what happens. All the information in the post comes from the Info link for the Page you are viewing. You might want to adjust that info on your own Page after seeing how it looks on someone else's Page.

And lastly, if you are viewing your Page, as your Page, the only link you will see is the Share link.

If you created a limited *business account,* visitors to your Page will see the ones noted in the preceding list. You will see Share only on your own Page. You will see Add to My Page's Favorites, Create a Page, Report Page, and Share on other Facebook Pages. Even though the Share link is there, if you click it and post, it doesn't go anywhere because you don't have a personal Profile to post it to. (This might be a Facebook bug.)

Editing Your Page

Now that you see what a Page looks like from the outside, you can go and see how it looks from the inside! This section explores all the ways you can edit your Page. You can see where you can add applications (apps), change the information people will see for your Page, change your Profile image, and many more things. Time to get started.

Go to your Page and click the Edit page button on the top-right side, as shown in Figure 3-7.

Figure 3-7:
This is the button to click to find the interface for editing your Page.

**Book II
Chapter 3**

Administering Your Facebook Business Page

You're now looking at your business Page's administrative dashboard, as shown in Figure 3-8. This is where you edit and modify your Page. Note the nice collection of navigation links on the left side of your Page. In the following sections, we briefly walk you through each of these links, going from top to bottom.

Figure 3-8:
The navigation menu for editing your Page is on the left side of your Page after clicking the Edit Page button..

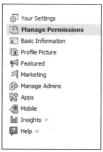

Your Settings

When you select the top link called Your Settings, you see two sections:

✦ Posting Preferences

✦ Email Notifications

As we explain at the beginning of this chapter, you now have both a personal Profile and business Page Profile. By default, when you're on your Page, any post you make shows as being from your Page Profile. The Page image thumbnail and name are what people see for those posts. But you can change this default and post as yourself — that is, as your personal Profile — by deselecting the check box in the Posting Preferences section.

The second part of this section lets you decide whether you want an e-mail notification every time someone posts to or comments on your Page. All admins of your Page will need to go in and adjust these settings to their preferences.

You want to know when someone posts or comments to your Page for a variety of reasons, but mostly you want to be able to respond quickly to any concerns or questions. You also want to know if someone has posted anything that you would consider spam so you can remove it quickly. Sometimes Facebook misses a post that would normally be caught and moved to your Hidden Posts section.

Depending on your business, a quick response raises your online reputation. So you can keep this checked to use Facebook's e-mail notification or try a third-party system. The authors of this book are enjoying the Hyper Alerts (www.hyperalerts.no/) notification system).

Look for the link under the e-mail notification check box called View All Email Settings for Your Page." See it? We suggest that you click it. When you do, you're taken to a page that shows all your e-mail notification settings. You might want to go through this, as we were surprised at how many email notification settings we needed to change, especially under "other Apps."

Look in this e-mail notification area for the section called Pages. There are four check boxes to consider here for receiving e-mail notifications:

✦ Makes you a Page admin

✦ Suggests Page to you

✦ Replies to your discussion board post

✦ Weekly Page updates for admin

You can make a decision about the first three, but we suggest you select the Weekly Page update because it gives you a nice summary of the activity of your Page for the previous week. You can see this info in your Insights section (see Book IX Chapter 2 for more about Insights), but in the meantime, this is a good e-mail to receive. It will be sent to the e-mail address you used to open your personal Profile with Facebook.

If you click the Change Email Settings For Individual Pages link (right under the four Page check boxes) a dialog box with all the Pages you have created comes up. You can easily select or deselect e-mail notifications for each Page here.

Manage Permissions

Clicking the Manage Permissions link opens an editing page that will determine how a person can interact with your Page. We want to explain each option on this page because these options directly affect how first-time and loyal visitors see and network on your Page.

✦ **Page Visibility.** We discuss the Page Visibility: Only Admins Can See This Page check box in detail in in Chapter 2 of this minibook. Selecting this check box hides your Page from the public until it's ready for viewing.

✦ **Country Restrictions:** If you leave this field blank, your Page will be visible to people located in all countries. Entering one or more countries means that only people located in those countries listed will be able to view your Page. By restricting the Country, anyone who isn't logged into Facebook will not be able to see your Page.

✦ **Age Restrictions:** The default is to allow anyone older than 13 to see your Page. If you need to restrict the viewing of your Page to people older than 17, 18, 19, or 21, you can set that level in the drop-down menu.

If you're promoting a business connected to alcohol, the Alcohol-Related age restriction sets the minimum age based on the location of the user. Only users in Canada and South Korea who are 19+, in Japan and Paraguay who are 20+, in India who are 25+, and elsewhere (including the United States) who are 21+ will be able to view your Page. However, Facebook makes the point quite clearly that you are ultimately responsible for who sees your Page.

✦ **Wall Tab Shows:** You have two choices here: All Posts or Only Posts by Page. We recommend selecting All Posts. Doing so allows anyone who has Liked your Page to post directly on the Page's Wall. If you want people to be able to comment under what you have posted, select Only Posts by Page. People will be able to comment, but only by posting under one of your posts. You can read Book IV, Chapter 2 where we discuss this more thoroughly.

✦ **Default Landing Tab:** A Landing Tab is what people see the first time they visit your Page, before they have Liked your Page. After they have Liked your Page, their next visit will take them directly to the Wall.

Use the pull-down menu to choose the Default Landing Tab from any links available on your Page's side navigation (for example, Wall, Info, or an application). Many businesses create a custom Default Landing Tab as a special welcome to their visitors, as it increases the likelihood of someone clicking the Like button. We explain how to do that in Book III, Chapter 2.

✦ **Posting Ability:** You have three (count 'em, three) check boxes to deal with here. You can specify whether users can write or post content on the Wall, add photos, and add videos. In the beginning, you can select all three, but make sure to educate yourself by reading Book IV, Chapter 2 where we discuss this in more detail. Sometimes you want (or don't want) random visitors to be able to post videos or photos on your Page. You can always remove random spam posts, but you can nip that in the bud by just not allowing it.

✦ **Moderation Blocklist:** You can add comma-separated keywords that Facebook then automatically marks as spam if they show up in a post to your Page or in a comment to a post. Remember to check your Hidden Posts (described earlier in this chapter) if you put any keywords here.

✦ **Profanity Blocklist:** The drop-down list gives you three choices; None, Medium, and Strong. I know I should come up with a witty description here, but &*%@# if I can! But seriously, if you think your Page might have people coming by and using profanity, go ahead and check Medium or Strong.

✦ **Delete Page**: The Permanently Delete This Page link can be used to erase this Page. Keep in mind that you cannot undo this action. Deleting a Page deletes everything, photos, posts, etc. Makes sure you have copied everything you want from the Page first. If you delete a Page for which you had already set a vanity URL (and you want to use that particular URL for a new Page), that URL will not be available for at least 14 days after deletion. If it isn't available after that, you will need to file an infringement form with Facebook to request to use it again. It might be easier to just hide the Page by selecting the Page Visibility check box at the top of this Manage Permissions section.

Basic Information

Remember all that work to figure out which type and category you wanted when first creating your Page? Remember the Info editing? Well, if not, that's okay. You can edit everything found on your Page's Info link from this Basic Information section.

The fields you find on the Basic Information tab are specific to the category and Page type you selected when creating your Page. You can change the category and Page type for your Page with the drop-down menus. The first drop-down menu allows you to choose a new category for your Page; the second drop-down menu allows you to choose a new Page type. Make sure that you click Save Changes before editing the fields, because those fields might change with the category change.

Fill in all the fields, remembering that you don't have to stick to what the fields are asking for. For example, the "Founded" field allows you to have up to 260 characters, but you don't have to use that many. This is what one of our writers put in that space:

2010 The Year of Becoming Socially Congruent! We start with being congruent at your very core – who you are – then work our way out to the way you use social media to market what you do. All of the layers need to be congruent, like nesting triangles.

You can also add your Twitter username, Web site address, LinkedIn profile page, any number of things. If you are including a Web address, make sure you include `http://` so that it will be hyperlinked.

When you first create your Page, the URL is long and unwieldy because it contains your Page's ID number. It looks something like this:

```
http://www.facebook.com/pages/Socially-Congruent-with-
     Phyllis-Khare/123451234512345
```

What you want is a "vanity" URL, or "pretty" URL. Facebook also calls it an "Alias." You want it to look like this:

```
http://facebook.com/SociallyCongruent
```

To claim a vanity URL, you must have at least 25 Likes for your Page. You need to ask your friends, or staff, or your large, extended family to go to your Page and click the Like button at the top of your new Page. How ever you do it, do it as soon as possible because you want to be able to claim your nice-looking URL for other promotional activities noted in Book IV, Chapter 1.

After you've reached 25 Likes on your Page, come back to your administrative dashboard and navigate to the Basic Information tab or go directly to `www.facebook.com/username.`. From there, follow these steps to create your vanity URL:

You can use the Username page to set your personal Profile username, too. Make sure you don't set your Page name to your personal name! Notice there are two sections, one for your personal name and one for your Pages. Your best bet is to set your personal account to your name first (such as www.facebook.com/phylliskhare) and then set your Page URL.

You may choose a username that Facebook suggests, or create your own. Click the Check Availability button to check for available usernames. A Username Available box comes up with several things to keep in mind about a username, as shown in Figure 3-9, such as making sure you have the right to use the name you've selected.

When you have something you like, click Confirm. Now you will have a nice, neat, URL for your Facebook Page. You can put this on everything; letterheads, Web sites, email signatures, just to name a few. We go into great detail on how to use this URL in the Book IV. In the meantime, put this URL in your next e-mail to your customers so that they can find you easily on Facebook.

Profile Picture

We show you how to add an image when we in Chapter 2s of this minibook. In case you didn't add an image then, you can upload a picture from your computer or take a picture with your webcam now.

Figure 3-9:
Setting your username.

Please take the time to create a very nice image to act as your Page image. The image size can be up to 540 x 180 pixels. The space you get for a Page image is quite a bit larger than that for a personal Profile picture and can really make a statement on your Page, as shown in Figure 3-10. Review Chapter 2 to get some good marketing ideas and to review the steps to modify your thumbnail.

Featured

The Featured link has two parts:

✦ **Likes:** The "Likes" section lets you Feature up to five Facebook Pages on the left side of your Page. You can specify which of your Liked Pages always rotate there by selecting five of them as Featured. The steps to Liking a Page as your Page and how to Feature a Page are coming up.

✦ **Page Owners:** The second section of the Feature tab, called Page Owners, raises the curtain on who the admins of the Page are. Some businesses want to keep that private; others want the world to know. Here is where you get to make that decision. When you Feature any or all of the admins, the admins will have their personal account thumbnail image and their name listed on the left column under the Featured Page Likes.

Figure 3-10: Make a statement on your Page with a full 180 x 540 pixel image.

To have Pages show up in the Likes section of your business Page, you need to do the following, and then we show you how to Feature five of them:

1. **Log in to Facebook as you normally do.**

2. **Click the Account link in the top-right corner of the page.**

3. **Click the Use Facebook as Page link.**

   This is where you go to toggle between your personal and Page Profiles. If you are an admin of several pages, you need to select the correct Page and click the Switch button.

4. **Navigate to the Page you want to include in your Like section.**

5. **Click the Like button at the top of that Page.**

When you return to your own business Page, you'll see the Page that you Liked will be listed on the left sidebar's Likes section of your own Page. After you Like more than five Pages, you'll need to decide which of these Pages you'd like to Feature in this spot.

To adjust which Pages are Featured on your Page:

1. **Log in to Facebook as you normally do.**

2. **Go to your Page.**

   You can do this next part as an admin or as your Page.

3. **Click the Edit Page button at the top-right corner of the Page.**

   This gives you access to your editing menu.

4. **Click the Featured link.**

5. **Click the Edit Featured Likes button.**

   Now you will see all the Pages you have Liked as your Page.

6. **Select the boxes of the five you want to Feature**

   If you don't want any Pages showing as Featured, deselect all boxes.

7. **Click Save.**

As we explain at the beginning of this chapter, you can Like Pages as your Page now, so if you have been on Facebook a while and Liked certain business Pages through your personal Profile, you can Log in as your Page and Like those Pages as your Page now.

When you click the Add Featured Page Owners button, you can select the check box next to the names of the admins you want to show to the world. Their personal Profile thumbnails will show up on the left side of your Page, as shown in Figure 3-11.

Figure 3-11:
Your
Featured
admins will
be visible
on the left
side of your
Page.

Note that you, as an admin, always see those Profiles in the admin area on the right top of the Page, but others do not see them unless you select their names to Feature them.

Marketing

The Marketing tab has seven very important links, which you should look at *very* closely. You'll get the short overview here; all of them are very big subjects, and some have whole minibooks dedicated to them in this book!

✦ **Advertise on Facebook:** Yes, we have a whole minibook dedicated to this topic. You can find it fully discussed in minibook VIII, but for now, we just want to point out that you can find the navigation link to Facebook's advertising section right here. Clicking this link brings you directly into the interface to create an ad. Facebook will help you by auto-populating some of the fields, but everything is adjustable. You have the opportunity to reach hundreds and thousands of people, or a small, highly targeted number of people on Facebook through this ad

✦ **Tell your Fans:** This is the same process we discuss in the Getting Started section when you first created your Page in Chapter 2 of this minibook. Basically, you can upload a contact file or find your e-mail contacts that are already on Facebook and invite them to view and Like your Page. After your Page is put together, you definitely want to come back to this link and complete this step.

✦ **Get a Badge:** Badges are predesigned banners (either vertical, horizontal, or two-column) that you can place on your Web site or blog to promote your Page. We suggest your create a Like Box instead of a badge, as we discussed earlier in Chapter 2, but this is where to go to create a badge.

When you click the Get a Badge link, you'll see four links on the left side with the different types of badges you can create; Profile badges, Like badges, Photo badges, and Page badges. Only the Like badge and Page badge are for a business Page. The other two are for your personal account.

Click the Like badge link. You have two steps; select the Page from the drop-down, then copy the code and place it on your website.

Click the Page badge, click the Edit this badge link, modify the badge until you like how it looks, save it, and then copy the code and place it on your site.

✦ **Add a Like Box to Your Website:** We highly recommended that you place a Like box on your regular Website. The process to add a Like box to your Web site is fully described in miniook VII, Chapter 2.

A Like badge and a Like box are two different things. A Like badge has only information about your Page and a link back to your Facebook Page, whereas a Like box allows people to Like your Facebook Page without leaving the Web site they are viewing. For example, if you have a Web site that has a Like box installed in its sidebar, people reading your blog can click the Like button in the Like box on the sidebar and that person will now be connected (be counted as a Fan) to your Facebook Page without their having to leave your Web site.

✦ **Create Alias:** This is the same thing as creating a username, or vanity URL, and is discussed in the "Username" section, earlier in this chapter. You can start the process to create a vanity URL here, or under Basic Information, as the link there is identical. This step is a must-do for all business Pages. At least 25 people need to have Liked your Page for you to be eligible to get an easy-to-remember (and type) username.

✦ **Send an Update:** You have many ways to get your message in front of the people who Like your Page. You can post a status update, create an ad, send public and private messages to your Friends, and send an Update. You can think of an Update as a way to get a message into Facebook's Message system, instead of it going into a person's News Feed.

Where do these business Page Updates go? Look on the left side of your personal Profile News Feed Page. Click the Messages link. Then click the sub-category called Other. Any Update from a Page you have Liked will be here. The drawback to this is that hardly anyone knows this is where to look for these updates.

Updates are best used sparingly. In our experience, a large percentage of your fans will not see them.

Even though, a great feature of this Update system is the fact that you can target your Updates. You can target by location, sex, and age. You can also upload and attach a video, attach a video recorded right from your webcam, or add a URL. Regular and targeted Update messages are explained fully in minibook IV, Chapter 2.

✦ **See All Updates:** If you have sent any Updates, the number will be in brackets next to this link. You can click the link and see all the Updates you've sent, as well as create a new one from this interface.

At the bottom of the Marketing page tab, in a tiny font, you see the Brand Permissions link. When you click that link, you go to Facebook's Brand Permission Center — Usage Guidelines page, where you can read all about Facebook's Trademark restrictions and how to keep from crowding the Facebook logo in a way that Facebook doesn't appreciate.

Manage Admins

Admins are people who can administer your Page. They can edit and delete items from your Page, ban users, post status updates and comments, and send messages to fans. Everything you can do with your Page, admins can do, too.

You, as the Page creator, are automatically an admin. When you, or an admin, create a status update on your Facebook business Page, it will look as though the Page made the update, not you personally (unless you change that in Your Settings, as discussed at the beginning of this chapter). The status update will have the Page thumbnail image and the Page name listed.

Here are some quick points about being an admin of a Page:

✦ You can have as many admins as you want.

✦ Always have at least one other person as your admin in case you're unavailable to make changes to your Page.

✦ All admins need to visit the Your Settings link on the navigation menu to adjust the email notifications settings and posting settings. Facebook defaults the email notification box for all activity on the Page to be checked. This means all admins will receive e-mail notification whenever someone posts or comments on the Page, unless admins deselect it. We discussed this earlier in the chapter under "Your Settings."

✦ As noted earlier in this chapter, all admins have equal rights, so any admin can add or delete another admin, including the one who created the Page in the first place.

✦ Remember, you need to switch over to viewing your Page as your Page to see new Likes and Notification icons for the Page, because just viewing the Page as an admin doesn't make those icons available.

✦ You can remove your admin status (or have another admin remove you) by following the next set of steps. You will then view your Page just like any other fan of your Page. You will not see the admin box on the right side of the Page with quick links to Insights or Ads. You will not see the Edit Page button. When you post, it will be from your personal Profile. You will not receive any email notifications for the Page.

✦ Facebook requires at least one admin of a Page. If you try to Remove yourself as an admin before adding someone else, you won't be able to remove yourself.

Here are the steps to add someone as an admin for your Page:

1. **Go to your Page and click the Edit Page button at the top-right corner of your Page.**
2. **Click the Manage Admin link on the left navigation menu.**
3. **Type the name or e-mail of the person you wish to add as an admin.**

   If you start typing the name Facebook, will bring up suggestions; just click the name to select it. You will need to be a Friend of this new admin to be able to add the admin this way.

   If you are not currently the admin's Facebook Friend, you can add the e-mail address that he or she used to open the Facebook account. The admin will receive a Facebook notification and will need to accept the invitation to be an admin of the Page.
4. **Click the Save Changes button. You need to enter your Facebook password at this point.**

Here are the steps to remove someone as an admin for your Page:

1. **If you'd like to remove yourself, or someone else as an admin of the Page, first go to your Page and click the Edit Page button on the right side.**
2. **Select Manage Admins on the left side of the page.**
3. **Click Remove next to the name of the person you want to remove.**

   If you are removing yourself, just click the Remove link next to your name. Remember, you won't be able to edit your Page or gain access to any of the Insights, Ads, Notifications, and so o, when you remove yourself as an admin. If you try to remove yourself as an admin before adding someone else, you won't be able to remove yourself.
4. **Click Save Changes.**

   You need to enter your Facebook password to complete the process.

 Another way to access your Page is to go directly to your Page manager at www.facebook.com/pages/manage/ and click the Edit Page link under the Profile image of the Page you want to edit.

Apps

Apps (or applications) are developed by third parties, or by Facebook itself, to expand the functions of Facebook. There are literally thousands of apps. You can connect an app to your Page to expand what people can do on your Page. You can search through all the apps Facebook has in its directory by going to www.facebook.com/apps/directory.php. Or, if you want a more focused approach, a nice place to explore all the apps that have

more to do with a business application are available through Appbistro at
http://appbistro.com.

When you create a new Page, you need to activate a few apps right away
because they create important links that people will be looking for in your
side navigation menu. These apps, developed by Facebook, are;

✦ Photos

✦ Links

✦ Events (if your business will be having them

✦ Discussion Boards (if relevant to your Page's goals)

The next chapter, "Arranging What Your Visitors See," explains all the steps
to add applications to your new Page as well as shows you how to move
application links up or down in your Page's left navigation.

Applications are so important to Facebook that we discuss them in all nine
minibooks of *this book*, and especially in minibook V.

Mobile

When you select the Mobile link, you're presented with the opportunity to
create four different kinds of mobile connections to your Page. With these
different options, you can upload status updates, upload photos, and so on.

✦ **With Mobile e-mail:** We go through your mobile e-mail options in
Chapter 1 of this minibook, but torecap, you can send a post or upload a
photo to your Page using an e-mail address created specifically for your
Page. Facebook puts your unique e-mail address in this section for easy
reference. From your mobile phone, what you type in the subject line
of the e-mail becomes the update to your Page, or if you are uploading
a photo, the subject line becomes the caption. Nothing that you type in
the body of the e-mail will show up, so leave it blank.

✦ **With Mobile Web:** You can see how your Page looks on a mobile phone by
typing in its URL in the phone browser. Facebook also puts the link to create
a vanity URL in this part of the dashboard. Remember, you need to have at
least 25 Likers before you can create a vanity URL, or what Facebook also
calls an Alias. You can go to http://facebook.com/username to create it.

For example, if you type **www.facebook.com/sociallycongruent** on
an Android phone, you are redirected to http://m.facebook.com/
sociallycongruent (notice the m). Turns out that your phone is so
smart, it knows when you are looking at Facebook from a phone, so it
directs you to the mobile interface for Facebook. Your Page will look a
bit different from how it looks on a computer, so make sure you check it.

You can also type **http://touch.facebook.com/yourpagename** to see how your Page will look to those viewing it on a phone.

✦ **With the iPhone or iPad:** First, install the Facebook App on your iPhone or iPad (there isn't an app built for the iPad — you'll need to add the one built for the iPhone) and log in.

To add your Page as a Favorite for quick access, follow these steps:

1. **Click the grid icon on the top-left corner of the app.**

2. **Click the + sign on the top-right corner.**

3. **Click the Pages button on the bottom right.**

4. **Find and select your Page.**

Doing these steps creates a quick access icon on the app. To find the icon, you might need to slide the app from right to left to get to the next page of icons. If you have an iPhone or iPad, you'll understand that sliding process.

5. **Click your Page's icon to access your Page.**

You can post photos from your iPhone or iPad with this app or post an update. Currently, you can't directly post a video. To post a photo, click the Camera icon to the left of the Status Update field and navigate to the photo. To post a status update, tap the What's on Your Mind? field and type your update.

✦ **With Text Messaging (SMS):** If you can access Facebook on your smartphone, you don't need to send updates via text messaging. Things change quickly, don't they? If you don't have a smartphone yet, you can set this up to text directly to your Page. Click the green Sign Up for SMS button and follow the steps to set it up with your phone carrier.

On the other side of this, you can tell people to Like your Page by sending a text message. Tell people to send a text message to 32665 (FBOOK) with the words "like yourvanityurl."

For example, say you are on a radio show. You can announce "Hey, you can Like my Page by texting Like AmyPorterfield to 32665! That's Like — a space — then AmyPorterfield (all one word) to 32665."

When someone does this, it is the same thing as clicking the Like button at the top of your Facebook Page. The Liker is now connected to your Page.

You will need to have your vanity URL (username) set up to do this. We discuss creating your username in the "Basic Information" section, earlier in this chapter.

Insights

Clicking the Insights link on your administrative dashboard takes you directly to your Insights dashboard.

Insights is Facebook's analytics system. You can see who uses your Page, as well as see their interactions, age, sex, where they live, their cat's name (no, not yet). . . . You can also see very detailed graphs about the users of your Page and their interactions with it. Get acquainted with the Insights dashboard because it can really help your see who your audience is and give you insight into what they respond to the most on your Page.

There is so much to this wonderful analytics program that we dedicated an entire chapter in Book IX to it.

Help

This link is your direct link to the Facebook Help Directory. Even though this link is simply named Help, it links directly to the business Pages Help section, rather than to some general Facebook help page. The main Help topics are

✦ Creating and administering your Page

✦ Promoting your Page and Page Insights

✦ Using Facebook Mobile to update your audience

✦ Usernames

✦ Page privacy for admins and followers

✦ Finding and interacting with Pages

✦ Upgraded Pages

✦ Bugs and Known Issues

✦ Have a suggestion?

We feel it's good to go straight to the horse's mouth (what does that mean, anyway?) when we have a question about Facebook. That's why this quick link to the Help section for Pages is handy to have on the editing menu.

Consider bookmarking these other sites for help reference:

✦ **AllFacebook:** www.allfacebook.com

✦ **Mashable:** www.mashable.com

✦ **Mari Smith's Free Facebook Resources link on her Facebook business Page:** www.facebook.com/marismith

Chapter 4: Arranging Your Navigation Menu

In This Chapter

✔ **Finding your new Page**

✔ **Understanding how applications act as navigation links**

✔ **Changing the order of the side navigation links**

✔ **Using additional administrative links**

*Y*ou and your Page admins need to be very familiar with how your Page looks to visitors on Facebook. In Chapter 3 of this minibook, we discuss how to choose and set the Landing Page new visitors see when first arriving on your Page. In this chapter, we tell you how to add some great side links for your visitors to enjoy.

Finding Your Page

The first question we get from marketers new to Facebook is, "How do I find my Page?" For a newbie, finding a Page is not intuitive, but you have a variety of ways to get to any business Page (yours or someone else's), and we explore a few of them here.

You can find your Page easily by using any of the following options:

✦ **Go to** www.facebook.com/pages: This page has three very handy links at the top right side of the Page:

  • *My Pages*: This link shows you other Facebook Pages that your personal Profile has Liked. These are not the Pages you have personally created.

  • *Pages I Admin*: This link brings up a new page with the Pages you have personally created or are administrator of. You can click the name of the Page to go directly to the Page or click the Edit Page link under the name to go directly to the editing dashboard of that Page.

  • *Create Page button:* Click this button and create a new Page.

✦ **Add the Page's username in the browser bar after** http://facebook.
com: After you have obtained a vanity URL (see Chapter 3 of this minibook to create one), you can also just add the username to the Facebook
URL in your browser bar, then bookmark it on your computer for easy
access. This is how the URL would look after you add the vanity URL:
http://www.facebook.com/yourusername

www.facebook.com/AmyPorterfield

www.facebook.com/SociallyCongurent

www.facebook.com/GrandmaMaryShow

✦ **Use the Facebook Search Bar:** This search bar is at the top of every
Facebook page. Start typing your Page's username and it will show up
for you to select.

If for some reason your business Page doesn't come up as you type, continue to type the name of the Page completely and then click the See More
Results link at the bottom of what is suggested.

You will now be on a Search page that lists multiple Pages, people, groups,
and so on with similar names to what you typed. You have the option of filtering these results via the options on the left sidebar. Those options are as
follows:

✦ All Results

✦ People

✦ Pages

✦ Groups

✦ Applications

✦ Events

✦ Web Results

✦ Posts by Friends

✦ Posts by Everyone

To find your business Page, select the Pages option. You should see your
Page's name now. Click it to go to your Page.

The nice thing about this Search interface is that you can see how the keywords in your Page Name are showing up on Facebook and on the Web by
scrolling down the Search Results page and seeing how those keywords
show up in other people's posts, and in classic Web searches. Select each of
the filters (Pages, groups, Events, and so on) to view the results.

Working with Left-Side Navigation Links

In Chapter 3 of this minibook, we introduce you to the left-side navigation of your business Page. The side navigation links that you and your visitors see on your Page are actually *applications* (usually referred to as apps). Apps are add-ons that provide added functionality to your Page. We explained them a bit in the last chapter and more thoroughly in minibook V. For this chapter's purposes, you just need to know that Facebook has several apps they developed ready for you to use on your Page, but you have to make them visible to your community. That's our focus in this section.

As we noted in the previous chapter, when you first create your Page, the public will only see three navigation links: Wall, Info and Photos. If you see the link called Getting Started (see Chapter 2 of this minibook), note that it is seen only by admins of the Page.

Book II
Chapter 4

Arranging Your
Navigation Menu

There are some great links you can add to this navigation menu right away, such as Events, Links, Notes, Video, and Discussion Boards. These apps were developed and designed by Facebook itself, so they are in the queue (so to speak), ready to be added to your Page. Later on, in all the following minibooks (especially in Books IV and V), we describe how to add custom-built links, too, such as Welcome links, store links, YouTube links, and hundreds of others! We go through those later.

Right now, we go through Facebook's apps and help you decide whether you want to add them to your Page.

You should know that after their initial visit to your business Page, most people will view only your Page's updates via their News Feed and will rarely visit your actual business Page. Sad, but statistically true. If you want your audience to visit your Page and explore your navigation links, you will need to provide strong calls to action in your status updates. Some examples of a *call to action* are a request to Like your Page and to join an Event or participate in a contest. Bringing people back to your Page develops strong bonds between you and the branding of your business.

Adding Apps to Add Links to Your Page Menu

As mentioned before, adding an app to your Page will add a link to the navigation menu that your visitors see on your Page. You can add as many apps as you want and rearrange them on the menu (Wall and Info are set in place and can't be moved). You can even rename many of them to customize what they say.

From your administrative dashboard, you can follow these generic instructions for adding a Facebook-built application link to your Page's side navigation menu (Events, Video, Notes, and Discussion Board). Occasionally, there will be variations with certain applications you are adding; we discuss those after showing you the basics of adding a link.

1. **Go to your Page and click the Edit Page button**.

   Clicking this opens up your editing menu on the left side of the Page.

2. **Click Apps.**

   The Apps tab shows you all the apps you currently have connected to your Page. From the list, find the app you want to add to the navigation menu for all to see.

3. **Click the Edit Settings link under the name of the app.**

   A dialog box appears. Most default applications (such as Notes, Photos, or Events) show two tabs: Profile and Additional Settings. Some applications (both default and custom) only show the Profile tab.

4. **Click the Add link on the Profile Tab.**

   There will be variations here depending on the app you're adding. We note those variations later.

5. **Click the Additional Settings Tab (if it's there).**

   Decide whether you want the app to be able to post to the Page Wall. For example, for the Photos app, click the permission box if you want photos to be posted to the Page wall each time you upload and publish a photo.

6. **Click Okay.**

   The app is listed in your Page's navigation menu for all to see.

Facebook currently shows several app links in the left navigation menu, followed by a *More* link that users click to display the rest of the list. We describe this feature a bit more in the *"Repositioning Links"* section, later in this chapter.

Now that you know how to turn on your default applications, you can use these instructions to install any of the Facebook-built applications we list in upcoming sections.

Events application

If your business has Events, you might want to add this link by following the steps in the previous section. To see an example of adding links for Events, take a Figure 4-1, which shows a local convention center's Event page. Notice how the events are arranged by Tomorrow, This Month, and then by Month name.

If you click an Event Title, you're taken to that particular Event's Page. Using Facebook Events for marketing is discussed thoroughly in Book VI, Chapter 1.

Figure 4-1: The Events application lists the events your business wants to showcase.

Photos application

This application is automatically on the navigation menu for new Pages. If you don't want this link to be visible to your Page visitors, you need to follow the instructions earlier in this chapter for adding an app, and then click Remove (instead of Add) on the Edit Settings tab. This removes the Photo link from the menu. If, in the future, you want this link to be available, just go back to that same tab and click Add.

Having this app as a link on your Page menu allows visitors see the photos you upload to your Page. You can arrange your photos into custom titled albums, but Facebook keeps your Profile images in one album for you called Profile Pictures (and you can't change the name of this album).

If you or someone post a photo to the Page Wall, Facebook will put it in an album called Wall Photos. You can't change the name of this album, either, but you can delete photos that end up in this album. We go through all the photo uploading, arranging, album naming world of images in Book IV, Chapter 1. This section is focused on turning on (or off) the app itself.

As we discuss in the previous chapter, you can also turn off the ability of a Liker posting photos to your Page in your administrative dashboard, under Manage Permissions.

After you have added the Photos app, people clicking that link on the menu will see a page with thumbnails of all your albums. When users click an album's thumbnail, they can see all the photos in that album as thumbnails. When they click any of *those* images, a *lightbox* opens. A lightbox is a dialog box that shows specific information — in this case, your photos. The lightbox has arrows on either side so that the visitor can move through the photo album one image at a time.

You can use photos like ads because you can upload an image of your promotional page or text and, in the caption section, place the hyperlinked URL that people can click to buy a product or sign up for something. Figure 4-2 shows an example of how much information you can put in the captions section. We spend some time on the marketing possibilities of photos in Facebook in Book IV, Chapter 1.

Figure 4-2: This is how people see your photos in the lightbox.

But what about those photos in the photo strip at the top of your Page? How can you manage those? See Chapter 3 of this minibook.

Links application

Every time that you, or anyone, posts a status update on your business Page that includes a link (URL) to anything on the Web, Facebook automatically also puts the complete post (including any comments it gets on the Wall post) on a handy little list that you can access through this menu link.

When you follow the instructions for adding an app, noted above, you can see that there is only one tab, Permissions. Click the Add link to add this app to the navigation menu. This menu link is a quick way to see all the URLs that have been posted to your Page, by you or a visitor (if you have that permission selected).

As soon as you post a URL to your Page Wall, it automatically is listed on this menu link, too. This includes any links to Web sites, blog posts, and YouTube video players. From our research, it seems that only the latest ten posts with links will be listed on this link page. You can decide whether this extra view of links is handy for your visitors or is adding to the length of the menu for no good reason.

Notes application

A Note is similar to an e-mail sent to several people listed in the TO: or CC: fields, except it is also public and can be seen by everyone. Everyone *tagged* will both get the message and see who else got the message, too. Tagging is a way to make sure that a particular person is aware of the Note. The people tagged will get a notification and be able to view the Note. (They will also be able to un-tag themselves if they don't want to be attached to it publicly.)

You can create a Note and tag people and Pages to view it. You can tag only your personal friends and Pages you've Liked, not people or Pages who have Liked your Page. So, Notes are limited in that way. But when you create a Note, it will put a Notification status on your Page Wall and go out to your Likers news feeds for *all* to (potentially) see.

You can also set your blog to auto-post on the Notes page. You can use the Networkedblog app (which we discuss in more detail in Book III, Chapter 3), or you might find that you don't need this Notes link at all, but it is worth exploring.

If you plan to add and use this link, there are a couple of ways to work with it; you can manually write a Note, or auto-post a Note from an RSS Feed.

Manually writing Notes

You might find that you're more long-winded than the regular status post space allows (420 characters). In that case, use the Notes application to express what you need to say.

You can consider this a blog, or an additional blog, or a larger posting space. You can create a special type of conversation between you and a few of your Likers using the Notes app. This could be a conversation space for a special group of people, such as your Key Players, or people who are enthusiastic about a particular subject.

1. **Click the Notes link in your Page's navigation menu.**

You might need to click the More link at the bottom of the navigation links column if Notes is not one of the links on display.

2. **Click the +Write a Note button on the top right of the Page.**

This opens an editing space where you can create a Title, type the text of the Note, tag people, add a photo, preview, save a draft, and publish.

3. **Fill in Title and Body of the Note.**

Note that you can use a few editing tools such as Bold, Italic, and others. A Note can be really long. How long? We don't know exactly, but we've seen up to five pages' worth fit in there! So write away!

4. **Tag People and Pages.**

To tag a person or a Page, just start typing the person's name in the Tag field, and Facebook will bring up your friends and the Pages you have Liked (with your personal Profile). Click the ones you want to Tag. See Figure 4-3.

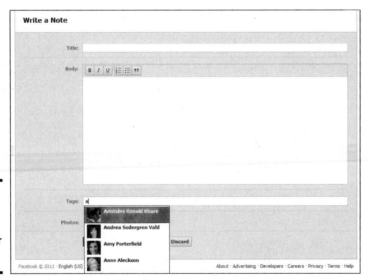

Figure 4-3:
Tag a
person or
Page in your
Note.

5. **Add a Photo.**

You can add a photo to your Note from your Page's photos or you can import a photo from your computer. When you click the Add a Photo link, you have the choice of uploading a photo or selecting the photos you've already uploaded to your Page (listed in albums). Just select the photo you want to add to the Note or import one.

6. Click Publish, Preview, Save Draft, or Discard.

You can decide how to proceed with this step.

- *Publish:* Your Note is published to the world! The Note will show up in your status update and Likers' News Feeds. Any people or Pages you've tagged will be notified. Anyone can read and comment on your Note.

- *Preview:* When you click Preview, you see exactly how your Note will look when viewed. It will have two links at the top: Publish or Edit. You can go back and Edit the Note by clicking Edit, or go ahead with the Publishing process by clicking Publish.

- *Save Draft:* The next time you want to edit the Note, you will need to look on the left side of your Page for the link called Notes. When you click it, two sublinks show up: Notes About (Notes in which your Page has been tagged) and Drafts. Click Drafts and you'll see a list of all your Note Drafts, as shown in Figure 4-4. Just click the Title to start editing. Non-admins won't see the link to your Drafts.

- *Discard:* Discarding a Note completely removes it from your Drafts. Discard is a way to say Delete before something is published.

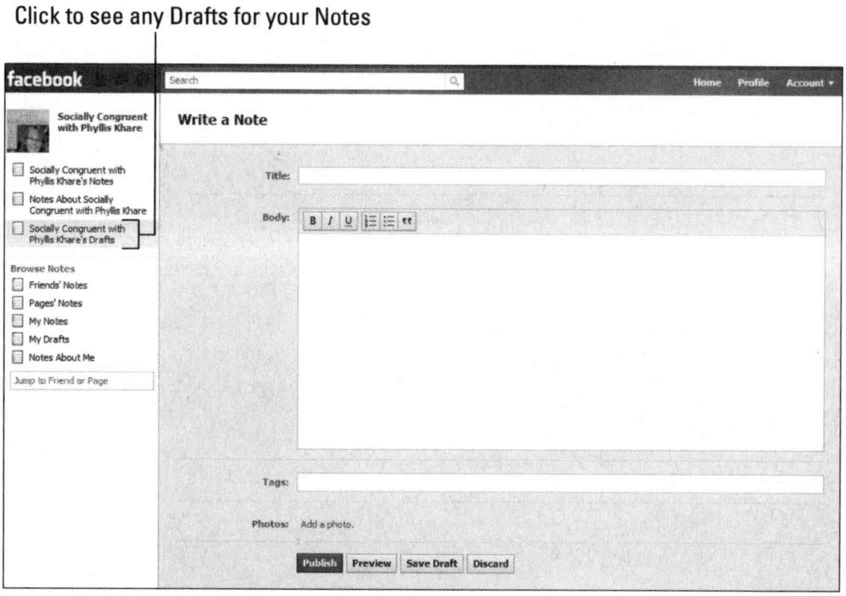

**Book II
Chapter 4**

**Arranging Your
Navigation Menu**

Click to see any Drafts for your Notes

Figure 4-4:
All your
Drafts are
listed here.

Auto-posting to Notes from an RSS Feed

You can pull in your blog posts and have them automatically post to the Notes link. The instructions on how to add your blog to Notes are discussed in detail in minibook III, Chapter 3. But you can add anything that has an RSS Feed to this app. An *RSS* (Really Simple Syndication) *Feed* is information that is pulled in from online publishers (bloggers, news services, social sites). You know whether a site has an RSS Feed if you see the (usually) orange RSS icon.

As long as you have the right to reproduce the content, you can auto-post anything that has a RSS Feed. You can, for example, add your Twitter Feed, your blog feed, or any feed that is *aggregated* (combined) from any number of Web sites. For example, you can aggregate your blog posts and your Twitter posts into one RSS Feed. After we explain how to add an RSS Feed to this Notes app, we show you a way to easily create an aggregated Feed.

You add a single RSS Feed address or an aggregated Feed Address the same way, as follows:

1. **Go to your Page and Click the Edit Page button.**

2. **Click Apps on the left menu.**

3. **Click the Go to App link for the Notes app.**

   Of the three links under Notes, make sure you click Go to App.

   You're taken to your Notes dashboard, shown in Figure 4-5.

Figure 4-5: Your Notes dashboard.

4. **On the very bottom of the left side of the page, click the Edit Import Settings link.**

   You are taken to a screen where you need to enter your RSS feed address, as shown in Figure 4-6.

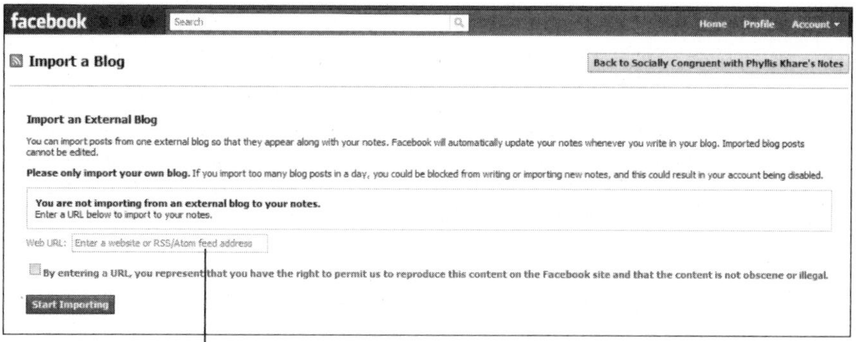

Figure 4-6:
This is the
place to add
an RSS Feed
to auto-post
on your
Notes Tab.

Put your RSS feed address here

5. **Enter your RSS feed address in the Web URL box.**

   This is where you paste your single RSS Feed address URL or an aggregated one (more on that in a minute).

6. **Select the box that says you have the right to reproduce the content.**

   Make sure this is true!

7. **Click the Start Importing button.**

As posts are shared on that external Website (the Feed address you are now importing to Notes), they will auto-post to your Notes app. You now have two choices as to where they will show up. You can have them post only to your Notes page or to both that page and your Page's Wall.

The place to modify those settings are found by doing the following:

1. **Follow Steps 1-3 in the preceding list to return to your Notes dashboard.**

2. **This time click the Edit Settings link under Notes.**

   There are three links under Notes; make sure this time you click Edit Settings.

3. **Click the Additional Permissions tab.**

4. **Depending on your preference, select or deselect the Publish Content to My Wall" check box.**

If you select this box, every time something posts to your Notes app from your Feed, it will also post it on your Wall (with a link to view it on the Notes interface). If you don't select the box, every time something posts to your Notes app from the RSS Feed, it will show up only on the Notes interface.

Here is a quick way to create a custom aggregated (combined) RSS Feed:

1. **Go to** http://www.xfruits.com **and create an account.**

You do that by clicking the Sign In link and creating an account.

2. **Go to the Home Page and the Click Aggregator RSS box.**

This takes you to a two-step process to create the aggregated RSS feed.

3. **Fill in the Title, Tags, and all the RSS Feed addresses that you want to aggregate into one RSS Feed.**

You can use your feeds from YouTube, Twitter, article sites, and other sites that give you an RSS feed.

4. **Click the Aggregate My Feeds button.**

This aggregates all your feeds into one feed address.

5. **Copy the URL of this new RSS Feed.**

Now you can use this combined feed to auto-post into your Notes Tab, which we explain next.

6. **Go back to your Facebook Page and follow the instructions for adding an RSS Feed, as noted in the earlier section, "Auto-posting to Notes from an RSS Feed."**

You will also need to Edit Settings to decide whether you want this Feed to show up on your Wall, or just on your Notes page.

Video application

Here's another app that might need some thinking through before you add it to the navigation menu. Facebook's video app might not be the best app for you to use on your Page. If your business uses a lot of videos, you might want to explore a few third-party apps before making a final decision to add this one or not. We discuss using the YouTube app for marketing in Book III, Chapter 1, and the Livestream app in Book VII, Chapter 4.

If you want to really expand the notion of using video on Facebook, you can also check out the VYou app at https://apps.facebook.com/vyoucom/?ref=ts . Now, back to the Facebook video app!

Here are a few points about the Facebook-built video app:

✦ The videos you upload can also be accessed from the Photo link. If you
   click Photos in the left navigation menu, there will be a Videos link at
   the top right of the albums page. Clicking that will show you a page with
   thumbnails of the videos you have uploaded. That video link will be
   there only if you have uploaded or recorded a video using the Facebook
   video app.

✦ If you post a status update on your Page using a YouTube URL, the video
   will not show up on this Video link page. You have to directly upload or
   record a video using the Facebook video app for it to be listed on the
   Video page.

✦ There's no "lightbox" interface for videos such as what Facebook provides for photos.

✦ If people share your Page's video by posting it to their Wall, people will
   have the option to Like your Page — with a Like button in the corner.

Book II
Chapter 4

Arranging Your
Navigation Menu

One of the more interesting features of the Facebook Video app is not that
you can upload a video from your computer but that you can record a
video directly from your webcam! Right there — right now — your pajamas
on! Seriously, though, if your business has updates that need to be posted
quickly, you might want to try out this feature. Facebook lets you record up
to 20 minutes. After adding the Video app, click the Video navigation link on
your Page, instead of clicking the Upload button, click the Record button.
Again, all this is discussed in Book III, Chapter 1.

Discussions Board application

This is one of the first Facebook-built apps you need to think about before
listing it on the navigation menu for all to see. If you decide to use it, get it
started as soon as possible. Nothing is worse than having users go to a Page
with this link showing — with its promise of a hearty discussion — and then
finding the page empty.

For those of you who remember when forums were all the rage, this format
will remind you of that. If your business needs a place for detailed back-and-
forth conversations around a distinct topic, you'll want to develop this link.

One very good thing about the Discussion Board link is that you can use it
for very clear-cut topics. For example, you can use it as your FAQ section or
as a way for people to respond to questions and make those answers readily
available (not lost on the Wall).

Take a look at a Coca-Cola's Page (www.facebook.com/cocacola) for an example of using the Discussion Board link for customer service. On the company's Discussion Board Page, you can see several topics that customers are venting about and to which Coca-Cola is responding. A Discussion Board takes the heat off the Wall and puts it in a place that's easier to respond to and a little less visible.

If you think that your conversations with customers can be more readily curated on the Wall, don't add this link.

Anyone who has Liked your Page can start a Discussion Topic, by the way. And they can say anything. Your Discussion Board could turn into a hotbed of spam, so consider your choice carefully.

Also, now that the navigation links are on the side of the Page, instead of at the top (as tabs) where they were in plainer view (before January 2011), it's a little harder to encourage people to click to go into the Discussions Board. Plus, it's another step for an admin of the Page to check and manage the area.

You add this link to your Page navigation menu by following the steps at the top of this chapter.

Say that you've decided to add the Discussion Board link, you know your audience, and you're sure that you can keep the spammers away by deleting their posts quickly. The following sections explain how you can start a topic for discussion and respond to comments about other topics.

Starting a new topic

Following is the process that you (or anyone) can use to start a new topic via the Discussions Board link.

1. **Click the Discussions link on your Page's navigation menu.**

   You might need to click the More link if the Discussions link is not showing.

2. **Click the Start New Topic button.**

3. **Type a name for your topic in the Topic text box.**

4. **Type your question or discussion text in the Post text area.**

5. **Click the Post New Topic button.**

Replying to an existing topic

As the admin of your business Page, you need to respond to comments and new discussion topics to encourage community interaction. To reply to an existing discussion topic, following these steps:

1. **Click the Discussions link in your Page's navigation menu.**

You might need to click the More link if it is not showing.

2. **Click a discussion title you want to add comments to.**

This opens a page showing all the conversations in this topic. You can add a reply at the end of all the comments so far. You can't reply to each comment submission, though.

3. **Type in your reply.**

You can put hyperlinks in this space, too.

4. **Click the Post Reply button.**

Deleting a topic or post

You can delete a Discussion Board Topic and all the conversation connected to it in one fell swoop, or you can delete a single comment or post at a time. The links you see for deleting are seen only by admins of the Page. Other people can't delete a topic, even if they started it!

To delete a Discussion Topic and all the conversations associated with it, follow these steps:

1. **Click the Discussions link in your Page's navigation menu.**

You might need to click the More link if Discussions is not showing. Now you'll see all the discussion titles in a list.

2. **Click the X to the right of the topic title you wish to delete.**

Each discussion topic title will have an X to the right of it. Clicking this X will delete the original post and all comments under it.

A confirm box will pop up.

3. **Click Okay.**

Now the entire Discussion and all the comments associated with it will be gone. If you want to delete just one comment at a time, follow these steps:

1. **Click the Discussions link in your Page's navigation menu.**

You might need to click the More link if it is not showing. Now you'll see all the discussion titles in a list.

2. **Click the title of the discussion that contains the comment you want to delete.**

3. **Find the comment you wish to delete and click the Delete Post link under that particular comment.**

A dialog page will come up asking you to confirm you want to delete the Post.

4. **Click the Delete Post button.**

**Book II
Chapter 4**

Arranging Your
Navigation Menu

Now just that particular comment will be deleted. You can continue to delete single comments this way throughout the whole discussion.

Marketing ideas for the Discussions Board link

As we mention earlier in this section, you might have a good reason to move the conversation off the Wall and onto the Discussions link. If you decide to use this app, make sure you monitor it daily.

Each time a post is created in the Discussion Board app, a notification is posted on the Page Wall that reads like this:

> "[Name of Page] discussed [Hyperlinked Topic Title] on the [Hyperlinked Page Name] discussion board."

Here's a full example of a Wall notification:

> RECENT ACTIVITY
>
> Socially Congruent with Phyllis Khare discussed Managing FAQs on the Discussion Tab on the Socially Congruent with Phyllis Khare discussion board.

Using this link for a FAQ page can be helpful. It's also good to have each question and answer as its own topic because this keeps the conversation organized, for a while at least. Even with this kind of organization, someone will come along and post a topic that is already answered under one of your topic posts. Oh, well. There goes the organization! But it might be worth a try, depending on your business. You also need to remind people on the Wall that you have a Discussion Page that has lots of information on it.

If you have a business that relies on tutorials in text format, you can use this Discussions application or the Notes application. Each topic can be presented as a how-to guide, and all the questions about the topic will naturally fall under that topic.

You could have a Page for a small college town to organize trips to several different local and regional airports. Name a Discussion topic for each of the airports. People needing rides click can the topic with the airport name they need a ride to and arrange rides within the Discussion area. The marketing angle for this particular Page would be that if one of the admins has a car service to one of the airports, that admin might get much more business as a result of this community-minded Page.

You can try all sorts of ideas with this application. The only drawback is that you won't be able to change the name of the link— it will always be Discussions.

✦ **You can create topics such as the following:** Generating New Product Ideas, What Should We Name Our New Book?, or Which Logo Suits Us.

✦ **You can use it for ride coordination for an event you are hosting.** You can set up Hotel Names as the topics and people can post their info under the hotel they are staying in to help coordinate rides.

✦ **If you have a travel-related business, you can set up Topics for certain cities or countries and post advice under each one.** People are generous with their travel advice. You might find this a good way to organize that information.

Many of these ideas are not marketing as much as they are organizational, but many companies rely on their reputation for being organized as a marketing theme.

You can place links in Discussion posts as long as you use a full URL address (that is, `http://nameofwebsite.com`). This is useful because it lets you add a direct link to any product or Web site in any Discussions post.

Repositioning Navigation Links

All left-side navigation links on your business Page, except Wall and Info, can be rearranged from top to bottom. However, you need to have more than eight links to be able to rearrange the links. When you have more than eight navigation links, go to your business Page and then follow these instructions to change the navigation order:

1. **Click the More link under the links in the side navigation menu.**

2. **Click the Edit link at the bottom of the list.**

   Your cursor changes to a cross with four arrows (hover over the navigation menu to see the cursor change). In addition, your navigation menu items now have an *X* next to each one, as shown in Figure 4-7.

3. **Click and hold the link you want to move.**

4. **Drag a link to its new position.**

   To drag a link, just hold down your mouse over the link title and, while holding your mouse button, drag it to a new spot and release the mouse.

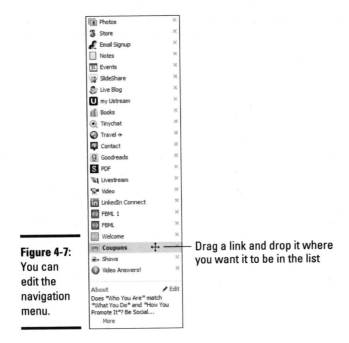

Figure 4-7:
You can
edit the
navigation
menu.

Drag a link and drop it where
you want it to be in the list

Working with the Right-Side Admin Links

As the administrator, when you're viewing your Page you will see a series of
links on the top right side, as shown in Figure 4-8. Only you, as an admin, see
these links. Everyone else sees the Friends who share this Page at the top of
that column.

When you're viewing your Page as your Page (if you need to be reminded
what that means, go to Chapter 3 of this minibook), you will not see the
Suggest to Friends link.

This box is seen only by admins of the Page

Figure 4-8:
These are
the admin
quick links.

The links at the top right of your business Page are considered "quick links" to important parts of your Page. They are as follows:

✦ **Admins:** You can see the thumbnail pictures of your Page's admins here. If you see a little green square in the bottom corner of an admin's picture, the admin is online and has his or her chat function open. Click the thumbnail and the chat interface opens for you to type a message to that admin.

You can make your Page admins visible to the public by clicking the Edit Page button and then selecting Featured in the left navigation menu. Then adding the Page Owners whom you want to be publicly viewable. Their personal thumbnail images will go on the left-side of your Page listed as Page Owners. We take you through those steps in the Chapter 3 of this minibook.

✦ **Use Facebook As:** This is the quick toggle to view Facebook as your personal Profile or as your Page profile. You can find out how to view these elements by reviewing Chapter 3 of this minibook.

✦ **View Notifications:** a quick link to the Notifications interface for your Page. We have a big section about Notification in minibook II (that's this one) Chapter 3.

✦ **Promoting with an Ad:** This is the quick link to the Facebook ad creation page. If you want to know all about Facebook ads, Book VIII is devoted to explaining how to create ads.

✦ **Viewing Insights:** This is a quick view of the important stats for your Page. We discuss Facebook Insights in great detail in Book IX, Chapter 2. This box gives you a quick way to click to the Insights interface.

✦ **Suggest to Friends:** Only admins can use this particular link to invite their personal Friends to Like this Page. Other people will have to use the Share link on the bottom left side of the Page — which creates a post to their personal Wall (or sends a private message). All that is discussed in Book IV, Chapter 1.

Book III

Adding the Basics to Your Facebook Page

The 5th Wave   By Rich Tennant

"I know it's a short profile, but I thought
'King of the Jungle' sort of said it all."

Contents at a Glance

Chapter 1: Posting to Your Page

In This Chapter

✔ **Becoming a pro at attachments**

✔ **Exploring the best practices for your posts**

✔ **Targeting your updates**

The most critical aspect of your Facebook presence is your posts. What you put on your Wall is the showcase of your business. After a Facebook user Likes you, he most likely won't go to your Page very often; typically, a user sees you only as an update in his News Feed. So, you have to be interesting, engaging, responsive, useful, and fun. No pressure, right?

You want your posts to establish you as an authority and expert in your field, and this chapter tells you what types of material you can use to accomplish that goal.

However, never forget that Facebook is a place where people come to be *social*. It's like a big cocktail party where people are having fun talking, so don't be a wet blanket and talk only about the big sale you're having. You don't want to be that irritating sales guy at the networking event whom everyone avoids — or worse, "un-Likes" you!

Helpful tips, useful information, and links and photos can go a long way toward making your Page engaging and popular. To that end, in this chapter, you find out how to post text updates, photos, links, and videos. You also discover how to target your updates to specific members of your community.

Posting Updates to Your Wall via the Publisher

To post an update to your community, you do so in what's called the Publisher. The Publisher is located on your Wall tab and contains the prompt "What's on your mind?" (see Figure 1-1).

Figure 1-1:
The Publisher is where you post information to your Wall that goes out to people who Like you.

The function of the Publisher on your Page is very similar to that of the Publisher on your personal Profile. When you post a status update to your personal Profile, however, it goes out to the News Feed of all your Friends, whereas an update to the Wall on your Page goes out to the News Feed of all those who Like you. Your Page's status update then shows up in the News Feed just as a person's status update shows up on the Feed of Friends.

Realize that when you post to your Page Wall, your post shows up in people's News Feed along with all the other posts of their Friends and Pages they Like. Don't refer to previous posts or things that are on your business Page that people can't see right then. If you want people to come to your Page to see those things, make sure you tell them to come to your Page. And make sure that each post can stand alone as a complete thought.

How long to make your post

Kind of like a Tweet, you have a limited number of characters available in the status update space: 420, to be exact. *Note:* After you type around 320 characters (depending on word structure), your post will be cut short, and a See More link pops up, as shown in Figure 1-2.

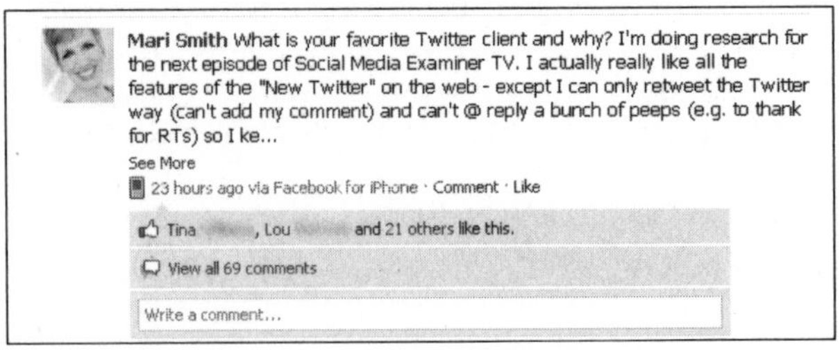

Figure 1-2:
A long status update gets truncated.

> **Mari Smith** What is your favorite Twitter client and why? I'm doing research for the next episode of Social Media Examiner TV. I actually really like all the features of the "New Twitter" on the web - except I can only retweet the Twitter way (can't add my comment) and can't @ reply a bunch of peeps (e.g. to thank for RTs) so I lke...
> See More
> 23 hours ago via Facebook for iPhone · Comment · Like
>
> Tina ____, Lou ____ and 21 others like this.
> View all 69 comments
> Write a comment...

Keep your post shorter so that people can easily read it and not miss anything valuable if they don't click the See More link.

How often to post an update

One of the most frequently asked questions is, "How often should I post?" The answer will vary depending on your goals and comfort level. Some people worry about "bothering" their community with too many posts. Or that some people will un-Like their Page or hide them if they post too much. We can assure you that most of your community won't mind your posts if you're doing them in the right way. That's why it's important to provide value.

Also, many people aren't on Facebook all the time and might not see your posts. Depending on how many Friends a user has or how many Pages a user Likes, your post might go through a News Feed fairly quickly.

For example, if you have one person who Likes your Page and has 10 Friends who post one update per day, and your Page is posting five updates per day, you'll be very visible, occupying one-third of their daily News Feed. However, say that you have a person who Likes your Page and has 500 friends who post one update per day: Your updates will just be 1 percent of their daily News Feed, and they may miss your posts. Bottom line: Don't worry about posting too often — people will miss your updates, and you want to continue to stay visible.

What types of material to include

When you go to create a post, think about your community. What do its members need? What's in it for them? Think of yourself as the funnel that guides the best information to your community — and that will be what keeps your community coming back for more. Also realize that you're participating in a conversation. Just as you do at a cocktail party, you want to respond when people comment on your post. Don't just post and run. (And don't post when you've had too many cocktails; you may regret it in the morning!)

Be sure to vary the types of material you post, too. Following are types of posts that you can use to market yourself as an expert, have fun, and plug your business all at the same time without being annoying:

+ **Pictures of a great Event you had**

+ **Video of behind the scenes happenings at your business**

+ **Questions that engage your audience and allow you to do some market research**

+ **Links to blog posts that solve people's problems within your niche**

Don't worry that you're giving information away for free. Your community will appreciate the information and look to you when they need help they can hire you for.

+ **Controversial news stories within your niche that will spark conversation**

+ **Events that you're hosting that will benefit your community**

+ **Links to resources that are helpful for your niche**

Again, this is just a partial list of post types. How do these market your business? By establishing yourself as the go-to person for your market. You notice that these posts aren't all about you and what you're selling. However, you're continually popping into the News Feed and reminding your community that you are there. You're branding yourself as an expert in your business.

Including Attachments

You might have noticed icons above the Publisher. You use these icons to attach an item to your post. They are, from left to right, Status, Photo, Link, or Video. We recommend varying your posts so that you use these attachments frequently. People like multimedia, and your status updates will be more visible when you use these features.

Posting Questions

Questions can be a great tool to get interaction from your audience. People love to give their opinion or chime in with their experience, as shown in Figure 1-3 in which 356 people answered the question posed.

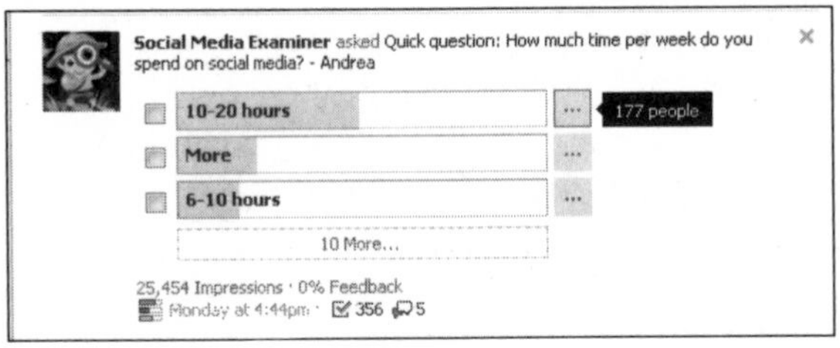

Figure 1-3: Questions can get a lot of response from your community.

> **Social Media Examiner** asked Quick question: How much time per week do you spend on social media? - Andrea ✕
>
> ☐ 10-20 hours · · · 177 people
> ☐ More · · ·
> ☐ 6-10 hours · · ·
> 10 More...
>
> 25,454 Impressions · 0% Feedback
> Monday at 4:44pm · ☑ 356 💬 5

You can also do market research, albeit unscientific, with these questions. As you can see, we found out that 177 people of the 356 responses spent 10@ nd20 hours per week on social media, which wasn't what we had expected.

The questions are in the form of poll answers, and you can choose to limit your answers to only ones that you allow or you can let your community members add their own selections. To use the Questions feature, follow these steps:

1. **From the Publisher on your Facebook Page Wall, click the Question link.**

   A box appears in which you can type your question, as shown in Figure 1-4.

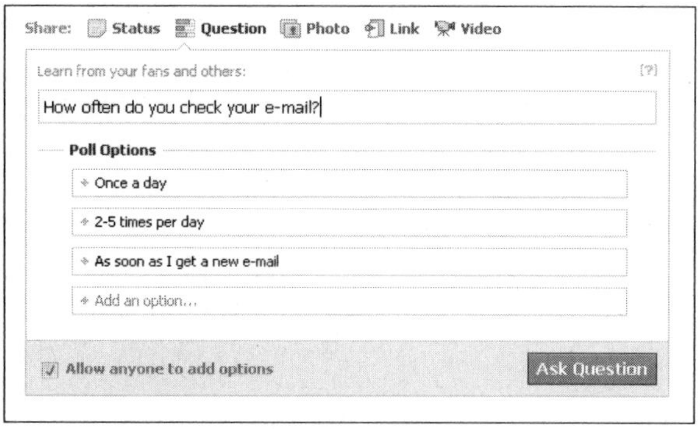

Figure 1-4: Type your question and poll options in the appropriate boxes.

2. **Type your question in the top box.**

3. **Click the box below the Poll Options and type a possible answer to the question.**

   As soon as you type in this box, another Poll Option box appears below your box.

4. **Add as many Poll Options as you want.**

   When you're done adding options, you see an extra empty Poll Option box that does not appear in the final question.

5. **If you do not want to allow people to be able to add options, deselect the box next to Allow Anyone to Add Options.**

6. **Click the blue Ask Question button.**

   Your question is posted.

This question will appear in the News Feed of everyone who likes your Page. Questions are also very viral, meaning that when people answer a question, their answer appears in their News Feed for their Friends to see, and it can then be answered by their Friends, as well.

You may wonder whether to allow people to add their own options to answer the question. Sometimes people enjoy putting in their own options and try to add something clever. Other times you may want to get more clear responses for research purposes, so you may not want to allow additional responses.

Questions also have their own Wall on which people can comment. To see this Wall, you have to click the question's hyperlink from your Wall. As shown in Figure 1-5, a pop-up box appears that shows more details about the question.

Figure 1-5: The pop-up box with all the details of the responses to the question.

Here is what you can see and do in the pop-up box:

✦ Responses in order of number of votes appear. If you allowed additional responses, you also see what people added.

✦ Number of votes appear when you mouse over the bar graphs.

✦ Click the three dots to the right of the bar to see another pop-up box with a list of all the people who voted for this option.

✦ If all the options can't be displayed, you can click the hyperlink to show the additional options (refer to Figure 1-4, which shows the 7 More hyperlink).

✦ Underneath the responses, you can see who asked the question, how many total votes the question received, and how many people are following the question. When people follows a question, they receive a notification whenever one of their Friends also answers the question.

✦ Under the Posts heading are all the people who have posted an additional response to this question on the Wall of the question. Each question has its own Wall on which people can discuss the question. So you may have the answers in the form of a poll, but people can elaborate on their responses on the Wall.

Attaching photos

Attaching photos is a great strategy for getting more interaction with your audience and marketing your brand because people love multimedia. A photo will be more noticeable that just a status update because it takes up more space in the News Feed. Disney Pixar posts a lot of photos of its movies with a little caption to engage. Take a look at Figure 1-6 for an example.

Figure 1-6:
Disney
Pixar gets
thousands
of Likes and
hundreds of
comments
on each
photo
posted from
its movies.

If you're a speaker, a photo of you speaking at an event will market your business in a more exciting way than if you just post an update saying, "Spoke at an event with business owners today." The great thing is that you can "show and tell" — that is, post the status and show the picture.

Or, say your business is a restaurant. You can post pictures of your food, kitchen, busy Friday night crowd, and so on. The possibilities are endless! Spend some time and think of all the picture posts you can have about your business.

To attach a photo, just click the Photo icon above the Publisher, as shown in Figure 1-7. You then have the choice to upload a photo.

Figure 1-7:
The Photo
icon
above the
Publisher
gives you
several
choices to
upload your
photos.

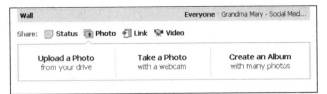

You can also post a photo as a link from a third-party site, such as Flickr or TwitPic. However, when you upload a photo as an attachment to the Publisher, it will be stored in your Photo tab for people to reference easily later. If you share a photo from Flickr as an attachment, it will just be a Wall post that is harder to get back to and enjoy.

Attaching links

We tell you the basics about attaching links in Book II, Chapter 3, but we dive a little deeper here with some of the marketing strategy. When you post a link, you can use the 420 characters of the status box, or Publisher, to introduce the link and entice people to click the story.

You can attach the link first and then write your comment in the Publisher or vice versa — it doesn't matter. Follow these steps to attach a link to your Wall post:

1. **From your Wall on your Page, click the third icon, labeled Link, next to the word Share, as shown in Figure 1-8.**

The Link box appears, and you can either manually enter the Web site address or paste it in.

Share: Status Photo Link Video
http://mashable.com/2011/02/12/trending-twitter-topics-chart-2/
Attach

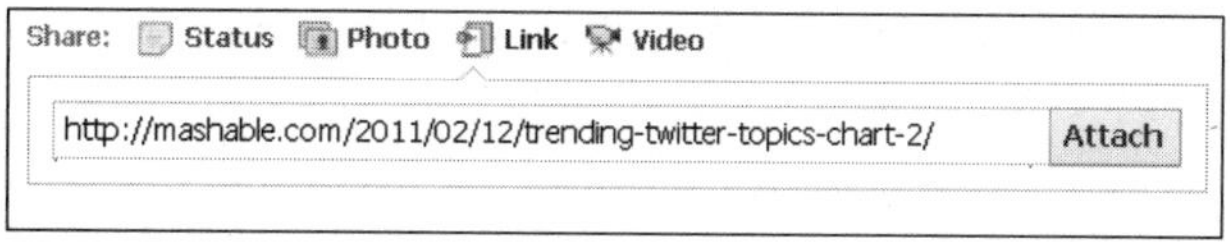

Figure 1-8: Add a link to your status update.

2. **Click the Attach button, on the right side of the Web site address, as shown in Figure 1-8.**

   The Web site will now be represented as a title and a short description next to a thumbnail image, as shown in Figure 1-9. These are pulled in from the Web site itself. You can edit this information by clicking the title or description. You also might have a choice in the thumbnail image to post, or you can click No Thumbnail if the image doesn't match the story.

Share: Status Photo Link Video
Top 10 Twitter Trends This Week [CHART]
http://mashable.com/2011/02/12/trending-...
Wondering which topics had Twitter abuzz this past week? Check out the full list of top trends.
1 of 1
No Thumbnail
Britney Spears still tops the Superbowl in Twitter's trending topics!
Everyone
Share

Figure 1-9: When you click Attach, the Web site has a title, a picture, and a short description, and you can add a comment.

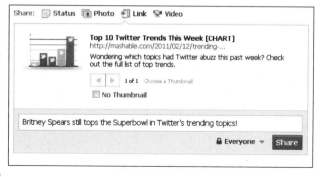

3. **Add some scintillating text to the Publisher.**

   This text might be a short description of, or plug for, the site you're linking to. The purpose of the text in this post is to give your community a reason to click the link.

4. **Click the blue Share button to post this status update with your link to your Wall.**

As mentioned in Step 2, you might be able to select from several thumbnail images to go with your link. The images are pulled from the site and might include images from advertisements on the Web site's side bar, so the images may not match the story. If you can't find an image that matches the link, you can select No Thumbnail.

The title and description are pulled in from the meta title and meta description on the Web site. Depending on the site, these might not even match the story on that site that you're trying to promote. The Webmaster of the site has the control over the meta title and description, but you can edit what shows up in your post by clicking the Title and Description before you attach the link.

Another thing you can do when posting a link is to post it right into the Publisher itself. This should automatically bring up the link attachment with the link already posted just as it would be above, with the Thumbnail choice. If you want to have a highlighted, clickable link in your comment area, just add the link in the comment area.

Deliberately, CNN frequently posts links to its news stories. The advantage to this is that the link is highlighted in the post and clickable, as shown in Figure 1-10. So now you have two ways for your community to get to this link: by clicking the highlighted link or by clicking the story below the post.

Figure 1-10: CNN posts the link within the publisher to make it clickable.

One other point of interest in this example CNN post is how engaging it is, with a teaser to the story that entices people to read more and click the link.

Don't post links to only your own Web site, though. Vary your content so that you become a funnel of information on the Web for your community. So where do you find these interesting links to post? Here are a number of ways to attract interesting material so that you can share it with your community.

✦ **Google Alerts:** Sign up for daily alerts to come into your e-mail on keywords in your niche. Sign up at http://www.google.com/alerts.

✦ **Google Reader:** Subscribe to other interesting blogs in your niche via an RSS Feed and check in with your blogs each day to find interesting posts. Sign up at http://reader.google.com.

✦ **Alltop:** This is a gathering of interesting blogs in various topics, arranged by topic and most recent posts at `www.alltop.com`.

✦ **Other Fan Pages in your niche:** Make sure to be a Fan of "competitor" Fan Pages to see what those folks are doing. It's okay to repost a link if it's an interesting bit of news.

✦ **Twitter:** A lot of interesting links are on Twitter. Follow the top people in your niche, and when you find something newsworthy, post it to your Page.

ReadWriteWeb does a very good job of combining links to its own blog posts and Web site with links to external sites. Find them online at `www.facebook.com/ReadWriteWeb`.

Attaching video

Video is a powerful tool to help your audience get to know you. You can easily upload a video into Facebook and you can even record one on the fly from a Webcam to post right away. When you click the Video icon in the Publisher, you will be given the choice to record a video with a Webcam or upload a video from your drive, as shown in Figure 1-11.

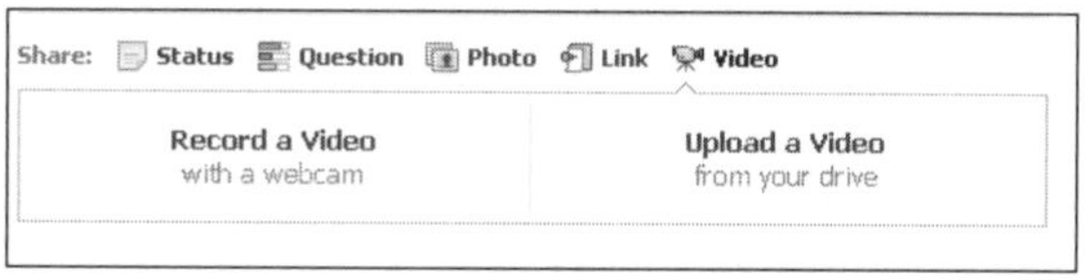

Figure 1-11:
Upload or record a video.

Upload a video shorter than 20 minutes, less than 1024MB, and made by you or your Friends per Facebook terms. Again, you always want to abide by their terms and conditions or your Page is in danger of being shut down. You will see the pop-up box as shown in Figure 1-12 to agree to Facebook's terms.

After you agree to the terms and conditions and your video uploads, you can edit some of the details, as shown in Figure 1-13.

After it's uploaded, the video will be able to play right within the Facebook status update and will stay on your Videos area -for your community to reference later.

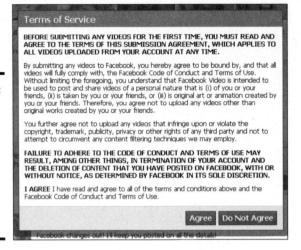

Figure 1-12:
Facebook's
terms and
conditions
pop up
when you
upload
a video
from your
computer.

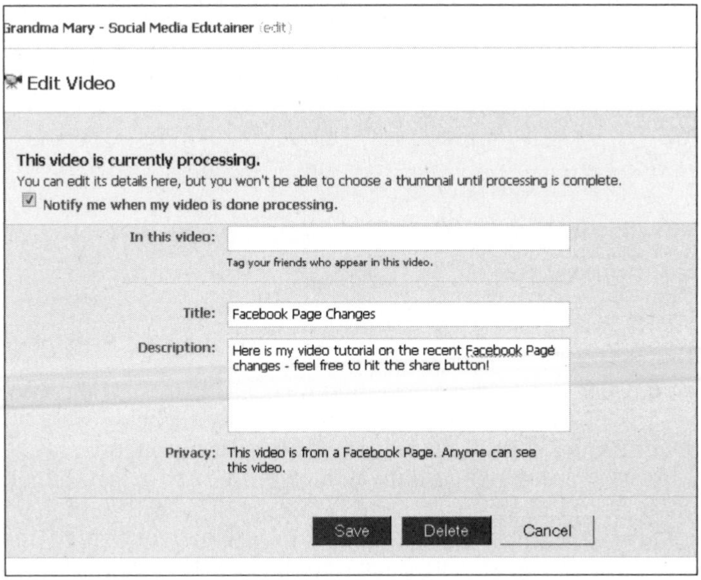

Figure 1-13:
Edit the
details
of your
uploaded
video.

Another advantage to uploading videos directly to Facebook is that when
non-Fans view your videos on Facebook, they will see the Like button for
your Facebook Page in the upper left of the video screen, as shown in Figure 1-14. This is a great way to make it easy for people to Like your Page.

You can also post videos by posting a link to a third-party video site, such
as YouTube or Vimeo. Most of these sites will allow the video to be played
within the update. However, these videos aren't stored on your Facebook
Page for people to see later.

Figure 1-14:
A Like button appears in the corner of your video for your non-Likers to easily connect with you.

Targeting Your Update by Location and Language

A little-known "trick" that you can do with the Publisher is to target your updates to certain members of your community. You can target your updates by geographical area or by language spoken. When you select the targeting, only those Likers that you specify in your target will see your status update in their News Feed.

So, if you have an Event happening in San Francisco, you can update only the people who live near there — meaning that your community in New York won't see those posts in their News Feed.

To use this feature, follow these steps after you type your status update:

1. **Click the lock icon to the left of the Share button in the Publisher, as shown in Figure 1-15. The lock icon has the default set to Everyone.**

   A drop-down menu appears.

2. **Choose Customize.**

   The Choose Your Audience pop-up dialog box appears, as shown in Figure 1-16.

**Book III
Chapter 1**

**Posting to
Your Page**

Figure 1-15:
Click the lock icon.

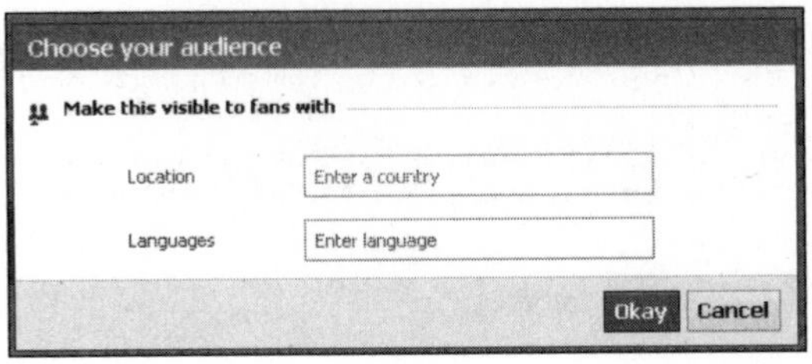

Figure 1-16:
Choose your
audience
to show
your status
update.

3. **Start typing a country name in the Location field, and when the drop-down menu showing the list of countries appears, select the country.**

   You must select a country on this list. After you select the country, you can identify the region further by City and State. If you put two countries on the list, though, you won't be able to choose city and states within multiple countries.

4. **Leave the default setting of Everywhere or select the By City radio button.**

   If you select By City, start typing in cities and select from the list provided. You can target many cities, as shown in Figure 1-17.

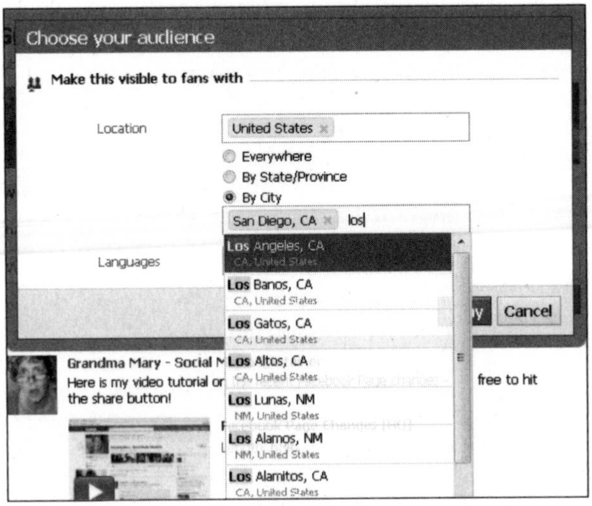

Figure 1-17:
You may
choose
multiple
cities from
the list.

5. **You can also target your updates to people who speak certain languages by typing languages into the box next to Languages.**

   You can do this in addition to or instead of targeting by geographical region.

Chapter 2: Understanding and Using iFrames to Customize Your Page

In This Chapter

✔ Defining iFrames

✔ Creating your own iFrame application for a customized Welcome Page

✔ Using third-party applications to create a custom Welcome Page

You may have seen customized Welcome Pages on some Facebook business Pages. A Welcome Page is actually a customized landing tab for visitors to your Facebook business Page who haven't Liked your Page yet. These Pages are referred to as Welcome Pages because you can set them to be the first thing new visitors see when they find your Facebook business Page — it's a virtual welcome! Anyone who has already Liked your business Page will go directly to your Page Wall when he or she visits. Only visitors who haven't Liked your Page will see this custom message first.

Having a Welcome Page to tell more about your business and remind people to click the Like button is a great way to increase your Likes without too much work. You can create these custom Welcome Pages with iFrames. In this chapter, you discover what iFrames are, how to create your own iFrame application and add it to your Page, and how to set your new iFrame as a default landing tab. We also introduce third-party applications that make creating a custom Welcome tab easy if you aren't comfortable coding your own iFrame (or don't have the resources to do so).

We go in-depth with the Facebook Developer Site in this chapter, and it's not for the timid. Feel free to skip over these steps and go to the middle of the chapter, where we give you some resources for hiring someone to write the code for you, or move later in the chapter, when we cover the simpler, third-party applications.

A Look at Some Customized Welcome Pages

These Pages, as you can imagine, are usually highly customized with branding and links that highlight a company. These Pages usually have a strong call to action (for example, Like our Page!) and some fun and practical links (for example, a video message, a newsletter sign-up link, or coupons for

Fans). The world is your oyster! Using a Welcome Page within your Facebook Page can further enhance your brand and make your Facebook Page stand out. In fact, studies show that when you have a customized Welcome landing Page on your Facebook Page, the number of people who click the Like button can double. Some examples of custom Welcome Pages are shown in Figures 2-1 through 2-3.

Figure 2-1: Red Bull has a graphic that encourages people to Like its Page.

Figure 2-2: T. Harv Eker reminds people to click Like and has a place to sign up for his newsletter.

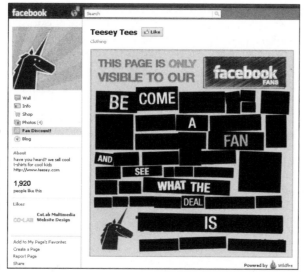

Figure 2-3:
Teesey Tees
has Fan-
only content
that appears
after you
Like its
Page.

Defining iFrames

So what are *iFrames*? iFrame stands for Inline Frame and is basically an HTML document embedded inside another HTML document on a Web site. An iFrame pulls the content from one Web site into another. So, in the context of Facebook, an iFrame pulls the content of another Web site into an area on your Facebook Page.

iFrames are very powerful because anything you can create on a Web site, you can bring into your Facebook Page, creating a unique and rich experience for your community. To use iFrames on Facebook, you need to have a place on the Web to put your content. By this we mean you need to have a server or host Web site where you can upload or FTP your photos, files, or whatever you will be displaying on your Facebook custom page. If you don't have a place to which you can upload your content, skip to the section "Using Third-Party Applications," later in this chapter. That's where we introduce you to several third-party applications that can host your content for you.

iFrames have been around for a long time on the Web but are a relatively new way to create a Welcome Page or other content on Facebook. Previously, the main way people created a custom Page on a Facebook Page was with an application called Static FBML (Facebook Markup Language). This application is no longer available, but we wanted to mention it because you may see references to Static FBML both within Facebook and on other Web sites.

Outlining the Options

To use iFrames on Facebook Pages, you have three different choices. You can build an application from scratch, you can hire someone to build the application for you, or you can use one of the third-party applications available. The following sections explain some of the considerations with each option.

Building an iFrame application

Building an application sounds daunting, but the process can be broken down into several easy steps. We walk you through the specifics a little later in the chapter, but for now, here is an overview of the steps for building an iFrames application:

1. Become a verified Facebook Developer. This is a simple process that requires either a mobile phone that can receive text messages or a credit card number for verification purposes only.

2. Design the content for your Facebook app. Typically this content is designed in an HTML editor such as Dreamweaver.

3. Upload the content for your Facebook app to your Web site. You will need to FTP the HTML document and necessary images to your server.

4. Configure your Facebook application. You configure your application in the Developer area of Facebook.

5. Install the application on your Page.

When you create and install your own iFrames application, it shows up on your Page's left navigation bar.

Although building your own application can be challenging, there are some advantages, as follows:

✦ You have complete control over your application (no extra references to third-party applications)

✦ You can change the small icon next to the navigation link. The third-party applications display their icon.

✦ You don't have to worry about something happening to the third-party application (something goes wrong in their application, the third party goes out of business, and so on).

Hiring someone to build the application for you

If you aren't savvy with HTML and are trying to do something more involved (such as embed videos or an opt-in form), you may want to hire someone.

The first stop might be the Facebook Developer Forum at `http://forum.developers.facebook.net`. This Forum has a section for jobs where you can post a project request. Most requests get several replies. Many people on the Forum are available for hire.

You can also look at sites such `http://elance.com` and `http://odesk.com`, which have a huge supply of freelancers who can help you out. Many have references and examples of their past work available. You can post your requirements, and the freelancers can bid on the project. You choose the freelancer who is the best fit for your needs.

Using a third-party application

Third-party Welcome Page applications are applications created by another company (that is, not Facebook) that are designed to simplify the process of creating custom content on Facebook. The idea is that you can just use a third-party application to create your Page and then add the app to your Facebook Page. You don't need to code anything, and you don't have to upload files to your Web site.

Here is a list of some of the applications you can use to create a custom Welcome Page. We discuss each of these later in the chapter.

✦ Wildfire: `http://iframes.wildfireapp.com`

✦ Involver: `www.facebook.com/StaticHTMLapp`

✦ TabPress: `https://apps.facebook.com/tabpress/`

✦ Static HTML: `www.facebook.com/apps/application.php?id=190322544333196`

✦ Tabsite: `http://www.tabsite.com`

✦ Lujure: `http://www.lujure.com`

More applications are being developed every day. We cover the step-by-step setup of some of these applications later in this chapter.

Third-party applications are developed by independent people or companies not connected with Facebook, and these applications may or may not work well. Occasionally, you'll come across some applications that are developed but then aren't updated, or you'll find that some applications don't work well from the start. If you're at all concerned about a particular application, we suggest visiting the Web site for the parent company that developed the app and noting which other companies are using the app. Many times, a Web site will have links to the Facebook Pages that are using their applications so that you can see it in action and have an idea of how it works as well as gauge the application's popularity. The apps we cover in this chapter all work very well; we just want to remind you to use caution when discovering new apps that may be available.

Exploring the Facebook Developer Site

The Facebook Developer site is where you begin your journey of creating your own application. To get to the site, log in to Facebook as your personal Profile and then go to www.facebook.com/developers. If you have never navigated to the Developer site before, it may ask you for permission to access your information. Click Allow, and you are taken to the Developer site. The Facebook Developer site home page is the blog with some of the latest information about Facebook new developments and possible bugs, as shown in Figure 2-4.

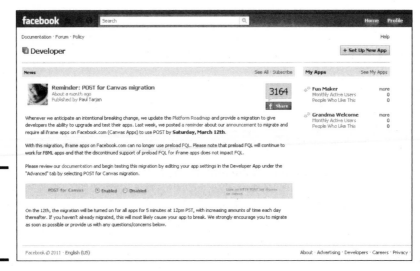

Figure 2-4:
The
Facebook
Developer
site.

Here are some of the elements on the Facebook Developer site that you can access and use:

✦ **Documentation:** Click this link in the upper-left corner to find information on creating code for the Facebook plugins, more information on creating applications, and so on.

✦ **Forum:** Click this link in the upper-left corner to access the Developer Forum where people are talking about bugs, issues, coding, job postings, and more. The Forum can be a great resource for asking questions if you're having trouble with coding your application.

✦ **Policy:** This is the Facebook Platform policy for developers. The policies covered here are more for people coding applications that users will interact with, such as games. The basic policies are intended to give users a good experience, respect for privacy, and so on.

✦ **Help:** In the upper-right corner, you see the Facebook Help link. This is for more basic help questions and is not very extensive. This Help Center is geared toward developers and covers topics such as "How do I verify my developer account?"

✦ **Set Up New App button:** Click this button to begin the process of creating an iFrame app that you can add to your Facebook Page.

✦ **My Apps and See My Apps:** The apps you have created are listed here, and you can navigate to them by clicking them individually or clicking the See My Apps link.

Creating Your Own Application

To create your own application, you start on the Facebook Developer site, and you first need to become a verified Facebook Developer.

Becoming a verified Facebook Developer

To become a verified Facebook Developer, you will need to verify that you are a real person through either a mobile phone number that can receive text messages or through a credit card number. You need to do this because applications on Facebook can be malicious and used to spread spam messages and viruses. So to combat this type of application developer, Facebook requires some method of tracking who is developing the applications.

To get the process started, go to `http://www.facebook.com/developers/` and click the Set Up New App button in the upper-right corner. If you've never set up an application before, you will see the verification message shown in Figure 2-5.

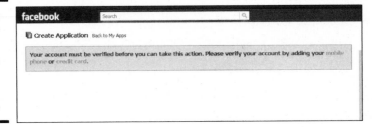

Figure 2-5:
Verify your
account
to become
a verified
Facebook
Developer.

The mobile phone verification process may not work well in countries out-side the United States. People have reported having trouble receiving the text message, so if you're outside the United States, you may want to use the credit card option.

Verifying through a mobile phone number

If you want to verify your account with a mobile phone number, follow these steps:

1. **Click the Mobile Phone link.**

   A pop-up box appears asking for your country code and cell phone number.

2. **Select your country code and cell phone number.**

3. **Click the Confirm button.**

   You will receive a text message with a string of numbers. That is your confirmation code. On your computer, you see the box to enter your confirmation code.

4. **Enter the confirmation code and click Confirm.**

   You are now a verified Facebook Developer!

Verifying through a credit card number

If you want to verify your account with a credit card number, follow these steps:

1. **Click the Credit Card link.**

   You are taken to a new window, and Facebook asks you to reenter your Facebook password.

2. **Reenter your password.**

3. **Click the Continue button.**

   You are now taken to the Payments area in Facebook to enter your credit card information. Your credit card is not used unless you do something that requires a payment, such as run a Facebook ad.

4. **Type your credit card information in the text box.**

5. **Click the Save button.**

You are now a verified Facebook Developer, and you can create an iFrame application.

Creating a basic iFrame application

So you've decided to try your hand at creating your own iFrame application. Excellent! Although creating an iFrame app isn't terribly difficult if you're familiar with basic CSS and HTML code, you need to have a few things ready before you begin.

First, you need to create the Web page that you will be displaying in the iFrame. Going through the steps to create your Web page is beyond the scope of this book, but you need to create the Web page to be 520 pixels wide to fit into the Facebook iFrame space.

Book III
Chapter 2

The possibilities for your Web page are literally endless. You can go from a simple design with just an image or have something more elaborate such as a ministore. Here are some possibilities:

Understanding and Using iFrames to Customize Your Page

✦ A single image (very easy to code)

✦ Several images fitted together that allow for links

✦ Embedded video

✦ Opt-in box for your newsletter with additional photos, video, or both

✦ Photos or video combined with Facebook comments so that people can interact with your page

If you create the Web page to be larger than 520 pixels, it will not fit into the space on your Facebook Page and will have scroll bars on the sides. We have found that you are better off creating the width of your Web page to be slightly less than the 520 pixels (more like 510 pixels) to be on the safe side.

After you have your Web page created and you have become a verified Facebook Developer, you are ready to create your iFrame app. Follow these steps after you have logged in to your personal Profile:

1. **Go to** www.facebook.com/developers.

2. **Click the Set Up New App button in the upper-right corner.**

You are now prompted to name your app, as shown in Figure 2-6.

Figure 2-6:
Name your
app.

3. **Type the name of your new application in the App Name text box.**

The name you choose will appear in your Page's left navigation menu.

4. **Select the Agree radio button to indicate that you agree with Facebook's terms.**

5. **Click the Create App button.**

You are taken to the Security Check Page.

6. **Type the text from the security check in the text box.**

7. **Click the Submit button.**

You are taken to the application Page, as shown in Figure 2-7. You land on the About section of the application.

Many of the fields on this Page are for applications that are for games or other Facebook applications that are designed to be used by many Facebook users and are optional for someone who is developing an iFrame Welcome Page. For the purposes of an iFrame Welcome Page, you have to fill out only the information on the About tab and the Facebook Integration tab on the left sidebar of this Page. We explain which fields you need to worry about and which ones you can skip.

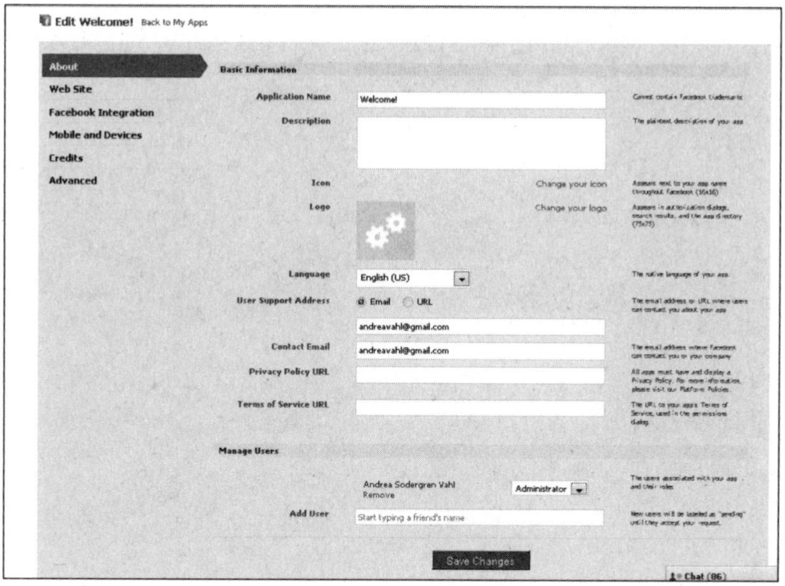

Figure 2-7:
Edit your
application.

8. **Fill out the About Page information for your application as follows:**

- *Description:* A description of your app (optional).

- *Icon:* Appears next to your navigation link in the left side-bar on your Facebook Page — 16 pixels x 16 pixels (optional). Although the icon is optional, we recommend using it to draw more attention to your custom Page.

- *Logo:* Appears in authorization dialog boxes, search results, and the app directory — 75 pixels x 75 pixels (optional). Because your app won't be getting authorization from the user or appearing in the app directory, you do not need to add a logo.

- *Language:* The language of your app.

- *User Support Address:* The e-mail address or URL where users can contact you about your app. You don't need to enter this because users won't be contacting you about your app.

- *Privacy Policy URL:* Add the URL to your Web site's privacy policy (optional).

- *Terms of Service URL:* You don't need a Terms of Service URL because you're not getting permissions from the users to access their information.

- *Add User:* You can also add an additional app user here by adding an e-mail address. If you have multiple people working on the Welcome Page design, you can add them here.

9. **Click the Facebook Integration link on the left sidebar, and you see the fields shown in Figure 2-8.**

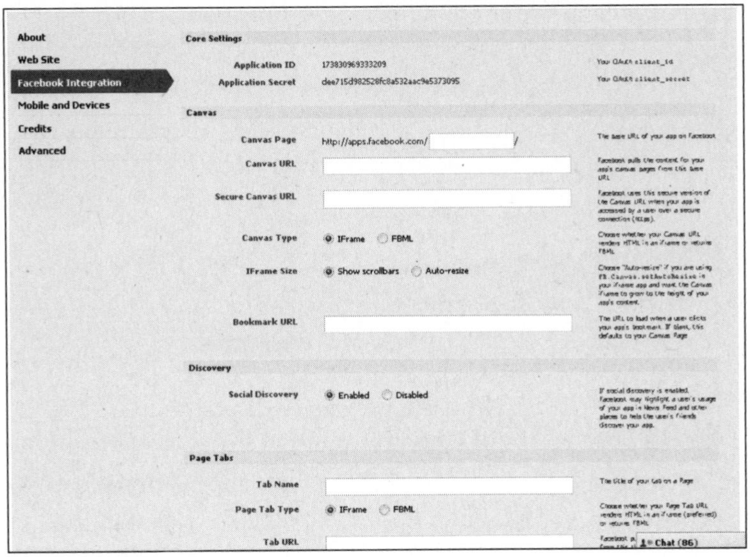

Figure 2-8:
The
Facebook
Integration
link.

Here are the items you must fill out on the Facebook Integration Page. Everything else can be left blank. The other fields are for apps that can be developed that are more interactive such as games. Refer to Book V, Chapter 2 for more information on creating that type of app.

- *Canvas Page:* Type the name of the application Page on Facebook. You can give this any title you would like.

- *Canvas URL:* Type the full path, including the folder name, of where you're hosting the Web page that you're displaying on Facebook. You must have the trailing slash (/) after the folder name. For example, your canvas URL may be similar to this:

   `http://domain.com/myfacebookwelcomepage/`

   Within that folder you will have uploaded the Web page, and you may want to call it index.html.

- *Canvas Type:* Select IFrame.

- *IFrame Size:* Select Auto-resize.

- *Social Discovery:* Select Disabled because you don't want people to discover your app outside your Facebook Page. If you were building an app such as a game, you would want this option enabled.

- *Tab Name:* Type the name you want to have as the navigation link on your Facebook Welcome Page (for example, Welcome, Sign Up, Click Like, and so on).

- *Page Tab Type:* Select IFrame.

- *Tab URL:* Facebook pulls content for your tab from this URL. This will be the full path to the Web page that you want to have displayed on your Facebook Welcome Page. In the example in Figure 2-8, the entire Tab URL is

```
http://www.andreavahl.com/theenlightenedmom1/index.html
```

10. **Click the Save Changes button at the bottom of the Page.**

The app has now been created, and you're taken to the My Apps Page, as shown in Figure 2-9. From here, you navigate to the Canvas Application Page, where you can install this app on your Facebook Page, as we explain in the next section.

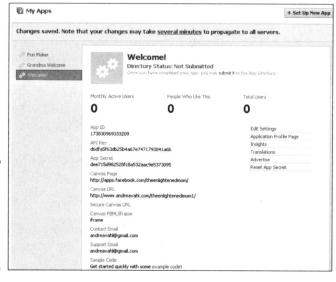

Figure 2-9:
Your iFrame
app has
now been
successfully
created.

Installing the iFrame application on your Facebook Page

Now that you've created your Welcome Page iFrame app, you need to install it on your Facebook Page. You can either go straight into these steps from the previous Step 10 or you can always navigate back to your application by going to the Developer Forum Page and navigating to your app under My Apps (reference Figure 2-4).

Follow these steps to add the application to your Facebook Page:

1. **Click the Application Profile Page link, as referenced in Figure 2-9.**

You are now taken to the Canvas Application Page, as shown in Figure 2-10. The Page looks very similar to a Facebook business Page, but it is for applications.

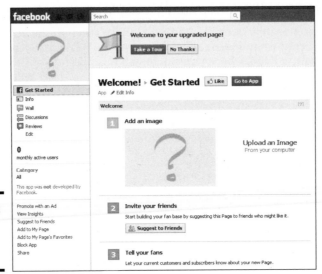

Figure 2-10:
The Canvas
Application
Page.

2. **Click the Add to My Page link on the left sidebar.**

A pop-up box appears with all the Pages where you are an admin.

3. **Click the Add to Page button next to the Facebook Page where you would like this application to appear.**

The Page name disappears from the list.

4. **Click the Close button.**

5. **Navigate to the Facebook Page where you added the application by clicking Account in the upper-right corner of the Page, and a drop-down menu appears:**

   a. Select Use Facebook as Page, and a pop-up box appears with all your Facebook Pages.

   b. Click the Switch button next to the desired Facebook Page. You are now taken to your Facebook Page.

   Your app is now installed on your Facebook Page. Navigate to it by clicking the title of the app on the left sidebar of your Page, as shown in Figure 2-11.

Figure 2-11: Your iFrame app now appears on the left sidebar of your Facebook Page.

Book III Chapter 2

Understanding and Using iFrames to Customize Your Page

Setting the iFrame app as your default landing Page

You may have created this application as a Welcome Page to encourage new visitors to click the Like button or to give them something special if they do click Like. In this case, you will want this Welcome Page to be the first thing new visitors see when they come to your Page.

To set this iFrame app as your default landing Page, go to your Facebook business Page and then follow these steps:

1. **Click the Edit Page button in the upper-right corner.**

   You are taken to your administrative dashboard and the default menu of Manage Permissions.

2. **Click the arrow in the drop-down menu area of the Default Landing Tab field.**

3. **Select the name of the iFrame app, as shown in Figure 2-12.**

4. **Click the Save Changes button.**

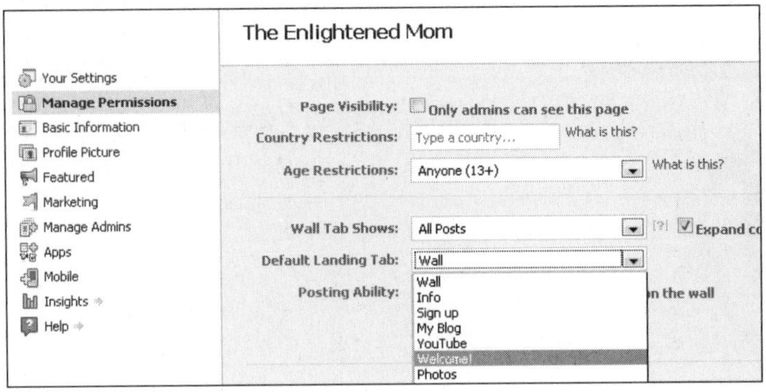

Figure 2-12: Setting your default landing tab.

Your default landing Page is now set to your new iFrame app. Anyone who has not clicked the Like button on your Page will see this iFrame app when they navigate to your Facebook Page. Anyone who already Likes you will go to your Wall if they navigate to your Facebook Page. See Book II, Chapter 3 for more information on the default landing tab.

Using Third-Party Applications

If you are not an experienced HTML coder and don't want to mess around with creating an iFrame app, there is still hope! Several third-party applications exist to make installing an iFrame app easier.

Many of the third-party applications host your content for you, which means you won't need to have your own Web host or server. (We go deeper into each application and the capabilities of each one in the next section.) Many of the apps give you the option of uploading a custom image or HTML code.

If you're good at coding a Web page, you can use this space to create a mini Web page, and the code is hosted by the app. If you're using HTML to code a mini-Web page, you have to host your own images that you are putting on the Page.

Many of these applications include the ability to have Fan-only content. (Some call it the "reveal tab" or "Fan Gating.") This feature allows you to have one image on top of some hidden content, and visitors cannot see the hidden content until they click Like. If they Like your Page already, the hidden content will be available at any time (refer to Figure 2-3).

Here's what you need before using these third-party applications:

✦ **Custom image:** Any picture format and sized at a maximum of 520 pixels width by 800 pixels height. You can use a smaller image if you like, but 520 by 800 is the maximum image size that you can display. A custom image is the minimum part of this list that you'll need. You can create a custom Welcome page with this image alone. Or you can add Fan-only content, which would include another custom image of the same dimensions or HTML code that would display a Web page underneath your custom image.

✦ **HTML code:** You can use this code to display a mini Web page. You can use just the HTML code alone or use that code underneath a custom image as some Fan-only content.

Book III
Chapter 2

> **TIP** You can tell what application a Facebook Page used to create its custom Page by the icons next to the navigation links on the sidebar. If you see a star that matches the icon on the Static HTML: iFrame tabs Page, the Page owner used this app to create the Page. This is sometimes useful information if you're spying on the competition to see what they're doing.

Understanding and
Using iFrames to
Customize Your Page

Wildfire

Wildfire's iFrame application, found at `http://iframes.wildfireapp.com`, is easy to use and gives you the ability to use Fan-only content. Wildfire uses the term *Fan-gated content* for the Fan-only content. You can use custom images or HTML code with Wildfire. The application has been free but the Wildfire Web site has indicated it plans to charge for this application, and by publication time this may already have occurred. According to its Web site, if you started using this feature before Wildfire charged for it, you will continue to get this feature for free.

Wildfire also has several different applications for Facebook, including contest applications that are covered in Book VI, Chapter 3.

To install the Wildfire iFrame app, follow these steps after logging in to your Facebook personal Profile:

1. **Go to** http://iframes.wildfireapp.com.

2. **Click the Install This App button.**

   You are taken into Facebook, and you see the screen shown in Figure 2-13.

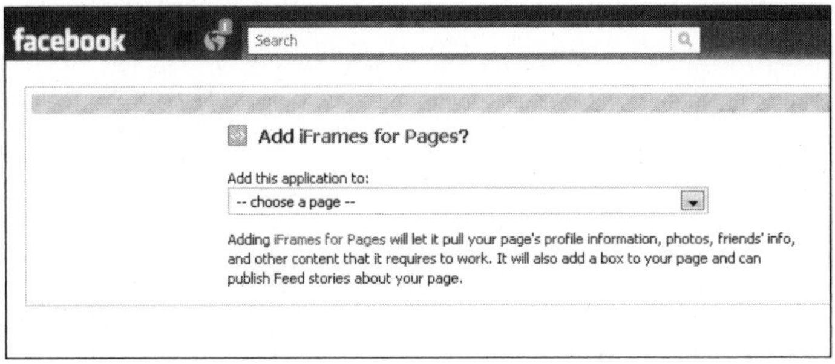

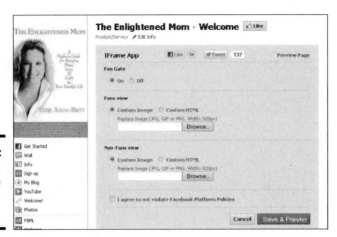

Figure 2-13:
Adding the
Wildfire
iFrame app
to your
Page.

3. **Select the Page where you want to add the application from the drop-down list.**

   After you select the Page, a blue button appears.

4. **Click the Add Wildfire's iFrames for Pages button.**

   You are taken to the app within your Page where you can add your basic information, such as name, e-mail address, and company information.

5. **Click the Submit button.**

   You see the configuration screen shown in Figure 2-14.

Figure 2-14:
Configuring
the Wildfire
application
is simple.

6. **Click the On radio button if you want to have Fan-only content (the default selection).**

7. **Select either the Custom Image or Custom HTML radio button under Fans View:**

   - *Custom Image:* If you have a custom image for the Fan-only content, click the Browse button and upload the image by navigating to the file on your computer. When you find the file, select it, and the filename will show in the text box.

   - *Custom HTML:* If you have custom HTML code that you would like to add as the Fan-only content, enter your code in the text box.

8. **Select either the Custom Image or Custom HTML radio button under Non-Fans View:**

   - *Custom Image:* If you have a custom image for the non-Fan view, click the Browse button and upload it by navigating to the file on your computer. When you find the file, select it, and the filename shows in the text box.

   - *Custom HTML:* If you have custom HTML code that you would like to add as the non-Fan content, enter your code in the text box.

9. **Select the I Agree to Not Violate Facebook Platform Policies check box.**

10. **Click the Save & Preview button.**

    You now see how your custom iFrame Page works, and you can click the Like button to verify that the Fan-only content works if you added Fan-only content.

Your Wildfire app setup is done, and you have a nice-looking Welcome Page.

Involver

Involver's application is called Static HTML for Pages and can be found here: www.facebook.com/StaticHTMLapp. It uses iFrames and also has the ability to add Fan-only content. You can use images or HTML code.

Involver has also developed several Facebook applications, such as a YouTube and Twitter app, which you can learn more about in Book III, Chapter 4. Note that Involver allows you to use two of their applications for free; after that, you're charged a monthly fee to use any additional applications. So if you're using two of their existing applications, you may want to choose one of the other iFrame applications for your Welcome Page.

To install the Static HTML for Pages app, use the following steps after you have logged in to Facebook as your personal Profile:

1. **Go to** www.facebook.com/StaticHTMLapp.

2. **Click the Add to My Page link on the left sidebar.**

A pop-up box appears listing the Pages you manage.

3. **Click the Add to Page button next to the Page where you want to install this app.**

4. **Navigate to your Page by clicking Account in the upper-right corner; then select Use Facebook as Page.**

A pop-up box appears listing the Pages you manage.

5. **Click Switch next to the Page where the app was added.**

You are taken to your Page.

6. **Click the HTML navigation link on the left sidebar of your Page.**

You may have to click the More link to see it. An orange Edit Settings button appears on your Page.

7. **Click the Edit Settings button.**

The Request for Permission pop-up box appears, asking you to allow the Static HTML for Pages app to access your information.

8. **Click Allow.**

You are taken to the Static HTML Settings Page, as shown in Figure 2-15.

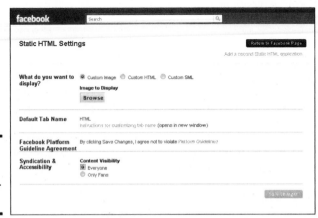

Figure 2-15:
Configure
Static HTML
for Pages.

9. **Select the radio button next to the type of information you want to display: Custom Image, Custom HTML, or Custom SML:**

   - If you select Custom Image, a browser box appears and you can browse your computer files to enter the image file.

   - If you select Custom HTML, a box appears where you can enter your HTML code.

   - Custom SML stands for Custom Social Markup Language and requires a license from Involver to use. You can find out more at `www.involver.com/sml`.

10. **In the Syndication & Accessibility section under Content Visibility, select the Only Fans radio button if you want to add an image over the content you added in Step 9. You will use the Only Fans option if you want to add Fan-only content.**

    If you select Only Fans, a check box appears next to `Display Custom Image to Non-Fans?`

11. **Select the check box, and you can browse your computer to add an image file.**

12. **Click Save Changes.**

    You see your images uploaded in a preview box.

You are now finished and can click Return to Facebook Page in the upper-right corner to verify that your Welcome Page is working properly. If you have set up the Fan-only content, you have to scroll down your Page and click Unlike on the left sidebar to verify that the non-Fan and Fan-only content is working properly. First, Unlike your Page to see what is displayed, and then Like the Page again to make sure that your app is working properly.

TabPress

TabPress is an iFrame application developed by HyperArts. This application supports Fan-only content and using HTML code. It doesn't allow you to upload the images directly in their application as the Wildfire and Involver applications do. To add images, you need to use HTML code to reference those images. Therefore, you need to first upload the images on your Web site and then write the HTML code to reference those images. If you're using only images, you might consider one of the other applications that allows you to upload your images directly.

You can access TabPress here:

```
https://apps.facebook.com/tabpress/
```

After navigating to the application, follow these steps:

1. **Click the Click Here link.**

   You are taken to the Application Page, which is similar to a Facebook business Page.

2. **Click the Add to My Page link on the left sidebar.**

   A pop-up box appears with the Pages you manage.

3. **Click the Add to Page button next to the desired Page.**

4. **Click the Close button.**

5. **Navigate to your Page by clicking Account in the upper-right corner; then select Use Facebook as Page.**

   A pop-up box appears listing the Pages you manage.

6. **Select Switch next to the Page where the app was added.**

   You are taken to your Page.

7. **Click the Welcome navigation link with the orange and green icon on the left sidebar of your Page.**

   You may have to click the More link to see it. The TabPress edit area appears, as shown in Figure 2-16.

Figure 2-16:
Configure
TabPress.

8. **Enter your HTML code for Non-Fans and Fans and then click Save/ Update Content at the bottom of the page.**

9. **Preview your Non-Fan and Fan content to make sure that it looks correct by clicking the Preview Non-Fan Content and Preview Fan Content buttons at the top of the page.**

Your Welcome Page is complete! You will not see the Welcome Page the same as others because you are the admin. You can log out of Facebook and view your Facebook Page to see how it looks.

Static HTML: iframe tabs

With the Static HTML: iframe tabs application, you can create Fan-only content. This application does not have the ability to upload an image directly, but you can use the HTML code to reference an image to display just as you can with the TabPress application. As mentioned previously, if you have only an image for your Welcome Page, you may want to use one of the other applications that will store your image for you.

To use this application, go to

```
www.facebook.com/apps/application.php?id=190322544333196
```

If you don't want to type in that long URL, you can put the title of the app, Static HTML: iframe tabs, in the search bar of Facebook, and you should see it in the drop-down search results. You'll know that you've found the correct app if you see a Star icon on the application Page, as shown in Figure 2-17. (With all the similar application names, it helps to know what you are looking for!) You can use HTML or FBML (Facebook Markup Language) in this application, so if you have created an older application with the FBML language that was used before, you can transition to this application for iFrames.

Figure 2-17: Static HTML: iframe tabs app.

After you're on the Static HTML: iframe tabs application Page, use the following steps to install the app on your business Page:

1. **Click the blue Add Static HTML to a Page button (refer to Figure 2-17).**

   You are taken to a screen with a drop-down menu to select the Page where you would like to add the app, as shown in Figure 2-18.

Figure 2-18:
Select the
Page where
you want to
add the app.

2. **Select the Page from the drop-down menu.**

   The Add Static HTML: iframe tabs button appears.

3. **Click the Add Static HTML: iframe tabs button.**

   You are now taken to your Facebook Page.

4. **Click the Welcome navigation link on the left sidebar of your Page with the Star icon.**

   You see the edit area for the app, as shown in Figure 2-19.

Figure 2-19:
Enter your
HTML
content.

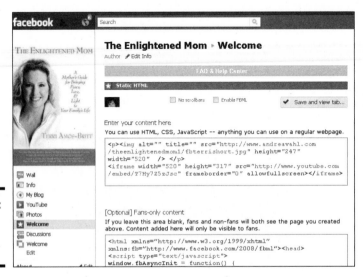

5. **Enter your HTML content and the optional Fan-only HTML content. If you're using FBML, check the FBML check box (refer to Figure 2-19).**

6. **Click the Save and view tab button in the upper right.**

    You are taken to another window where you have to view your tab as a Fan, view your tab as a non-Fan, or go back to the editor.

7. **Click the View Your Tab as a Non-Fan link to make sure it looks right.**

8. **Click the Welcome Navigation link again on the left sidebar to get back into the application.**

9. **Click the Save and View Tab button in the upper right.**

10. **Click the View Your Tab as a Fan link to make sure that the content looks good.**

    You have now set up your Welcome tab!

Tabsite

Tabsite is another iFrame application that you can use to create multiple subpages within one page. Tabsite is more complex to configure because it is very versatile. We don't cover all the steps here but want you to be aware of this application.

Tabsite has a free option with two tabs and different paid options. Figure 2-20 shows an example of a custom iFrame Page built with Tabsite. In the figure, each blue bar takes you to a new subpage so that you can create a mini Web site within the page.

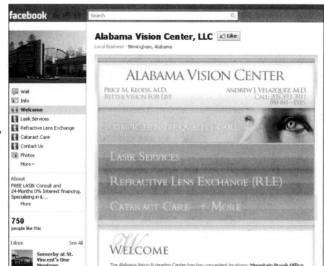

Figure 2-20:
You can have multiple subpages within each Tabsite page.

You can find out more about the application at www.tabsite.com. It is also covered in Book V, Chapter 1.

Lujure

Lujure is another iFrame application used to create custom Pages. Lujure has a drag-and-drop design process that makes it easy to add different elements to your iFrame Page without knowing how to code HTML. Because of the flexibility and configurability of Lujure, we don't cover all the steps here. Lujure has some nice video tutorials on their Web site. Lujure has free and paid options available; you can find out more at http://assemblyline.lujure.com. An example of a custom iFrame Page created with Lujure is shown in Figure 2-21.

Figure 2-21: A Welcome Page created with the Lujure application.

Changing the Name of Your Navigation Link

Many of the iFrame applications have a default Navigation link that is titled Welcome. This is a very appropriate name for a landing page, but if you're creating something different, you may want to rename the navigation link to something more descriptive for the content you're creating. Changing the name of the navigation link isn't difficult and in fact amounts to using the same process for all the third-party applications we cover in this chapter.

To change the name of the navigation link for your Welcome Page, follow these steps from your Facebook Page:

1. **Click Edit Page in the upper-right corner.**

   You're taken to your Page dashboard.

2. **Click the Apps link on the left sidebar.**

   You see all the apps you have installed on your Page.

3. **Find the app of the iFrame application (for example, TabPages, Static HTML, and so on) that you have installed and click Edit Settings.**

   A pop-up box appears, and you can change the name of the navigation link and click OK.

Chapter 3: Importing Your Blog Posts to Your Facebook Page

In This Chapter

✔ Obtaining the Web address of your RSS Feed

✔ Deciding which Facebook application to use to import your blog

✔ Installing and configuring the NetworkedBlogs application

✔ Exploring RSS Graffiti

✔ Using Facebook Notes to import your blog

✔ Looking at Social RSS

*I*f you have a blog, the easiest way to add new content on your Facebook Page is to import your blog posts. Easier yet would be getting this job done automatically.

You're in luck because several Facebook applications are available to do just that. When you post something new on your blog, the application automatically creates a new entry on your Wall, which in turn goes out to the News Feeds of people who Like you. This automation means one less task for you to have after you post a new blog entry.

In this chapter, we tell you how to use four of the most popular applications for importing blog posts to your Facebook Wall. Each application requires your RSS Feed's URL, so the chapter starts by telling you how to find that URL.

Importing your blog automatically will save you time and hassle. Luckily, you have lots of choices how. Try one. If it doesn't work for you, you can always stop that application and install a different one.

Getting the Address of Your RSS Feed

No matter what blog-import application you decide to use, you need to know the Web address, or *URL,* of your blog's RSS Feed. *RSS,* which stands for really simple syndication, is a standard that the Internet uses to pull information from Web sites in an organized manner. It pulls only the text, leaving all the fancy graphics that appear on your blog behind.

The address of your RSS feed is typically something like this: www. *YourWebSite.com*/feed. Depending on how your Web site is set up, though, this address could be something quite different. If you don't know the address of your RSS feed, check with your Web developer. If that's not an option, here's a handy trick for discovering your feed address.

On Internet Explorer

If you're using Internet Explorer, follow these steps to find your RSS feed address:

1. Go to your Web site or blog in Internet Explorer.

Right above the Web site, you should see the RSS icon in orange, as shown in Figure 3-1. If the icon is showing gray, the browser cannot find an RSS Feed on your site, and you need to contact your Web developer.

Figure 3-1: The RSS icon will appear orange right above your Web site if an RSS Feed is detected.

2. Click the main RSS Feed listed (if there is more than one).

In Figure 3-1, Amy's blog also shows the Comments Feed for all the comments posted on her blog. You'll be taken to the view of the RSS Feed, and the address for that Feed will display in the browser address window.

On Firefox

If you're using Firefox, follow these steps to find your RSS feed address:

1. Go to your Web site or blog in Firefox.

The browser window should have an RSS icon if the browser detects an RSS feed.

2. **Click the RSS icon in the browser window.**

   You should see the Subscribe to the Blog on this Web site option.

3. **Click Subscribe to the Blog on this Web Site.**

   The address for the Feed will display in the browser address window.

Finding the RSS feed by looking at HTML code

Another handy trick to find the RSS Feed is to look at the HTML code of the Web site. You can do this from any browser although the steps vary depending on your browser. In this section, we offer the steps using several browsers.

If you are using Firefox:

1. **Go to the Web site or blog.**

2. **Click View from the menu bar.**

   A drop-down menu appears.

3. **Select Page Source.**

   A new window opens, showing the HTML code.

If you are using Internet Explorer:

1. **Go to the Web site or blog.**

2. **Click View from the menu bar.**

   A drop-down menu appears.

3. **Select Source.**

   A new window opens, showing the HTML code.

If you are using Google Chrome:

1. **Go to the Web site or blog.**

2. **Click the wrench icon in the upper right corner.**

   A drop-down menu appears.

3. **Select Tools.**

   A drop-down menu appears.

4. **Select View source.**

   A new tab opens, showing the HTML code.

**Book III
Chapter 3**

**Importing Your
Blog Posts to Your
Facebook Page**

If you are using Safari:

1. **Go to the Web site or blog.**

2. **Click the page icon in the upper-right corner.**

A drop-down menu appears.

3. **Select View Source.**

A new window appears, showing the HTML code.

After you have the tab or window open with the HTML code for any of the browsers, press Ctrl+F on your keyboard to search for a phrase. Enter **rss** to find the RSS feed address. Using Amy Porterfield's Web site, as an example, you find the following when you search on the term *rss*:

```
<link rel="alternate" type="application/rss+xml"
title="Amy Porterfield | Social Media Strategy Consultant
RSS Feed" href="http://amyporterfield.com/feed/" />
```

The RSS feed address is right after the `href=` term and is `http://amyporterfield.com/feed/`.

Introducing the Facebook Blog Import Applications

After you have the address of your RSS Feed (as we discuss in the previous section), you're ready to begin using one of Facebook's applications to import your blog. But which one? Here is a list of some ways to import your blog automatically into Facebook:

✦ NetworkedBlogs application

✦ Social RSS application

✦ RSS Graffiti

✦ Facebook Notes application

The Facebook Notes application is developed by Facebook, and the others are developed by a third party. All these applications have some benefits, and deciding which one to use is a matter of preference. As a metric, the number of users can indicate popularity. NetworkedBlogs has more than 1.9 million monthly users, Social RSS has more than 788,000, and RSS Graffiti has more than 395,000. Notes doesn't have the usage statistic available.

To help you decide which application is right for you, the following sections describe each one and show you how easy they are to set up, what features they have, and what the imported posts look like. All these applications are free, although Social RSS has a paid option for a higher level of service.

Using NetworkedBlogs Application

NetworkedBlogs is the most popular method for automatically importing your blog posts into your Page. You import your blog both to your Page and your personal Profile. After you import your blog, a tab appears on your Page that contains your previous posts for people to reference; see Figure 3-2.

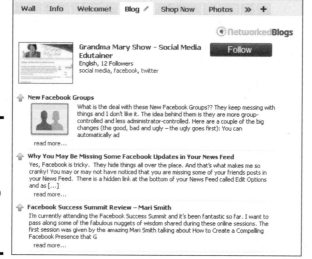

Figure 3-2: Your blog posts are stored on the Blog tab when using Networked Blogs.

Clicking one of these links takes a viewer directly to that blog post. Each post is also automatically posted on your Wall, and the post will look similar to the one in Figure 3-3. The first few lines of the blog post, as well as a picture from the post, are automatically pulled in. You can tell where the post came from by the note underneath the post that says via NetworkedBlogs.

Figure 3-3: See where the post came from.

If you don't have a picture embedded in your post, the NetworkedBlogs application will display a screenshot of your whole blog as the thumbnail picture next to your Wall post.

Installing NetworkedBlogs

The NetworkedBlogs application can be a little tricky to navigate, but it has a good FAQ section that can help you through the process. To install the NetworkedBlogs application, follow these steps:

1. **Log into Facebook as your personal Profile.**

2. **Go to** http://apps.facebook.com/blognetworks.

This takes you to the NetworkedBlogs Application Page.

3. **Click the Add to My Page link underneath the logo on the left sidebar.**

A pop-up box appears, listing the Pages you manage.

4. **In the pop-up box, click the Add to Page button next to the Page where you want the app installed and then click the Close button on the pop-up box.**

After NetworkedBlogs is installed on your Page, you have to configure the application to let it know what blog is yours, set up your Profile within the application, and then test it to make sure it's working.

Configuring NetworkedBlogs

To configure the application, follow these steps:

1. **Click the Edit Page button in the upper-right corner of your Page to get to your Page dashboard.**

2. **Click the Apps link from the left sidebar of the Page.**

A list of all your applications appears, and NetworkedBlogs should be one of them.

3. **Click the Go to App link under the description.**

You see a screen that prompts you to continue as your personal Profile (see Figure 3-4).

Figure 3-4:
You need to continue as your personal Profile.

4. **Click the Continue as Your Profile Name button.**

The Networked Blogs screen appears, as shown in Figure 3-5.

Figure 3-5:
Networked
Blogs
needs to be
configured
to add your
blog.

5. **Click the Add Your Blog link under the question, "What do you want to do next?" as shown in Figure 3-5.**

Both the Add Your Blog and the Registered with NetworkedBlogs links will take you to the same screen. At that screen, you fill in the information for your blog, as shown in Figure 3-6.

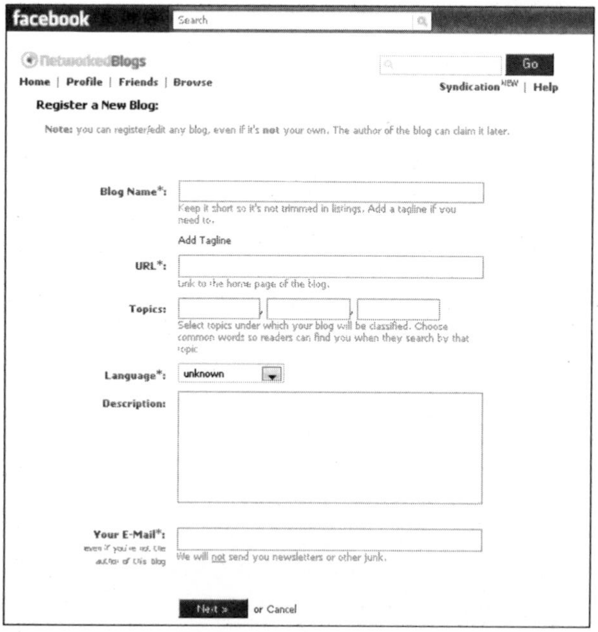

Figure 3-6:
Fill this
information
in for your
blog.

The starred items in Figure 3-6 are mandatory; everything else is optional. You can edit any of this information later. Use these tips for filling in this information:

- *Blog Name:* The title of your blog. Keep it short and then add a Tagline with the link below the Blog Name if you have a Tagline.

- *Tagline:* This gives you a little more space to tell people what your blog is about.

- *URL:* The home page of the blog.

- *Topics:* Three keywords that indicate your blog is about. They can be any keywords that people who use the NetworkedBlogs App can use in their search to find blogs that they are interested in.

- *Language:* The language your blog is written in.

- *Description:* This shows up in the NetworkedBlogs directory, so make it interesting and tell people why they would want to read your blog.

- *E-mail:* For Networked Blogs verification. You don't receive e-mail from NetworkedBlogs.

6. **Click the Next button at the bottom of the screen, as shown in Figure 3-6.**

   A new screen appears, asking whether you are the author of the blog for which you just entered the information.

7. **Click the Yes button.**

   Another screen appears; this one determines which method you want to use to verify that you are the owner of your blog.

8. **Choose which method you would like to use to verify your ownership of the blog: Ask Friends to Verify You or Use Widget to Verify Ownership.**

   You can have your Facebook Friends verify that you own the blog; if you select that option, you can select nine friends to send the request for verification. The problem with that option is that not everyone sees that request in his or her notifications (people don't always know to look there), so your verification can take a long time. The better option is to use the widget to verify ownership if you can.

Verifying ownership of your blog

If you select the Ask Friends to Verify You option, a screen with all your Facebook friends appears, and you can select who will get a request to verify that you own your blog. After you select the Friends who will verify the ownership of your blog, you're done. You can move to the next section on Setting up syndication.

If you choose the widget to verify ownership, you just need to install this widget temporarily until the NetworkedBlog application verifies that you put the widget on your blog (you will get a notification), and then you can remove it. You may choose to keep the widget to promote the fact that you're a part of NetworkedBlogs. If you keep the widget on your Web site, people can click the Follow This Blog button to follow your blog through the NetworkedBlogs app.

If you opt for the widget option, you are taken to the screen shown in Figure 3-7. Continue by following these steps:

Figure 3-7: Choose between a widget and a badge.

Book III Chapter 3

Importing Your Blog Posts to Your Facebook Page

1. **Select the blue Install Widget if you have a self-hosted WordPress blog or Tumblr, or Blogger.**

   The widget is for sites that allow JavaScript, and the badge is for sites such as WordPress.com that don't allow JavaScript.

   Most self-hosted blogs will work with this option unless you have your blog on WordPress, Posterous, or Drupal.com. If you have your blog on one of those sites, select the blue Install Badge button. You will be taken to a screen with some code to cut and paste, as shown in Figure 3-8. There are also some more detailed instructions at the bottom of this screen on how to install it on a Blogger.com or WordPress.com.

A self-hosted blog is typically a blog where you pay for hosting. The WordPress.com, Blogger.com, Drupal.com and Posterous.com sites are free sites to host your blog, but they have some limitations.

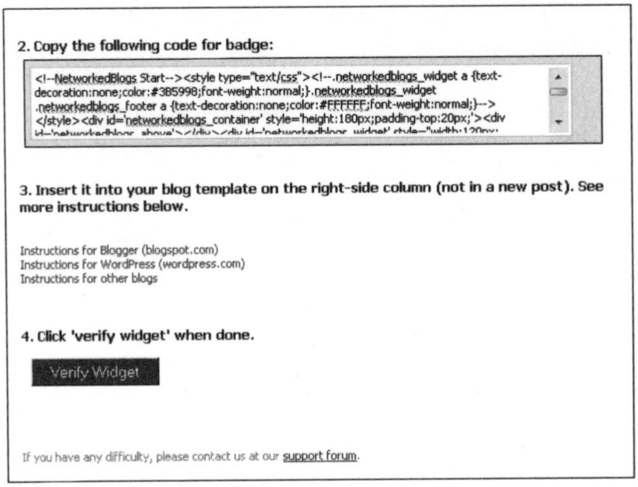

---

2. Copy the following code for badge:

<!--NetworkedBlogs Start--><style type="text/css"><!--.networkedblogs_widget a {text-decoration:none;color:#3B5998;font-weight:normal;}.networkedblogs_widget .networkedblogs_footer a {text-decoration:none;color:#FFFFFF;font-weight:normal;}--> </style><div id='networkedblogs_container' style='height:180px;padding-top:20px;'><div id='networkedblogs_above'></div><div id='networkedblogs_widget' style='width:120px;

3. Insert it into your blog template on the right-side column (not in a new post). See more instructions below.

Instructions for Blogger (blogspot.com)
Instructions for WordPress (wordpress.com)
Instructions for other blogs

4. Click 'verify widget' when done.

Verify Widget

If you have any difficulty, please contact us at our support forum.

Figure 3-8:
Cut and paste the code and install it on your blog.

---

2. **Highlight the code and copy it (press Ctrl+C on a PC or ⌘-C on a Mac).**

3. **Click the blue instructions link related to your blog: Instructions for Blogger, WordPress, or for Other Blogs (choose this option if you're installing the widget).**

4. **Follow the instructions to install the widget or badge and then click the blue Verify Widget button.**

   If you install the widget correctly, you get a Verification Successful message.

5. **Click Next.**

   Your verification is complete. You can now remove the NetworkedBlogs widget or badge if you wish.

Setting up syndication

Syndication tells NetworkedBlogs where you want your new blog posts to be posted in Facebook (and NetworkedBlogs can automatically tweet your new post, too). To set up your syndication, follow these steps:

1. **Click the Syndication link in the upper-right corner of the NetworkedBlogs Application.**

   You see a screen showing your syndication settings.

2. From the drop-down list, select the blog you want to configure. You can add Facebook Targets and Twitter Targets, as shown in Figure 3-9.

Figure 3-9:
Click Add
Facebook
Target to
select your
Facebook
Profile or
Page.

If you get stuck, the NetworkedBlogs application has a decent Help section, with screenshots, at

`http://apps.facebook.com/blognetworks/help_faq.php`

After you successfully configure your NetworkedBlogs application, when you post a new blog post, the application will automatically post it to your Page or personal Profile, depending on how it's configured. The post is usually up within a few minutes after you post to your blog, but we have seen it take as long as an hour. Just be patient if you don't see it right away.

If you find that your blog post isn't updated in the NetworkedBlogs application, click the Pull Now link, as shown in Figure 3-10, to go and find any new blog posts on your blog and bring them into the application.

Figure 3-10:
Click Pull
Now if your
blog post
hasn't auto-
matically
been
brought
into the
application.

Many people ask whether they should post their business blog to their personal Profile as well as their Page. Our recommendation is that you should unless you feel very strongly against "bothering" your friends and family. You probably aren't posting that often to your blog, and your friends and family should know what you are doing in your business. Many referrals can and should come from your friends and family, and seeing a blog post may spark a connection for them to Share your post with one of their Friends.

Getting more readers by increasing your ranking inside the app page

Within the NetworkedBlogs application, you can follow other blogs. And when you do this, they appear in your NetworkedBlogs News Feed when you click on Home within the NetworkedBlogs App, just under the NetworkedBlogs logo. Oh, no! Not another News Feed! Yes, but this News Feed can be helpful when keeping track of the blogs that you want to follow.

You can also increase your blog readership by trying to increase your ranking within the NetworkedBlogs application. The more followers and high ratings you have, the higher your blog comes up in the Browse area in the NetworkedBlogs application for your topic. This is another place that you can use to gain more attention to your blog and your business.

Begin by browsing the blogs within NetworkedBlogs by topic: Click Browse and then select Topics or Popularity. The more followers and ratings you can get, the better your chance of coming up in the top 50. To get more followers and ratings, start by asking your Facebook Friends to follow and rate your blog within the NetworkedBlogs application.

Reposting a blog post using NetworkedBlogs

You can repost the blog post through NetworkedBlogs to your Profile or Page any time you'd like. You can always post the direct link to your blog post on your Wall, but if you'd like to repost with the NetworkedBlogs Application, here are the steps:

1. **Click the Networked Blogs link from the left sidebar of your personal Profile home page.**

   You are taken into the application, which shows the News Feed of the blogs you follow.

2. **Click the Profile link underneath the NetworkedBlogs logo at the top of the page.**

   You go into your personal Profile information.

3. **Scroll down to the Blogs I Write section and click your blog to access the blog information area.**

4. **Scroll down to the Blog Feed section to go the post you would like to repost to your Profile or Page. Then click the Syndication link, as shown in Figure 3-11.**

5. **From the information about how many times the post has been posted, select where you would like it reposted.**

Figure 3-11:
The syndication link gives you the ability to repost to your Profile or Page.

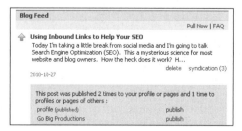

6. **Click the Publish link next to the where you would like it reposted.**

We recommend reposting some of your blog posts from time to time if they're still relevant and helpful to your audience. You'll be getting new people who are a part of your Page who might not have seen the post when it first came out. Even long-time members of your community may have missed the post or the chance to read it, so they will welcome the opportunity to view your helpful blog post. As long as you are using this reposting feature prudently, it's a good thing to do occasionally.

Installing Social RSS

Another Facebook application that you can use to automatically import your blog posts is Social RSS. Social RSS is a little easier to set up than NetworkedBlogs, but the free version might not work for you if you're posting more than three times per week. See the section on upgrading to the paid service for more information.

To start using the Social RSS App, follow these steps:

1. **Go to** `http://apps.facebook.com/social-rss/tabsettings.php` **while logged into Facebook as your personal Profile.**

   You see a Request for Permission screen to allow Social RSS to access your basic information.

Book III
Chapter 3

Importing Your Blog Posts to Your Facebook Page

2. **Click Allow**

   You will see the Social RSS configuration screen, as shown in Figure 3-12.

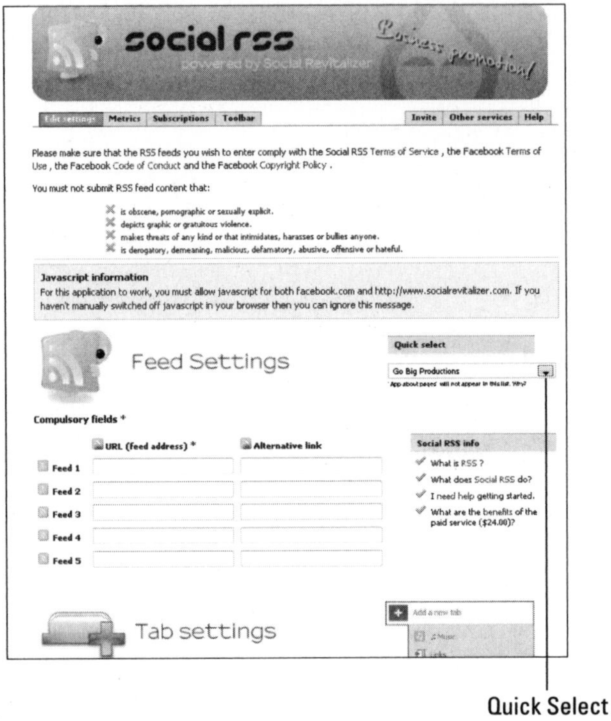

Figure 3-12:
Configure
the Social
RSS
application
here.

Quick Select

3. **Use the drop-down menu under Quick Select to select what Facebook Page you want to add the RSS Feed to, as shown in Figure 3-12.**

   A pop-up box appears to load your feed settings. When it's finished loading, you are shown a screen asking to Add Social RSS to your Page.

4. **Click the Add Social RSS button.**

   You are then taken back to the Social RSS app, where you can add your RSS Feed address.

5. **Enter your RSS Feed address under the Feed 1 box under the URL heading.**

   See the first part of this chapter for more about this address.

6. **Scroll down and configure the Tab settings.**

The Tab settings configuration, which allows you to send the feed to your Wall and also to auto-Like the post, is shown in Figure 3-13.

This shows how the help appears when you click a field.

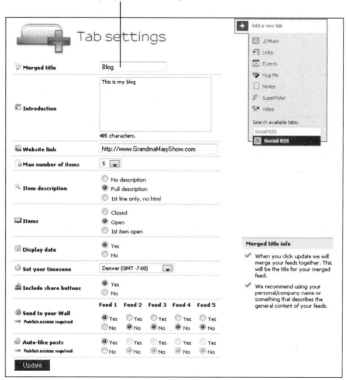

Figure 3-13:
Send the feed to your Wall and auto-Like the post.

If you click any of the fields shown in Figure 3-13, you see information about that field on the lower right of the screen. Here is more information about what to put in each field:

Merged title: This will be the title of your link on your left sidebar on your Page. If you are pulling multiple RSS Feeds in with the Social RSS App, they will all appear on the same Page. If it is just your blog, then you can title it Blog. If you have multiple feeds coming in, you may want to call it "Industry News" or whatever characterizes those streams best.

Introduction: A brief paragraph about your blog or what the set of RSS Feeds are about. The Introduction will appear at the top of the page of posts.

Website: Your Web site address for people to click.

Max number of items: The maximum number of stories that will be showing at a time on your Social RSS tab on your Facebook Page. You can select from 1-10.

Item description: Choose whether to show the whole item description, just the first line of the description or no description at all in your posts. We recommend Full Description.

Items: You can also choose whether to have the posts open or closed by default or just the first post open. We recommend Open.

Display date: Choose whether or not you want the publish date attached to your posts.

Set your time zone: If you do choose to display the dates, you then have to set your time zone.

Include share buttons: If you select this option there will be a link with all your posts so that people can easily share this to Facebook and other social sites. We recommend you select "Yes".

Send to your wall: Select if you want the post automatically put on your Wall (which then sends it to all your connections' News Feed). We recommend you send your own blog posts to the Wall and then it is up to you whether you want any of the other RSS feeds you may have imported to your Wall also. The free version of Social RSS only allows for 3 updates to your Wall per week so if you anticipate the other RSS Feeds to have more than that, select no for the other RSS Feeds.

Auto-like posts: You can also auto-like your RSS Feed posts. With the new Facebook notifications for Pages, this feature isn't necessary anymore unless you just want to Like your post.

7. **Click the Update button at the bottom of the Page.**

   You will be asked to Allow Permission for the Social RSS App to post to your Wall.

8. **Click Allow.**

   You will see a pop up box that says your Feeds have been successfully updated and the box also will promote the Paid service of the Social RSS App and give you an opportunity to use the 14-day free trial.

9. **Click Try Free Trial if you want to try it; otherwise, click OK.**

Figure 3-14 shows what the post will look like when it's automatically imported into your Wall.

Figure 3-14:
An example
Social RSS
Wall post.

Using Social RSS

After you have Social RSS configured, it automatically adds your posts to your Page Wall (if you selected that option) and to your RSS/Blog tab on your Page. You can always edit the settings or add more feeds from other places.

You also can add a feed to your personal Profile from the Social RSS application. Just select My Profile from the drop-down menu in the Social RSS configuration area, as shown in Figure 3-15.

Figure 3-15:
You can
also publish
your RSS
Feed to your
personal
Profile.

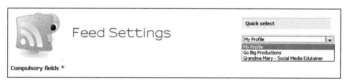

Beyond that, Social RSS is doesn't have too many other features unless you upgrade to the paid service (described next), which will give you some added statistics.

Deciding when to upgrade to paid service

The Social RSS application does have a paid service ($24 per year, as of this writing), which grants you more posts per hour (up to five per feed per hour, with a maximum of five feeds). By comparison, the free Social RSS currently allows for only three posts to your Wall per week. So, if you're blogging every day, that's obviously not going to work. If you're sending multiple feeds to your Wall, that's another reason that the free service might not work for you.

The other benefit to the paid service is the information it provides you. For example, the paid version of Social RSS tells you how many

✦ Users are sharing your blog post

✦ Users are clicking through to your Web site

✦ Interactions you have on each post

If you want to consider this program but aren't ready to commit, check out its free 14-day trial.

Using RSS Graffiti

Another Facebook application that you can use to post your blog entries automatically on your Facebook Wall is RSS Graffiti. In fact, you're not limited to importing only blog posts: You can use this application to bring in any RSS Feed from anywhere, similar to Social RSS. You can control how many posts per day are pulled in, just in case the RSS Feed you enter has more posts than you want to share with your community.

Adding additional RSS Feeds can help you add content to your Page. You may want to use RSS feeds to import industry news, or other helpful blogs. There are some RSS Feed directories out there, but you're better off bringing in a feed from a site that you know, like, and trust.

RSS Graffiti is highly configurable. You can configure the post style, the scheduling of updates, and the times the messages are posted. All these features translate into many settings, which you can change. Most of the settings can be left at their default values.

To get started with RSS Graffiti, follow these steps:

1. **Go to http://apps.facebook.com/rssgraffiti while logged into Facebook as your personal Profile.**

    You see the welcome message in the RSS Graffiti app and note that authorization is required. The default view for the RSS Graffiti application is your Personal Profile, which you can post to as well as post to your Page Wall. We cover the steps to post to your Page Wall here.

2. **On the left side of the application, select the Facebook Page where you want the RSS Feed posted (see Figure 3-16).**

3. **Click the Click to authorize button to allow posting to your Facebook Page.**

    A Request for Permission screen asks you to Allow RSS Graffiti to post to your Page Wall.

Figure 3-16:
Select the
Facebook
Page where
you want to
post your
RSS Feed.

4. **Click Allow.**

You are taken back to the application and your status shows Configured.

5. **Click the Add Feed button.**

You need your RSS Feed address, as we show you at the beginning of this chapter. You are taken to the screen to configure your feed.

6. **Enter the RSS Feed address in the Feed URL box, as shown in Figure 3-17, and then click the Click Here to Fetch and Preview link to verify the feed.**

As we mentioned earlier, there are many features you can configure with RSS Graffiti but the default settings work well for most people. So at this point, you can click the Save button (see the upper-right of Figure 3-17) and your RSS Feed will post to your Wall when there is a new post.

RSS Graffiti currently is not showing as a link in the Page sidebar, so if you want a place to show your most recent blog posts on your Facebook Page, we recommend using one of the other apps listed in this chapter.

You can edit your RSS Feed settings later to use some of the more advanced features. Here are some of the things you can change to customize your feed:

✦ **Source URL:** You can use this to override the URL pointing to the Web site. Leave it blank to use the Feed URL address.

✦ **Post Style:** With the current Facebook Page layout, this option should be left at Standard.

**Book III
Chapter 3**

**Importing Your
Blog Posts to Your
Facebook Page**

✦ **Time Filtering Options on the Filter tab:** Posts will not be published on your Wall before this date and time. Older posts will not be published unless you change this option. You can indicate how long a post must be up in minutes before it is posted to your Wall with the Eligibility Age field. You might want to use this if you sometimes make minor edits to posts shortly after you publish them. That way, you have a buffer of time before the story is posted to your Facebook Wall.

✦ **Message options on the Transform tab:** You can add messages to each post using these options. You may choose to add a Static message that says New Post from My Blog or something similar.

✦ **Schedule tab:** Options on this tab include how many posts are brought in and how often RSS Graffiti is checking for new posts coming in from your feeds.

✦ **More tab:** Options on this tab include adding your Twitter account and setting a Bit.ly account.

Be careful about adding just any RSS Feed to your Page. After all, you don't control that content, and you might not agree with a post brought in.

Figure 3-17:
Enter your feed and preview.

Click this link

Importing Your Blog Posts with Facebook Notes

Some people use Facebook as a blog by posting their content as a Note on the Notes tab. When you post a Note, you can add a picture, add links within your Note, and adjust the formatting to make your post look very professional

When you post the Note on the tab, it will then be shown on your Page Wall as well. See Book II, Chapter 3 for more information on adding Notes. Figure 3-18 shows the Note appearing on the Wall. When you click the link, the full Note appears.

Figure 3-18:
Using Notes
as a type of
blog.

**Book III
Chapter 3**

Importing Your
Blog Posts to Your
Facebook Page

There also is an option to pull your blog feed automatically via the Notes feature. We have found it to be a little slow at times to post your blog post, but it's very easy to set up. To use this method of automatically posting your blog to your Page, follow these steps:

1. **On your Facebook Page (and logged in as your Facebook Page), click the Edit Page button in the upper-right corner.**

   You are taken to your Page dashboard.

2. **Select Apps from the left sidebar and find the Notes App from the list.**

3. **Click the Go to App link below the Notes description.**

   The Notes App is now displayed, as shown in Figure 3-19.

4. **Click the Edit Import Settings in the lower-left corner, as shown in Figure 3-19.**

   You are taken to a screen where you enter your RSS feed address, as shown in Figure 3-20.

Figure 3-19:
The Notes
App.

Click to add your RSS Feed.

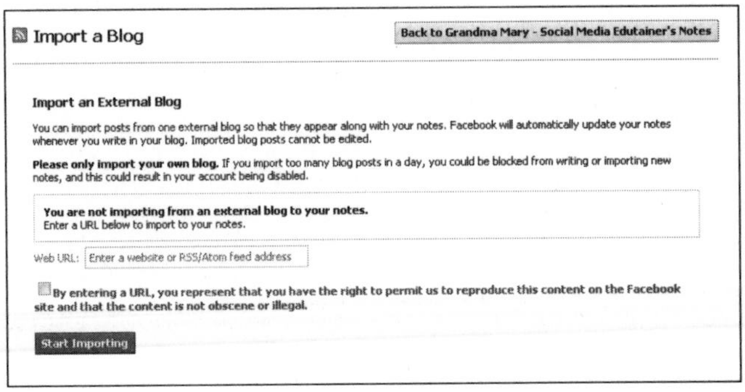

Figure 3-20:
Import your
blog via the
Notes tab.

5. **Enter your RSS feed address in the Web URL box.**

   We find it better to enter the RSS address rather than the Web site.

6. **Select the check box that says you have the right to reproduce the content and then click the Start Importing button.**

   Your blog post will now be published to the Wall and stored on the Notes link on the left sidebar of your Page.

Don't worry about duplicating content. Some people ask whether they should post on their blog and then repeat that information on their Facebook Page and on Twitter and maybe also sending out a newsletter with the link to the post. Don't worry that people are going to get sick of that post. Most likely, they will see it in only one or two places unless you're posting the same thing over and over. After all, you're trying to get the word out about your blog post, and people need multiple opportunities to be able to read it.

Chapter 4: Connecting Your Social Media Accounts

In This Chapter

✔ Connecting to Twitter in various ways

✔ Using HootSuite and TweetDeck

✔ Adding LinkedIn to your Page

✔ Using SlideShare to add PowerPoint and Word documents

✔ Adding YouTube videos

Y ou likely know what Twitter is and how to use it. Same goes for YouTube. You might not have heard of HootSuite and TweetDeck, though, or how to use them to your advantage when you coordinate your social networks in tandem with Facebook marketing.

Bottom line, in this chapter, we show you the benefits (and a few considerations) of connecting your Facebook presence with social networking venues to compliment and diversify your Facebook marketing campaigns. And, yes, we also show literally how to connect these to you can put them to your best use.

To Connect or Not Connect

So, do you want to tweet everything you post to your Page, or post to your Page from Twitter, or update them simultaneously? More important, should you? First consider the implications of linking the two accounts.

Most social media thought leaders agree that posting in both Twitter and Facebook all the time isn't a good idea because your Facebook community will be different from your Twitter community — they expect different things. Twitter typically has more quick interactions and conversations, while the Facebook community expects less updates and more threaded conversations.

Also, if you're participating in other social media sites, we recommend connecting them with your Facebook Page because people on Facebook might not be aware of where to find you on YouTube, Twitter, or LinkedIn. And adding your other accounts can give your users a richer experience with SlideShare presentations and YouTube videos.

To help you coordinate all your social networks, consider using tools like HootSuite and TweetDeck to simplify your life by creating a single dashboard to monitor your various social profiles and update from one place. We show you how to use both of these tools in this chapter.

Connecting Facebook and Twitter

How to connect Twitter and Facebook? Let us count the ways! There are many ways to link your Facebook Page to your tweets. (For those of you not familiar with Twitter, a *tweet* is equivalent to a status update in Facebook, but only 140 characters long.) Here are some of the options for how you can connect Facebook and Twitter; we cover each method in detail:

✦ **En masse:** Send every post on your Facebook Page to your Twitter account automatically.

✦ **Selectively:** Selectively post from Twitter to your Facebook account by adding a hashtag to the tweets that you want posted on your Facebook Page. Keep reading to see what a hashtag is and how it works.

✦ **Both:** Update Twitter and Facebook simultaneously *and* selectively by using HootSuite or TweetDeck.

Linking your Facebook Page to Twitter

If you want to send everything that you put on your Facebook Wall to Twitter, you can do that easily and automatically through Facebook. This isn't a bad thing to do because typically, you're posting to your Facebook Page less frequently than you would post to Twitter. And, the Twitter community accepts more frequent posts than the Facebook community.

However, just keep in mind that Facebook status updates are 420 characters long — way longer than the 140-character limit of a tweet. In a bit, we'll show you how to handle that limitation.

Sending all your Facebook updates to Twitter can be a good way of connecting your community on Twitter to your Facebook Page. Just be mindful that some people don't like the duplication with Twitter and Facebook: that if you're going to tweet, just tweet as Twitter was meant to be used, without trying to fit more than the original 140 characters into your tweets.

That being said, you decide what is right for you and your brand. Automation between Facebook and Twitter can be a good thing for the following reasons:

✦ Saves you time

✦ Adds more content to your Twitter feed

✦ Can bring your Twitter community to your Facebook Page

To make the connection, log into your Facebook account and then follow these steps:

1. **Go to www.facebook.com/twitter.**

You can either open a new window in your browser or just type the URL into your browser window. You see the screen shown in Figure 4-1.

Figure 4-1: Send your Facebook Page updates to Twitter.

2. **Click the green Link a Page to Twitter button.**

You're taken to a page that shows the Pages of which you are an admin; see Figure 4-2.

3. **Click the Link to Twitter button next to the Page you want linked.**

You go to Twitter to authorize this action; what you see is shown in Figure 4-3. If nothing happens when you click the Link to Twitter button, your pop-up blocker may be blocking the access to the site and you may need to allow access.

If you're not logged into your Twitter account, you'll be asked to log in at that time to authorize the postings.

Figure 4-2:
Your admin Pages are listed.

Figure 4-3:
Twitter requires that you authorize the postings from your Page.

4. **Click the Allow button to allow posting to your Twitter account.**

    You'll then be redirected back to Facebook where your Page is now confirmed to be linked to Twitter, as shown in Figure 4-4.

    Your Facebook Page is now linked to Twitter, and everything you post on Facebook will be tweeted on your Twitter account.

Also notice in Figure 4-4 that you can unlink your Facebook Page from Twitter. If you ever decide to stop tweeting your Page posts, just go back to www.facebook.com/twitter and click the Unlink from Twitter link to stop the tweeting.

Figure 4-4:
Your
Facebook
Page and
Twitter are
now linked.

What happens to too-long Tweets

As we mention, status updates in Facebook are potentially longer than the ones allowed in Twitter. So what happens if you post something in Facebook that's too long to tweet, but you have Facebook and Twitter linked? Well, Facebook automatically cuts off the tweet and posts a link to the actual Facebook update so someone could click it to read the entire post.

Figure 4-5 shows a too-long tweet that was sent from a Facebook Page.

Figure 4-5:
A too-long
tweet
sent from
Facebook.

Someone following the post on Twitter who wants to read the rest of that sentence just clicks the link at the end of the tweet to be taken to the Facebook update, as shown in Figure 4-6.

Figure 4-6:
The whole
status
update is
now visible
within
Facebook.

Notice in Figure 4-6 the two links that the person viewing the tweet could now click to go to your Facebook Page:

✦ The link preceding the status update that reads Grandma Mary - Social Media Edutainer

✦ The link above the status update: in this example, `Grandma Mary - Social Media Edutainer's Profile`

Linking Twitter to your Facebook Page

Conversely, you can also go the other way and send your tweets to your Facebook Page from Twitter with the Selective Tweets application covered in the next section. This works well if you're on Twitter a lot and want to share something quickly with your Facebook audience.

You can make this connection by using the Selective Tweets application within Facebook, as covered in the next section.

You can also make the Twitter-to-Facebook connection by using a Twitter tool, such as HootSuite or TweetDeck, which we cover later in this chapter.

Using the Selective Tweets app

Selective Tweets is a Facebook app that you can easily add to your Page. With this app, you decide when to update your Page at the same time as you tweet by just adding the hashtag `#fb` (for *Facebook*) to any tweet, which indicates that the tweet should also be posted to your Facebook account. And, when you add that hashtag, your tweet will also be sent to your Facebook page as a Wall post.

A hashtag is just the # symbol, connected with some words or letters.

To add Selective Tweets to your Page, first log in to Facebook as your personal Profile. You can find the Selective Tweets application at `www.facebook.com/selectivetwitter`. Go there, and then follow these steps to install the application:

1. **Click the Add to my Page link underneath the blue Go to Application button.**

   A pop-up box appears with your Pages for which you are the admin.

2. **Click the Add to Page button next to the Page you would like to have your tweets sent to.**

   That Page name disappears to indicate that the app has now been added to that Page.

3. **Click the Close at the bottom of that pop-up box.**

4. **Navigate to your Page by clicking Account in the upper-right corner of Facebook and then select Use Facebook as Page.**

   A pop-up box appears with a list of your Pages.

5. **Click the Switch button next to the Page you want to go to.**

6. **Click Edit Page button in the upper right corner your Page.**

   You are taken to your Page dashboard.

7. **Click Apps in the left column.**

   You see Selective Tweets as an installed application; see Figure 4-7.

Figure 4-7: Selective Tweets is now installed.

Book III
Chapter 4

Connecting
Your Social Media
Accounts

8. **Click the Go to Application link, under the description of Selective Tweets.**

   You're taken to a screen where you can enter the Twitter account you would like tied to this Page; see Figure 4-8.

Figure 4-8: Add your Twitter name and grant permission for Twitter to post to your Wall.

9. **Enter your Twitter username and then click the Grant Permission link; see Figure 4-8.**

10. **When a pop-up box asks you whether you want to grant Twitter permission to post to your Wall, click Allow.**

11. **Click the Save Changes button.**

Now you can send selected tweets to your Page by entering the #fb hashtag at the end of tweet, and Twitter will post that tweet (minus the #fb hashtag, of course) to your Page Wall.

Don't post a lot of Twitter-specific lingo to your wall, such as messages with @reply or tweets with other hashtags in them. Your Facebook community might not be on Twitter and won't understand all the symbols and messages.

Using Twitter Tools to Update Facebook

You can also use a Twitter tool — or Twitter client, as sometimes called — to update your Profile or Page. Two of the most popular Twitter tools are HootSuite and TweetDeck. Both are designed mainly for Twitter, but you can also use them to update multiple other social media platforms at the same time, such as LinkedIn, Facebook, MySpace, Foursquare, and others.

Exploring Hootsuite

HootSuite is a free, Web-based app you use to manage multiple social media accounts. Because it's Web-based, you can run the application from its Web site (to the cloud!) and have access to it from any computer. By comparison, TweetDeck is a program that you download onto your computer and run it from your desktop. It's also worth mentioning that HootSuite and TweetDeck both have mobile apps for your smart phone.

Walking you through the entire setup of HootSuite and TweetDeck is beyond the scope of this book, and the installs are pretty intuitive. We just want to show you how you can align your Facebook accounts with these applications and how they work.

HootSuite is a free app but does have some nice perks if you upgrade to its paid Pro Plan at $5.99/month. The Pro Plan includes features such as adding more than five social media accounts, adding a team member to be able to monitor the same social media accounts, and Google Analytics integration.

To start using HootSuite, go to www.hootsuite.com and click Sign Up to get started and walk through its configuration steps.

With HootSuite, you can add multiple social profiles by clicking the Settings icon on the left side of the page and then selecting Social Networks as shown in Figure 4-9.

Figure 4-9: Add social profiles to HootSuite here.

You'll be taken to a screen like that shown in Figure 4-10, where you can add your different social profiles by clicking the Add Social Network link. With the Hootsuite tool, you can update Twitter, Facebook, LinkedIn, Ping.fm, Wordpress, MySpace, Mixi and Foursquare. You can add your Facebook personal Profile as well as any Facebook Page that you administer. Having your personal Profile and Facebook Pages all in one place with Hootsuite means that you can do all your updating in one place. You can also see your News Feed and comments within Hootsuite.

Figure 4-10: Configuring the social networks in HootSuite.

Figure 4-11 shows what HootSuite looks like. The Compose Message field (upper-left corner) is where you enter your status update for Twitter, Facebook, LinkedIn, or some combination of all these Web sites.

Figure 4-11:
The
HootSuite
dashboard.

Next to the Compose Message field is a series of icons, all indicating the different social media profiles that you can update at one time. In Figure 4-11, left to right, you can see icons for Twitter, Facebook, Facebook Page, and LinkedIn. So say that you want to post a message and send it to your Facebook personal Profile, your Facebook Page, Twitter, and LinkedIn: You could check all those profiles, enter your message, and then click Send Now to update all your profiles simultaneously. Figure 4-12 shows an example of how you would update several social sites at once.

Figure 4-12:
Click the
profiles you
want like to
update with
the same
message.

HootSuite can also schedule your status updates. So, if you're going to be gone for the day or for vacation, you can schedule a few updates to post to your social profiles when you're gone. HootSweet.

Scheduling updates is good for your business so that you are not completely out of sight while you're gone. Many businesses even let their community know that they will be gone but will be posting useful content or some of their best past blog posts. This technique is a good practice because your community members then know not to expect immediate return messages if they respond to a posting.

To schedule a post with HootSuite, compose your message just as you would a normal message, select your social media profile where you would like the message sent, and then click the calendar icon below the update window, shown in Figure 4-13, to choose the time and date to send the message.

Figure 4-13: Click the calendar icon to schedule your message.

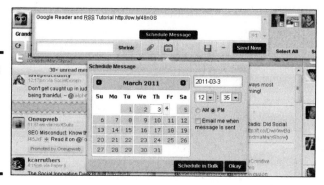

After you have the time and date set, click Okay and then click the Schedule button that replaces the Send Now button.

Using TweetDeck

TweetDeck is also a great (and free) option for updating and connecting your social media accounts. As we mention, it runs on your computer (and also has a mobile app). Just go to www.tweetdeck.com and click Get It Now to download the application and go through the setup process.

Figure 4-14 shows a screen shot of the TweetDeck application. In the What's Happening? box (top of the screen) is where you put your updates. The social media profiles are across the top; click the names to update several profiles simultaneously. To send your post, just press the Enter key on your keyboard after you're done typing your update in the window. You can also click the Send button on the right side just under the update window.

To add social media accounts to TweetDeck, click Settings (the wrench in the upper-right corner of Figure 4-13) and then Accounts in the pop-up window, as shown in Figure 4-15.

Figure 4-14:
The
TweetDeck
application.

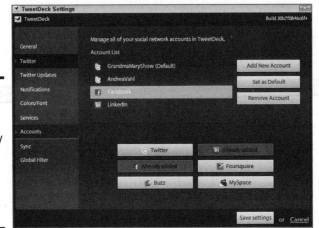

Figure 4-15:
Add social
media
accounts by
clicking the
Accounts
link in the
Settings
box.

With TweetDeck, you can add Twitter, Facebook, LinkedIn, MySpace, Foursquare, and Google Buzz. Add the social media profiles where you participate.

TweetDeck has a link shortener built into the update window. When you insert a URL into your post, TweetDeck automatically shortens your link. You can also schedule your updates just as with HootSuite.

To schedule a post, just click the clock icon just under the right side of the update window. A pop-up box appears as shown in Figure 4-16 to allow you to schedule the post.

Figure 4-16:
Schedule your updates in TweetDeck by clicking the clock icon.

Other posting clients

Other clients are available will post to your Facebook personal Profile, your Page, and other social media profiles from one place. Some of these have *analytics* to track your number of followers, keywords, and retweets built in, or the capability to schedule your updates in the future. Some have free features and some are covered in a subscription price:

✦ **Ping.fm** (www.ping.fm): Ping.fm can send updates to more than 30 social networks simultaneously, so if you have profiles on a lot of social sites, Ping.fm could be a good solution for you. It doesn't have scheduling ability but it does integrate with some of the other tools, such as HootSuite and Seesmic, that do have that feature. Ping.fm also has a mobile app and e-mail integration so that you can send an e-mail to Ping.fm that will post to your social networks.

✦ **Seesmic** (http://seesmic.com): Seesmic has a Web app, a mobile app, and a desktop app that will update Twitter, Facebook, LinkedIn, Google Buzz, Ping.fm, and Foursquare. Seesmic also has scheduling ability to schedule your posts for later.

✦ **SocialOomph** (www.socialoomph.com): Social Oomph is a Web-based tool that is primarily focused on Twitter but you can have it update Facebook personal Profiles and Pages with the paid version of Social Oomph. You can also add the Selective Tweets app (see the section on Selective Tweets earlier in this chapter) to update your Facebook Page or Profile with the #fb hashtag to use the free version of SocialOomph.

✦ **PeopleBrowsr** (www.peoplebrowsr.com): PeopleBrowsr is a Web-based app and has the capability to post to more than 10 social networks, including Twitter, Facebook and LinkedIn. PeopleBrowsr is free to use but has a very robust analytics service for a fee.

Connecting LinkedIn to Your Facebook Page

LinkedIn and Facebook don't have many features to interconnect. You can't post to LinkedIn directly from Facebook, but there is an app that allows you to add a navigation link on your Facebook Page sidebar to your LinkedIn profile or LinkedIn Company profile. The app is called My LinkedIn Profile and is found at

```
http://www.facebook.com/apps/application.
    php?id=6394109615&v=info
```

You can also find the application by entering My LinkedIn Profile into the Facebook Search box.

To add this app to your Facebook Page, log into Facebook as your personal Profile and go to the preceding URL; then, follow these steps:

1. **Click Add to My Page underneath the logo on the left side.**

   A pop-up box with a list of all your Facebook Pages appears.

2. **Click the Add to Page button next to the Page where you would like the app added.**

   The Facebook Page where you added it will disappear, indicating that the app has now been added to that Page.

3. **Click the Close button on the pop-up box.**

4. **Go to your Page, click Account in the upper-right corner, and select Use Facebook as Page.**

5. **Click the Switch button next to the Page you want to go to.**

   You are taken to your Facebook Page Wall.

6. Click the Edit Page button in the upper-right corner.

You see your Facebook Page dashboard.

7. Click Apps on the left sidebar menu.

You see all of the installed applications for your Page.

8. Scroll down to the My LinkedIn Profile and click the Go to App link underneath the description.

You're taken to a Request for Permission page to allow My LinkedIn Profile to access your information.

9. Click the blue Allow button.

You are taken to the My LinkedIn Profile app, shown in Figure 4-17.

Figure 4-17:
My LinkedIn
Profile app.

**Book III
Chapter 4**

Connecting
Your Social Media
Accounts

10. Enter your LinkedIn personal profile URL or, if you have created a LinkedIn company profile, you can choose to add that URL instead.

11a. Verify your LinkedIn personal profile URL as follows:

a. Log in to LinkedIn.

b. Click the Profile menu to see your profile.

c. Scroll down to the Public Profile field to verify your LinkedIn profile URL.

11b. Verify your LinkedIn company profile as follows:

a. Log into LinkedIn.

b. Click the Companies menu to see a drop-down list.

c. If you have created your LinkedIn Company profile, the company name will be showing in the drop-down menu; select your company and see its URL displayed in the browser window.

12. **After you have entered the LinkedIn URL for the profile of your choice into the Facebook My LinkedIn Profile app window, click the blue Save button (refer to Figure 4-17).**

A message appears on the page saying that changes have been saved. You can now navigate back to your Page and the LinkedIn app will show as a link on your left sidebar with your LinkedIn profile, as shown in Figure 4-18.

Figure 4-18: Your LinkedIn profile now shows on your Facebook Page.

Adding PowerPoint Presentations and Word Documents with SlideShare

If you have a SlideShare account, you can connect PowerPoint presentations and Word documents that you have uploaded to SlideShare in a tab on your Page. Use SlideShare to showcase all your PowerPoints on your Facebook Page and to add more content that establishes your expertise in your niche. For example, Mari Smith, a Facebook expert, has a number of PowerPoint presentations available on her Page for her community to reference; check it out in Figure 4-19.

Figure 4-19:
Mari Smith's
SlideShare
tab.

One important caveat concerning the addition of SlideShare to your Page is that you must add the SlideShare to your personal Facebook Profile. It is not possible to directly add the SlideShare app only to your Facebook Page. We first take you through the steps of adding the app to your personal Profile. Next, we show you how to complete the process and add the app to your Page. To add this application to your personal Profile, follow these steps after logging to Facebook in as your personal Profile:

**Book III
Chapter 4**

Connecting
Your Social Media
Accounts

1. **Go to** http://apps.facebook.com/slideshare **to add the SlideShare app to your personal Profile.**

   You see the Request for Permission page to allow SlideShare access to your basic information.

2. **Click Allow.**

   A pop-up box appears, stating that you have installed the application; you can add a bookmark, as shown in Figure 4-20, if you want.

3. **Click the Next button and, when asked whether you want to add your e-mail account for Slideshare notices, enter your address if you want this to happen.**

4. **Click the Next button.**

   You are taken to the screen shown in Figure 4-21, where you can either sign up for a new Slideshare account or connect to your current account at the bottom of the page.

Figure 4-20:
Confirmation of your SlideShare installation.

Figure 4-21:
Sign up for a new SlideShare account or connect to your existing one.

5. Click the Here link at the bottom of the page.

You are taken to a page to enter your SlideShare login information.

6. Enter your login information and click the Link to SlideShare button.

Your presentations are now showing on your personal Profile.

Next, you need to add the SlideShare app to your Page. To do that, follow these steps while logged in as your personal Facebook Profile:

1. Go to the SlideShare app page here:

```
http://www.facebook.com/apps/application.
    php?id=2490221586
```

You need to use this URL because this location allows you to add the app to your Page.

2. **Click Add to My Page underneath the logo, as shown in Figure 4-22.**

   A pop-up box appears, listing all the Facebook Pages you administer.

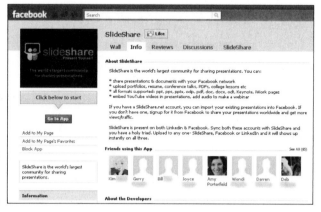

Figure 4-22: Add SlideShare to your Page Application link.

3. **Select Add to Page button where you are adding SlideShare application.**

   The Page disappears from the list indicating that the app has been added.

4. **Click the Close button.**

   The pop-up window closes.

5. **Go to your Page, click Account in the upper-right corner of Facebook, and select Use Facebook as Page.**

6. **Click the Switch button next to the Page you want to go to.**

   You are now taken to your Facebook Page Wall.

7. **Click the Edit Page button in the upper-right corner to see your Facebook Page dashboard.**

8. **Click Apps on the left sidebar menu to see all the installed applications for your Page.**

9. **Scroll down to the SlideShare app and click Go to App under the SlideShare description.**

   You are taken to a screen that says "You are using Facebook as [*your Page name*]. To access this Page, you need to switch from using Facebook as your page to using Facebook as yourself."

10. **Click the blue Continue as [*your personal Profile name*].**

You're taken to a Request for Permission page to allow SlideShare to access your information.

11. **Click the blue Allow button.**

You're taken to a screen to sync your SlideShare account with your Facebook Page, as shown in Figure 4-23.

Figure 4-23: Click Yes to sync your SlideShare account to your Page.

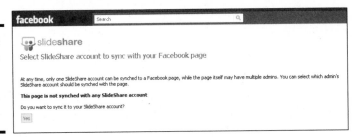

12. **Click Yes.**

The screen now shows a message indicating that the SlideShare account is now synched between your personal Profile and your Page.

Your PowerPoint presentations or Word Docs that are uploaded into SlideShare are now showing on your Facebook Page as well as on your Facebook Profile. When you upload a new PowerPoint, it will post in your SlideShare app but will not automatically post to your Wall. To post a SlideShare presentation to your Wall, you need to go into SlideShare, get the link to that presentation, and post it as a link to share it that way. The SlideShare app is just a handy reference area for all your presentations in one place.

Adding a YouTube Video

If you have a YouTube channel, you definitely want to take advantage of sharing your videos with your community. Video is a powerful tool that will connect you to your audience and help them get to know, like, and trust you.

To connect your Page to your YouTube videos, you can

✦ Post the YouTube video as a link in your Publisher.

✦ Create a tab on your Page with a Facebook YouTube application.

✦ Design a special tab that will showcase your YouTube videos.

Posting your video as a link

If you want to post a YouTube video as a link, it will play in the News Feed, as you might have seen with other YouTube videos.

Make sure you're posting the link to the specific video, not a link to your YouTube Channel.

For example, in Figure 4-24, you can see the Grandma Mary Show YouTube channel. On this channel, you can watch the videos on the right side by clicking them; they then appear in the larger field on the left. But to get the specific link to the video to share it, you need to click the Share link underneath the video. When you click it, you see the specific video link appear (right next to Paste This Link into an E-mail or Instant Message).

Figure 4-24: To share the video link, click Share to reveal the link to cut and paste into the Facebook Publisher.

Adding a Facebook YouTube app and tab

You can also add a YouTube tab to your Page with several different YouTube applications. A few of them are paid applications that range in price from $10/year to 4.99 per month, depending on the application.

Following are URLS for some of the YouTube apps:

✦ `http://apps.facebook.com/uchannels`: You'll pay a $55 annual or $4.99 monthly subscription fee to add this app to your Facebook Page. The app can automatically post new videos to your Wall.

✦ http://www.facebook.com/YouTubeApp: Involver's YouTube app can be accessed from here or from http://www.Involver.com. We like this app because it's free and features your most recent video more prominently. It doesn't post automatically to your Wall with the free version, but if you upgrade to the pro version, you can get automatic publishing.

✦ http://apps.facebook.com/videobox: Free app that lets you pick and choose which apps to display on your tab. Doesn't automatically post to your Wall.

✦ http://apps.facebook.com/youtubetabapp: Requires a $10 per year subscription to add this app to your Facebook Page.

Figure 4-25 shows an example of how a YouTube tab can look with the YouTube application found at http://apps.facebook.com/videobox.

Figure 4-25:
You choose what videos to display on this application.

As you notice in the YouTube app list, some applications might or might not have the capability to automatically post a video to your Wall — and that's a big deal because you need to alert your community members about your new videos as you put them onto YouTube so that they get it in their News Feed. If a video is on a tab, that can be a nice reference place for anyone coming to your Fan Page, but you do want to also put new videos as a post on your Wall. In this case, you want to add the new videos to your Publisher, as we mention earlier.

As mentioned, Involver also has a free YouTube channel tab application that you can add to your Page. Involver has free and premium paid applications for Facebook. You can access the applications at www.involver.com. With Involver, you can add two of the available applications for free, and then you will have to upgrade to a premium subscription to add additional applications. The Involver YouTube tab is shown in Figure 4-26.

Figure 4-26:
The Involver
YouTube
app.

Chapter 5: The Fine Print: Legal and Other Considerations

In This Chapter

✔ **Where to find the fine print**

✔ **Complying with the FTC**

✔ **Posting content for regulated industries**

*R*emember when you signed up for Facebook and you selected the box to agree to Facebook's Terms and Conditions? You sat down and read all that fine print right then and there before agreeing, right? Surrre you did. As most of us do, we just click OK or agree or whatever we need to do to get into the site as quickly as possible.

The good news is that the Facebook Terms and Conditions are fairly manageable. No online bullying, no virus uploading, no general law breaking. But don't overlook point #1 under the Safety section:

> You will not send or otherwise post unauthorized commercial communications (such as spam) on Facebook.

Vague at best. Allow us to explain this a bit better in this chapter, with some guidelines for staying on the right side of Facebook — and U.S. federal — law as you embark upon your Facebook marketing endeavors.

Digesting Legal Considerations

The first step to figuring out the legal considerations is to find them! The main site for the Terms and Conditions is www.facebook.com/terms.php. Within this list of terms, you can find links to many other lists of terms such as Advertising Guidelines, Developer Applications, Privacy, and more.

Facebook does monitor these Terms and Conditions although not always thoroughly because, after all, Facebook can't be everywhere at once. And, yes. Facebook will indeed disable your account if you violate these terms. We've frequently seen enforcement against sending spam. You might (or might not) know that you can send messages to people who aren't your Friends. This capability is helpful sometimes if you need to get a message to someone privately who Likes your Page but who isn't a personal Facebook Friend.

The problem with sending messages to people you aren't Friends with on Facebook is that you don't know how much is too much. Facebook doesn't specify how many messages you can send without getting banned. And typically, you aren't going to be sending many messages to people you aren't Friends with, so you will be riding on the right side of Facebook law.

If you go to any person's Profile on Facebook whom you aren't Friends with, you will see a Message button in the upper-right corner of the page. If you click the button, you can send that person a message even though you aren't friends with the person. In Figure 5-1, you see a Profile of someone named Chris, and you can see that we're not Friends with Chris. We can't see some of his personal information — but, we can send him a message.

If you send a message to too many people you don't know, though — especially if the message contains a link to a Web site — you'll get a warning from Facebook. And if you continue sending messages like this, your account will be disabled. Not good. So the message here is, you can send messages to people you don't know, but don't send too many simultaneously. We recommend sending 10 or fewer messages a week to people you don't know if you need to contact people you aren't friends with on Facebook.

Figure 5-1:
You can
send
anyone on
Facebook
a private
message
from your
personal
account.

You cannot send any Facebook e-mails as your Facebook Page. You can send Facebook e-mails only as your personal Profile, in any case — to Friends or non-Friends.

Understanding FTC Regulations Concerning Testimonials and Reviews

Businesses often use their Facebook Page to sell their own products or possibly to market other people's products and get a commission on the sale of that product. Using testimonials and reviews can help sales because people like to see *social proof* of a product (if one person likes it or gets good results, maybe we will, too). Testimonials and reviews are a good marketing tool. But you do need to be aware of some of the FTC regulations concerning reviews and testimonials if you intend to use them in your marketing efforts.

In October, 2009, the Federal Trade Commission (FTC) released updated guidelines on how testimonials and reviews were allowed to be shown by advertisers. The FTC's job is to protect consumers from fraudulent business practices and general marketing sliminess.

These new regulations can be found online at

www.ftc.gov/os/2009/10/091005endorsementguidesfnnotice.pdf

We're guessing that no one is probably very eager to read this 81-page legal document, but you do need to be aware of the changes as a result of these guidelines that could affect the way you do business.

One of the big unknowns with all these regulations is how they will be enforced. The FTC, of course, can't monitor every Facebook Page, Web site, and e-mail sent out. But like with every rule/law/terms set forth by a governing body, it's best to try to comply from the beginning. All it takes is one disgruntled customer to bring the infractions to light, and no one wants to end up with some hefty fines from the FTC.

A fine mess to not get yourself into

The FTC fine was rumored to be $11,000 per infraction. However, Richard Cleland, Assistant Director, Division of Advertising Practices at the FTC, said, "That $11,000 fine is not true. Worst-case scenario, someone receives a warning, refuses to comply, followed by a serious product defect; we would institute a proceeding with a cease-and-desist order and mandate compliance with the law. To the extent that I have seen and heard, people are not objecting to the disclosure requirements but to the fear of penalty if they inadvertently make a mistake. That's the thing I don't think people need to be concerned about. There's no monetary penalty, in terms of the first violation, even in the worst case. Our approach is going to be educational, particularly with bloggers. We're focusing on the advertisers: What kind of education are you providing them, are you monitoring the bloggers and whether what they're saying is true?"

That tempers the fear a bit, but as we mention, you should follow the FTC guidelines from the beginning to avoid any issues.

Affiliates

The first change that might affect you is the disclosure of material connections between you and a product you're promoting. If you're familiar with affiliate marketing, this can affect what you might post on your Page. *Affiliate marketing* is when a business compensates someone for sales brought in by that person's marketing efforts. The person promoting the company's products is typically compensated with a percentage of each sale, like a commission. Many companies, including Amazon, have affiliate programs to encourage sales through this independent sales force.

But the new FTC guidelines, noted here, state that you need to disclose a material connection between you and the business that might compensate you for promoting its product.

255.1 Consumer endorsements

(d) Advertisers are subject to liability for false or unsubstantiated statements made through endorsements, or for failing to disclose material connections between themselves and their endorsers. Endorsers also may be liable for statements made in the course of their endorsements.

Many people comply with this regulation by stating that the link is an "affiliate link" when promoting a product or program — and this is compliant with the FTC guideline. An example is shown in Figure 5-2.

Figure 5-2:
Promoting
affiliate links
to products.

Here's another way to be compliant: Post the explanation of the product being promoted as well as the link to where someone could buy the product, with a statement to the effect of, "This is an affiliate link but I do not promote anything I don't believe in wholeheartedly." Your audience will understand that sometimes you bring products to them, much as you would your own product, that fit their needs. As long as you aren't continually selling to them, they don't mind. Some people disclose that a link they're posting isn't an affiliate link so that people are clear that they aren't making any money by promoting this product.

255.2 Consumer endorsements

(b) An advertisement containing an endorsement relating the experience of one or more consumers on a central or key attribute of the product or service will likely be interpreted as representing the endorser's experience is representative of what consumers will generally achieve with the advertised product or service in actual, albeit variable, conditions of use. Therefore, an advertiser should possess and rely upon adequate substantiation for this representation. If the advertiser does not have substantiation that the endorser's experience is representative of what consumers will generally achieve, the advertisement should clearly and conspicuously disclose the generally expected performance in the depicted circumstances, and the advertiser must possess and rely on adequate substantiation for that representation.

This means that you need to be careful with claims relating to your product. If you have a weight loss or health product, you now can't claim, "Tim lost 100 pounds in his first 2 weeks with our product. *Results not typical." Even if this were a true claim, the FTC would like a clearer representation of expectations with your product. The reasoning behind this is that consumers tend to ignore the "results not typical" warning, and the FTC's job is to protect consumers. A good addition to the preceding statement would be "Typically our clients see an average of x number of pounds over x time."

Content Compliance Issues for Certain Industries

Certain industries have more regulations than others regarding what they can share online. Some industries have specific regulations outlined by law, and other companies have an outline of self-governed policies relating to social media and online activities. If you're in the one of the following industries, you have some form of guidelines relating to online activity:

+ Financial advisors

+ Investment advisors

+ Mortgage brokers

+ Banks

+ Insurance agents

+ Publically traded companies

+ Pharmaceuticals

+ Healthcare

Any financial industry institution needs to be cautious about what information they share. Financial institutions are expected to keep records of customer communications, which could include online social media communications. And they also need to be concerned with sensitive customer confidentiality issues when interacting with clients.

Publically traded companies need to be cautious about any forward-looking statements. The Regulations Fair Disclosure policy, introduced in 2000, states that all publicly traded companies release information to investors and the public at the same time. If this policy isn't followed, insider trading or selective disclosure charges could be filed.

Pharmaceutical companies need to worry about claims being made online and also outlining adverse effects of their products. This could include any statements made within the community itself.

Insurance agents are allowed to give advice only to people in the state in which they are licensed. This can pose a problem on a Page where there are people from other states because you can restrict who can be Liked your page by country, but not by state. If you're an insurance agent, make sure that your posts stay away from giving straight insurance advice.

Healthcare industries have to be careful of patient confidentiality, and this even includes the fact that the patient-doctor relationship exists. They also have to beware of giving any medical advice. Figure 5-3 shows a Page of Doctor Karen Becker, a veterinarian. Her info area clearly states that she cannot give out advice. We recommend pointing that out, or have a link to your disclaimer on your Web site.

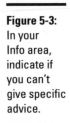

Figure 5-3:
In your Info area, indicate if you can't give specific advice.

If you're in one of these industries, you're probably aware of regulations and guidelines already set forth by the governing bodies related to your industry. But it's just a gentle reminder to be aware of your Facebook posts, tweets, and comments out there on the Web.

Bottom line, you can still have a Facebook Page to connect to your community, but you might have to keep posts slightly more social. You can post about things you are doing in the community, things happening in the office, ask fun questions, and other things to promote your business in a general way.

Book IV

Building, Engaging, Retaining, and Selling to Your Community

Contents at a Glance

Chapter 1: Building Visibility for Your Page

In This Chapter

✔ **Letting everyone know where you're located on Facebook**

✔ **Sharing and suggesting your Page with your existing customers and connections**

✔ **Sharing photos to attract people to your Page**

*B*ooks II and III explain how to design a functional Facebook Page. In this minibook, you find some practical ways to increase the visibility for your Page by letting people know where you're located on Facebook and learning how to share and suggest your Page.

Imagine that you open a new storefront. You want to send out notifications to everyone on your lists, both existing and potential customers, so they can find you. You need to do the same for your Facebook Page.

Some of your existing customers and connections are already on Facebook, but some (depending on your customer demographics) are not. At the ready are Facebook's built-in systems for attracting people to your Page and some time-tested off-line strategies to bring people not on Facebook to your Page.

When you open the doors to your new Facebook location, you'll be stepping into a new type of marketing, one based on conversation, content, value, and sharing. The next few Pages contain ideas you can use right away to add Facebook to your existing company materials and Web site, and some basic techniques using the Facebook Photo Album that are sure to attract people to your Page.

Inviting Your Existing Customers and Connections to Your Page

Think of your Facebook Page as a new brick-and-mortar space. It has an address and is open 24/7. You just moved in, and it's time to let people know about it. The point is to build a bit of a buzz about your new place so people will Like the Page and share it with their Friends.

Some businesses create a Page launch day. This way, they can make a big splash with their entry on Facebook. Others go slowly and build their presence on Facebook over time. Pick the way that suits you and your business, but make sure you do all the following (that apply) to invite your existing customers and connections.

You need to have at least 25 people Like your Page to be eligible for a *vanity URL*. Plan ahead and get your 25 people right away so you can use a more elegant Facebook address — such as `http://www.facebook.com/SociallyCongruent` — on your hard-copy materials. See Book II, Chapter 1 on how to securing a vanity URL.

A vanity URL doesn't contain numbers like this:

```
http://www.facebook.com/Pages/manage/?act=40641063#!/Pages/
    Socially-Congruent/147368801953769?ref=ts
```

Changing your hold message

If your business has a phone on-hold system, update it and add your Facebook address. Here are several great (made-up) examples:

Thank you for calling. We're so sorry you have to wait. Waiting makes me cranky, but if you are at your computer why don't you go check out my new Facebook Page! Go to Facebook dot com forward slash Grandma Mary Show that's all one word GrandmaMaryShow. Show me some love and "like" me! Now back to the lovely hold music.

Thank you for calling. If you are listening to this hold message maybe we are out brewing some tea! If you're like many of our customers — you have Facebook up and running — find Planetary Teas and see what's steeping there.

While you're holding, you might as well go over to my Facebook Page (yes, I'm on Facebook). In fact, you might find a discount or two over there that might come in handy when I pick up your call! Go to Facebook-dot-com-forward-slash-Ellen-Finkelstein.

Adding your Page address to your e-mail signature

Most businesses want to add their Page name to their e-mail signature right away. You don't have to have your vanity URL yet to do this because you can hyperlink a long URL to simple text. If you don't have a signature yet, we show you how to fix that, too.

Follow the instructions for the e-mail client you use to create an e-mail signature that promotes your Page.

If you use Outlook 2007, follow these instructions. Other versions of Outlook will be similar, but it's always good to check Outlook's tutorials on how to modify your e-mail signature.

1. **Open Outlook and sign in to your account.**

2. **Choose Tools⇨Options.**

3. **From the Options dialog box that appears, click the Mail Format tab.**

4. **Click the Signatures button.**

Doing so pulls up a Signatures and Stationery creation box. Make sure that you're on the E-mail Signature tab, as shown in Figure 1-1.

5. **Either select an existing signature to edit or click New to create a new signature, as shown in Figure 1-1.**

- *Editing an existing signature:* Select the existing signature, enter your new text, select it, and click the Hyperlink icon, as noted in Figure 1-1. This pulls up the Insert Hyperlink dialog box. Add your Facebook Page URL in the address field and click OK.

- *New Signature:* Click New, and a box will open up to give this new signature a name. Name it and click OK. Then design your signature in the editing box. Again, to add a hyperlink to your Facebook Page name, <u>type</u> the name of the Page, select it, click the hyperlink icon, and add the URL in the Address field.

6. **Click OK.**

When you create a new e-mail message, your existing signature auto-populates in the new email. To change the e-mail signature from within the message, select the Insert tab in the new e-mail window, select Signatures in the ribbon, and click the name of the new signature. Outlook replaces the signature in the new email message with the one you choose.

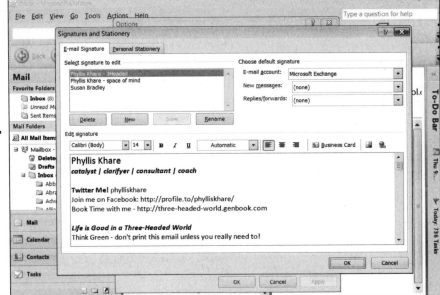

Figure 1-1:
On this
E-Mail
Signature
tab you can
either edit
an existing
signature
or create a
new one.

If you use Yahoo, follow these steps to add a hyperlink to your email signature:

1. **Open Yahoo and sign in to your account.**

2. **Click the Options link (on the right) and then choose More Options from the menu that appears.**

3. **Click the Signature link (on the far left).**

   You are now on the Signature creation Page. Look to the top right of the editing box. You might need to toggle to Rich Text if this editing box defaults to Plain Text.

4. **Design your signature, and type in the text you want hyperlinked to your Facebook Page,**

5. **Select the text to hyperlink to your Facebook Page.**

6. **Click the Hyperlink icon and paste in your Facebook URL. Then click OK.**

   OR

   Enter your Facebook Address, select it, and click the hyperlink icon to add the URL in the Insert Link to field, as shown in Figure 1-2.

7. **Click Save Changes at the top of the Page**

   Yahoo supports only one signature per account at this time.

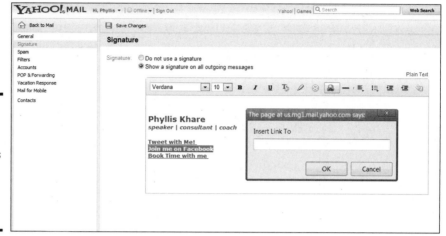

Figure 1-2:
The Yahoo
Signature
Page makes
it easy to
add your
Facebook
link.

If you use Gmail, you design your signature a little differently than in Yahoo and Outlook. The good news is that you can add an image to your signature; however, you can't upload it from your computer. You need to *host images in the cloud* – which means using a service such as Flickr, or even Facebook, to store the images online.

1. **Open Gmail and sign in to your account.**

2. **Click the Options icon at the top-right corner of the Page (it looks like a gear).**

   Note: The Gmail Options link might look different depending on which browser, and which version of that browser, you're using. The link might just be labeled "Settings."

3. **From the Settings Page that appears (the General tab), find the Signature section (about halfway down the Page). Select the e-mail address to which you want to add the Facebook address.**

   You can have as many signatures as you have Gmail addresses.

4. **Design your signature with your name and contact info. Enter the name of your Facebook Page, select it, and click the hyperlink icon.**

5. **Type or paste your Facebook Page URL in the Web address field.**

6. **Click OK. If you are finished and don't plan to add an image, click Save Changes at the bottom of the Page.**

**Book IV
Chapter 1**

**Building Visibility
for Your Page**

7. **(Optional) To add an image (a photo or logo image) to your signature, follow these steps starting from the Signature editing box.**

    a. *Click the Image icon (that's the one with the land and sky image).*

    b. *In the Add an Image dialog box that opens, enter the image's URL.* This is what makes Gmail's signature program different from the others. You can't just upload an image from your computer. The image has to exist somewhere online ("on the cloud"). Gmail will connect to that address online and pull it into the signature each time you send an email.

    If the image you want to use exists only on your computer's hard drive, you can upload it to your Facebook photos, or to an image site such as Flickr. After you upload it, right-click it (Ctrl-click on a Mac, and), then choose Copy Image URL (or it might say copy link address) from the menu that appears.

    c. *Paste the URL in the Image dialog box as shown in Figure 1-3.*

All images online have an address or URL. You can use any image on your Web site or any image hosted on Facebook or photo-hosting sites such as Flickr.

8. **Paste the image URL you copied in Step 5 into the Image URL field and then click OK.**

A preview of the image will now be there to check.

Using other people's images could be an infringement of copyright. Use only those images for which you have permission to use.

9. **Click the Save Changes button on the bottom of the Page.**

Figure 1-3:
Add the image URL, and it will load automatically in each e-mail you send.

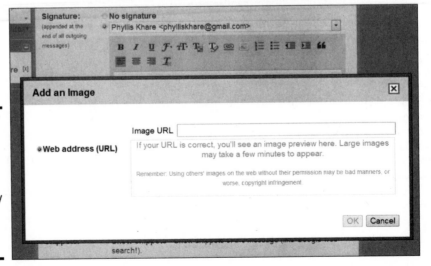

Figure 1-4 shows a full signature example, including an image, created with Gmail.

You can add some simple text to your signature with the link spelled out (not hyperlinked), such as:

> You might Like Us on Facebook, too.
>
> `http://facebook.com/yourcompanyname`
>
> Do you hang out on Facebook? Come say Hi at `http://facebook. com/yourcompanyname`

TIP

You can also use an Internet browser extension or application to create a dynamic signature that contains a Facebook icon linked to your Page. The best one we've found that works on all major browsers is WiseStamp. When you go to `www.wisestamp.com`, the site figures out which browser you're using and shows you the correct download link. Then just follow the instructions provided.

By the way, "dynamic" means if you include a link to your blog, for example, every time you publish a new blog post, the name of the post automatically appears in your signature hyperlinked back to your blog!

Figure 1-4: Signatures with added links and an image to your Facebook Page.

Figure 1-5 shows an example of a WiseStamp signature. When your e-mail recipients click the Facebook icon, they go straight to your Facebook Page.

Figure 1-5:
Use
WiseStamp
to create a
memorable
signature.

Including your new Facebook address on hard-copy mailings

Some businesses dedicate a hard-copy mailing to their customers telling them about their new Facebook Page. You can include the announcement in a regular mailing or create a special one, but if your customers *read* what you send them, you need to make the announcement in that medium.

Many companies are now including on all their hard copy a small social connection area that shows their online connections, including their Web site address, YouTube channel, Twitter username, LinkedIn Company Page address, and more. Here is a great example from a hard-copy magazine, as shown in Figure 1-6.

Figure 1-6:
The whole
social media
connection
bar in a
magazine.

Updating your letterhead and stationery

You need to have your vanity URL before you update your letterhead. As we discuss earlier in this chapter, you need 25 people to Like your Page to be eligible to get one. Then you can add an elegant URL, like `www.facebook.com/SociallyCongruent`, to your stationery, as shown in Figure 1-7.

Figure 1-7:
A Facebook
address can
be added
to any
letterhead
design.

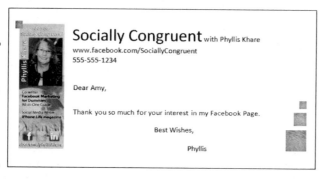

Including a Facebook icon on your Web Page

Web Pages now commonly feature a Facebook icon. In fact, a Web site without one seems to be missing something. You eventually want to integrate everything Facebook has to offer with your Web site. See Book VII (on advanced marketing) for everything Facebook offers. For now, a simple first step is to connect your Web site to Facebook.

**Book IV
Chapter 1**

**Building Visibility
for Your Page**

Putting a linked Facebook icon on your Web site or blog is very easy. All you need is your Facebook Page URL address and an icon image. You can even do this before you've secured your vanity URL. You can have a graphic designer create an icon image for you or use an existing one, as shown in Figure 1-8.

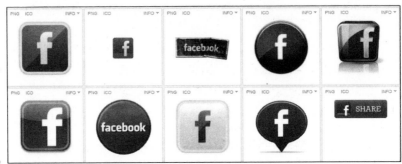

Figure 1-8: Standard Facebook icon images you can use.

A great source of Facebook icon images is IconFinder, www.iconfinder.com. Enter **Facebook** in the search bar, and then select the icon you prefer. Note the drop-down box that gives you three options: No License Filtering, Allowed for Commercial Use, and Allowed for Commercial Use — no link required. I suggest option number 3, as it's the simplest to use.

After you select the appropriate category, find an icon that blends well with your Web site. Select it and then select the size you need. If you don't know what size you need, download all the sizes and save them to your computer. You need to then send these images to your Webmaster to place on your Web site or do it yourself.

If you're using a WordPress, Joomla!, or Drupal template for your Web site, you might find that Facebook icons are built in to the template offerings, and all you need to do is put in your Page address to activate the icon on your Web site. Many plug-ins for those systems allow you to add a Facebook icon and link it to your Page. You need to explore your Web site creation system and see whether this feature is available.

If you're using an HTML system to create your Web site, you can create your own linked image and then upload the new Page to your server. If that last sentence made no sense to you, you need to talk to your Webmaster or Web site designer.

Linking to your Page from your Facebook personal Profile

If your Page is a service that you offer, go back to your personal Facebook Profile and add a little bit to your Info tab about your new Page's location. If your business is something you want to keep completely separate from your personal Profile on Facebook, you can skip these steps. Minibook II, Chapter 2 covers how to edit your Info tab.

1. **Click your name next to your picture on your Facebook personal Profile.**

You are now on your Wall.

2. **Find the Info link under your picture and click it.**

3. **Click the Edit Profile button on the right side of the Page and add text to the About Me section.**

You can use the About Me section to add your new Page address and an invitation to join you there, as shown in Figure 1-9.

4. **Click the Save Changes button.**

Here's an example, from a personal Profile directing people to a Business Page.

Figure 1-9: This is where to add your business Page location on your personal Profile.

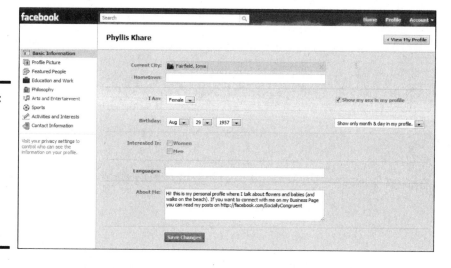

Another creative idea is to put your business Page URL on your personal Profile image. You have to do a little photo-editing, but the result will help move people over to your Page. See Figure 1-10.

Figure 1-10: This is how you can modify your personal image to help show people where your business Page is located.

Inviting your other social networks to visit your Page

Maybe you've been active on Twitter or various niche social media sites, and now you want to invite the people you've met there to visit your Page. You can get people to click the link to check you out, but you want them to Like you, too.

If you follow the suggestions in Book III Chapter 2, you have a nice Welcome Landing Page with interesting content. People will stay and Like your Page if they feel a connection with you and your business.

A good way to develop a flow to your Page, so that people are asking questions or commenting on your posts, is by inviting your most engaged members of your other social networks.

Here are some examples of how you can connect your Facebook Page with other social media:

✦ **Twitter:** Add your Facebook Page link to any auto Direct Messages you already have going out to new followers.

✦ **LinkedIn:** Add your Facebook link to any message you send and make sure that it's listed on your Profile.

✦ **YouTube:** Add your link to any YouTube channel in the info section, and to the first line of each video's information section. You can also use the Linked Tube service (www.linkedtube.com) to create a clickable link right on the video itself.

Every social media system has a place to add links; be sure to go to each one you already use and add your new Facebook Page address.

After you add the link to your Page on your other networks, you can start to invite people to your Page through your regular posts and updates. One of the attractive things about a Facebook Page, for example, is that you can have a longer conversation than the 140-character limit in Twitter, so your Twitter followers might enjoy a longer conversation with you on Facebook.

On a regular basis, create a post that links back to your Page on all your other social networks. You can also post the direct links to any photo or album you've created. See the upcoming section, "Sharing your albums and photos." This is a nice way to invite people to see your Page and hopefully stick around and Like it.

Growing your Page manually or buying automatic Fans

The debate between growing your Page manually and buying automatic Fans is a controversial subject. As much as we'd like to take the middle ground on this, we recommend that you grow your Page manually, organically. It's always better to have people on your Page who are real, engaged Fans of your product or service rather than paying companies through any "get fans fast!" services you hear about or see online.

Think creatively about contests, games, applications, and other forms of Page-building rather than buying your way into Facebook fame. See Books V–VIII for those strategies.

Sharing Your Page with Your Friends on Facebook

You have two major ways at your disposal when it comes to inviting your personal Friends to Like your Page:

✦ As an admin of your Page, you can suggest your Page to your personal Friends.

✦ You and everyone else can Share the Page. Sharing a Page will put the invitation on the sharee's personal Profile Wall.

If you don't want any of your personal Friends to be invited to be connected to this Page, you can skip suggesting and sharing altogether.

Still, you might want to go through the steps to Share your Page because these steps are the very same thing you will want your supporters to duplicate to show your Page to their Friends. Understanding how sharing works will allow you to craft the best message to solicit their help in expanding your reach.

There are countless other ways to bring people, other than your Facebook Friends, to your Page, but these two ways are built in to Facebook's own system and can be used effectively to create a momentum toward an engaged community for your business. After you have a few friendly faces who have Liked your Page, you can start to use some of the advanced marketing ideas in Books V–VIII.

Suggesting your Page

Facebook recently changed the process to suggest a Page to Friends. Now only the admins of a Page can use the "Suggest to Friends" feature. Everyone else will need to use the "Share" feature.

As an admin, to invite your personal Friends to your business Page, go to your Page and click the Suggest to Friends link (on the right side), as shown in Figure 1-11.

Figure 1-11: The Suggest to Friends link.

In the dialog box that appears, you have two ways to find and select names of Friends:

✦ Start to type of name of someone to select certain people.

✦ Click a person's Profile image to select that person.

The total number selected shows up on the top right of the box.

If a person's Profile picture is grayed out, they have already been invited to Like the Page, as shown in Figure 1-12.

You know your friends better than anyone. Don't over-do the inviting because getting an invitation week after week for the same Page, either through Suggesting or Sharing or posting, can be really irritating. To find other ways to attracting your friends to your Page, keep reading this book!

If you've set up your own personal Friends Lists in your personal account, you can select your Friends by opening the Filter Friends drop-down list and selecting the list you want to invite. If you take the time to create personal Friend lists, you can really use them in your marketing efforts on Facebook.

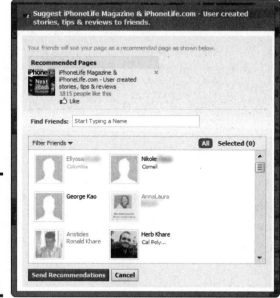

Figure 1-12:
This is how people look after they have been invited to Like a Page.

Friends Lists are created in your personal Profile. You can't create any Business Page Lists. One of the times these personal lists are important for your Page, is when you're asking your Friends to Like your Page by using the Share or Suggest links.

When you're done selecting your Friends, click the Send Recommendation button. The top of the Suggest box shows what your Friends will see — a small image, name of the Page, how many people currently have Liked it, and the "Thumbs Up" icon to Like the Page (see Figure 1-13).

Currently, you don't get a chance to add a personal message to the Suggest to Friends type of invitation.

Figure 1-13: Short and to the point: a Facebook Page recommendation.

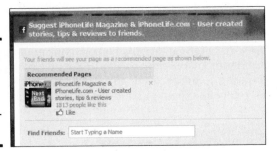

Your Friends can either ignore the message or click the link that takes them to your Page and click the Like button. They will also get a message that goes to their Messages section in their account.

Sharing your Page

The other main way of inviting your Friends to your new Page is by using the Share link at the bottom of your Page, as shown in Figure 1-14. When you click this link, an invitation will post to your personal account Wall, and your Friends will have the opportunity to see it in their News Feed.

Depending on what Feed your Friends use (Top News or Most Recent), they may or may not see your invitation sent this way; see Book III, Chapter 1. You should post an invitation to your Friends in many different ways — on and off Facebook — to have them connect to your new Page.

Clicking the Share button initiates something very important: It pulls up a box that auto-fills with some of the information on your Page's Info link. The items on this link are defined by the type of Business Category you choose, as discussed in Book II, Chapter 1. If you've filled in your Info link fields fully, you will see a description of your business, including your Page image, all ready to send.

Figure 1-14:
Invite
Friends via
the Share
link.

You do not — we repeat — *do not get to directly edit the text in this box*. You *can* go to your Info link and edit the information there, and then start over with the Share link.

However, you do get to add a comment in the status box above the invitation. After you craft the new invitation status box text, you can decide to whom you will send it.

At the top of the box, as you can see in Figure 1-15, you will see a drop down where you can select one of the following: On your own Wall; On a friend's Wall; In a Group; In a private message. Select where you want it to go, write something in the message field, and click Share Page.

You can also change who can see it by clicking the lock icon and deciding whether Everyone, Friends of Friends, or Friends Only (which might be the default) can see it. You can also select Customize and then set who can and who can't see this invitation.

The next few figures show a few examples of what the Share invitation will look like, depending on which business category you choose.

In the first example, the company is a magazine with the category of Product/Service. It populates the invitation only with the Company Overview text from the Info link, as shown in Figure 1-16.

Figure 1-15:
Set who
gets to
see your
message.

Figure 1-16:
Only part
of the
Info link is
used in the
invitation.

In the second example, the category is Public Figure, which populates the
invitation only with the Personal Information from the Info link, as shown in
Figure 1-17. Look how much information can be sent!

Figure 1-17:
Only the
Personal
Information
field is used
here.

Figure 1-18 shows what gets pulled up for a Page with the category of
Musician/Band. It populates the invitation only with the Biography part of
the Info Tab.

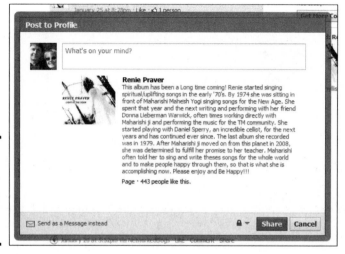

Figure 1-18:
The
Biography
section is all
that is used
here.

In the next example, after selecting TV Show, it populates the invitation only with the Plot Outline text of the Info link, as shown in Figure 1-19.

The people who end up Sharing your Page this way won't have control over the information that populates the invitation box, so you can see why it's important to have the right category and to fill in the Info section fully.

Sending requests to promote your Page

It's perfectly okay to privately message some of your closest friends and business partners to ask them to Share your Page with their Friends on Facebook. You can call them on the phone (imagine that!), e-mail them with your new Facebook address link, hand-write an invitation over drinks (it's been done), or use the built-in instant messaging (Chat) system that Facebook offers. If your Friends like using the Chat system, you can have a nice little conversation with them and talk about your new Page.

You can see which Friends are online by clicking the Chat menu at the bottom right of any Facebook Page. A green dot will appear next to a Friend who is online and available to chat, and a moon will appear next to a Friend who is idle. On Profiles and anywhere else on the site, clicking a chat icon will start a conversation with that person.

To send a Chat message, simply type your message and then press Enter/Return.

Figure 1-19:
The plot outline is all that populates this invitation.

Finding and thanking your key enthusiasts

Acknowledging the people who spread the word about your Page is always a good idea. You can offer an incentive or reward for their efforts. The trick is figuring out who is helping you out! Currently, the only way is to ask. So take the bull by the horns and pop the question in the form of a Page update, as in, "Who has shared this Page today?," and offer them discount coupons or codes.

We've seen many creative uses of thanking enthusiastic supporters. The folks behind one Page we know offer free live training to anyone that evening if they can get their Like count up over a certain number. For example, if they can add 50 new Likers to their Page by 5 p.m., everyone is invited to a free training on how to use iFrames to create a video landing tab! Using this strategy has been very effective for this business.

Adding Photos to Attract People to Your Page

No matter whether you have a physical product or are in a service industry, photos sell and attract. There are many ways to use photos to invite people to your Page and to keep them actively engaged.

Collect many high-quality photos of your product, or action shots of your service, or anything that relates to your Page's focus. Continue to collect these photos and make sure to post them on a regular basis. About 2.5 billion photos are uploaded to Facebook every month, and it continues to be one of the best ways to market no matter what social media platform you're on.

Read the information in this section to develop a marketing strategy with photos in Facebook.

Creating a strategy with photo albums

Consider your business before you click the uploading photos link, though. Think about what would be interesting to people who already know you, and what would be interesting to those who have never heard of you. Use the photo system in Facebook to its fullest, keeping in mind best practices for your niche or industry.

Take a moment and think of some really interesting Photo Album names that would promote your business. You will always have the Album called Profile Pictures, which will always contain all the photos you use for your Profile image, but every other album you create can be named by you.

For example, if you're selling a physical product, create an album called Happy Customers and upload shots of happy customers using your product. Create an album called Found in Chicago for photos of your product on the shelves of a store in Chicago. You could use this idea in a contest; see more in Book VI on making Facebook come alive with events and contests.

If you're selling a service, create an album called Here I Am, *Doing It* (replace *Doing It* with your service), and upload photos of your staff doing their work, or you in a session of your service. How about an album called Award-Winning with photos of your awards and achievements?

Your business might use humor in attracting a strong group of Fans — we mean, Likers. If you think that putting up a picture of your dog and labeling him the Acting CEO works for your customer base, then go ahead and have fun with it! The people who really like your Page will most likely Share these photos, so make them relevant to your business. They can be funny — and goodness knows we all could use a laugh.

Uploading photos to your Facebook Page

Uploading photos to your Facebook Page is the same process as uploading to your personal Profile, except you start from your Page. Facebook recently re-designed Pages to be more like a personal Profile, with a photos bar at the top of the Page.

This photo bar is discussed in detail in minibook II, Chapter 3.

Uploading photos to Facebook is a snap. Here's how:

1. **Log into your personal Facebook account and go to your Page.**

2. **Click the Photos link on the left side of your Page.**

3. **In the new Page that appears, click the +Upload Photo button on the right side of the Page.**

   Yet another new Page appears.

4. **In the new Page that appears, click the Select Photos button, and then use the dialog box that appears to browse your computer for the photos you want to upload.**

5. **Select the photos you want to add to your album by using Ctrl+click.**

6. **While your photos upload, fill in a name for your album (remembering the strategies we described in the preceding section), the location, and the Quality, and whether the photos are Standard or High definition).**

7. **After the photos are loaded, click the Create Album button.**

8. **In the (yet newer) Page that appears, add a description to all the images you uploaded, as shown in Figure 1-20.**

This is a very important step because this text stays with the photo no matter where it's viewed. Try to incorporate your full Web site address, or full Facebook Page address. These addresses will be hyperlinked and clickable.

Include the `http://` part, your product name, or contact info in the caption field to make it clickable.

9. **Beneath the photo that you want to make your album cover, select the This is the album cover checkbox.**

Figure 1-20 shows the This is the album cover checkbox.

10. **Click Save Changes.**

You can publish the album right now or wait. If you're uploading and creating albums at midnight, you might want to wait and publish them later the next day or at a strategic time. We show you how to publish in the next section.

Figure 1-20: Adding a description is an important step.

Create photos using Photoshop or other photo-editing software to create beautifully design photos that will become your album covers. Upload these and select them as the cover, and you create something very clear and easy to select when viewing and sharing, as shown in Figure 1-21.

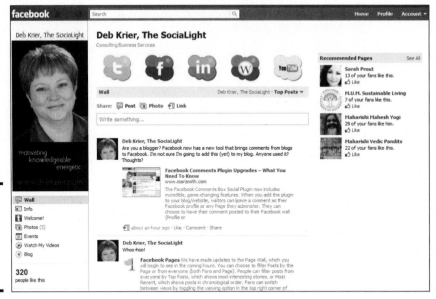

Figure 1-21: Imaginative examples for album cover images.

Sharing your albums and photos

The marketing strategy behind sharing your albums and photos is something you need to sit down and design. Maybe every Friday, you send out a new album; or every Tuesday, you send out a Product spotting in another city.

If you didn't publish your album when you uploaded the photos (see the preceding section), do this now for it to show up on the Page's Wall.

1. **Go to your Page and select the Photos link.**

2. **Select the album you haven't published yet.**

You'll see all your albums in a grid. Select the one you want to publish now.

3. **Click the Edit Album Info link on the left side of the Page.**

4. **Click Edit Photos.**

The Publishing options appear.

5. **Click Publish Now.**

This posts the album to your Page's Wall, and everyone who has Liked your Page will have the opportunity to see it in their News Stream.

You can also re-share this album or individual pictures, after publishing, from two places:

✦ Your Wall

✦ The Album itself

If you see your album or photo on the Page Wall, you can click the Share link under the photo, as shown in Figure 1-22.

Figure 1-22:
You can click the Share link under the photo on your Wall.

Sharing photos and albums these two ways will send the images only to your personal Friends. You can put in a call to action, asking people to share the album with their Friends in the Message field when you share.

The second way is to follow these steps:

1. **Go to your Page and select the Photos tab.**

2. **Select the album you want to share.**

3. **Click the Share This Album link in the bottom-left corner of the Page.**

You can then choose Send as a Facebook Message, or Post to Profile instead, as shown in Figure 1-23. The link to this Photo album will go to their Messages section. You can also send the album to folks outside the Facebook platform by using an e-mail address, but they will need to join Facebook to see it.

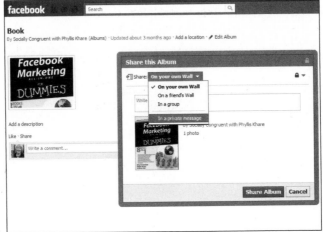

Sharing with people other than your personal Friends on Facebook

You can send any photo or album directly to anyone outside your personal Facebook Friends by following the steps in the preceding section, except this time, select Send as Message Instead and put in an e-mail address rather than a Facebook name.

Facebook will send an e-mail with a link to the photo. *Note:* If the person you send it to is on Facebook, he'll be able to view it. If he doesn't have a Facebook account, the link will take him to a Page with the message that he can't view the photo unless he joins Facebook.

You also have a direct URL to each album that you can send to anyone, and they will be able to view it. Or you can post anywhere online. To find this direct URL

1. **Go to your Page and select the Photos link.**

2. **Select the album that you want to share.**

3. **Click the Edit Photos link.**

   At the bottom of this album editing Page, you'll see the direct link. It will look something like Figure 1-24.

4. **Copy the link and send it out in an email.**

If the person you sent the URL to doesn't have a Facebook account, he will be able to view the album, and the invitation to join Facebook will be there, too.

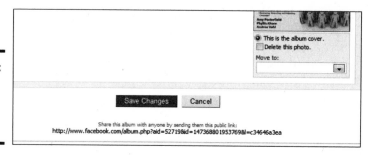

Figure 1-24: The URL for a direct link to the album.

Chapter 2: Engaging and Retaining Your Community

In This Chapter

✔ **Engaging people to keep them coming back to your Page**

✔ **Understanding and making the most of different News Feeds**

✔ **Learning the art of responding to comments**

✔ **Banning and removing people and comments as a last resort**

*E*ngagement is the Holy Grail for Facebook Pages. To engage your target audience, you need to be clear about your purpose and branding, and let your own personality (or your brand's) shine through. Best practices dictate that you can post almost anything to your Page as long as you connect it to your particular focus and adhere to the express purpose of having conversations with current and potential customers.

For example, if your Page is about sustainability practices, you might post a personal picture of your children adding to the compost bin or chasing the chickens running around in your yard. In contrast, posting a video on your sustainability Page of your favorite American Idol is not in line with that particular focus (unless, of course, he raises chickens and sings about them in the video).

In Book II, Chapter 3, we explain how to use the regular posting features, status updates, video posts, audio, events, and other aspects of posting. In this chapter, we explore how to use those features to engage your community even further.

Specifically, we tell you how to use questions, polls, and surveys to create conversations on your Page. We also explain why you need to understand Facebook's EdgeRank (how it effects who sees what on your Page) and how to create posts to your viewing advantage.

We explain the difference between what your visitors see in your Top Posts and Most Recent feed, and how that all ties into admin settings for your Wall. And finally, we show you how to remove unpleasant guests from your Page.

Creating Posts and Updates That Engage Your Readers

Some types of posts resonate with your audience better than others. In the beginning, you might want to try a variety to see which ones work the best. Once you discover the formats that your audience responds to most favorably, you can post in those formats on a regular schedule so that people expect and even look forward to your posts. Doing so sets the stage for the conversations to start.

For example, if every Friday you post a coupon code, a clue to a treasure hunt contest, or a free training ticket, people will start to remember and look for your posts on those days.

More than three million businesses, brands, and celebrities have created Facebook Pages, but the great majority of them are still trying to figure out how to attract an audience, authentically engage the people who might Like them, and develop increased revenue. Many brands, on the other hand, have well over one million Likers and have figured out the best ways to engage their particular base so that a viral effect starts and they recruit even more people to their brand or cause. How do they do it? They use several strategies, detailed in the following sections, that you can try.

Asking questions

There are two different types of questions we need to discuss here. One is a regular question that you ask in a regular status update; the other uses Facebook's Question tool. We discuss exactly how to create a Facebook Question in Book III, Chapter 1, but in general, asking questions might be a great way to engage your audience.

Asking questions or inviting your audience's opinion on something instantly creates a personal connection. People like to tell you their opinion on subjects that are dear to them. Your most enthusiastic Likers have an opinion about your brand, your marketing message, or your community involvement (or lack of it). Asking them to express those opinions can open the door to lots of conversation and involvement.

But which system do you use to ask the question? If you want the question to find its way into the News Feed of the people who have Liked your Page, we suggest using a simple question as a regular post. If you want the question to find its way outside your Page connections, use the Facebook Question tool in the status box (as we describe in Book III, Chapter 1).

Some companies are finding that combining questions with video can create an even stronger engagement than using just one or the other. In a great article, "4 Easy Ways to Engage your Facebook Fans," posted on one of the best resources for social media marketing, Mashable.com (`http://mashable.com/2010/03/19/facebook-fan-engagement`), you can find many detailed examples on techniques to engage an audience, one of which is to include questions when you post a video. One company found they received 100 times more media impressions (people sharing the videos) when people also responded to a question about the video.

Here are some engaging ways to ask a question:

✦ Find topical news stories that connect to your business and ask what people think about it. Post the question with the news video for a bigger response.

✦ Pose a question you get from your potential customers and ask your enthusiasts how they would answer it.

✦ Ask a simple question, such as, "Who wants a coupon?"

✦ Use "fill-in-the-blank" questions. For example, the Life is Good Facebook Page `www.facebook.com/Lifeisgood` asked the question: "A positive life lesson I'd share is _____." There were over 1300 comments and over 500 Likes in just a few days!

The prospect of receiving discounts is always one of the top two reasons for consumers to "Like" a brand on Facebook. So asking the question, "Who wants a coupon?" usually gets a good response. Creating coupons for your Page is discussed in Book VI, Chapter 2.

Polling your audience

You may find that polling your audience creates a higher level of engagement with your Page than many other types of strategies do. By taking a poll, you may also discover audience preferences that will direct your promotions and communications in a different direction than you would have thought to go. Your customers and potential customers are the ones you need to serve, and using polls helps gather insight into what they really want.

Here are a few tips to create a simple poll:

✦ Make them short.

✦ Make each question simple and direct.

✦ Make sure to post the results quickly so that people can see that their opinions have registered.

✦ Draw some conclusions, post them, and ask the responders whether you drew the right ones — an excellent way to re-engage them in conversation.

You can ask several kinds of questions. You can

✦ Pose Yes/No questions to your audience.

✦ Present your audience with multiple-choice questions.

✦ Ask your audience to rank a list of items.

Polldaddy (http://polldaddy.com) offers a good app that you can use to create a simple poll to place on your Page. Note that you can't put the Poll itself on your Page Wall. You can refer to the link it's on and point people there with a regular post, or send out an Update. You can also make this the landing page for your new visitors. We talk about how to adjust those settings in Book II, Chapter 3.

Promoting your fans and enthusiasts

Back when Facebook used the "Fan" and "Fan Page" vocabulary, it was a bit easier to write about the people who connected to your Page. Now you have to make "Liker" sound as though it's a normal thing to say. For the purpose of this section, we're revisiting the use of the word "Fan" because it more aptly describes the person who, on his or her own, promotes and shares your content with a wider audience. Such a person Likes you — she really Likes you!

Nothing in marketing is more powerful than word-of-mouth promotion. We all know that. How do you find and encourage people to open their mouths and speak favorably on your behalf? First, acknowledge *them*. You know how it feels when you have been acknowledged for something you've done. You can give that feeling to someone else on your Page in a variety of ways:

✦ Thank a random Fan by giving him something of value. Make this a regular feature of your Page.

✦ Ask your Fans if they've volunteered for any charities, or donated toward one. Then challenge your Fans to match their goodwill, or write a blog post about the charity and mention your fan by name.

✦ Publicly thank the people by name who are sharing your posts with others.

✦ Have your Page be a place for Fans to share what they do, by dedicating a day to those posts. For example, if your Page is dedicated to sustainability, be a forum for Fans to share their best resources. Have a "Resource Wednesday," or a "Sharing Saturday," or whatever suits your Page.

Many Pages use a "Fan Page Friday" concept that is similar to "Follow Friday" on Twitter. Figure 2-1 shows how that looks on Grandma Mary's Page (www.facebook.com/GrandmaMaryShow).

Figure 2-1:
Fan Page
Friday is a
time-tested
strategy for
developing
your Page.

Tagging key players in updates

How do people know you've thanked them on your Page? If they happen
to see your status update come through their News Feed, they'll see their
name. But what if they don't catch your update in the News Feed? If you Tag
them by using the "@" system, they see the post on their Wall and get a notification that they have been Tagged in a post by you. This works for your
Friends and Pages you Like.

1. **Type the @ symbol in the Status Update box on your Page and then
    start typing the name of the friend or Page you want to Tag (making
    sure not to put a space between the @ and the name you type; see how
    "@Amy" appears in Figure 2-2).**

    A list of all your friends and Pages with that name appears.

2. **Click the correct name or Page name.**

    The name you click appears in the status update box, hyperlinked to
    that person's personal account or Page.

3. **Finish crafting the message.**

4. **Click Share.**

    The person or Page sees your message on his or her Wall and notifications.

**Book IV
Chapter 2**

**Engaging and
Retaining Your
Community**

You can Tag only people you are Friends with via your personal Profile and you can Tag only Pages that you have Liked as your Page (see Book II, Chapter 3 for a complete explanation of the different types of Profiles you have as a Page admin). Tagging can be a particular challenge if you have a very large group of people who Like your Page, but you are not personally connected to Tagged people on your personal Facebook account.

Figure 2-2:
Using the @ symbol to put a hyperlinked name in the status update box.

Using public posts to thank people

Key players are your cheerleaders, enthusiasts, and walking advertising system. On Facebook, these key players can influence hundreds, even thousands, of people with their comments. Most of us take our friends' recommendations more seriously than those of strangers that we may have found searching online. After you establish who *your* key players are, thank them and encourage them to interact even more.

Through your Insights dashboard, you might find that women 24 to 34 years old comprise your highest viewing demographic. Thank the members of that age group, too, by providing something that is valuable to them generally. For example, create a post that provides a link to something they might value, such as discount codes for diapers, as a way to thank them for being part of your Page.

If you find through your Insights dashboard that a huge number of people from California visit your Page, say hi to them and thank them. For example, you could say, "Hi to all the people in California who have liked this Page!

Post a picture of you outside your favorite hiking trail with our Brand Z hiking shoes!"

You can find a textbook case of using questions, polls, and acknowledgement on the NFL Page (`http://facebook.com/NFL`). Just scroll through the posts to see the mix of video, polls, questions, discounts, and giveaways. But most important, note the number of people who Liked the post; also note the number of comments generated by that post. You can see many of these things in Figure 2-3.

Figure 2-3: A variety of posts engage the fans of the NFL Page.

Creating incentives for repeat visits

The majority of the 600 million people on Facebook go through a process that may look a little like this: They log in and see the Top News Feed (the one that Facebook aggregates for them, which might not include your Page posts). Next, they scan through the top 15 or so posts and maybe click through or comment on a few posts. They try to remember where Facebook hid the Friend's birthday list, and they generally surf around. They don't look at the ads on the side of the Page (that you spent money for), and they quickly go to their favorite game, look at the clock, and realize the enormous amount of time that just got sucked out of their lives!

Another scenario for a smaller percentage of people looks like this: They log in, switch over to view the Most Recent News Feed, and scan through several pages of the stream commenting, liking, and sharing posts with their friends. They notice the ads on the side and think, "How did I get targeted for this one?"

Another scenario that we've found for a younger demographic (20–35 year olds) looks like this: They don't need to log in because they never log out; they check Facebook via their cell phone pretty much all day. They select Status Updates and that's all they view — period.

Currently, more than 150 million active Facebook users access Facebook through their mobile phones (and devices). According to Facebook, these people are twice as active on Facebook as nonmobile users are! Make sure that you view your Facebook Page through your phone so that you can see what they see. View it with the direct browser link at `http://touch.facebook.com` and through iPhone and Android applications.

So, looking at these three scenarios, how do you get people to not only view your Page after they initially Like it but also return regularly? Do they need to return to your Page? Can you send everything you want them to see in a post? These are questions you need to ask about your business.

Human nature is often predictable. We like incentives. According to research, and especially research on Facebook, we like discounts, coupons, competition, acknowledgement, and personal conversation.

Take the time to measure and note your audience demographics. Note whether your readers prefer coupons or contests. (If you don't know, ask them!) Pay attention to what kinds of status updates they respond to and then do more of what's working. . Think "incentive" all the time. Find things that activates those human qualities that foster engagement.

Here's a list of actions to try based on all the information so far in this chapter:

+ **Ask questions:** Use both types (see "Asking questions," earlier in this chapter) to see which works best for you. Encourage conversation by responding to all questions with an answer and another question!

+ **Give things away:** Give coupons, discount codes, e-books, and other stuff related to your business. Make it a regular activity to encourage return visits.

+ **Acknowledge people:** Reward your community through activities such as Fan Page Friday, Fan Friday, charity support, random acts of thanking.

+ **Use Facebook-approved contests:** We cover contests in detail in Book VI.

✦ **Respond quickly:** People are impressed when an actual human responds to a customer question or comment.

✦ **Share the best:** Share your best videos, best tutorials, best resources, best quotations — whatever is appropriate for your business to share.

You know what motivates *you* to seek something out. Analyzing your own behavior can lead to insights about what may work on your Facebook business Page.

Developing a posting schedule

One aspect of engaging readers is how often you post. Good social media consultants tell you to post at the rate your audience expects.

Your audience's expectations for your rate of posting depend on what you post. If you post breaking news in your field, for example, your audience depends on you to disseminate information as it becomes available. This can make for frequent posting.

Here are some examples to show how other Pages handle frequency of posting:

✦ Mari Smith, a well-known social media speaker, directly posts 5 to 10 times a day with up to 15 or more comments on other Wall posts on her Page (www.facebook.com/marismith).

✦ iPhone Life magazine (www.facebook.com/iphonelifemagazine), an online and hard-copy magazine for iPhone enthusiasts, posts three to eight times a day using a Facebook app called NetworkedBlogs (described in Book III, Chapter 3) and once or twice more manually a day.

✦ GeekBeatTV (www.facebook.com/geekbeattv), a channel from the well-known Internet TV Station Revision3, posts once or twice a day with lots of comments.

✦ NPR (www.facebook.com/NPR) posts as often as once an hour.

Here are some examples of how often small businesses with a local reach post:

✦ Noah's Ark Animal Foundation (www.facebook.com/NoahsArkIowa), a no-kill shelter in Fairfield, Iowa, whose mission is to rescue, protect, and find loving homes for stray and neglected dogs and cats, posts once a day and has a wonderful adoption strategy using beautiful photos and video of their dogs and cats. They sponsor Meow Mondays, Woof Wednesdays, and Foster Fridays, and in between they post news about their dog park project.

✦ Finnywicks (www.facebook.com/Finnywicks), a local toy store, again in Fairfield, Iowa, only posts once a week and highlights a new toy that has just arrived.

Large and small businesses use a variety of posting schedules and strategies. Figure out what is unique about your business, what your fans want to see, and how often they want to see it. Put that all together on your Page.

Targeting Your Updates to Facebook's Different Feed Streams

To know how to send out your posts, you need to understand how the two News Feeds (Top News and Most Recent) are populated and seen on a personal Facebook account. The Top News feed aggregates the most interesting content (from Pages and Friends) based on a Facebook algorithm called *EdgeRank,* and the Most Recent feed shows you the actions and posts (most of) your friends and Pages you have Liked are making in real-time. Facebook's own research says that 95 percent of users only view the Top News feed. In our own experience we can tell you that most people don't know they can toggle between Top News and Most Recent.

You can switch between Top News and Most Recent from your personal Facebook account. Simply click the appropriate link, as shown in Figure 2-4.

Figure 2-4:
Switch
between
Top Posts
and Most
Recent

You can also see a drop-down arrow for Most Recent where you can further filter what you see into only posts by Pages, only posts with links, only posts with photos, only status updates, and only Questions.

What does this mean for your Page? First and foremost, you need to understand what EdgeRank is so that you can deliver your updates in the best way for your Likers to (potentially) see them.

Understanding EdgeRank

You want more than anything for your Page to have high visibility and show up in a person'a Top News feed. A Page with *high interaction* gets better EdgeRank and ends up in the Top News Feed, which means more people will see your posts. The formula Facebook uses to determine the visibility of a Page is called *EdgeRank,* which is based on three factors:

✦ **Affinity:** How often two people interact on Facebook. Affinity scores increase the more you (and your Page) and an individual exchange messages, Wall posts, comments, and links. The more often a person Likes your Page posts, the better the affinity between your Page and the individual, and the more likely your Page posts will show up in the person's Top News Feed.

✦ **Weight:** How many comments and likes on a post. Weight value increases the more comments, likes and other variables it has based on what Facebook is weighting at the moment (Places, video, and photos seem to have the most weight).

✦ **Decay:** How old the post is. Decay is automatically weakening the EdgeRank as it grows older in the timeline — as time increases, value decreases.

Like and make a comment for each post made on your Page to engage conversation. You can comment as yourself (if you have selected that option) or as the Page. Commenting as both is good unless it seems odd to do so. Doing this one action (commenting) will help increase the Weight value.

If one of your Likers clicks the Share link for one of your posts, and Likes it, too, the shared post will have a better chance at showing up in their Friends' (those with the highest affinity scores with the sharer) Top News feeds. Whew — did you get that? And that's just the tip of what this algorithm is all about.

We don't explain how EdgeRank is formulated (because it's fairly complicated), but we can explain a few strategies to help boost your Page's score. You can also read this very good article on EdgeRank and strategies to maximize your Page's visibility www.socialmediaexaminer.com/6-tips-to-increase-your-facebook-edgerank-and-exposure/

EdgeRank optimization strategies

✦ Encourage people to Like your posts. Ask them directly — as in "Like this post to show your support for. . ."

✦ If you have a Facebook Places Page, consider merging it with your regular Facebook business Page because doing so increases the weight, or relevance, of what is posted. Before you do that, please see Book II, Chapter 1.

**Book IV
Chapter 2**

Engaging and
Retaining Your
Community

✦ Be sure to post photos, videos, and use Facebook Questions on a regular basis, as they have more weight in the formula. Even better is to have your Likers post their photos.

✦ Post when your audience will see the posts. Are they looking at Facebook daily, or only on the weekend? Post when they are online and looking (find out how in Book IX).

✦ Ask your closest friends and key players to make comments on your Page as much as possible, and return the favor, as this starts the conversation rolling and helps shy people feel safer about commenting.

Following these easy strategies will help boost your EdgeRank and help deposit your posts in your Likers Top News Feeds. It may also be helpful to educate your friends and Likers how this system works. Many people have asked why they don't see posts from certain Pages and people — EdgeRank is the reason.

Creating and Participating in Conversations with Your Audience

Creating and participating in conversations is why we are on Facebook. Having an authentic conversation that involves and motivates people feels good and draws more people to the conversation. All the writers of this book have found new and wonderful people through personal conversations on Facebook.

When you can converse with someone about a customer service issue, or tell someone through a post how happy you are with that person's product and he or she responds to you quickly and treats you with respect, a bond is created that will bring you back to that business again and again. The business is counting on this reaction, and that's why so much attention is being given to the art of conversation in Facebook.

Revisiting the settings for posts to your Wall

When you created your Page (see Book II, Chapter 1), you made the decision to have the posts on the Wall be either just your own (Only Posts by Page) or open for posting by the public as well (All Posts). Most Pages have selected the All Posts options, as it encourages conversation, because anyone can post something, whereas the Only Posts by Page option only allows people to make a comment to something already posted by you (the Page).

Now that you've started to have conversations with people on your Page, you might want to modify those original settings. To review and possibly change those settings, follow these steps:

1. **Go to your Page and click Edit Page button on the right side of your Page.**

The left editing menu appears. Look for the Manage Permissions link.

2. **Look for Wall Tab Shows. Use the drop down to select either All Posts or Only Posts by Page. See Figure 2-5.**

3. **Click Save Changes.**

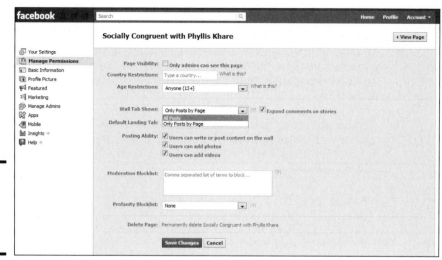

Figure 2-5:
Modifying
the Wall
view for
your Page.

Understanding the different views people see on your Page

It would be a wonderful thing if we all saw the same thing on a Facebook Page, but because of EdgeRank, we don't. What Joe sees on the Grandma Mary Facebook Page is different from what Jesse sees because of the different interaction (EdgeRank) they have developed with the Page and Grandma Mary. By understanding all the different views a person can have on *your* Page, you'll be more educated in how to generate and participate in conversation with them.

Someone can view your Page in two ways:

✦ In Top Posts order

✦ In Most Recent order

Facebook defaults the Page view to Top Posts, just as it does for Top News on a personal account. What one person sees in this view is different from the next person, based on EdgeRank. So, in other words, *every visitor to your Wall sees the order of posts differently.* This is the same whether you have the Wall Settings set to All Posts or Only Posts by Page.

The viewer needs to toggle the view to Most Recent to be able to view the posts in chronological order.

If you prefer that people see your posts in chronological order, you will need to educate them how to toggle the link at the top of the Wall feed, to Most Recent. Some Pages occasionally create a post to remind people how to toggle the view. Here's some suggested text to use for that post; "You can view the posts on this Page in chronological order by clicking the arrow next to Top Posts (in the right corner under the photo strip) and choosing Most Recent."

On top of all this, there are three check boxes in Manage Permissions that will determine what a visitor can post to your Page, and thereby change what other people see (videos and photos have more weight in the Top Posts view). They are:

✦ Users can write or post content on the Wall

✦ Users can add photos

✦ Users can add videos

We suggest selecting all three check boxes and monitoring what gets posted. If you find that your visitors are spamming your Page with videos or photos, you can go back to Manage Permissions and deselect the check boxes.

Being responsive and allowing conversation

If the Holy Grail of Facebook marketing is engagement, being open to all types of communication is the way to go. Regardless of whether you select the Wall view to be All Posts or Only Posts by Page as the default for posting, you still need to comment, ask questions, be responsive, and generally be available to the people who Like your Page.

Many businesses use this conversational quality in Facebook to nurture a community of people who they can run ideas by, or test new products with giveaways. By having a friendly, responsive Page, you can realize many opportunities for testing and expanding your business.

Also, as the admin of your Page, you get to direct the conversation but be open to the conversation going in a different direction than you anticipated. More than anything, the people on Facebook are looking for a community of like-minded people, and your Page can be that place for them.

Even if you have a controversial subject on your Page, you gain respect by behaving like an adult when you need to be responsive. Allow the conversation to flow, but also moderate, remove or report users and Pages if it gets out of hand.

Keeping the Conversation Civil

Most of the time, the conversation on Facebook is fun and enjoyable. Occasionally, however, someone will decide to post things on your Page that are not congruent with your business. In other words, they post spam or rude and derogatory statements.

We hope you never run into situations where you need to remove or ban someone from your Page, but you have a responsibility, as the admin of your Page, to keep the conversation going in a positive direction and in line with what your Page is all about.

Removing a Post

To remove a post from someone or from another Page (or even something you posted) from your Page, follow these steps.

1. **Put your cursor on the right side of the post and a hidden gear icon appears.**

2. **Click the gear and then click Remove post, as shown in Figure 2-6.**

   A message appears, asking "Are you sure you want to delete this post?"

3. **Click Remove Post.**

Once you remove a post, you can't undo the action, so be sure you really want to remove it before you click the Remove Post button. The person who created the post is not notified that the post was removed. The only way they know it was removed is if they come back to your Page and look for it and can't find it.

Note: Removing a post doesn't ban the poster from posting again.

Figure 2-6:
It's easy to remove a single post by clicking the gear next to the post itself.

Banning, blocking, and reporting a poster

Removing a post is one thing; banning, blocking, and reporting take it up a notch. Banning and blocking is for posts that are not appropriate for your Page, and Reporting is for posts that cross the line into spam, abuse, or violent words.

Be aware that anyone can create a new Facebook account and Like your Page and again post inappropriate comments. You need to be vigilant about keeping an eye out for the bad apples in the bunch.

There are two ways to ban a user or a Page from posting to your Page. If you have a few Likers, the first way is really easy to use. If you have millions of people who have Liked your Page, in the words of the Jedi, "May the Force be with you" — as Likers are not listed alphabetically when you use this method. If you have a great many followers, the second way is the only way to go.

Banning someone when you have a small following

If you only have a few Likers and want to ban someone, or another Page, from your Page, go to your Page and follow these steps:

1. **On the left column of your Page, click the People Like This link under the number of people who Like your Page.**

    A dialog box with a list of all the users who have Liked your Page appears. You'll need to find the name of the offending person.

2. **Select the *X* to the right of the user's name you want to ban.**

    This pulls up a dialog box, as shown in Figure 2-7.

3. **Check the box next to Ban Permanently.**

4. **Click Remove.**

This person or Page will not be able to re-Like your Page and post again unless they create a new account with a different name.

Figure 2-7: Banning someone permanently from your Page.

Banning when you have a large following

The other way to ban someone, or another Page, from your Page, especially if you have a large number of people who have Liked your Page, is to ban them directly from an offending post they have made.

1. **Put your cursor on the right side of the offending post and a hidden gear icon shows up.**

This pulls up a dialog box that has several links, one of which is Remove Post and Ban User (or Remove Post and Ban Page).

2. **Click Remove Post and Ban User (or Page).**

This opens a dialog box to Disallow Posts from this User (or Page).

3. **Click Remove Post and Ban User (or Page).**

This action permanently bans this person, or Page, from your Page and removes all content they have posted.

Reporting a post as abusive

Sometimes, a post crosses the line into what you consider abusive. Facebook describes abusive as spam or scam; contains hate speech or attacks an individual; violence or harmful behavior; or nudity, pornography, or sexually-explicit content.

If you need to report a post as abusive, follow the steps for deleting a single post (see the previous section, "Removing a post"), but this time, click the link called Report as Abuse and select the radio button that describes it (spam, scam, or whatever accurately describes the post), as shown in Figure 2-8. Then click the Submit button.

After you submit the post, Facebook investigates the report and decides whether it needs to ban the user or the Page completely from Facebook.

Figure 2-8:
Select the appropriate radio button to report a post as abusive.

Is this post about you?

Yes, this post is about me:
- I don't like this post
- This post is harassing or bullying me

No, this post is about something else:
- Spam or scam
- Contains hate speech or attacks an individual
- Violence or harmful behavior
- Sexually explicit content

Continue   Cancel

Users can block your posts, too

Just as you can block or ban users from posting on your Page, so can users turn the tables on you by blocking your posts. All they have to do is go to one of your posts in their News Feed and select the gear icon on the right side of the post. A dialog box then appears with the following options: Hide this post; Hide all by this user or Page, Unlike Page, or Mark as Spam.

Selecting Hide keeps them a Liker of your Page but leaves your posts out of their News Feed. You can find out how many people (but not specific names) have hidden your Page's posts in your Insights dashboard. A complete description of the Insights dashboard is in Book IX, Chapter 2.

If users select one of your posts as Mark as Spam, Facebook investigates you and your Page for any Facebook violations.

Chapter 3: Better Engagement with the Help of Facebook Like Links and Buttons

In This Chapter

✔ Understanding the Facebook Like link and button

✔ Seeing the implications of using the Like button code outside Facebook

✔ Learning how to create a simple Like button code for your Web site

This chapter explains the Like *link* and Like *button* and how to use them to engage your audience on Facebook and outside the Facebook environment. A fuller discussion of the enormous implication of using this Facebook integration tool occurs in Book VII, Chapter 2.

The Button vs. the Link

There are two ways you will see the Like interface on Facebook itself. One is as a link. (See Figure 3-1 for an example of how you see a simple link on a Facebook post.) The other is a button, as shown in Figure 3-2.

Figure 3-1:
The Like link on posts on Facebook.

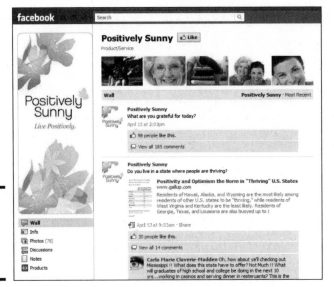

Figure 3-2:
The Like
button on a
Facebook
Page.

By now, if you have spent any time on Facebook, or the Internet for that matter, you will have run across the Like link and button in many places.

Here are a few places you'll find them:

+ As a link at the bottom of each post in your Facebook News Feed

+ As a link on the bottom of each comment from any post in your News Feed

+ As a link on Facebook ads

+ As a button at the top of any Page you haven't Liked yet

+ As a button on blog posts outside Facebook

+ As a button on a Facebook box on Web sites outside Facebook

The Like *link* is generated automatically for you in Facebook posts and comments. The Like *button* is also automatically generated on your Facebook business Page and can be manually placed on any type of online interface to which you can add HTML code. The Facebook Like button that is installed on your Web site allows people to share content from that site with their Friends back on Facebook.

In the next section, we give you a simple overview of where you may see the link and button, how these elements differ from one another, and why they are both important to you as a marketer on Facebook.

Answering Common Questions

If you are new to the Facebook environment, you might have questions as to the mechanics of what happens when Like buttons and links are clicked. In this section, we go through a few common questions and give you some understanding around these actions. We hope this provides an understanding of what your Fans will experience when they click the Like button at the top of your Facebook Page or on your Web site Facebook Like box widget. It should also provide an understanding of what happens when they click any Like link on your Page posts, or any ads you create.

Facebook marketing doesn't work unless you have a group of people who are connected to your Page. They get connected through Liking your Page. All the fun stuff we can do on Facebook for marketing really depends on this Liking aspect. Without Liking, none of those social sharing advantages fully come into play. You can make Liking your Facebook Page easy by placing the Facebook Like button in as many places as possible! The questions and answers that follow explain how fans can use the Facebook Like link and button. This Q&A can also help you determine which options are best for you.

Q. What happens when someone clicks the Like link on one of your Page posts?

A. As shown in Figure 3-3, a Like link will always be there when you post on your Page.

Figure 3-3: There are many reasons to click the Like link on a post.

When people click the Like link on a post on your Page, it increases engagement on your Page, thereby adding to a better EdgeRank for your Page.

If several people Like the post, it will add the number of Likes together and put that number next to a thumbs up icon on your Page and wherever the posts shows up on a fan's News Feed. If someone clicks the thumbs up icon, the comments will open up and then by clicking the thumbs up number again, a box will come up with the names of the other people who have also Liked the post. There will be a button to add these people as a Friend, too.

When you view your Page as your Page and click the Notifications icon (top-left corner on your Page), you will see who has Liked a post on your Page. If you click See All Notifications, you will see all the notifications for the last week.

You, as your Page, can also scroll through the posts on your Page and click the numerical notation and Like any Pages (as your Page) in that list by clicking the Like button next to their name. (If you have already Liked the Page, there will not be a Like button.)

Each time someone clicks the Like link on a post, the post has a better ranking from Facebook. See our explanation of EdgeRank in Book IV, Chapter 2 to see how the Facebook algorithm comes into play with people clicking the Like link on a post.

Q. What happens when someone clicks the Like link on a comment on one of your Page posts?

A. As shown in Figure 3-4, each comment has a Like link, too.

Again, clicking the Like link for a comment adds to the engagement on your Page, and you want that! Clicking the Like link under a comment someone has left on your Page acknowledges that you have read it — and Like it! They will get a Facebook notification (found by clicking their Notification icon) in their personal account that you Liked their comment.

Figure 3-4:
Liking a
Comment
someone
posts on
your Page
acknow-
ledges that
you have
read it.

Q. What happens when someone clicks the Like button at the top of any Facebook Page?

A. As shown in Figure 3-5, the Like button at the top of a Page tells you that you haven't Liked the Page yet.

Figure 3-5: This is the Like button you want people to click!

This is one of the most important Like buttons on Facebook. This is the button you want people to click!

After users click your Like button at the top of your Page, several things that happen:

+ Your Page now appears in the Likes and Interests section of the users' personal Profile.

+ A notification goes on their Wall that they Liked your Page, unless they modified their privacy settings to disallow those types of postings on their Wall.

+ The users potentially see your posts in their News Feed. (This is a big topic and is discussed more thoroughly in Chapter 2 of this minibook.)

+ You can now target your ads to users who have Liked your Page.

+ You can target your Facebook Updates to users who have Liked your Page (see minibook IX Chapter 2, *Exploring Facebook Insights*)

After people Like your Page, you have started your community. Facebook calls this *connections*. Your connections consists of the people with whom you'll have conversation and who will be spreading the word about you. They are connected to your Page by the act of Liking it. You have gained permission, by their Liking of your Page, to communicate with them directly.

Now you can post to their News Feed, send them updates, and target any ads to all your Likers or subsets of them. It is a very good thing.

Q: What happens when someone clicks the Like link on your Facebook ad?

A. As shown in Figure 3-6, a Facebook ad can have either a Like link or no link at all. If no link appears under the ad, the ad is either notifying users of an Event or it links to a site outside Facebook through the hyperlinked title of the ad.

Figure 3-6:
Some Facebook ads have a Like link; some don't.

When a user clicks the Like link on an ad, that user immediately becomes a Liker of the Page that the ad is representing.

You can verify this process for yourself by clicking the title of an ad and seeing that you haven't Liked the Page. Then go back to the ad and click the Like link, return to the Page (are you still with us?), and refresh it. You should then see that you're included in the group of Likers for that Page.

So, in other words, the Like link on an ad is the *same thing* as the Like Button on the top of a Page. Clicking the link on the ad and clicking the Like button on a Page do the same thing.

The added benefit of having a Like link on an ad is in having the opportunity to explore the analytics concerning who Liked the ad and draw some conclusions about the community you're developing. We delve into those ad analytics in Book VIII.

Q. What happens when someone clicks the Like button on your individual Web site or blog posts?

A. The blog post shown in Figure 3-7 has a Like button so that readers can show their support of the post. You can install a similar button by inserting code on your Web site, or using a Like button plugin in WordPress.

Figure 3-7: The Like button on your blog post can be configured to allow users to post a comment back to Facebook without leaving your blog.

When someone clicks a Like button on a blog post, they are Liking the post, not the Page (or the Website). When a user clicks a Like button on your Web site or blog, a short summary of the content, called a "story," with a link back to the content on your site, is posted to the Facebook Wall of that user and also sent out into the News Feed with the potential to be seen by all the user's Friends.

Sometimes a Web site owner will change the text on this button to say "Recommend," but it does the same thing (as noted above) as if it said Like. There is also a way to modify the code to allow someone to post a comment as they Like the post (refer to Figure 3-7).

Depending on which code you use (more about that in Book VII Chapter 2), users have the ability to not only Like your post (and have that notification show up in their News Feed), but they can also make a comment that will show up on Facebook, all without leaving your Web site.

Q: What happens when someone clicks the Like button on a Facebook Like box widget on your Web page? (A Like Box is shown in Figure 3-8.)

Figure 3-8:
Clicking
the Like
button in a
Facebook
Like box
(Widget) on
your Web
site is like
clicking on
the Like
button
on your
Facebook
Page itself.

A. If you include a Like Box widget on your Web page or blog (discussed in Book VII Chapter 2), your website or blog page has a direct link to your Facebook business Page. This means when a user clicks a Like button on your Page inside the Facebook Like Box widget, a connection is made between your Facebook Page and the user. Clicking that Like button in the Like Box is the same as clicking the Like button at the top of your Facebook Page.

Your Facebook Page will now appear in the Likes and Interests section of the user's personal Profile, and the user will now see your posts in his or her News Feed. Your Facebook Page will show up in the same places that Facebook Pages show up around Facebook (for example, through a search), and you can target your ads to those people who clicked that Like button.

Clicking the Like button on a Like Box on a Web site gives the same benefits to the Page owner as clicking the Like button on your Facebook Page does.

Placing the Like Button Code

The Like *link* is generated automatically for you in posts, comments, ads, and on your Facebook business Page.

The Like *button* can be placed on pages outside Facebook by generating HTML code and then inserting it in your Web site's code so that it is part of every blog post you make, as shown in Figure 3-9.

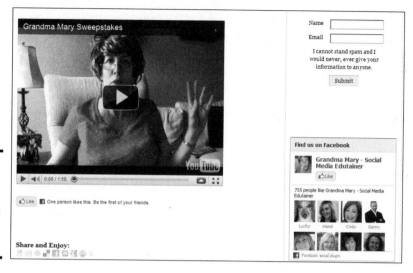

Figure 3-9:
This is
how a Like
button looks
on a blog
post.

Depending on how you configure the code (more about that in Book VII, Chapter 2), users can have the ability to not only Like your post (and have that notification show up in their News Feed), but they can also make a comment that will show up on Facebook, all without leaving your Web site.

If talking code throws the geek meter up to overwhelm, then take a minute to read the following very simple instructions and see if you can figure it out. If not, then talk to your Web master and have them generate the code and place it for you.

If you have a WordPress blog or Web site, there are plugins that do the same thing as this Facebook generator. An easy one to use is Facebook Like Button Plugin *for* WordPress (http://wordpress.org/extend/plugins/fblikebutton). All the steps to install this widget in WordPress can be found in Book VII, Chapter 2.

Generating the code for a Like button

The following steps are to create code for a Like button. We are not going to go into the deeper development of code using Open Graph Tags (that would provide you with additional analytic data from Liking activity). In fact, we are going to go through what Facebook calls Step One, only.

1. **Go to** http://developers.facebook.com/docs/reference/plugins/like. You are now on the page that will generate the code for your Like button.

2. **In the form, enter the URL of the Web page you want users to Like your posts.**

Type in the complete URL of your Web site including the http:// part.

**Book IV
Chapter 3**

Better Engagement
with the Help of
Facebook Like Links
and Buttons

3. **Decide whether you want to include the Send button with your Like button.**

   We suggest you select the box to include it.

4. **Choose your layout style from the drop box.**

   There are three choices: standard, button count, and box count. You can click each one to see a preview of how it would look.

5. **Click to select the box next to "Show faces" if you want to show the Profile images of the people who Like your post.**

   The faces will show up on the standard button style only and will appear next to the button. Having faces of your Facebook Friends on a blog post helps build social trust, and will encourage them to Like something if they see their Friends have already. Note that users will see only the faces of their Friends, not of everyone who has Liked it.

6. **Type in the width you want to use for your Like button.**

   Choose a width that complements the layout of your Web site or blog. The default size of 450 pixels works for most sites.

7. **Choose the verb you want to display in the button from the drop-down list. You can choose Like or Recommend.**

   Some people suggest that you choose Like most of the time because it is more widely recognized by Facebook users.

8. **Choose the font for your button in the drop-down list.**

9. **Choose the color scheme for your button in the drop-down list.**

10. **Click Get Code.**

    A dialog box pop ups with two different code boxes. You can choose between iFrames code and XFBML code.

The XFBML code is more versatile, but you need to know how to use JavaScript SDK. The XFBML code allows you to dynamically re-size the button height and with a bit of code tweaking, to know in real time when someone clicks the Like button. Using XFBML creates a comment box to give people the ability to add a comment to the Like. You might have seen that on other blogs — when you click the Like button, a little text field opens that gives you a chance to type in a comment. (Refer to Figure 3-7.) If users do add a comment, the story published back to Facebook is given more EdgeRank!

Modifying code takes a little expertise. If you enjoy working with code and are a DIY kind-of person, Facebook has some support and training for you at `http://developers.facebook.com/docs/reference/javascript/`.

If you aren't concerned about the deeper analytics of tracking and just want people to Like and Share your posts on Facebook, you can configure the code from the preceding steps and copy either the XFBML or iFrames code that is generated.

11. Copy the code you want.

Now you can place the code on your Web site or give the code to your Webmaster to place on your site.

Detailed steps on how to place the Facebook Like button code on your WordPress site is in Book VII Chapter 3, but here's a hint: Inside your WordPress dashboard, look for the Editor of your Theme. Navigate to the Single Post single.php and paste the code above this code: `<?php the_content(); ?>` and Save changes. Now your Like and Send buttons will be on all your single post pages!

Book IV
Chapter 3

Better Engagement
with the Help of
Facebook Like Links
and Buttons

Chapter 4: Expanding Your Existing E-Commerce onto Facebook

In This Chapter

✔ Creating a new storefront on Facebook to feed into your existing e-commerce store

✔ Opening a self-contained store exclusive to Facebook

✔ Exploring e-commerce application options

✔ Installing third-party e-commerce apps on your Page

*N*othing says "engagement" like shopping. By providing your loyal enthusiasts with a way to buy your products and in the same stroke share the news of their purchase with their friends on Facebook, you could start a momentum toward brand awareness with the potential of increased revenue. If we remember correctly, that's one of the main reasons to have a Facebook Page in the first place!

It all comes back down to *social proof*. Social proof, or social trust, or social authority, as some call it, is when you have a reputation for being the expert (or the best provider) on the subject of your business on social media platforms. In terms of Facebook, social trust is built when people see that their Friends have already said, in effect, "This is good." Imagine this scenario from your customers' perspectives — if they look at one of your hats for sale on your regular Web site, and you have Facebook's Open Graph API implemented, or they click your Facebook Page shopping link, and right next to the Add to Cart button they see four of their Friends' Facebook thumbnail images who have already bought the hat, it brings social proof (trust, authority) and better customer engagement to your store. (And, we hope, another sale for you!)

Here's a comment we read on a shopping site on Facebook: "I like that I can still chat with my Facebook Friends while shopping in the same window. Easy way to get their input on my potential buys!"

It is this kind of social proof and real-time interaction that leads to sales, and it's one reason that the largest corporations in the world are now on Facebook. In this chapter, we explore the world of social shopping and all the different ways you can add your e-commerce to the Facebook environment.

Understanding Facebook Storefronts

Why should you consider using your Facebook Page as an e-commerce store? Because

+ The average user spends about 1.2 days a month (and growing) on Facebook.

+ Facebook is becoming *the* hub of all kinds of activity, including shopping.

+ Free shopping applications make it easy for anyone to have an online storefront or store.

+ Engagement goes up when you offer discounts, coupons, or other exclusive deals as Facebook shopping incentives.

Potential customers on Facebook like to stay on Facebook. They might see in their News Feed that one of their Friends has Liked your Page and go explore what you have to offer. You need to keep in mind that people might spend more money if it is easy to stay and shop on your Facebook Page.

Facebook offers two different types of shopping interfaces:

+ **Partial storefront:** This is a place to browse products, but when visitors click the Buy button, they are whisked away from Facebook to the company's Web site store to complete their purchase.

+ **Complete storefront:** This is a fully functioning store where shoppers can browse goods and purchase them without leaving the Facebook environment.

Large companies use Facebook stores

In 2009, many large corporations started exploring the e-commerce possibilities on Facebook, by using already created e-commerce apps or developing their own applications.

Procter & Gamble partnered with Amazon.com to develop a Facebook app that would allow customers to stay on Facebook, purchase items, and have the entire shopping process handled by Amazon.com's Web Store.

In addition, Disney developed its own shopping app to sell movie tickets, and eBay has a Facebook storefront app that enables registered eBay sellers to share items they're listing to their News Feed. Etsy store owners have a Facebook app that creates a beautiful dedicated link with their Etsy store on it. It usually has a grid configuration and opportunities to Like and Share with your Friends on Facebook.

Using PayPal to Accept Payment

We're just about ready to explain how to choose and install a storefront Facebook application, but first you might need to create a PayPal account for your business (because most apps use PayPal for their payment options). The main benefits of using PayPal are that many of your users will already have PayPal accounts, and those who don't can use a credit card with the PayPal interface. The benefit for your company (besides being able to accept credit cards) is that you don't need to open a bank merchant account to start collecting payments.

Setting up a PayPal account is quick and easy, but verifying the bank account that you associate with PayPal can take several days. After you have your PayPal account set up and verified, you can start the process of installing and connecting any third-party shopping application (which we discuss in the very next section!).

If you need assistance in setting up a PayPal account, I suggest you go directly to their Web site `www.paypal.com` and click the Business tab.

Finding E-Commerce Apps that Fit Your Needs

There are many storefront applications you can integrate with your Facebook business Page. In this section, we show you how do find them and choose the one that's right for your business.

Many of the hundreds of stand-alone Internet shopping sites (such as eBay and Etsy) are realizing that they need to create apps that will integrate their sellers' stores with Facebook to stay current and in the space where potential customers are already spending their time and money.

If you are currently a retailer, or are considering promoting a product or service, you should check with the e-commerce system you're currently using to see whether that system already has a Facebook integration application.

If you're starting from scratch, though, you can employ many ways of finding the right e-commerce app for your business on Facebook:

✦ Search Facebook for "e-commerce" and explore the applications listed in the search results.

✦ Note which storefront apps other companies are using on their Facebook Pages.

✦ Search `http://AllFacebook.com` or `http://mashable.com` for articles on Facebook shopping applications.

**Book IV
Chapter 4**

Expanding
Your Existing
E-Commerce onto
Facebook

Or you can just test the ones listed in the sections that follow. We tested all these before choosing the ones that fit our various businesses. After you have selected the storefront application you want to use, it's easy to put the app on your Page (and those instructions are at the end of this chapter). First, though, we need to talk about some of your options.

Storenvy

Storenvy (`http://www.storenvy.com/`) is a partial storefront application. It has a marketplace of independently-owned stores. You can open an online store for free, and the Storenvy Facebook app lets you put an interface on your Facebook Page. When people click to buy your products, they go to your page on the Storenvy site. It requires no set-up fees, no monthly fees, no listing fees, and no transaction fees. You can have an unlimited amount of products, up to five images per product, and fully customize your store. See Figure 4-1 for an example of a Storenvy e-commerce interface on Facebook.

Figure 4-1: A Storenvy e-commerce interface on Facebook.

Payvment

Payvment (`www.payvment.com/facebook/`) is a professional-grade store application that you can add to your Facebook Page. You can open a store for free. Payvment requires no set-up charges or monthly fees, and it does not take any amount out of your transactions. Pricing may change when it comes out of beta.

Payvment has a Facebook shopping mall interface (`http://apps.face-book.com/shoppingmall/`) filled with all its merchants. You can put items from different merchants into one shopping cart and pay one time. You can easily Like and Share items with your Facebook Friends.

If customers leave your Payvment store on your Facebook Page, without purchasing the items in their cart, those items will remain in their cart so that the next time they go to purchase something anywhere on Facebook (using that same Payvment app on someone else's Page), those items will still be in the cart, queued up for purchase!

See Figure 4-2 for an example of a Payvment e-commerce interface on Facebook.

Figure 4-2:
A Payvment
E-commerce
interface on
Facebook.

ShopTab

ShopTab (`www.shoptab.net/`) is a partial storefront application that is easy to set up. To use ShopTab, upload your products to the ShopTab interface at their Web site online and then add the ShopTab application to your Facebook Page. ShopTab allows people to look through your products on your Facebook Page, but when users click to buy a product, they are taken to the ShopTab Web site to complete the purchase.

This application does not have a free version, but it does have a free trial.

Etsy

Thousands of artists and crafters are listed with Etsy (`www.etsy.com`) with Facebook Pages. See Figure 4-3 for an example of a Etsy e-commerce interface on Facebook. Notice how easy Etsy has made it for anyone to Share each item on Facebook by just clicking the Share button beneath the product.

**Book IV
Chapter 4**

Expanding
Your Existing
E-Commerce onto
Facebook

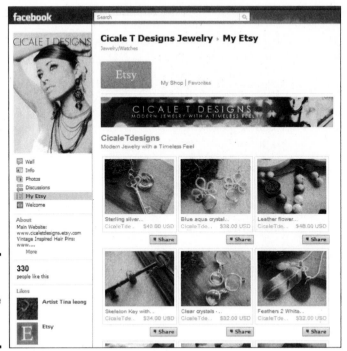

Figure 4-3:
An Etsy
e-commerce
interface on
Facebook.

Moontoast

Moontoast (www.moontoast.com) has a really nice interface on Facebook through its Embedded Store option. An Embedded Store just means the whole transaction takes place without leaving Facebook. A good example of this complete storefront application is Reba McEntire's storefront (www.facebook.com/Reba). Moontoast provides only an enterprise solution (pricing is available by phone consultation), so if your company fits that category, you might want to talk to Moontoast directly. See Figure 4-4 for a Moontoast interface.

TinyPay

Tinypay.me (http://tinypay.me/) is another service you can use to create a link back to an e-commerce site. To use this service, you create a product page on tinypay.me, and the tinypay.me Web site creates an embed code that you can place on your Facebook business Page using the Involver Static HTML iFrames app (more on that coming up). You can also just post the product's URL in a Facebook Page status update and forgo the whole applications process completely!

Figure 4-4: A Moontoast e-commerce interface on Facebook.

Add to Cart button   Check Out button

Tinypay.me acts like a partial storefront because clicking the link takes you to a page off Facebook where the user can buy your product. This service is very easy to implement. See Figure 4-5 for an example of a Tinypay.me e-commerce interface on a Facebook Page, and see Figure 4-6 for how the app interface looks (where you paste the html embed code). Please note that the Page owner also included code for a table, so the items were arranged nicely on the Page.

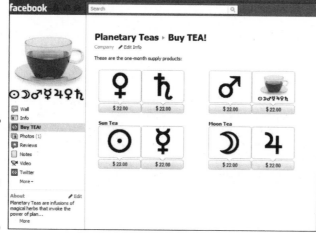

Figure 4-5: A Tinypay. me e-commerce interface on Facebook.

**Book IV
Chapter 4**

Expanding
Your Existing
E-Commerce onto
Facebook

Figure 4-6:
This is where you paste the embed code in the Static HTML app by Involver.

Here's an important thing to think about when choosing the best shopping interface for your business: Are your customers looking for and buying products on Facebook using their iPhones or iPads? Many of these storefront apps use Flash, and as of this writing, Apple does not allow Flash on any of its iOS devices.

Installing a Facebook Storefront Application

In the "Finding E-Commerce Apps that Fit Your Needs" section earlier in this chapter, we list many excellent e-commerce store applications that are currently available (eBay, Etsy, and others) for integration with your Facebook Page.

After you have settled on an application, the process to install a storefront application is exactly the same as adding any type of application to your Page. Follow these steps to put any Facebook shopping application on your Page:

1. **On your Page, click the Edit Page link top-right of your Page.**

   You are taken to your administrative dashboard.

2. **Click Apps in the sidebar of your dashboard.**

   The screen shows you all the applications you currently have installed on your Page.

3. **Scroll down to the bottom of the Applications list and click the Browse More Applications link.**

   You are taken to all the Applications available in Facebook.

4. **In the Search box in the upper-left corner of the screen, enter the name of the application you want to install on your Page.**

   The application appears in the Search Results area.

5. **Click the application's link.**

   You are taken to the Application's Page.

6. **Click the Add to My Page link underneath the logo on the left sidebar.**

   A pop-up box appears with all the Pages you manage.

7. **Click the Add to Page button next to the Page you want to work with.**

8. **Click the Close button on the pop-up box.**

Now you need to go back to the apps link, find the app you just added to your Page, and do the following:

1. **Click the Edit Settings link under the app you just added.**

   A new dialog box appears.

2. **In the dialog box, click the Add link and change the text for the new link where it says Custom Tab Name (Facebook still calls this link a Tab).**

3. **Click Save and then Okay to close the dialog box.**

4. **Click the Go to App link.**

   This will take you back to the apps interface off Facebook or to an interface on your Page (depends on the app) to modify what is on the Page.

If you're installing a partial storefront application (that is, one that allows visitors to browse your products but requires them to complete the purchase at another Web site), you need to go the Web site for that application and enter the products you want to sell in your store. Then your product information will be fed to the Facebook app link.

If you're installing a complete store application, you can load product information either right there on Facebook or on the application's Web site. Then your customers can view product information and purchase those products right there on Facebook.

Creating a Link to Your Website Store on Your Page

With a Facebook Page, you have many opportunities to link back to your already existing e-commerce Web site without installing an application. For example, you can

**Book IV
Chapter 4**

Expanding
Your Existing
E-Commerce onto
Facebook

✦ Create status updates with the specific URL of any products you mention.

✦ Upload promotional videos with links back to your Web site's store.

✦ Highlight your store URL on your Page's Info Tab.

✦ Include your store's link in your business Page's Profile image.

✦ Implement any of the other strategies we discuss in miniooks II and III.

But a very good way to connect a commerce site to Facebook is to just create a storefront link that takes you back to your regular Web site e-commerce Page.

You can link to your My Etsy e-commerce page, eBay page, Amazon e-Store, tinypay.me pages, or any site where you sell your products. Just remember that many of these sites offer their own Facebook apps and creating a storefront link with their official applications might look (and perform) better than just a link back to your Web site's storefront.

Using Other Applications to Create a Custom Link for Your Storefront

There are several applications you can use to create a custom link on your Page's side navigation menu that will link to your E-commerce Web site. Here are a few to explore. The following are not considered shopping applications, but instead offer ways to create custom links for your Page that can be used for anything — including links to your e-commerce Web pages.

Page Modo

Page Modo (www.pagemodo.com) is priced from Free to $59 a month for Enterprise businesses. It has a very easy interface with many templates to choose from. You can customize your template with images, links, videos, *hidden codes*, and many other things. Hidden codes are also called reveal codes. This means that after someone clicks the Like button on your Page, new text (coupon codes, videos, all sorts of things) will be seen (revealed). To edit how this page looks, you go to your account interface on pagemodo.com. This system creates only one custom link for your Page.

TabSite

TabSite (www.facebooktabsite.com) is priced from free to $15 a month. The free version allows you to create a custom link that will go to a page that has one main tab and two sub-tabs. The editing interface for a TabSite tab is reminiscent of a Word document, as you can see in Figure 4-7. After this app is installed on a Facebook Page, a new Welcome link appears in your left navigation menu.

One Tab and two subtabs are created using the free version of tabsite; you can increase the number of main tabs and subtabs for a fee

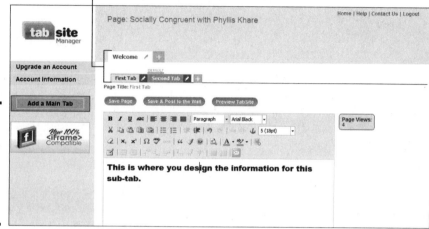

Figure 4-7:
The interface for creating a custom link with two sub-tabs.

Lujure Assembly Line

Lujure Assembly Line (http://assemblyline.lujure.com) is a new interface we're very excited about. It is different than the other options we've discussed because you just drag and drop applications onto a canvas, as shown in Figure 4-8. You don't have to know any kind of code to create a beautiful custom e-commerce storefront. The interface was built with the non-coder in mind. Assembly Line comes in a free version as well as several paid versions.

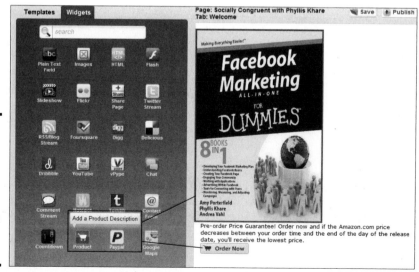

Figure 4-8:
You can drag and drop applications to create your custom storefront link.

Book IV Chapter 4

Expanding Your Existing E-Commerce onto Facebook

RootMusic

RootMusic (www.rootmusic.com) is an option to consider if you have a band or are a musician. This app offers a fully customizable storefront link for your music. RootMusic connects your SoundCloud e-commerce site to this link for easy purchasing.

Go to Appbistro (http://appbistro.com) to find applications that are best suited for your type of business. Remember when you chose your particular category of business for your Facebook business Page? This is the information Appbistro uses to determine what apps it presents to you. Appbistro is a treasure chest full of applications you can try out on your Page. We consider it a kind of Yellow Pages for Facebook Applications.

There are many ways to add your e-commerce to your Facebook Page. The few we present in this section can get you started. The only limit is your imagination.

For example, if you fancy yourself to be a "TV Shopping" site, you can use the Livestream app to create a custom link with your Live Video streaming right there. You could introduce your new products and have people call your order department to buy. A weekly or daily show on Facebook would be so cool! Start here: http://apps.facebook.com/livestream/manager.

Book V

Understanding Facebook Applications

The 5th Wave   By Rich Tennant

"Jim and I do a lot of business together on Facebook. By the way, Jim, did you get the sales spreadsheet and little blue pony I sent you?"

Contents at a Glance

Chapter 1: Facebook Applications 101

In This Chapter

✔ Understanding what a Facebook application is

✔ Finding existing applications to include on your Page

✔ Adding, deleting, and modifying applications

✔ Finding out how to use existing applications for marketing

An *app*, or application, is how you can expand the way Facebook interacts with your audience. iPhone and mobile phones have educated most people about what an app is. "There's an app for that" has become a well-used phrase for many years. Literally thousands of apps can be used on mobile phones, and developers have built hundreds of applications for use in Facebook.

Facebook apps are what make your Page unique and interesting. If all you present on your Page is the Wall, Info, and photos, it looks as though you haven't put any attention on presenting your business. On the other hand, you want to be very clear on which types of apps to put on your Page. Having too many bells and whistles is not charming, either!

There are apps that have been developed by Facebook itself and those that are developed by third parties (developers). The ones developed by Facebook itself are

✦ Photos

✦ Notes

✦ Events

✦ Video

✦ Links

✦ Discussions

These are really easy to activate on your Page, as we show you in this chapter. We like to call them ready-to-go apps because you don't need to go outside your Page to find them.

Facebook puts apps developed by third-party developers in categories (many apps are in several categories) on a Directory page. The categories are

+ **All Apps:** A listing of all the apps

+ **On Facebook:** Sub-categories are Business, Education, Entertainment, Friends & Family, Games, Just For Fun, Lifestyle, Sports, and Utilities

+ **External Websites:** Apps that are connected to Web sites

+ **Desktop:** Apps that are connected to computer desktop applications

+ **Mobile:** Apps that are connected to mobile apps

+ **Pages:** External Web sites

+ **Prototypes:** Facebook-developed apps that are under review

Many people prefer to find and install Facebook apps from another interface called Appbistro (`http://appbistro.com`). In this chapter, whenever we suggest that you look for an app through Facebook's Directory, you can instead go to Appbistro's site if you prefer. It is a very user friendly space.

Understanding How Facebook Users Make Use of Apps

Currently, more than 52,000 apps are available on the Facebook platform. These applications are the fuel that drives the Facebook experience.

There seem to be three camps of Facebook application users: those who are there for the personal conversation and ignore or block applications, those who are there to enjoy the applications and play games, and finally the business owner who is looking for ways to drive eyeballs to his Page using appropriately targeted applications.

You are free to place as many already existing apps on your Page as you want, or create your own custom-designed apps. In Chapter 2 of this book, we discuss how to create your own app. In this chapter, we focus on already created apps and discuss how they can be used for marketing.

If you view Facebook on an iPad (or iPhone, iPod, or any iOS device), check to see whether your apps use Flash (such as the Scribd app from Involver); if so, you won't be able to view the content on that device. Again, it's something to keep in mind as you build your Page. Test all the apps you install on your Page on all platforms: iOS, Android, Web-based, and so on.

Viewing your installed applications

As a new Page owner, you already have a few apps in play. How do you find them? Follow these steps:

1. **On your Page, click the Edit Page button on the top right of your Page.**

Your Page dashboard appears.

2. **Click Apps in the sidebar of your dashboard.**

The screen then shows you all the applications you currently have available to be installed on your Page, as shown in Figure 1-1.

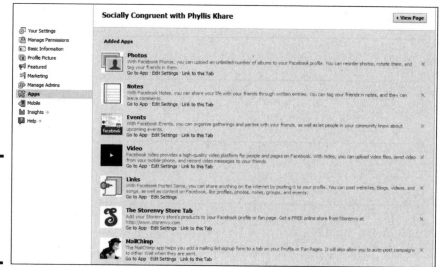

Figure 1-1:
The list
of apps
ready to be
installed on
your Page.

By clicking the App link, you see which apps are ready to be installed on your new Page. For example; a new Product/Services Page has these six apps:

✦ Events

✦ Photos

✦ Video

✦ Links

✦ Notes

✦ Discussion Boards

Below that list is the Browse More Applications link.

Each app has one, two, or sometimes three links beneath it: Go to App, Edit Settings, and sometimes, Link to This Tab, as shown in Figure 1-2.

Link to This Tab link

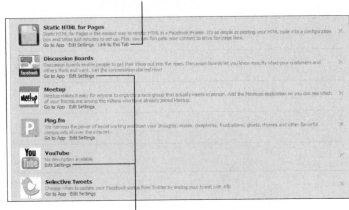

Figure 1-2:
Under each
app name
are two or
three links.

Edit Settings link

✦ **Link to This Tab:** If you click the Link to This Tab link, it opens a dialog box with the direct URL to that particular place on your Page. So, for example, if you want to send a direct URL to your Discussion Boards, you can look for the Discussion Boards application, click the Link to This Tab link, and copy and paste the URL in a message to send someone directly to that place on your Page.

✦ **Edit Settings:** If you click the Edit Settings link, a dialog box appears offering you the option of adding or removing it from your side links and giving you opportunity to change the text for the link, as shown in Figure 1-3.

Adding the Tab creates a side link; you can
type in any text you want for the side link

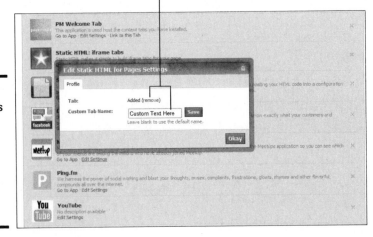

Figure 1-3:
The options
for adding
an app
to your
Page and
changing
the text of
its link.

✦ **Go to App:** If you click the Go to App link, you go directly to the editing page for that app or to a page to set options for the app.

For example, if you click the Go to App link for the Photo app, you go directly to a page where you can set your options for allowing Fans to add their photos to your Page. If you click the Go to App for the Events app, you go directly to the page to start creating an Event, as shown in Figure 1-4.

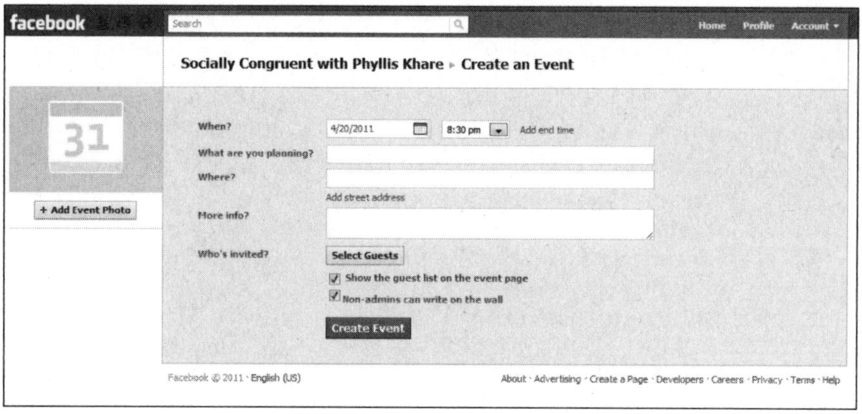

Figure 1-4: Sometimes clicking the Go to App link takes you directly to the creation page for that app.

You should go through all the apps already listed and decide whether you want them to have public links on your Page. Pages come with the Wall, Info, and Photos already listed on the side menu, but not Video, Links, Events, Notes, or Discussion Boards. If you want those available for your Likers to use, you have to add them to the side menu by clicking the Edit Settings link and clicking Add.

Finding the Facebook Application Directory

Facebook's Application Directory lists all the available Facebook apps. You can access it at www.facebook.com/apps/directory.php or follow these instructions:

1. **On your Page, click the Edit Page link top-right of your Page.**

You are taken to your Page dashboard.

2. **Click Apps in the sidebar of your dashboard.**

The screen lists all the applications you currently have installed on your Page.

3. **Scroll down to the bottom of the applications list and click the Browse More Applications link.**

This Page is called All Apps.

You find three sections on the All Apps Page:

✦ **Featured by Facebook:** When we looked at this recently, Facebook featured 11 pages of apps (2 to a page). The pages ran the gamut from SlideShare to Bartab. If you click any of them, you go to the application Page.

✦ **Apps You May Like:** When we looked at this, Facebook recommended 20 pages (10 to a page) that we might like. Again, clicking any of them takes you to their application Page.

✦ **Recent Activity from Friends:** The third section shows applications your Friends are using. If the same application is being used by several of your Friends, Facebook groups them together and gives you a link to see more.

Seeing applications your Friends are using

This particular section is important for marketers because it shows you what other people are using and viewing. For example, the YouTube application is very popular with our Friends, so we know that they're used to seeing it and viewing videos with it. So that's a big clue that tells us which app to add to our apps on our Page.

Our Friends are pretty Facebook savvy and find all sorts of great Facebook applications. We can go to this section, see what apps they're using in their posts, and explore the possibilities of using them on our Page, too.

You can find the name of the app someone is using in the small print right below the post, as shown in Figure 1-5.

Figure 1-5: You have to look closely to find the name of the app that your Friend has used.

Look for the name of the app that was used to create the post

If you click the My Band: Profile Pages for Bands and Musicians application link, you see an expanded view of which of your Friends are using this app.

Adding an App to Your Page

Adding an application to your business Page is easy, but you have to do a few steps in the proper order. After you get into the rhythm of adding an app, it becomes very easy. Follow these steps:

1. **On your Page, click the Edit Page button top-right of your Page**

You are taken to your Page dashboard.

2. **Click Apps in the sidebar of your dashboard.**

The screen then shows you all the applications you currently have installed on your Page.

3. **Scroll down to the bottom of the applications list and click the Browse More Applications link.**

You then see a list of all the applications available in Facebook.

4. **In the search box in the upper-left corner of the screen, enter the name of the application you want to install on your Page.**

5. **Click the application's name.**

You are then taken to the application's Page.

6. **Click the Add to My Page link on the left sidebar.**

A pop-up box appears with all the Pages you manage.

7. **In the pop-up dialog box, click the Add to Page button, as shown in Figure 1-6.**

8. **Click the Close button in the pop-up dialog box.**

Now you need to go back to your Page and follow these final steps:

1. **Go to your Page and click the Edit Page button.**

2. **Click the Apps link on the menu and find the app you just added.**

It will be on the list somewhere (it's not alphabetical or chronological).

3. **Click the Edit Settings link under the app you just added.**

A new dialog box will come up (refer to Figure 1-3 to see what it looks like).

4. **Click the Add link and change the text for the new link where it says Custom Tab Name (Facebook still calls this link a Tab).**

5. **Click Save and then Okay to close the box.**

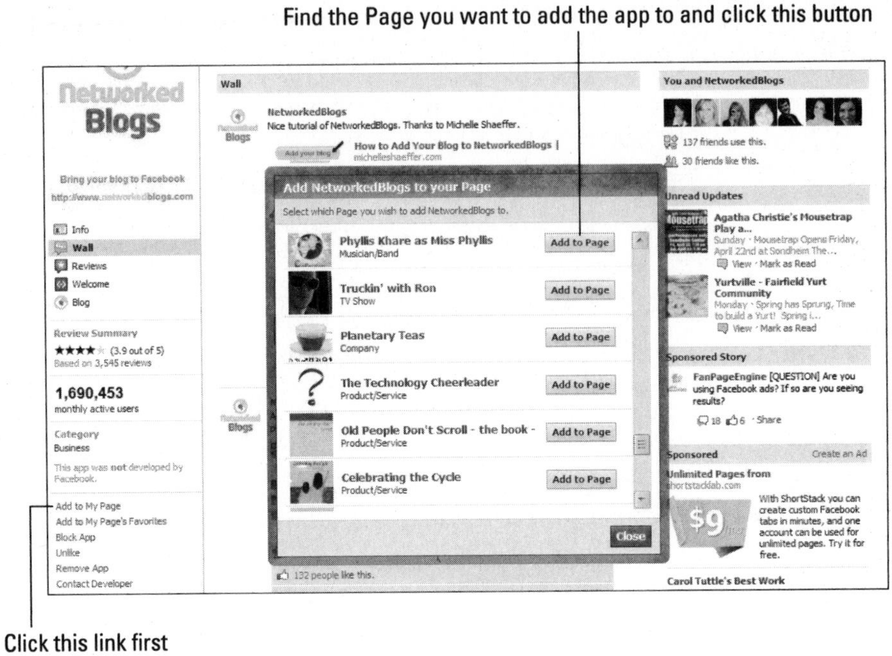

Find the Page you want to add the app to and click this button

Figure 1-6:
Find the Page that you want to add the application to and click the Add to Page button.

Click this link first

6. Click the Go to App link.

This takes you back to the app's interface off Facebook or to an interface on your Page (depends on the app) to modify what will end up on the Page.

Mobile viewers using a Facebook app might not be able to see some of your applications. Always view new applications through your mobile phone to be sure that mobile viewers can see them, too.

Deleting an App from Your Page

Sometimes you have an app that just doesn't click with your audience. If that's the case, don't worry: Applications are very easy to remove from your Page.

You can either remove the app from your Page, but still have it available on your list of applications, and/or you can completely remove the application from your Page.

To remove the application link from your navigation menu, but still have the application, follow these steps:

1. **On your Page click the Edit Page button on the top-right corner.**

2. **Click Apps in the sidebar of your dashboard.**

   The screen shows you all the applications you currently have installed on your Page.

3. **Click the Edit Settings link under the app you want to remove.**

4. **Click the Remove link, as shown in Figure 1-7.**

Figure 1-7:
Clicking the
Remove link
removes
the link from
your Page's
navigation
menu.

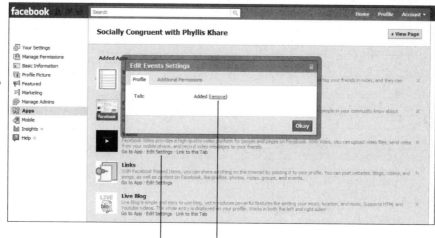

Click Edit Settings. . .   . . .then click this

To fully remove the application from your Page, follow these steps:

1. **On your Page, click the Edit Page button on the top-right corner.**

   You are taken to your Page dashboard.

2. **Click Apps in the sidebar of your dashboard.**

   The screen shows you all the applications you currently have installed on your Page.

3. **Find the app that you want to remove.**

   You might need to scroll down the Page to find it.

4. **Click the X on the right side of the application line, as shown in Figure 1-8.**

   This removes the application from your Page. If you want to use it in the future, you need to start from the beginning and add it to your Page again.

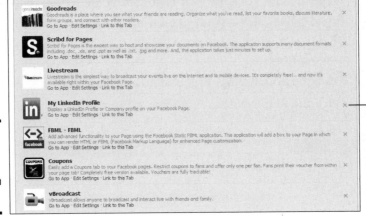

Figure 1-8:
Click the X
to remove
the app from
your Page.

Click to completely remove this app from your Page

Using Existing Applications for Marketing

Go to www.facebook.com/apps/directory.php to view Facebook's
Application Directory. The many apps on Facebook are organized under the
following headers on the left side of your screen:

✦ All Apps

- Business

- Education

- Entertainment

- Friends & Family

- Games

- Just for Fun

- Lifestyle

- Sports

- Utilities

✦ External Websites

✦ Desktop

✦ Mobile

✦ Pages

✦ Prototypes

Out of the tens of thousands of apps on Facebook, a few really good ones rise to the top that you might find useful by connecting them to your Facebook business Page. We explore some of them and discuss how to use them effectively in the social environment called Facebook.

When you click any of the links in the Directory, two or three more sections open on the Page to the right. Depending on the link you click you may see:

✦ Featured by Facebook

✦ Apps You May Like

✦ Recent Activity from Friends

> If a Friend is using one of the apps in the category you selected, you will see the post using that app. For example, if you're viewing the External Website category, you might see a few posts listed from Friends who have used the Meetup app or Twitterfeed (both external Web site apps for Facebook).

If you click All Apps — Business, for example, you also see, in the bottom section of the Page, these links that will sort them:

✦ Popular

✦ Recently Added

✦ See All

One of the nice things about this Directory is that you can see how apps are rated on a five-star system by users. Remember, this is a social network, and the power of its users can make or break an app. If you hover your mouse pointer over the star review for an app, you can see how many reviews it has received. Also, you can see how many of your personal Friends are using this particular app, as shown in Figure 1-9.

In the next few sections, we look at the different categories of Facebook apps and see how to use a few of the already existing apps for marketing. Many of these apps are discussed in full detail in Book III and Book IX. This list is an overview of the possibilities of what you can add to your Page. For a more detailed understanding of the marketing potential of some of these apps, please explore the other places they are discussed throughout this book.

Also, many of these apps offer both free and premium services. You'll need to look at them with your business in mind and choose accordingly.

You can see how many of your Friends
are using this app and how it's ranked

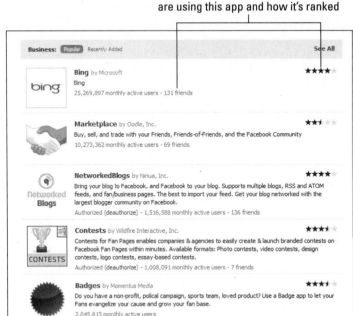

Figure 1-9:
You can see
how many
of your
personal
Friends
are using
this app
and how it
has been
rated by the
Facebook
community.

Business

Depending on the type of Page you are creating, you might find a lot of applications in the Business section to add to your Page. We're going to recommend a few for you to explore. Remember, to add these to your Page, follow the instructions earlier in this chapter in the section "Adding an App to Your Page."

✦ **NetworkedBlogs** (http://apps.facebook.com/blognetworks) is actively being used by over 1.5 million people on Facebook. This app can save you time by automatically posting your blog posts directly to your Facebook Page. A nice feature of this app is that it lets you repost any blog post to your Page Wall. If you have a blog, consider adding this app to your Page, but be aware that the more you manually post (as opposed to automating posts), the better your EdgeRank. We discuss this app in detail in Book III, Chapter 3.

✦ **Social RSS** (http://apps.facebook.com/social-rss/tabsettings.php?ref=ts) recently redesigned its services. It allows you to add your blog or any RSS feed to your Page. This can be really handy if you want to pull in specific posts from all over the Internet, not just your blog. For example, if you want to post your tweets to your Wall, you can add your Twitter RSS feed to this app. This app is also discussed in Book III, Chapter 3.

✦ **slideshare** (`http://apps.facebook.com/slideshare`) is another app you might want to consider adding to your Page, especially if you give presentations or have a process that you want to explain in a PowerPoint-type format. You need to open an account on `www.slideshare.net` first, upload a presentation from your computer, and then go back and synch your app to your account. When users click the slideshare link on your Page, they are presented with an interface that contains your presentations and popular presentations on their Web site.

✦ **Marketplace** (`http://apps.facebook.com/marketplace`) is an app that you might find very useful. It is part of an online classified company called Oodle. The company enables local property managers, real estate agents, and car dealers to post their listings on Twitter and Facebook. You can add Oodle's Marketplace app on Facebook and list your products there and on its online portals. A good example of this is the Hoffman Audi New London site on Facebook: `http://www.facebook.com/hoffmanaudinl`. It's not just for property managers, real estate agents, and car dealers, though. You can also post "stuff" like electronics, jobs, animals, services — it's a full-service classified ad app.

Many of the services that you might already be using outside the Facebook environment have apps, such as Eventbright, MailChimp, SurveyMonkey, PayPal, LinkedIn, and others. Go to their Web sites and look for any Facebook integration. Some of these services have actual Facebook apps; some give you code to place in an app like Static HTML, which will create a nice link on your Page. See Book III, Chapter 2 to find out how to use Static HTML.

Check each application's Reviews link before adding it to your Page. You can find the Reviews link on the application Page, as shown in Figure 1-10.

Education

In the Education subcategory list, you find a lot of apps that seem to be just games. We're a little confused as to why many of them are categorized as Education, but who knows? Maybe "God Wants You to Know" could be educational.

One very good app in this category that may be very useful for your business Page, especially if you are an author who wants to connect with a community of readers, is Goodreads.

Goodreads (`http://apps.facebook.com/good_reads`) is currently active with over 120,000 users. It corresponds to its Web site (`www.goodreads.com`). You can add your own authored books and those you'd like to recommend to others. The dedicated link creates a nice view of the books you want to discuss or share, as shown in Figure 1-11.

Figure 1-10:
Read the
Reviews link
and make
sure that the
application
is a good
one to add
to your
Page.

Reviews

Figure 1-11:
The
Goodreads
app has
a nice
Facebook
design.

Entertainment

If you're a musician or have a Facebook Page for your band, you might want to add several apps in this category to your Page:

✦ **Band Profile** (www.facebook.com/rn.mybandapp) currently has more than 8 million active users on Facebook! This app is powered by ReverbNation (www.reverbnation.com). It creates a link called Band Profile, and it pulls info from your account at ReverbNation. People can join your Fan list, join your mailing list, share the music, play your music, watch your music videos, see where your next show will be, and see your Fans — in other words, it's a complete site for your music on your Facebook Page.

✦ **Tinychat** (http://apps.facebook.com/tinychat) has been a popular tool for Twitter users for a few years. Its Facebook app allows you to open a video chat from within your Facebook Page and host discussions. You can send notifications to your personal Friends or type in an e-mail address to send them a link to connect. From a marketing perspective, consider using this as a weekly event to chat with your customers, clients, or as an impromptu chat when something topical that relates to your business comes up.

You can find other video apps in this entertainment category, and we would consider them "Business" apps, too. Use these video apps to connect with your audience without leaving the Facebook environment. They are Vpype www.facebook.com/vpype, which is used by some very active social-media marketers on Facebook, and Livestream, which is used by Facebook itself for its live events http://apps.facebook.com/livestream/manager. If using video appeals to you and your business, check out a fuller use of the Livestream app in Book IX.

You might want to spring for the paid versions of these applications; otherwise, you might have ads appear on your live and archived video presentations.

Friends and Family

If your business Page has a family focus, you might find a couple of apps useful. Again, many of these are connected to already-popular online sites. Circle of Moms (www.facebook.com/circleofmoms) is one of those apps.

If you have a business Page that is targeted to pet owners, you might want to check out Catbook (http://apps.facebook.com/catbook). Then go see its other apps — Dogbook, Rodentbook, Horsebook, and, well, you get the idea!

Literally hundreds of apps are in the Friends and Family category, but they have no real purpose on a business Page. (But hey, we could be wrong.) Happy hunting!

Games

When people think of Facebook apps, they most often think of games. Game apps are really what Facebook counts on for revenue. You've probably heard of FarmVille and Mafia Wars. Those are Facebook apps. If your business Page is connected to the gaming world, these apps might interface well on your Page. Otherwise, you should probably steer clear of these because they are really built for your personal account.

Just for fun

If you are outside the United States, you can check out what seems to be a very popular app called Phrases. It has more than 28 million active users. Facebook has not allowed this app to be used in the United States for some reason. Maybe we would use it so much it would crash the system! It is an app that lets you design your own application that generates quotes that are sent out to your Likers.

We considered recommending My Year in Photos, but beware. Many apps, such as My Year in Photos, pull photos from your personal account, not your Page photos. As you look through apps to add to your Page, be sure to notice which ones do that.

Lifestyle

Etsy, the Web site that specializes in selling handmade items, has a nice app in this category for those who have a business built around crafting (http://apps.facebook.com/myetsy). We mention this app in the section about e-commerce in Book IV, Chapter 4. It lets you create a link that pulls from your Etsy account at Etsy's main Web site (www.etsy.com). You can even set this link to be the default landing tab for new visitors coming to your Page.

Finding apps with Involver

Another way to find really good apps for your business Pages is by using Involver (www.involver.com/applications). Involver has many apps that are quite relevant to a Facebook business Page, including an RSS feed, the YouTube channel, Photo Gallery, File Sharing (which is a great way for authors to give away chapter previews or book teaser copy). An app of note is the Scribd app. First you upload a PDF to the scribd.com Web site, and then it's automatically available on the Page link for viewing, sharing, downloading, e-mailing, and getting embed code for the PDF — all from your Facebook Page. Make sure that you test the apps you're interested in. Some are better than others, and some have costs associated with them. You can read more about Involver in Book III, Chapter 4.

Sports

You may have noticed the use of polls and quizzes on sports Facebook Pages. The NFL Page is an excellent example for anyone with a sports-related business (www.facebook.com/NFL). Many of its apps are custom built, but you can try using apps from Fan Appz (http://fanappz.com) to build your own polls and quizzes. Fan Appz has a free version, a professional version at $50 per month, and an Enterprise solution. The Pro version includes no Fan Appz or 3rd Party Ads, a Google Analytics Integration, YouTube and 3rd Party Video Support, and Facebook Places Integration, among other perks.

Building a quiz will take some time, but if your audience on your Page likes quizzes, it's time well-spent to produce more engagement with your Page.

You could also play any of the Facebook games built around sports to meet new people and hopefully attract them to your Page. This is an interesting way to expand your "territory of influence," so to speak. Some games you might want to explore are Fantasy Football, Citizen Sports, and Premiere Football.

Utilities

If you have a Constant Contact e-mail service account, you should probably think about adding its app called Constant Contact Labs - Join My Mailing List to your Facebook Page (http://apps.facebook.com/ctctjmml). Many of the major mailing list services have apps for Facebook, such as Mailchimp and iContact.

Now that we've run through some of the apps listed as on Facebook, you may have noticed that we haven't covered the ones listed in the following sections on the App Directory Page. Don't worry, though — many apps are listed in several different categories.

+ **External Websites:** Flixster, Bing, Pandora, TripAdvisor, Meetup, and other apps.

+ **Desktop:** Seesmic, RealPlayer, TweetDeck, and other apps.

+ **Mobile:** Mobile Arcade, Qik Video, and other apps.

+ **Pages:** Causes, Where I've Been, and other apps.

+ **Prototypes:** Apps that are built by Facebook engineers appear under this heading. These are experimental apps and are sometimes buggy. They can also change or be taken down at any moment, so you'll need to check them frequently if you use them. Some of the ones listed right now are Enhanced Event Emails, Photo Tag Search, and Slideshow.

As mentioned previously, many apps are listed in several categories in the Directory. Think of it as a shopping experience; you see the same shoes in several stores, so to speak. And as we mention early in this chapter, you should choose the apps that are most appropriate for your business, and don't overload your fans with needless link clutter on your Page. Choose wisely.

We want to mention appbistro again (`http://appbistro.com/`) because this app has a nice interface for finding apps for your Page.

One last thing about apps. Not only are there apps you can add to your business Page, but Facebook itself has an app for your mobile phone. The interface is optimized for mobile phone viewing, which means you'll find pluses and minuses for Facebook business Pages when viewing them through a mobile app. For example, on an Android device, using the Facebook app, when you go to a business Page through a link in the News Feed, you see only two tabs: Wall and Photos. All the apps that you've added, along with any custom-designed links you might have built for your Page, are not available for viewing on a mobile phone (currently). Take a good look at your demographics. Are your visitors viewing your Page only through a mobile phone? If so, keep that in mind as you build your Page. You might need fewer apps and instead more posts to your Wall.

Now, what if the app you have in mind is not listed anywhere in any app directory? The next chapter takes you through the world of creating your own custom app for your Page.

Chapter 2: Creating New Streams of Income with Apps

In This Chapter

✓ Submitting your Facebook application

✓ Finding users for your app

✓ Marketing your app

*D*eveloping a Facebook application is not terribly difficult if you have some programming experience. If you're not a programmer, hiring one who can develop an app for you is also not terribly difficult. Making money from your application is where it can get tricky. You can find over 550,000 active applications on Facebook, and only a very small percentage of them make money. But if you start with a winning idea or game, add some viral tonic, and stir in a little persistence, you may have the recipe for a money-making Facebook application.

Getting to Know Facebook Apps

A wide range of applications and games are currently used on Facebook. They can be as simple as the Give Hearts Application, which is pretty self-explanatory and just gives "hearts" to other Facebook users, or as complex as the Networked Blogs application, which imports your blog automatically to Facebook.

Other applications are developed for brands and Pages to use specifically on their Facebook Page, such as the Store Locator on the Einstein Bros Bagels Page, as shown in Figure 2-1. You can use applications to do everything from just display an image to displaying a mini Web site on your Facebook Page. Many people refer to these applications as iFrame applications, but they're the same applications that we develop in this chapter. The application is designed to be used for private use on your Facebook Page, just as the Store Locator application is in this example. See Chapter 2 of this minibook for more information about using iFrames to customize your Page.

Figure 2-1:
Einstein Bros Bagels developed this app to help people find a location.

You can monetize your application in one of a few ways, and it's a good idea to have a clear strategy in mind before you develop your application. Here are the most common ways people make money with their applications:

✦ **Advertising:** The first money-making model for an application is advertising. You can make money with advertising within your app by putting banner ads linking to things that provide a commission (typically referred to as *affiliate marketing*) or via a pay-per-click model. Figure 2-2 shows an example of a banner ad within the Quiz Whizapplication.

✦ **Virtual goods or the "pay-to-play" model:** This model is most often used by games. Playing is free, but a player can earn and buy credits to do more things within the game. Games like FarmVille, Texas Hold'em, FrontierVille, and Mafia Wars all use this model.

✦ **Freemium model/subscription services:** The *freemium* model means that your application does some things for free, but you then require users to pay for more advanced features. This can be a one-time fee for the premium service or a subscription service. An example of this is the PageNotifier application, which notifies you of comments on your Page. You can use it for free and get one e-mail message per day to notify you of new comments, or you can sign up for more frequent scans for a small monthly fee. If you have a good idea for a need you can serve with different tiers of service, this can be a great model to follow.

Figure 2-2:
A banner
ad for
Mandalay
Bay within
the Quiz
Whiz
application.

Creating Your Own Branded App

When you have your brilliant application idea and your money-making strategy in mind, it's time to create your application. Facebook needs to approve your application first, but it allows most applications that are submitted as long as they follow these core principles:

✦ Create a great user experience

• Build social and engaging applications

• Give users choice and control

• Help users share expressive and relevant content

✦ Are trustworthy

• Respect privacy

• Don't mislead, confuse, defraud, or surprise users

• Don't spam — encourage authentic communications

In case you don't have programming experience and want to hire a developer, Facebook has a list of preferred developers at `http://developers.facebook.com/preferreddevelopers`. You can also find developers in the Facebook Developer Forum, but make sure that you take a look at their portfolios of work.

As you begin to create your application, here are some of the basic terms you need to know:

✦ **Canvas Page:** When you build an application on Facebook, your application shows up via a *Canvas Page,* which is an iFrame hosted by Facebook. An *iFrame* is just a way of displaying content from another site onto Facebook's site. This is where people connect with your application.

✦ **Integration points:** How people connect to your application and where and when you post information about your application can affect how easily your application can go viral. In this chapter, we cover several *integration points* where users can come across your application. The main place to integrate is in the user's News Feed. For example, when a user starts using your application, you can post a notification about it in the user's News Feed, as shown in Figure 2-3. You can also post information when a user gets to a certain level in your game. We cover integration points in more detail later in this chapter in the "Integration points" section.

Figure 2-3:
News Feed
stories
when
people
add your
application.

✦ **Authentication:** By default, your application can access all the general information in a user's Profile, including name, Profile picture, gender, and Friend list. But if your application needs to access other parts of the user's Profile that may be private, your application can request extended permissions. Be aware that applications that request more permissions tend to have a lower click-through rate on the Permissions screen. Users tend to be uncomfortable with giving away lots of permissions. Figure 2-4 shows the Request for Permissions screen shown to users.

Figure 2-4:
Several
permissions
are needed
for the
TripAdvisor
application.

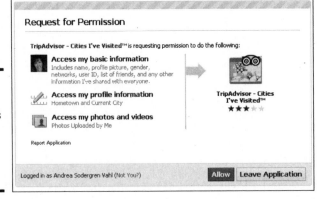

Getting into the programming of your application is beyond the scope of this book, but even if you are hiring someone to code your application, it's a good idea to get familiar with the Facebook Developers area to see what help is available. It's also good to know the steps to start your application and to add to the information in your application so that if you have to change any of the basic information, you can do that on your own.

To create your application, follow these steps:

1. **Go to** www.facebook.com/developers/createapp.php.

   You will see a screen where you can name the application.

2. **Enter the name of the application; review Facebook's Terms by clicking the Facebook Terms link.**

3. **Click the radio button next to Agree and then click Create App.**

4. **You are then asked to enter the Captcha code as a security check. As always, good luck reading the code. Enter the code and click Submit.**

   You are then taken to the Edit Application area, as shown in Figure 2-5.

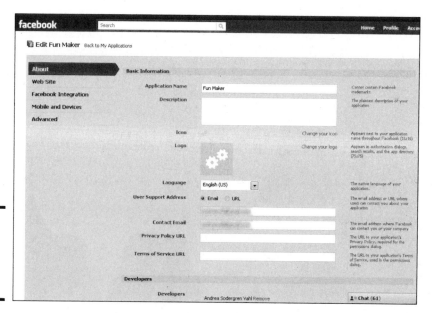

Figure 2-5:
Edit your
application
from this
page.

5. **Fill out the following fields on the About Page:**

   • *Description:* A description of your app (optional)

   • *Icon:* Appears next to your app name throughout Facebook and is 16 pixels x 16 pixels (optional)

- *Logo:* Appears in authorization dialogs, search results, and the app directory and is 75 pixels x 75 pixels (optional)
- *Language:* Language of your app.
- *User Support Address:* The e-mail address or URL where users can contact you about your app
- *Privacy Policy URL:* The URL of your Web site's Privacy Policy
- *Terms of Service URL*
- *Add User:* Add an additional app user here by adding an e-mail address

6. **Click the Web Site tab on the left side of the Page.**

7. **Enter your Web site's URL in the Site URL box.**

   If you would like authentication on the subdomains, enter the site in the Site Domain field also. You would use this feature to make sure that the Facebook user gave you all the same permissions for different domains that you might use in the Application.

8. **Click the Facebook Integration tab on the left side.**

   You see a form like the one shown in Figure 2-6.

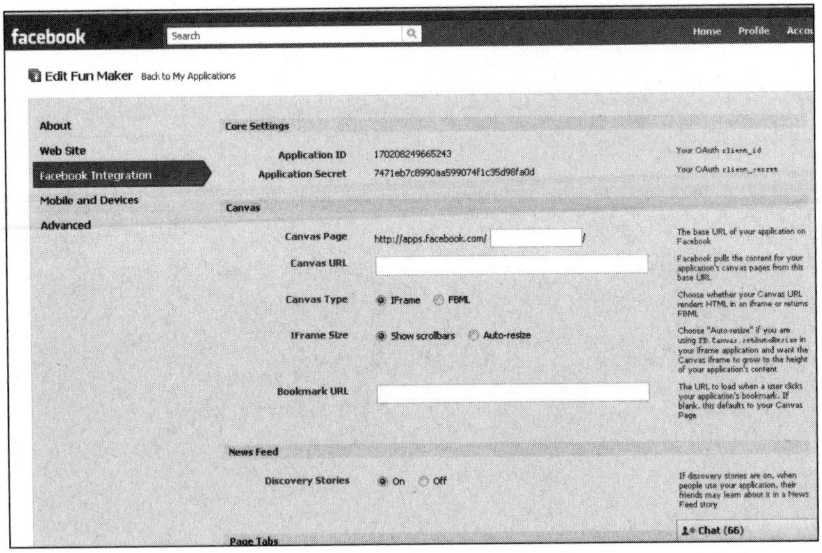

Figure 2-6:
Fill in the Facebook integration information here.

The Canvas Page is the unique name for your URL of the application on Facebook. Because the name has to be unique, it can be a challenge to come up with one that is not already taken. Pick a name that is similar or the same as your application name. You can use letters, underscores, or dashes, but numbers are not allowed. Enter this name in the Canvas Page field.

In the Canvas URL field, enter the URL of the Page on *your* server that will host the application.

Select the iFrame radio button next to Canvas Type because that will be the default application type as FBML is being phased out. .

From here, you can fill in the remaining sections based on your application's needs.

As you develop your application, keep these important best practices in mind:

✦ **Make sure that your application doesn't take too long to load and use.** People are typically used to fast Web interactions, and speed is important. Reduce the number of server calls (accessing the data on the server) that you need to make from your application to help increase the speed.

✦ **Spend time creating your icons and screen shots.** Make sure that they are enticing and interesting. This helps the application get noticed by other users or by people browsing the Application Directory (we discuss the Application Directory later in this chapter).

✦ **Craft your description and About Page well.** Spend some time emphasizing why your application is better, different, or more fun than other similar applications.

✦ **Test your application heavily before use.** Facebook has added the ability to create up to 50 test users associated with each application to test the functionality of everything from using the application to inviting Friends to the application and more. Go to `http://developers.facebook.com/docs/test_users` to get the code to create test users.

✦ **Think about mobile.** As more users begin using Facebook on their mobile devices, make sure that you are participating there too.

✦ **As mentioned, minimize the number of permissions you ask for and ask for only what you need.** If people see that the application has too much access, it may deter them from using your app.

✦ **Keep on top of Facebook changes.** Facebook changes the application programming interface (API) with little or no warning, and it's up to you to see what, if anything, it breaks in your application (you can learn more about the API an other core concepts here: `http://developers.facebook.com/docs/coreconcepts/`). Facebook may give you some idea of changes to come, but you don't always know the exact moment they will take place. Watch out! The Developer's Forum can be a good place to go when something has changed because the developers share what works for them to adjust to the new change.

Finding resources for app developers

Two places on Facebook are great resources for app developers. One is the Developer site on Facebook (`http://developers.facebook.com`). The other is the Developer Forum (`http://forum.developers.facebook.net`), where other app developers can help each other.

These two sites are your foundation for information. The communications from Facebook are critical, and the Forum is invaluable for help with code, questions about how to monetize your app, ideas on advertising, and so on.

Another great place to get information is the Inside Network of Web sites. Here you find a collection of four sites: Inside Facebook, Inside Social Games, AppData, and Inside Mobile Apps. They can be found at `www.insidenetwork.com`.

The AppData site is a great place to search for apps and look at their statistics. AppData has organized the applications much better than Facebook's own Application Directory. Figure 2-7 shows the listings by application and also by developer.

Figure 2-7: The AppData site in the Inside Network site is a good resource.

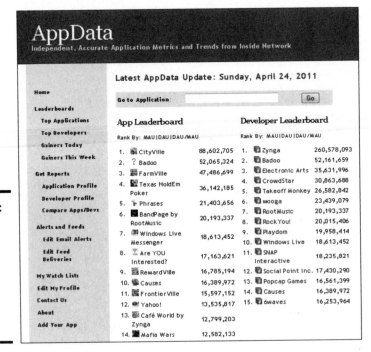

AppData is also a good place to submit your application after you have completed it. Notice the Add Your App link in the lower-left corner of Figure 2-7. By clicking it, you can submit your application to the AppData directory.

If you have developed a game, keep informed about new happenings through the Facebook Developer's Forum but also through blogs like the www. insidesocialgames.com.

Developing a budget for creation and marketing

You need funds to develop your application before you see any return, but where do you get these funds? You have a number of ways to get funding for your application, including venture capital, private investors, and your own bootstrap efforts.

In the past, Facebook ran fbFund, which awarded grants to application developers, but it was discontinued in 2010. It was funded by a couple of venture capital firms, Accel Partners and The Founders Fund. You may still see information about this fund on Facebook's site, but it has been discontinued.

If you choose to work with venture capital or private investors, keep in mind that you will have to have a solid plan and realistic projections for your application.

Make sure that you have a budget for the creation phase of developer and design work, but also keep in mind the promotion of the application. There's no point in creating an application with no marketing budget. Your marketing efforts should include a Facebook Ad campaign (see Book VIII for more on how to set up your campaign) and perhaps some advertising in other networks such as www.rockyoumedia.com or www.slide.com/advertise. You can also find some applications using the free service at www.applifier.com for application Ad exchanges, as shown in Figure 2-8. An ad exchange is where you cross-promote other apps on your app with ads while you receive the same type of cross-promotion on other apps. These ads help drive awareness for your app with people who use apps on Facebook. Applifier is primarily for game applications.

Figure 2-8:
Applifier is
a free Ad
exchange
program
to cross-
promote
games.

If you are bootstrapping (that is, you don't have extensive funding sources) your application development and don't have a budget for advertising, the integration points are going to be critical for your success. Make sure that you are using the News Feed posts effectively and making it enticing for people to invite their Friends to use your application. When people are drawn to an application because their Friends are using it, you can get better participation.

Submitting apps

To submit an application to the Facebook Application Directory, you must first make sure that it has at least five total users or ten monthly active users. You can get these users by strong-arming your Friends and family to sign up to use the application, or you could run a Facebook Ad to get new users to your application. See Book VIII for more information about setting up an Ad campaign for your application.

After you have the minimum number of users, use the following steps to submit your application:

1. **Go to** www.facebook.com/developers.

   You see your applications listed on the right, as shown in Figure 2-9.

2. **Click your application title, and you are taken to your application dashboard area, as shown in Figure 2-10.**

   Here you see that your Directory status is Not Submitted.

3. **Click the blue Submit It link, as shown in Figure 2-10.**

If you are making an application to be used for your own Page or the Page of a client, do not submit it to the Directory.

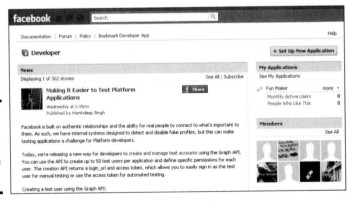

Figure 2-9:
Your
applications
are listed on
the right.

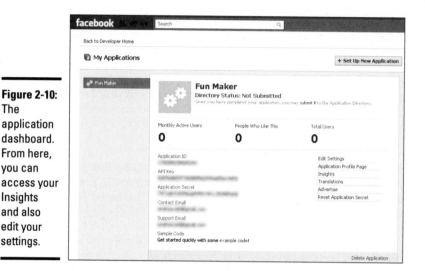

Figure 2-10:
The application dashboard. From here, you can access your Insights and also edit your settings.

Getting featured by Facebook

How to get into the Featured by Facebook section of the Application Directory is a bit of a mystery. You can find the Application Directory at www.facebook.com/apps/directory.php. The featured applications shown in Figure 2-11 don't seem to be based on the number of users or even the number of stars in the reviews.

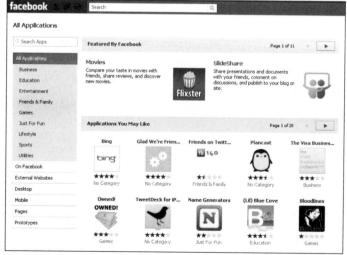

Figure 2-11:
Applications in the Directory can be listed almost randomly.

Also a mystery is the Applications You May Like section. They may come from an algorithm that considers applications you already use combined with applications that your Friends use.

Even the apps that come up when searching the Apps Directory are unusual. If you search the Directory on a term such as *video* or *books,* the list returned shows the applications in a seemingly random order, with lower-rated apps that have few users sometimes coming before apps of higher ratings and more users.

Sometimes when you search for a specific app even by name, it may still be buried in the search results or, worse, not show up at all. But it is still a good idea to submit your app to the directory because it may be found there by someone searching for apps.

The feeling among developers is that the Directory isn't too important for the growth and success of your app. Not too many people actually browse the Directory (or even know it's there!) to find their applications unless they are looking for something very specific. More important is getting people to use it and share it with their Friends.

Another place to submit your application is to external app directories such as AppBistro or the Inside Network's AppData listing (refer to Figure 2-7). AppBistro can be found at `http://appbistro.com/` and then click How It Works at the top of the page for more information on the submission process. Inside Network's AppData can be found at `http://www.appdata.com/`; click Add Your App at the bottom of the left sidebar.

Using Your Branded App

After you have your application coded, the real test comes. Will people use it and share it? Facebook users can be a finicky bunch. Even if an application is incredibly useful, that doesn't mean it will go viral. Here are some things that you can do to help your application be usable, shareable, and interesting:

✦ **Watch for bugs.** Your early adopters test your app for you. You want to be very responsive to things that don't work or they will leave. Watch your Wall on your application Page for users reporting bugs. If you have a Discussion tab on your Page, they may report bugs there also. Check them both frequently. Get things fixed quickly and respond to their posts, or let them know that you are working on it. Your early users are critical to the success of your application. Figure 2-12 shows a site handling its bugs proactively by putting a link to have people report bugs easily.

Figure 2-12:
At the
top of the
application,
you can
easily
submit bug
reports (or
give the
site a good
review).
Smart.

✦ **Balance how much you post and communicate with your users.** You need to publish stories to News Feed to increase the exposure for your app, but if you post too much, you risk people leaving your application or blocking it.

✦ **Pay attention to feature requests.** If you have several people asking for the same new feature, adding it may improve the usability of your application.

✦ **Update your app regularly.** An app that languishes without even minimal updates can show that the developers don't really care.

Driving users to your app

After you get your application up and running, you want thousands to start using it right away, right? Well, patience can be the key here. You need a certain number of users before your app can start growing by leaps and bounds. You can start off getting new users by asking your Friends and family to use it and then have them encourage others to use the application, but that will only get you so far.

Integration points

The integration points mentioned earlier are also a key. The number of integration points offered by Facebook has gone down with the removal of tabs for applications on personal Profiles and the removal of Profile boxes. Here is a list of the current integration points:

✦ **Application Directory:** You have a listing in the Application Directory after you meet the minimum five-user requirement and submit your application.

✦ **About Page:** This is where people can find out about your application and start using it or add it to their Page if it's an application that can be used by Pages. It has the look of a business Page, which can confuse some people regarding how to install the application or start using it.

Figure 2-13 shows an About Page. In this figure, you can see that it looks a lot like a business Page. The way that you can tell that it is an application is that underneath the title of the Page (Pixorial, in this case), you see the classification App. You also see the blue Go to App button. This Page tells you about the app and then links you to the actual app.

Figure 2-13: Update your users by posting on your About Page.

✦ **Canvas Page:** This is the Page within Facebook that runs your application.

✦ **News Feed:** You have the ability to post in your user's News Feeds. You can post several types of things. You can post a notice when someone starts using your application. You can also post an attachment such as a video or picture.

Limitations on how and what you can post are covered in more detail later in this section. You also have a maximum number of times that you can publish to the News Feed for a user. This limit gets raised as you get more users who are using your application.

✦ **Notifications: If you have obtained the appropriate permissions**, you can send her notifications and e-mails. This can be helpful to get people back to using your application if they become inactive. Again, you have to use this strategically so that people don't block your application.

✦ **Requests:** This is the way people can invite their Friends to use your application. Requests can also show up in the sidebar of the user's home page (reference Figure 2-16). Requests can also be for games where people give each other gifts to draw people into the game.

✦ **Bookmarks and counters:** Your application or game can be bookmarked on left side of the user's home page, as shown in Figure 2-13. This makes it easy for users to find the application again. The counter can be set to show actions within the application that the user needs to take. Notice the 7 next to FarmVille in Figure 2-14 — it means that the user needs to take seven actions. This can help bring users back to your application.

Figure 2-14:
Bookmarks appear on the left side of the user's home page.

✦ **Like button:** When people click the Like button on your application Page, an update appears in their News Feeds.

The News Feed is a critical integration point because you want your application to be showing to the user's Friends. But it's a balance. If you post too much, people will hide your application or block it. If you force users of your application to post too many updates to their News Feed, the Friends of the user might not like all the posts, and will decide that they don't want to use the application.

Facebook has some guidelines about how you implement the requests and stream stories. Here are things that are and are not allowed by Facebook when using the integration points:

✦ **You cannot incentivize users to share information about your application by promising them a reward only if they do so.** For example, you cannot offer users "10 Gold Coins" for your game only if they publish the story to the News Feed. But you can ask if they want to share a story to their News Feed about winning "10 Gold Coins" and give them the option to skip it if they don't want to share it.

✦ **You cannot prefill News Feed stories so that it looks like the person wrote the comment.** This puts words into the users' mouths and makes it look as though they wrote the post (that is, "This game is awesome!" with a link to the game so that it looks like the user wrote those words).

✦ **You must provide an easy way to skip publishing a story to the News Feed or using the integration points.** If you have an option for a user to invite his Friends, for example, he must be allowed to skip that step if he chooses.

Advertising

Advertising can be a great place to attract new users to your application. See Book VIII for more information about how to create your Ad campaign. Even established applications continue to run advertising campaigns to attract users. Figure 2-15 shows the Ad that the Wildfire application is running.

Figure 2-15: The Wildfire application advertises on Facebook Ads.

As we cover in Book VIII, you can really target who you show your Ads to in Facebook.

Keeping users in your app

To keep users coming back to your application, make sure to give them a reason. Give them new content to find or something different to expect each day. Also, engage your users and establish relationships with them if you can. Requests can help keep users using your application or game. Requests are defined in the Integration Points section, previously in this chapter. The requests are going from one Facebook user of your app to their Friends. These show up in the sidebar of the home page, as shown in Figure 2-16.

When a person starts using an application, depending on the permissions you requested when you set up your application, you may be able to e-mail him or her. Again, use restraint so that users do not block your application. Figure 2-17 shows an e-mail from FarmVille that hopes to engage users.

Figure 2-16:
When you click App Requests on the left sidebar, all the applications that have sent requests to appear here. Game Requests appear as their own menu item.

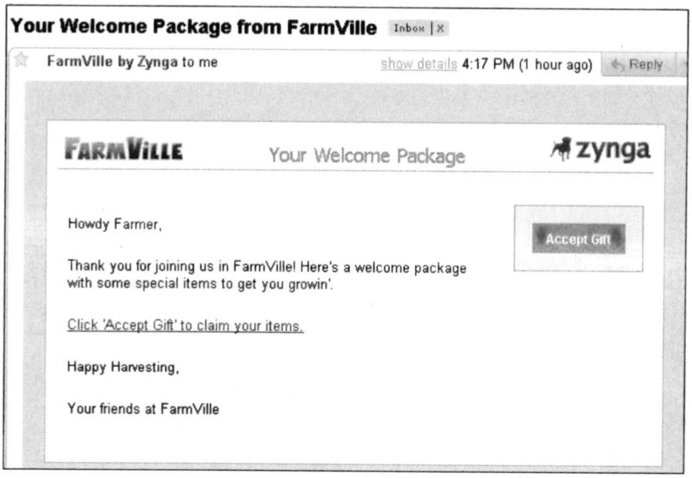

Figure 2-17:
Welcome gifts and other special communications can keep your users engaged.

Making your app go viral

The magic *v* word — viral — is what it's all about in the world of Facebook applications. How does an app go viral? A lot has to do with the integration points and what people see in their News Feeds. Also, very important with the viral nature is how people can bring their Friends into the application. If you can create something that will get people's Friends invited to the application by making the invitation fun and exciting, you have struck gold.

If you can get people to say, "You *have* to try this; it's awesome!" to all their Friends, you have a much better chance of succeeding. Above all, make sure that it's easy for people to invite their Friends to your application.

Promoting your app across different platforms

It's a good idea to make your app available outside of Facebook if possible. Although Facebook isn't going anywhere anytime soon, you don't want your entire future to rest on Facebook's whim. Some solutions for this are creating an iPhone app or making some of your functionality available on a Web site.

For example, Pixorial, shown in Figure 2-18, is a Facebook video-sharing application, but it also has a Web site that allows people to access its videos and e-mail them to people who are not on Facebook or send them to different places on the Web.

Figure 2-18:
The Pixorial external Web site.

Creating an iPhone or Android application involves more challenges and requirements than creating a Facebook application, but it can be worth it for the cross-promotion. If you can get smart phone users to start using it, they may also use your application within Facebook.

Developing an application can be fun and financially rewarding, but it also can be a lot of hard work. Start out with a plan, watch what is happening in the marketplace, and have patience. Hire a good developer if you don't have the coding experience. Try different techniques of engagement if one isn't working for you, and good luck!

CityVille: The making of a viral app

CityVille is a game developed by Zynga, the largest Facebook game developer. So it had a leg up when it came to marketing. Within the first 24 hours that CityVille was out, it had almost 300,000 users, and at the end of one week the numbers topped 3 million. The game is currently closing in on 90 million users. How did Zynga do it?

First, it leveraged the users of their other games, FrontierVille and FarmVille, and then had a massive international launch. If that sounds daunting for your application, don't worry: Zynga had to start somewhere, too. Zynga has created easy-to-use games that involve user's Friends by having them work together to unlock rewards.

The users can work toward a goal or spend real money on virtual goods that help them get to that goal faster. These actions then cause the user to be more invested in the game. The users are also playing with their Friends and are keeping up with their Friends' progress by playing more than they might if they were playing alone. So while CityVille has shattered growth records on Facebook, they are leveraging Zynga's preceding games that are very similar in concept. The lesson here is to create something that works and then rinse and repeat.

Book VI

Making Facebook Come Alive with Events and Contests

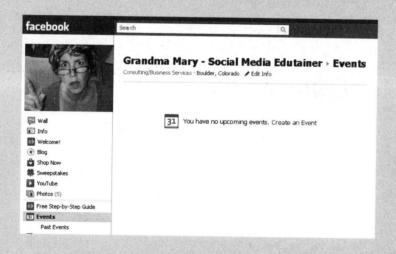

Contents at a Glance

Chapter 1: Creating Facebook Events

In This Chapter

- ✔ **Entering the Event basics**
- ✔ **Sharing your Event with your community**
- ✔ **Working around Event limitations within your Page**

Using the Facebook Events feature can create a lot of buzz around an Event, your store, an online event, or even a product or book launch. Facebook Events show up on people's Walls and within their Events area and are even searchable by anyone on Facebook. Add to the mix the fact that any time a Friend interacts with your Event, that person's Friends all see something in their News Feed about the Event, which gives it a lot of free publicity courtesy of Facebook.

If you have been on Facebook for very long, you have probably received an Event invitation yourself, so you may be familiar with Facebook Events. If not, don't worry; in this chapter, you learn how to set up an Event, the best practices for getting the word out about your Event, and tips on using Events with your Page.

Getting Started with Facebook Events

Facebook Events can be a powerful way to get your Event noticed and shared within the Facebook community. But just as with any marketing activity in Facebook, you need to be mindful of the balance between sharing your Event and spamming people with unwanted posts about it.

Because Facebook Events show up in multiple places within Facebook, they are more visible than just a Wall post. Facebook makes it easy to have Friends invite other Friends to events, and if an Event is public, anyone who has a Facebook account can RSVP.

Don't make your Event public if your Event is at your home. There have been cases in which random strangers have shown up to Events that were posted on Facebook publicly and have vandalized the home.

As mentioned, Facebook Events can be beneficial for many different types of events: charity events, book tours, virtual webinars, open houses, big sales at your store, and more. Figure 1-1 shows a book signing created by Gary Vaynerchuk; note that one of the authors was invited by a Friend on Facebook. News of a Facebook Event can spread through Friends inviting other Friends.

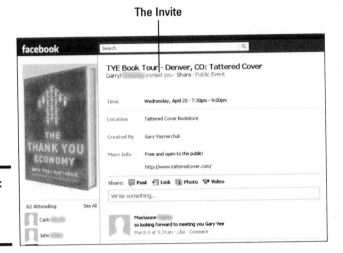

Figure 1-1: A book signing event.

Social Media Examiner has done a great job of promoting its virtual webinars through Facebook Events (Figure 1-2 shows an example). It uses the Event Wall actively to answer questions about the Event and give new information about the Event.

Figure 1-2: The Social Media Success Summit was a virtual Event.

Facebook Events are seen in potentially five different places, which is why you want to create Facebook Events. You give your connections five different ways to find out about your Event, as follows:

✦ The right sidebar of your home page lists two or three upcoming events (the most current ones are displayed).

✦ The Events link on the left sidebar of your home page shows all your Events.

✦ When an event is created, it appears in the News Feed of all your Friends (if you create the event on your personal Profile) or in the News Feed of all your Likers.

✦ When people are invited to an Event, they may get a notification in their notifications area if they have their Event notifications enabled.

✦ When people are invited to an Event, they may also get an e-mail about your event if they have the e-mail notifications enabled.

It's important to note that when you create a Facebook Event on your Page, you will not be able to invite guests (see the section "Uncovering Limitations," later in this chapter). But other people can invite guests if they RSVP to your Event.

On the right sidebar of your home page, you see the most current events coming up, as shown in Figure 1-3.

Figure 1-3: Events appear on the home page.

Having the Events listed on the home page of Facebook makes them very visible to potential customers, which is a perfect reason to create Events for your business. The Events listed are the ones that are either happening now or are the next upcoming event. So this area is good for reminding people of an Event coming up shortly, but not as effective for events farther in the future.

You will also find a link to all your Events on the left sidebar of your home page. When you click it, all the Events you have been invited to appear on the Events page, shown in Figure 1-4.

Figure 1-4:
All your
events on
the Events
page.

When you get invited to an event, it also shows up in your notifications area (see Figure 1-5). This is another way that your Event gets increased visibility.

Figure 1-5:
You get
notified
when
someone
invites you
to an Event.

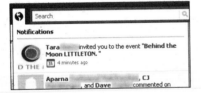

You can create Facebook Events through your personal Profile, and you can create them through your Facebook business Page (or Page; we use those terms interchangeably). We recommend creating an Event through your Facebook Page because it's better for your branding and complies with Facebook's terms that disallow you from using your personal Profile for your own commercial gain. There are some limitations with creating Events on your Page, and we cover how to best get around those limitations later in this chapter, in "Uncovering limitations of Facebook Events."

Adding the Events app to your Page

When you first start your Facebook Page, the Events application is available, but it may not be immediately visible in your Page navigation links on your left sidebar. Events is a Facebook application, meaning that it was created by Facebook and not a third party.

Your Events link should (but might not) show up in the left sidebar underneath your Page picture, as shown in Figure 1-6.

Figure 1-6:
Look for the Events link first underneath your Page profile picture on the left sidebar.

To add your Event link on your Page sidebar, follow these steps:

1. **Click the Edit Page button in the upper-right corner of your Facebook Page.**

   You are taken to the Page dashboard.

2. **Click the Apps link on the left sidebar to see all the apps you have available on your Facebook Page.**

3. **Find the Events app, as shown in Figure 1-7 and click the Edit Settings link.**

   A pop up box appears.

Figure 1-7:
The Events application in the Apps area.

4. Click the (Add) link next to the Tab: Available text and then click the Okay button (see Figure 1-8).

   The pop-up box disappears and you now have the Event link showing in the left sidebar of your Facebook Page.

Figure 1-8: Add the navigation link to your sidebar by clicking Add.

From the Apps area, you can create an Event by clicking the Go to App link shown in Figure 1-7. Or from your Facebook Page, you can click the Events navigation link on the left sidebar and then click the Create an Event link, shown in Figure 1-9.

Figure 1-9: Click the Create an Event link to start creating your Event.

Entering the Event details

When you go to the Event Application or click Create an Event after clicking the Event link on your left sidebar, as detailed in the steps in the preceding section, you are taken to the screen where you can enter the Event details, shown in Figure 1-10.

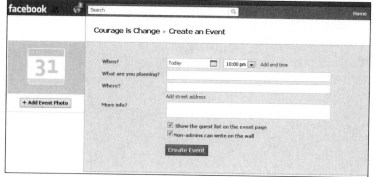

**Book VI
Chapter 1**

Creating Facebook
Events

Figure 1-10:
Enter the
Event
details here.

Enter your Event details in the following fields:

✦ **When?:** Enter the time and the duration of the Event. For typical events, you will have a beginning time and an end time. If you're promoting an ongoing occurrence, such as a book launch, you can specify a range of time during which you'll be promoting the event. The benefit of using a range of time is that your Event will show up in people's sidebar for the duration of your Event.

✦ **What are you planning?:** Put the title of your Event here; this title shows up when you post your event. So make it compelling and descriptive!

✦ **Where?:** Fill in this field with a description of where the Event is to be held. If you're holding an online event or virtual type of Event, you can add more description here to market it, such as "In your pajamas at home" or "An online exclusive event." The information in the box also shows up if you post a link to this Event or Share this Event; so again, you want to make it descriptive. To add the exact location, click the Add Street Address link below this box.

✦ **More info?:** Give details concerning what the event is about, what you plan to do, why someone should attend, and so on. Put the main information in the first 50 words because that's what people see. After 50 words, a More link appears for users to click to see the rest of the description. So if someone needs to pay to register for your event (currently there is no way to do this through Facebook) and go to another site where you are accepting payments, put the link to this site in the first part of your description.

After you enter everything into the fields described in the preceding list, make sure to add a picture. Even if you don't have a specific picture to go with the Event, find one on the Web (making sure that you have the appropriate permissions or that it's royalty free) or use your logo. You want a picture to go with your Event to make your display eye-catching and more visibly interesting than mere text is.

If you are hosting a large event, plan ahead to design a picture or image specifically to go with your Event. You will have more branding for your Event and get a better response.

When your Event is ready, click the Create Event button. Clicking this button publishes the Event to your Wall, as shown in Figure 1-11, so make sure it's ready to go.

Figure 1-11:
Your Event
is published
immediately
to your Wall.

Grandma Mary - Social Media Edutainer created an event.

Social Media Lunch and Learn - Facebook, Twitter and LinkedIn for Business
Friday, January 7, 2011 at 12:00pm
Colorado Conference Rooms, Boulder, CO

Post Insights not yet available, please check back later.

2 minutes ago · Like · Comment · Share · RSVP to this event

You can't start working on an Event and save it for later additional work. So before you start, make sure that you have all the details ready! As soon as you click Create Event, it will be published.

Synching Events with your personal calendar

After you have created an Event or even RSVP'd to someone else's event, you can easily export this event to your personal calendar. To do so, click the Export link at the bottom of the Facebook Event page, and a pop-up box appears to allow you to choose where to send the Event as shown in Figure 1-12.

Figure 1-12:
The pop-up
box lets
you choose
where to
export the
Facebook
Event.

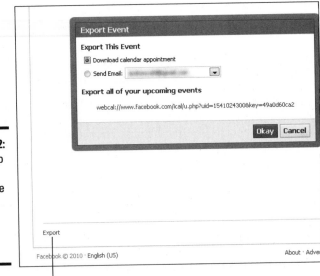

Export link

Editing your Event

In case you need to make a change to your Event after you have created it, editing your Event is very simple. From your Facebook Page, use the following steps:

1. **Click the Events link on your left sidebar.**

   You see your Events listed, as shown in Figure 1-13.

Book VI Chapter 1

Creating Facebook Events

Figure 1-13: Your Events are listed when you click the Events navigation link.

2. **Click the title of the Event to be taken into the Event details area.**

3. **Click the Edit Event button in the upper-right corner of the Event as shown in Figure 1-14.**

   You can now edit any of the Event details just as if you were creating the Event for the first time.

4. **Click the Save Event button after you have made your changes.**

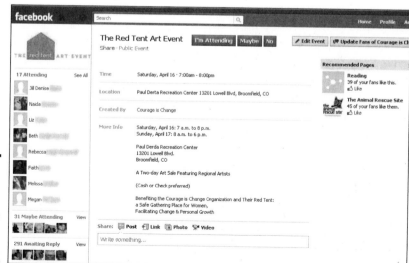

Figure 1-14: Click the Edit Event button in the upper-right corner.

Cancelling your Event

It's easy to cancel a Facebook event if you need to. Keep in mind that you can edit the information on the Event if needed as covered in the previous section. But if you have accidentally created multiple Events or you just need to cancel one, follow these steps:

1. **Go to your Event by clicking the Events link in your left sidebar (refer to Figure 1-13).**

2. **Click the title of the Event.**

   You are taken to the Event details area.

3. **Click the Edit Event button in the upper-right corner of the Event.**

4. **Click the Cancel this Event link in the lower-right corner (see Figure 1-15).**

   A pop-up box appears, in which you can write a personal note to those who have been invited, as shown in Figure 1-16.

5. **Click the blue Yes, I'm Sure button.**

   Your event is cancelled. As the box says, the cancellation cannot be undone and you will no longer be able to see the Event at all.

Figure 1-15: Click the Cancel this Event link in the lower-right corner.

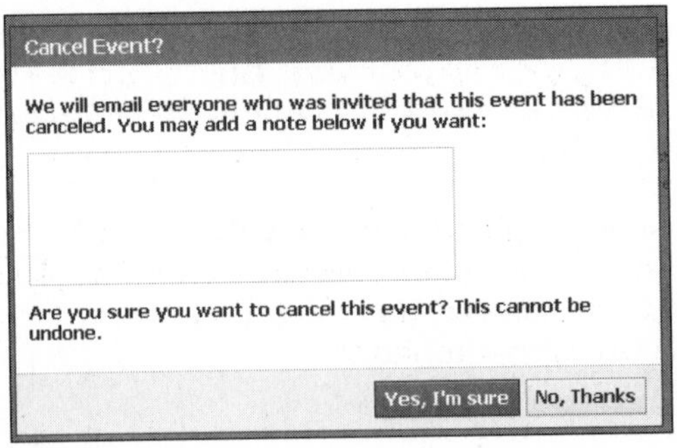

Figure 1-16: Write a note to let people know why the Event is cancelled and to give further instructions.

Uncovering limitations of Facebook Events

Creating a Facebook Event on your Facebook Page is different from creating the Event on your Facebook personal Profile in two main ways. First, you can't invite anyone to your Event.

When you create an Event on your personal Profile, you can select the guests whom you want to personally invite from your list of Facebook Friends. They then receive a notification that you invited them to your Event; they also get an e-mail notification if they have that feature enabled. But because Facebook Pages cannot invite their Fans, you have to get the word out about your Event by posting it to your Wall and encouraging others to invite their Friends.

The second limitation is that when you create the Event as your Page, you can send only an Update to your Fans about the Event. (We tell you how to do so later in this chapter, in the "Sending updates about an Event" section.) Updates are not very visible as we explain later. When you create a Facebook Event on your personal Profile, you can send Facebook e-mails to the people you have invited to let them know about any changes or updates to the Event. Facebook e-mails are very visible and helpful when you need to let people know about a major change.

Even though there are these limitations with creating an Event on your Page, we still recommend that you use your Page for any business activities. Facebook Events can still be a beneficial way to promote your Event to your community.

Promoting an Event

After you create your Facebook Event, you need to make sure you promote it. A great way to do that is by making your promotion fun and exciting for your community. You may want to post a few "teaser" announcements about your event to let your community know to be watching your Page. Something like "Big news coming tomorrow about something you won't want to miss" can work well to create some buzz before you post the actual Event.

The first step to promoting your event is to share it directly with your community. You have the initial Wall post when the Event is created, but it is important to remind people often about your event just in case they missed the post in their News feed.

There is a line between getting the word out about your Event and over-promoting it. To avoid crossing this line, make sure that you still have plenty of value in your other posts. Also, don't just post your Event over and over or people will Unlike or hide your Page!

Inviting your community to your Event

Because you cannot invite your community via a standard Facebook invitation, the main ways to get the word out about your Event are by posting your Event to your Wall as a link, tagging your Event in a Wall post, and using Updates. Remember to vary your posts and keep them fun.

Notifying your Page community of your Event

Your Event was posted to your Wall when you created it, but you should re-post your Event regularly. Some people will have missed that initial Wall post, and others may need reminding to RSVP to your Event. To continue to get the word out about your Event, make sure to share the Event as a link on your Page several times a week. You can find the link to the Event by going into the Event after you create it as shown in Figure 1-17.

Find ways to vary your posts about your Event. Give away a promotional item, feature a particular vendor or sponsor of your Event, or add something new to the Event to give you a reason to make a new announcement about it.

Highlight the URL and select the Ctrl and C buttons on your keyboard to copy it.

Figure 1-17: Find the URL of your Event as a regular link to post it to your Page wall.

Just attach the link to an Update as you would any other by clicking the Link button in your Update and pasting it in the Link area. The picture for your Event will be the one posted next to the Event.

Because you have posted your Event as a link, it is easy to share with other people. If the link to your Event is in the News Feed, people can click Share, and a pop-up box will appear that lets them fill out their own invitation to the event in the status area as shown in Figure 1-18. Ask people in the status part of the message to click the Share button to spread the word about your Event!

Figure 1-18:
Encourage
people to
click Share
to post your
Event to
their News
Feed.

Tagging events

Another way to keep people informed of your Event is to use the status
updates feature for both your personal Profile and your Page to tag the
Event so that people can easily click over to it. To tag the Event, just type
your message into the Publisher on your Wall, use the @ symbol, and start
typing the name of the event, as shown in Figure 1-19. The Event name
should come up and you can select it.

Figure 1-19:
Tag your
Event as
a different
way to link
to it.

Selecting it makes it a clickable link like the one shown in Figure 1-20.
Tagging covered in more detail in Chapter 3 of Book 4.

Make sure to remind people about the Event often by reposting the link
or tagging the Event. Consider posting something about your Event two to
three times per week at different times of the day. You will want to post at
different times to connect with different members of your audience who may
be logging into Facebook at different times. Normally, the best time to connect with the most people is in the morning, so make sure you have at least
one post per week in the morning.

Figure 1-20:
An Event
tagged
by Social
Media
Examiner to
promote it
and remind
people to
RSVP.

Sending Updates about an Event

You can also send an Update to your community about the Event. Updates are the way that business Pages send messages to people who Like their Page. An Update is not as visible as a Wall post. To send an Update to your community, go into the Event, and in the upper-right corner, click the Update Fans Of link, shown in Figure 1-21.

Figure 1-21:
Click the
Update
Fans Of link
to send an
update to
your Page
community.

A pop-up box appears that allows you to add a message your Update about your Event, as shown in Figure 1-22.

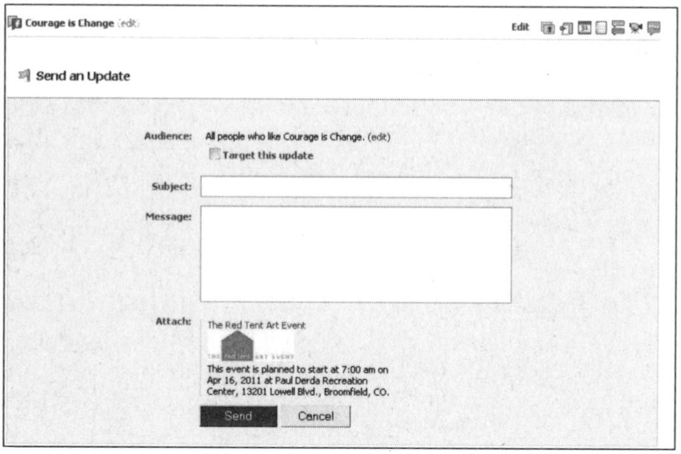

Figure 1-22:
Add your message to your Update and click Send.

Updates appear in the Messages area (see Figure 1-23), but people are not notified when they get an update from a Page, so be aware that many people don't think to check the Updates. Wall posts are more effective for reminding your community about your Event.

Figure 1-23:
Updates from Pages appear in the Messages area.

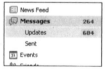

Encouraging interaction within your Facebook Event

Your Facebook Event contains its own Wall on which people can post messages about the Event. They can also post Event pictures and videos. If people are posting in the Event, make sure that you are responding and connecting. People may have questions about the Event, and you want to answer those as quickly as possible. Other people likely have the same questions, and the sooner you address any issues that arise, the better for your business.

If your Event is a reoccurring one, post some pictures of past Events to show people how fun or well-attended it has been. You may also want to post a picture of the past Event on your Page Wall and then tag the Event (refer to Figure 1-20).

You may also ask some of your close friends who are coming to the Event to post on the Wall of the Event to get buzz going, as well as to provide social proof. *Social proof* means that when you can see your friends or other people giving good feedback about something, you're more likely to respond favorably to it or to give it a try.

The Event Wall postings do not get sent out to the News Feeds of people attending the Event but are visible when people look at the Facebook Event.

Sharing your Facebook Event outside Facebook

Part of your promotion strategy should be to Share your Event on other sites as well. When you drive traffic to the Facebook Event, you also increase exposure to your Facebook Page. When you are sending out the link to your Event, just cut and paste the URL (refer to Figure 1-17). Here are some places to Share your Event:

✦ **Blog or Web site:** If you have a blog, post a blog entry when your Event is announced. If you have a professional logo, place it in the sidebar of your blog or Web site with a clickable link that goes back to the Facebook Event.

✦ **E-mail subscribers:** Send an update about your Event to your subscribers. If they're not on Facebook, they won't be able to RSVP there, but they will be able to view the Event. Give them an alternative way to RSVP if they're not on Facebook.

✦ **Twitter, LinkedIn, and other social media:** If you're on Twitter, tweet the link to your Event each day after you have announced your Event. Also send a message to your LinkedIn connections and any other social or professional networks you subscribe to if appropriate. For example, make sure that you're inviting only local people from your LinkedIn network if your Event is local. Or if you are connected to colleagues with a completely different business focus than your Event, don't invite them.

A word about creating a Facebook ad for your Event

Another method for promoting your Event is by running a Facebook ad. Putting together such an ad is fairly easy to do and doesn't have to cost a lot of money. Advertising your Event can be an effective tool to reach your target demographic and connect to new people on Facebook. When you create a Facebook ad for an Event, people can RSVP easily by clicking the RSVP link on the ad.

We don't cover how to create a Facebook ad for an Event in this chapter, but you can find out how to set up your ad in Book VIII, Chapter 2.

Chapter 2: Building Excitement with a Contest

In This Chapter

✔ **Choosing a type of contest**

✔ **Outlining the details of your contest**

✔ **Setting targets for success**

According to a recent poll by Econsultancy, the number one reason people will Like a Facebook Page is to be notified of special offers and promotions (`http://econsultancy.com/us/blog/7136-why-do-people-follow-brands-on-facebook`). With that in mind, it's a good idea to run a contest on your Facebook Page.

A contest also gives people a reason to connect with you, makes your Page more fun, and attracts more people to your brand and your site. But what will your contest look like? You have a lot of options to consider when setting up your contest, and in this chapter, we explore how to design your contest, set your targets, and make sure that you are riding on the right side of Facebook law.

Thinking about Running a Contest?

The first thing you should consider when running a contest is your goal. Are you looking for more people in your Facebook community, more subscribers to your newsletter, or more brand awareness? If you begin with the end goal in mind, the pieces will fall into place.

All different types of businesses can benefit from Facebook contests. A contest can draw attention to your business and give you a list of people who want your product or service. You can draw attention to a product or service that you offer as a way to market it. For example, if you're a consultant, you can offer a consulting package that people may not know about. If you're a florist, you could offer a "Fresh Flowers for a Month" package to get your community thinking about treating themselves to flowers every week. If you're a Web designer, you could give away a free Web site redesign to prompt others to use your services. When people enter your contest, you have a list of people who are interested in your product or service.

Make sure that you structure your contest to align with your end goal. Here are some ways to achieve your goals when running a contest:

+ **Grow your Facebook community:** If you want more people to join your Facebook community, make Liking your Page a requirement for entry.

+ **Add subscribers to your newsletter:** Be sure to let contest entrants know that they will be added to your e-mail list when they enter (and make sure that they have a way to unsubscribe to comply with spam rules).

+ **Increase brand awareness:** You can also have entrants check in to your Facebook Place to enter the contest, which can drive awareness of your business location.

Your prize does not have to be expensive or lavish. It just has to be something that your community wants. (A Facebook Page called Chocolate for Breakfast gave away a premium chocolate prize pack and received more than 700 entries in one week!) You might also receive a glowing recommendation and referrals from the winner of your contest.

Your contest is part of your marketing budget. A well-run and well-publicized contest can be much more effective than a print ad for increasing awareness and engagement.

Designing Your Contest

How you design your contest can have a big impact on its success. How long will it run? Will you pick a random winner or have a photo contest that is judged? Will you ask people to invite their Friends to enter? Will you have an option to sign up for your newsletter?

One guiding principle for designing your contest is to make it fun. People enjoy the chance of winning something for free. Make it valuable for your audience and beneficial for you.

Also, you need to decide how to administer the contest according to Facebook's contest and promotional rules. The easiest way is to run your contest through a third-party application, which we cover in Chapter 3 of this minibook. You can also consider designing the contest application yourself (see Book V, Chapter 2 for more information about creating applications).

You have several issues to consider when designing your contest:

+ **Type of contest:** It can be a sweepstakes where the winner is drawn at random or a contest where people vote for the winner.

✦ **Requirements for entry:** Will you have users upload a photo or video, send a short essay about why they should win, Like your Page, or just enter their name and e-mail address? The possibilities are endless. If you make it too difficult, you may not get as many entrants. Make sure that you make it fun, and it will have a better chance of having people spread the word about it.

If you intend to have people upload content, it can be more entertaining to have the winner picked by a community vote. This will give people a reason to come back and check on the progress of their favorite pick.

✦ **Prizes:** While it helps to have a big budget to offer something like a Family Trip to Yellowstone, as offered by Challenge Butter in Figure 2-1, you can still offer something valuable to your community even if you are a small business. Spend some time considering the prize, and you may even poll your audience to see what they would like.

✦ **Length of contest:** How long will your contest run? If it requires voting, how long will the voting period be after the contest? Will you have a "judging" period to narrow the entrants and then allow people to vote on the ones you have selected? Many places recommend a one-month contest period to give time to get out the word-of-mouth factor. This is definitely appropriate if you have photo or video requirements for entry. A sweepstakes can be shorter if needed. You will have to factor in how much time you want to allow for promotion. If you are running it for a month, you will need to be promoting it heavily for a month, so factor this into your marketing schedule.

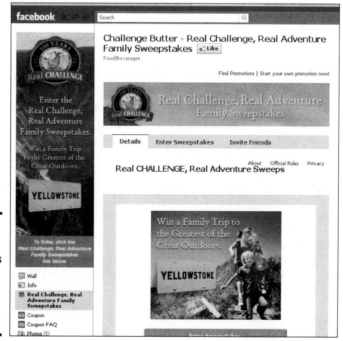

Figure 2-1:
Challenge Butter offers an enticing prize to contest winners.

Facebook has strict rules about contests. The biggest rule is that contests and promotions may not be administered through Facebook unless they are administered through an application. You can build the application yourself or use a third-party application designed specifically for contests and sweepstakes (such as Wildfire, Votigo, and so on). You cannot collect entries, conduct a drawing, or notify winners through Facebook. For more information, see the section "Understanding legal restrictions," later in this chapter.

Choosing a contest type

You can run two main types of contests: a true contest where there is some vote to choose the winner (or the winner could be judged by you) or a sweepstakes where the winner is chosen at random.

You can set up the contest in a variety of ways. One such way is to have someone upload a picture that is judged by your community. Realtor.com ran a holiday lights picture contest that involved having people upload pictures of their houses decorated with holiday lights. The Facebook community then voted for their favorite picture, and the winner won a $100 gift card. As another example, a coaching professional had people write a short statement about why they wanted to come to her weekend retreat. She then judged the entries herself and picked a winner for a free registration to her retreat.

Sweepstakes are prevalent on Facebook. The barrier to entry is low because people typically just have to enter their name and e-mail address and Like the Page. Because no judging is involved, the winner is chosen at random. If you use a third-party application such as Wildfire to run your sweepstakes, the application will assist you with choosing a random winner.

Choosing between a contest and a sweepstakes will depend on your goals. Typically, contests are better for engaging your current community and sweepstakes are better for growing your community. If you use the Wildfire application to administer your contest or sweepstakes, you can also choose to give away coupons. Here are some considerations when choosing between a contest, sweepstakes, or a coupon/giveaway:

✦ **Contests:** A contest will increase your community involvement by having users vote and may drive more of the entrants' Friends to your Page as they ask them to vote for them. But if the entry requirements are too involved, you may not get the turnout you had hoped for.

✦ **Sweepstakes:** A sweepstakes is better for growing your Facebook community or e-mail list. The requirements for entering the sweepstakes are typically entering a name and e-mail address and possibly Liking the Page, which is very easy for most people to do. You will get more entries but possibly not as many people sharing it with their Friends.

You may get people entering your sweepstakes who are only interested in the prize and not interested in your company. If you can make the prize connected with your business, you will have a better chance of connecting with the right audience.

✦ **Coupons or giveaways:** Depending on which contest application you use, you can run a coupon or giveaway. Figure 2-2 shows a coupon promotion created with the Wildfire application. You can also find these promotions under the Promotions application at `http://apps.facebook.com/promotionshq` (which is run by Wildfire). The Promotions application is the application that you can add to your Page to administer the coupons. Chapter 3 of this book covers the various contest applications supported by Facebook.

Figure 2-2:
Coupons and promotions appear in the Contest/ Sweep-stakes area within Facebook.

A coupon or a giveaway is great for attracting attention to your product, building brand awareness, or a launching product. Coupons and give-aways in Facebook are easily shared with Friends, and people love to get special deals.

The coupons will not be very visible in this place alone, so you will have to promote them. Atlanta Bread is promoting their coupon for a free cookie on its Facebook Page (see Figure 2-3) and its Web site (see Figure 2-4).

Figure 2-3: Atlanta Bread promotes its coupon on its Facebook Page.

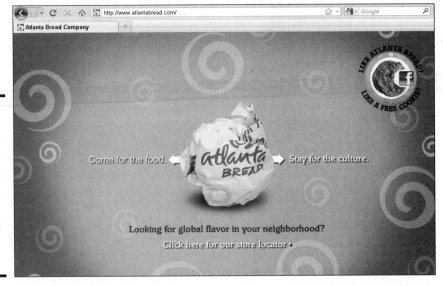

Figure 2-4: Atlanta Bread promotes the coupon on its Web site and drives traffic to its Facebook Page.

Coupons are a nice feature here, but you might want to consider Facebook Deals as well. Facebook Deals are free to set up.

See Book VII, Chapter 6 for more information about Facebook Deals.

Reaping the benefits of a well-run contest

Before you put your contest out there, make sure that you have everything in place to kick it off with a bang. You will be spending money on the contest application, and you want to make sure that you are getting the maximum benefit. You also want to make sure that it's well thought out so that you don't get negative results. The following sections describe some of the good and bad consequences of running a contest.

Benefits

The following are some of the benefits of running a contest:

✦ **Increase in traffic to your Facebook Page:** If you are promoting your contest well and encouraging people to sign up on your Page, you will have increased traffic. Make sure that you set up the marketing schedule so that you promote consistently throughout the contest.

✦ **Rewarding your community:** A contest can reward some of the members of your community and keep them interested in your Page.

✦ **Increase in participation:** By opting in to your contest, your community is participating more, which will encourage more participation in the future, especially if you are having a true contest where people vote.

✦ **More Likes:** We hope that you're requiring that people Like your Page when you run your contest.

✦ **More newsletter subscribers:** Not everyone is on Facebook all the time reading your updates (shocking, we know). E-mail is still a great method of communication when you really need to get the word out about something in your business.

✦ **Buzz:** Well-run contests can generate buzz and get people excited about your product or brand.

Disadvantages

Some of the disadvantages of running a contest are as follows:

✦ **Time:** Promoting and marketing your contest can take time. To promote it well, it can take a lot of time, possibly time away from your core business. Make sure to plan your contest during a time when you won't be caught trying to do too much at once.

Polling your audience for ideas

Sometimes you may not be sure what prize you want to offer or what would get the most response from your community. The best way to overcome this obstacle is to ask your users. You can create a poll or survey easily with sites like SurveyMonkey.com or Zoomerang.com. You can use the Question tool in the Facebook Publisher to create a poll for your Page. You can ask, "What prize would you like to receive if I held a Facebook contest?" and then add prize options that people can vote on. See Chapter 1 of Book III to learn more about creating a poll for your Page.

You may be deciding between two or three prizes, and by involving your audience in the decision, you will build more excitement for the prize and also build more buzz around the contest. If you don't have any ideas, your audience can help suggest things, but you may not get a consensus.

✦ **Money:** Your contest will cost money to run; the actual prize will obviously also cost money. Depending on how nice the prize is, you can spend a lot of money. If you don't receive the benefits you were hoping for, such as a large group of new Likers or people who enter the contest, sometimes giving out that prize can feel painful. Again, planning and promotion can help you get the benefits you are looking for.

✦ **Possible community dissatisfaction:** Some people just don't like contests. If judging is involved, people may get angry if they feel it wasn't done properly. This can create some "bad buzz" around your brand. One way to combat this may be to think of a special gift for everyone who entered. That gift doesn't have to cost much money. It could be a special e-book given only to them or a special discount just for them. Even just a personal note to thank them for entering and for their participation can go a long way.

Now that you know the pros and cons of conducting a contest, how do you ensure that your contest is successful? The key is the system in place to handle the entries and the marketing. Your system will be the third-party application or the application you design yourself.

The nice thing about the third-party applications is that they handle the entries, voting, posting of the rules, and selection of the winner all within Facebook guidelines. The applications make it easy to run a contest that is professional and well designed.

Understanding Facebook and legal restrictions

You should definitely understand Facebook's promotion guidelines before starting your contest. While you may see others violating the terms, Facebook does state that it can remove materials relating to the promotion or even disable your Page or account. So it pays to follow the rules!

The biggest rule that you should follow is to not administer any promotion through Facebook except through an application. You can use a third-party application designed to administer contests (such as Wildfire, Votigo, and so on) or you can program an application yourself to collect entries which is more involved.

But what does it mean to not administer a promotion through Facebook except through an application? Basically, you cannot collect entries, conduct a drawing, or notify winners through Facebook directly; the notifications have to be done though a different tab on your Facebook Page. For example, you cannot

+ Put a post on your Wall that says "Everyone who responds to this post is entered to win a gift card"

+ Have people upload a photo to your Wall to be entered in a contest

+ Announce the winner of your contest with a post on your Wall

+ Have anyone who Likes your Page be automatically entered in a drawing (you can have this be a condition of entry, but it cannot be the only way that someone enters the contest)

You can promote a contest that is being held on your Web site through Facebook, but the administration of the contest cannot take place using the Facebook Wall.

Here are some legal restrictions that you need to be aware of:

+ The promotion cannot be open to anyone under the age of 18. However, Facebook does have people under the age of 18 on its site (13 is the minimum age).

+ If you have set up a sweepstakes, due to legal restrictions, it cannot be open to people in the countries of Belgium, Norway, Sweden, or India.

+ You cannot have as a prize or promote the following items: gambling, tobacco, firearms, prescription drugs, or gasoline.

Again, the nice thing about the third-party applications such as Wildfire and Votigo is that they are set up to follow Facebook's guidelines. For the full set of guidelines, go to `www.facebook.com/promotions_guidelines.php`.

Defining Success

Before you start your contest, make sure that you know what you are aiming for so that you know whether you were successful. How many entries are you hoping for? How many new Web hits? How many new mentions of your brand? If you fall short of your goals, you can analyze what you could have changed in the promotion or execution of your contest. We cover the analysis in Chapter 4 of this minibook.

Setting targets

How do you set reasonable targets for entries to your contest? That can be a bit of a challenge if you have never hosted a contest before. You may look at your first contest as your training ground for future contests (and yes, it's a good idea to do multiple contests!).

The number of entries depends on several factors:

✦ **Size of your Facebook community:** If you're starting your contest with 25 people who Like your Page, a target of 12 entries from your Facebook Page may be reasonable.

✦ **Size of your e-mail list:** If you have an e-mail list of 500 and an open rate of 50 percent, you might estimate that of those who open your e-mail, 10 percent will enter. That would mean 25 entries from your e-mail list.

✦ **Other social-media lists, such as Twitter, LinkedIn, Forums, and so on:** You will also want to promote your contest on Twitter, LinkedIn, and other places that you frequent online. But the entry rate on these sites might be lower still. You can probably estimate that 1 percent of your Twitter following and your LinkedIn connections would enter depending on how engaged you are with these connections.

✦ **Web-site hits:** If you have your contest listed prominently on your Web site, you can also estimate that some of your Web site visitors will enter your contest. Entries might be fairly low — possibly around 0.5 percent of your Web site traffic.

✦ **Size of the prize:** You will get a higher opt-in for a bigger prize.

✦ **Length of contest:** The longer the contest goes, the more time people have to opt in. But don't make it too long so that people get tired of hearing about the contest. One month is a good rule of thumb, and it can be shorter for sweepstakes-type contests.

✦ **Other promotional efforts:** These efforts could involve guest posting on another blog where you promote your contest, advertising your contest, or distributing flyers about your contest in your local community.

You may want to set a conservative goal of 5 percent opt-in for your e-mail and Facebook community and smaller percentages of other places that you participate on the web. Then take a look at that number and see whether that is a worthwhile number for the money and the time you will be spending.

Keep in mind that goodwill and buzz are hard to measure and hard to put a price on.

Setting your plan

After you set your targets, set your promotion and marketing plan for your contest. Make sure to get the word out on all channels to engage your audience. Here are places to market your contest:

✦ **Blog or Web site:** If you have a blog, make sure that you have a blog entry ready for when your contest kicks off. If you have a Web site, make sure that you have a link or banner to click on so that visitors to your Web site can enter the contest or sweepstakes.

✦ **Facebook Page:** Obviously, you will be posting often on your Facebook Page about the contest because it is easy for your community to enter on Facebook.

✦ **E-mail subscribers:** Start with your current customers to get the buzz going about your contest. Let them know how they can enter, and ask them to spread the word.

✦ **Twitter and other social media:** If you are on Twitter, make sure that you are tweeting the link to your contest daily. Send a message to your LinkedIn connections if appropriate.

✦ **Facebook Ads:** Facebook Ads (see an example in Figure 2-5) are a natural place to get people to enter your contest. You can target your demographic in the setup of the Ad and send users directly to the link on your Facebook Page that has the entry form to your contest.

Figure 2-5:
Ad for winning a shopping spree in Denver.

Win $1,000 at GoLite ✕

Win a $1,000 shopping spree at the GoLite Holiday Outlets stores in Denver.

You will also need to have your measurement plan in place. The other nice thing about the third-party Facebook applications is that they have extensive analytics on the entries, as shown in Figure 2-6.

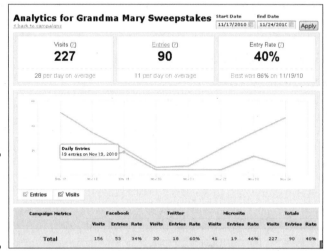

Figure 2-6:
A snapshot of the analytics on Wildfire.

We cover more of analyzing your contest results in Chapter 4 of this minibook. Make sure that you have Google Analytics on your site so that you are tracking clicks to your contest entry form.

Now that you have your plan in place, you are ready to set up your contest, which we cover in Chapter 3 of this minibook. Remember to keep it fun and exciting so that your community will help spread the word about your contest and make it go viral.

Chapter 3: Using Third-Party Contest Applications

In This Chapter

✔ **Browsing contest applications**

✔ **Selecting the right application for you**

✔ **Setting up the application within your Page**

T he easiest way to manage your Facebook contest is with a third-party contest application. These applications have been designed to work within Facebook's contest guidelines and make getting started a snap. You will have a professional look to your contest and, in many cases, get analytics included with the package so that you can analyze your results.

As with other Facebook applications, you will have to go through a few steps to add the application to your Page, and in this case, the applications are not free. Luckily, they are very affordable, and you can get a lot of nice features to help you facilitate a well-run contest.

In this chapter, we look at how to find those often-elusive third-party applications, how to get them set up, and how to notify the winners and deliver your prizes.

Finding a Contest Application

Finding contest applications in Facebook can be challenging. The Facebook search function for the apps does not always find all of the apps available. In most cases, it's best to just go directly to the Web site of the third-party application to find directions on how to add the application to your Page.

Three of the applications, Wildfire, Woobox, and North Social, are self-service applications, which means that you can set them up from start to finish on your own. We look at the steps to set them up later in this chapter. The other contest applications require you to contact the vendor to get pricing and more information and are typically better for large campaigns. The other contest applications have more customization capabilities but they also are more expensive. In this chapter, we focus on the steps to use the self-service applications.

Each application has its pluses and minuses, and you should make sure that you are going with the one that fits your needs. If you're running a larger campaign, get quotes, look at the third party's past performance, and ask for referrals.

Whichever third-party application you use, be ready with all your other promotional efforts and take some time to analyze your results. We cover both of these aspects of your contest in greater detail in the next chapter.

Comparing contest applications on the Web

If you would like to compare your contest application options, here are the Web sites of the current third-party Facebook contest developers:

✦ **Wildfire** (www.wildfireapp.com): Wildfire is the most popular contest application. It's an easy self-service application that you can set up yourself, and it doesn't cost too much to use.

✦ **North Social** (http://northsocial.com): North Social has a sweepstakes application but not a contest application. North Social bundles all its Facebook apps for one monthly fee. It is also a self-service application.

✦ **Woobox** (www.woobox.com): Woobox is similar to North Social in that it is a self-service application with a sweepstakes option, but it's not a contest option, and all its apps are bundled for one monthly fee.

✦ **Votigo** (www.votigo.com): Votigo has a contest and sweepstakes option but is not self-service, meaning that you can't set your contest up on your own. Votigo focuses on larger brands such as Kohl's and MAC cosmetics. If you want to use its contest application, you need to contact Votigo through its Web site to get pricing and details.

✦ **Fan Appz** (http://fanappz.com): Fan Appz has only a sweepstakes option, and you can't set it yourself up. You have to contact Fan Appz to get it set up.

A contest involves having people upload a picture or video or submit an essay, and there is some type of voting or judging. A sweepstakes selects the winner at random and contestants need only to enter their name and e-mail address. See Chapter 2 of this minibook for more details on contests and sweepstakes.

Both Votigo and Fan Appz are not self-service applications and are completely custom apps, so we don't focus on how to use them in this chapter (just wanted to you to be aware of them). Contact those companies to get more information.

Many of these sites have examples from contests they have administered or video tutorials on how to get started. These tutorials are very helpful in showing how the contest applications work and can be a good place to start when deciding which application to use.

Searching for contest applications within Facebook

If you want, instead of going to a contest application that you already know about directly, you can try to search for a new one. New apps are added to Facebook all the time, and there may be a more recent contest app that would work well for you. Custom applications such as Votigo and Fan Appz will not show up here.

The Apps Directory search feature doesn't always list the proper applications clearly, which can be confusing. When you enter *contest* into the Apps Directory, found at `http://www.facebook.com/apps/directory.php`, you will find applications of contests that have been developed for a specific use as well as some of the applications that are designed for general use.

If you do search on *contests* in the Apps Directory, you will find the Wildfire Contests application, as shown in Figure 3-1.

Book VI
Chapter 3

Using Third-
Party Contest
Applications

Figure 3-1:
Wildfire's
Contests
application.

Likewise, searching on *sweepstakes,* you will find the Wildfire, North Social, and Woobox Sweepstakes applications, as shown in Figure 3-2

Figure 3-2:
The
Wildfire,
North
Social, and
Woobox
Sweep-
stakes
appli-
cations.

Installing and using the applications can vary from one application to another. Sometimes you will be able to install the application, such as the Wildfire application, from within Facebook. Others, like North Social, direct you to their Web site to get the full installation instructions.

A third-party Facebook application search tool is available that does a better job of searching through applications than the Facebook Application Directory. It's called Appbistro and can be found here: http://appbistro. com. This tool may come in handy as new applications are being added to Facebook every day.

Getting to Know the Contest Applications

In this section, we cover the contest and sweepstakes applications that you can install and set up yourself: Wildfire, North Social, and Woobox.

Exploring Wildfire

The Wildfire application is the most widely used contest and sweepstakes application. As mentioned earlier, it is a self-service application that you can easily set up on your own.

Wildfire has the advantage of having an integrated place to enter many contests and sweepstakes from within Facebook. It's not always easy to find, but it may cause some people who may not have otherwise seen it to "stumble across" your contest. Figure 3-3 shows the screen where people can browse contests run by Wildfire and can be found on the Wildfire apps page here: http://apps.facebook.com/sweepstakeshq/. As shown in the figure, users can browse by category, most popular, most recent, top prizes or ending soon.

A Wildfire campaign starts at $5 per campaign plus a daily fee for basic ones and up to $250 or more for their premium campaigns.

Looking at North Social

North Social also has a self-service sweepstakes application that is easy to set up. It does not have a contest application, but it does have many other Facebook Page applications that you can use for one monthly fee in addition to the sweepstakes application as shown in Figure 3-4. The other applications include exclusive coupon offers, a sign-up for your newsletter offer, an RSS feed, and more.

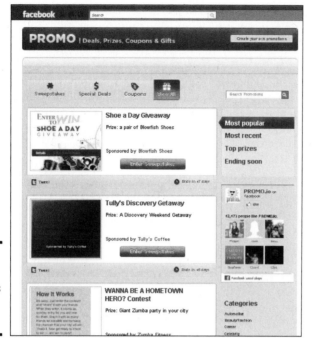

**Book VI
Chapter 3**

**Using Third-
Party Contest
Applications**

Figure 3-3:
Listing of all
the contests
run by
Wildfire.

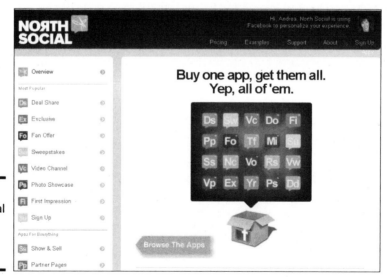

Figure 3-4:
North Social
and the
available
apps.

North Social does require you to use image files, which you will need to create. The image file will serve as the graphics for your contest on your Facebook Page. You can easily create graphics with a simple program like Paint, but you may want to have a professional look from a graphic designer if you can't create professional-looking graphics yourself.

North Social prices by the month and by how many people are in your community. One benefit is that you get access to all their applications, but you may not want to get locked in to a monthly subscription cost indefinitely. A campaign for a Page with less than 1,000 Likers would be only $20 per month (plus a 2-week trial).

Investigating Woobox

Woobox has a monthly subscription fee that will allow you to access all its applications. Currently, it has two free apps: Coupons and Static IFrame Tab. You can use the Static IFrame Tab application to create custom Welcome Pages (which we cover in more depth in Book III, Chapter 2).

Woobox also has the Sweepstakes app and Group Deals app; you can access these apps through the $29-per-month subscription service. Woobox has some nice features, such as requiring people to Like your Page before they can access the sweepstakes entry form and giving people extra chances to enter if they get a Friend to enter.

Delivering the prizes

You may also want to know how the winners are selected and notified. Facebook rules prevent you from notifying the winner on your Page Wall. The Wildfire and North Social apps will help with randomly selecting the winner. With Woobox, you will have to download the entries and randomly select one, and we show you the best way to do that in the Woobox section later in this chapter.

If you are using Wildfire to run a contest that incorporates voting, the Wildfire application keeps track of the votes. You will be able to notify the winners with an e-mail that is generated by Wildfire, as shown in Figure 3-5 (this e-mail is generated for both the contest and the sweepstakes applications).

If you have to mail the prize to the winner, make sure that you mention in your rules that you need a proper mailing address. State that if you can't contact the winner to get a proper mailing address, a new winner will be selected.

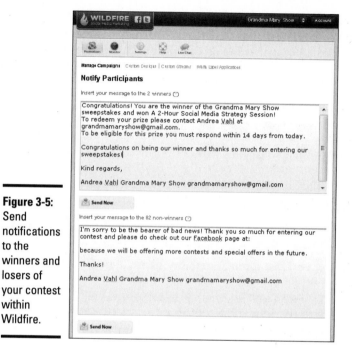

Figure 3-5:
Send
notifications
to the
winners and
losers of
your contest
within
Wildfire.

You also may want to give a time frame in which the winner has to respond to the announcement and claim the prize. Give the winner at least three days to respond, with a maximum of one week. That way, the contest won't be too old and you can still generate some excitement if a new winner must be selected.

Keeping to a budget

As you set up your parameters, you can see exactly how much the campaign will cost before you start. You will pay for the campaign up front, so there should not be any danger of going over your budget after you commit to the contest.

Wildfire charges you according to the length of the contest or sweepstakes and what features you require. North Social and Woobox operate through a monthly subscription fee.

Your prize will likely be the most expensive part of the contest campaign, and the bigger the prize, the better the response, in general.

Designing Your Contest with the Wildfire Application

You can start designing your contest or sweepstakes with the Wildfire application either within Facebook or on the Wildfire Web site. As you design your contest, your progress will automatically be saved so that you don't have to do the work all at once.

If you are going to have a special tab on your Facebook Page for your contest, you will have to add the Wildfire application to your Page before the contest is actually published to your Page.

The easiest way to sign up with Wildfire is to go directly to its Web site at `http://www.wildfireapp.com/` and follow these steps:

1. **Click the red Sign Up! button and on the screen that appears, enter your account information.**

2. **Fill in your first and last name, company name, e-mail address, and password, and select the Agree to Terms check box (review the terms by clicking the terms of service link if you wish). Then click the Create Account button to create your account.**

   You are taken to the site to create your campaign, as shown in Figure 3-6.

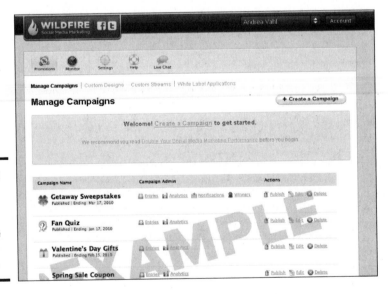

Figure 3-6: After signing up, you can create your first campaign.

3. Click the Create a Campaign link (refer to Figure 3-6), or click the Create a Campaign button in the upper-right corner.

A pop-up box appears, as shown in Figure 3-7.

Figure 3-7: Choose which type of campaign to run.

4. In the pop-up box, select the type of campaign that you want to run.

You are then taken to the Create a Sweepstakes Campaign screen, as shown in Figure 3-8. We chose the Sweepstakes option as an example.

5. Fill out the campaign details for your campaign (refer to Figure 3-8 for an example).

When you're filling out the Description of Grand Prize field, you might want to take a look at the Text Formatting guide hyperlink. If you click it, you see different phrases that you can type into the field to make bold phrases or allow a big header within the text. You can also add a second prize by clicking the Add a Second Prize link. You might want click the Advance Features link to give your prize a dollar value and place it into a category. The categories are used when people browse the Wildfire promotions.

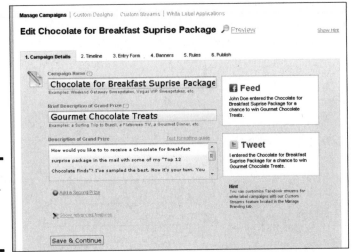

Figure 3-8:
The Sweep-
stakes
sign-up
example.

6. **After you've finished filling out the campaign details, click the Save & Continue button at the bottom of the form.**

   This takes you to the timeline selection (see Figure 3-9).

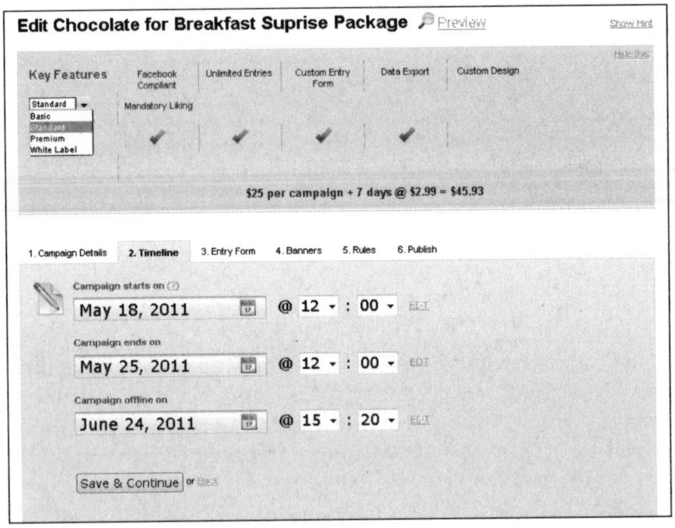

Figure 3-9:
Choose your
timeline.

7. **Choose how long you want the contest to run and then click the Save & Continue button at the bottom of the form.**

   Chapter 2 of this minibook provides suggestions on how long you should run the various types of contests.

In the box that appears (refer to Figure 3-9 where shown.), you can choose what type of campaign you want to run. We recommend the Standard Campaign option as a minimum because you can export the data from your campaign for analysis.

After clicking Save & Continue, you are taken to the Entry Form tab, as shown in Figure 3-10.

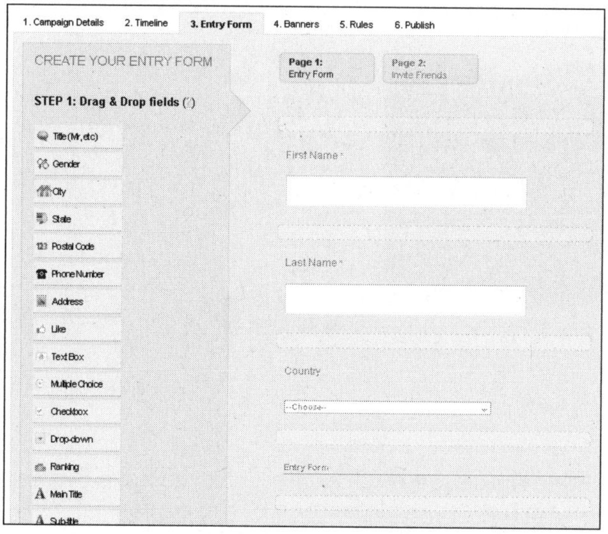

Book VI
Chapter 3

Using Third-
Party Contest
Applications

Figure 3-10:
Decide what information you need on the entry form.

You can decide what information you need from the contestants. You can also choose to have them opt in to your e-mail newsletter, which is only available in standard campaigns and up.

8. Click the Save & Continue button at the bottom of the form.

You are taken to the Banners section, where you can upload your banner, as shown in Figure 3-11.

If you don't have a custom banner, don't worry. It can just help personalize your campaign. If you can use the banner from your Web site, that can help with your branding. Or you can just use the template banner available for you to add your information about your contest. You can also add a 90 x 90–pixel Feed Banner that will show in the News feeds when people enter. Having a Feed Banner has been shown to help increase entries.

Figure 3-11:
Upload your banner or use the template banner.

9. **After you've uploaded the banner, click the Save Banner button and the Continue button at the bottom of the screen.**

   The Rules section appears.

10. **Enter the rules for your contest.**

    Make sure that you are following local contest laws. Also enter the Disclosure Statement and Privacy Policy.

11. **Click Save & Continue at the bottom of the page.**

    You are taken to the Publish tab, where you can decide where to publish your contest. You have to pay for your campaign before you publish it. To pay, click the Pay Now button in the top center of the page and fill in your payment information.

If you haven't done so yet, you are prompted by Wildfire to add the application to your Page. Here is how you add the application to your Page (you must be logged into Facebook as your personal profile for these steps):

1. **Find the Wildfire application that you will use (such as Contests, Sweepstakes, or Coupons).Here is how you find the applications:**

   - **Sweepstakes application:** `https://www.facebook.com/apps/application.php?id=28134323652`

   - Contests application: `http://www.facebook.com/apps/application.php?id=95936962634`

   - Coupons (called Promotions): `http://www.facebook.com/apps/application.php?id=48008362724`

2. **On the left sidebar, under the picture, scroll down until you see the Add to My Page link and click the link.**

   A pop-up box appears, showing all the pages where you are an admin.

3. **Click the Add to Page button next to the Facebook Page where you want the application added.**

   The Page disappears from the list, indicating that the application has been added to that Page. Click the Close button to close the pop-up box.

4. **Navigate to your Page by following these steps:**

   a. Click Account in the upper right corner of the page and you see a drop-down menu.

   b. Select Use Facebook as Page. A pop-up box appears with all the Pages you an Admin of.

   c. Click the Switch box next to the Page you want to navigate to.

5. **Click the EditPage button in the upper-right corner of your Facebook Page.**

   You are taken to your dashboard.

6. **Click the Apps link on the left side and find the Wildfire application (Contest, Sweepstakes, and so on).**

7. **Click Go to App under the application.**

   You see a screen that allows the connection with your Fan Page, as shown in Figure 3-12.

8. **Log in to your Wildfire account from this page.**

   In the screen that appears, you can add the contest to your Page by clicking on the Add to Fan Page button.

You're almost ready to publish the contest to your Page. Before you do, make sure that you have everything in place. You should have your promotional plan in place so that you get the maximum buzz! We go over promotional ideas and planning in Chapter 4 of this minibook.

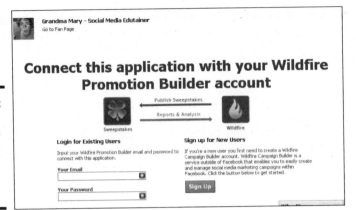

Figure 3-12:
Connecting
the Wildfire
application
with your
Facebook
Page.

When you're ready with your promotional plan, log in to your Wildfire account from the Wildfire Web site and click the Publish link next to your campaign. Then click Publish Now, which is next to the Fan Page icon under the Campaign Channels heading.

Using the North Social Application for Your Contest

North Social also has a sweepstakes application that you can set up on your own. You pay a monthly subscription fee based on how many people Like your Page. The monthly fees start at $19.99, so it is very affordable to use. After you subscribe, you have access to all the applications that North Social offers, so if you can use multiple applications, North Social can be worthwhile to keep. If you are just going to use the sweepstakes application one time, set up a reminder to cancel your subscription when you are done with your campaign.

One nice feature that North Social has is the capability to use the "Fan-only" graphic for the Sweepstakes Page. What this means is that non-Fans, or people who don't currently Like your Page, will see a graphic informing them that they need to click Like to enter your contest. Then, after they click Like, they can enter. The catch is that you have to create this graphic yourself.

To use North Social, you need two mandatory custom images: the Main image, which describes your sweepstakes, and the Thank You image, which is what people see after entering your sweepstakes. These two images must be 520 x 650 pixels.

You can also have an optional a Landing Image, which you can use to have Fan-only entry to your sweepstakes. This image lets people know that there is a sweepstakes and they have to click Like to enter. The Landing Image must be 520 x 650 pixels.

There is also an optional Thumbnail image that you can have displayed next to your sweepstakes description if people share the sweepstakes on their Wall. This image gives your contest better branding and helps you look more professional. The Thumbnail image must be 64 x 64 pixels.

The necessity for custom image files could be a barrier for some people who might consider using this application. If you don't have the ability to create professional images for your contest within your company, you can consider hiring a designer to create them for you. You will find a wide range of prices available from people who create graphics. You can hire a graphics designer from places such as http://www.odesk.com or http://www.elance.com.

The benefit to having custom graphics for your sweepstakes is that you will have a very professional sweepstakes entry page. As an example of what the North Social application looks like on a Facebook Page, Figure 3-13 shows the a North Social t-shirt giveaway sweepstakes.

Figure 3-13:
The North
Social
T-shirt
sweep-
stakes.

You also need to sign up for an account at North Contact, which is North Social's list management and form creation tool. North Contact forms are the way you collect the names and e-mail addresses of the entries into your sweepstakes. Before you get started with the Sweepstakes setup, make sure you apply for a North Contact account here: `http://www.northcontact.com/`. The account is free but it takes 24–48 hours to get your North Contact login details, so make sure you allow time for this information to be sent to you.

North Social has a good video tutorial on setting up your campaign and adding the North Contact form to your sweepstakes setup. You can watch the tutorial here: `http://northsocial.com/apps/sweepstakes/`.

Using the Woobox Sweepstakes Application

Woobox has some useful sweepstakes features. It is easy to set up and has a Fan-only graphics page that is built in. Or you can create one yourself to customize your campaign.

You can also give people extra chances to win if they share your sweepstakes with their Facebook Friends, which can give people an incentive to spread your sweepstakes around. One downside of Woobox is that you don't have much space in the Description area to talk about your sweepstakes. But you can use custom images to convey more information about your sweepstakes.

To get started using the Sweepstakes application, first go to the Woobox Web site at `http://woobox.com/`. Then follow these steps:

1. **Click the red Signup Now button.**

   You are taken to a sign up page.

2. **Enter your Name, Company Name, e-mail, and password and click Create Account.**

   You are prompted to choose an account level. Most account levels will fall under the Pro selection (the default selection), which is \$29/month. If you have more Likes, select Pro100 or Pro250 accordingly.

3. **Enter your billing information and click the Purchase Account Level button.**

   You are taken to the Your Offers screen to add an offer. Before you add an offer, link your Facebook Page to your account so that you can require people to Like your Page before entering your sweepstakes.

4. **To link your Facebook Page to Woobox, click the Setting link in the upper right of the screen.**

   You are taken to your Business Settings. You can enter your business settings (name, address, phone, Web site) if you like, or you can do that later.

5. **Click the Connect a Facebook Page hyperlink.**

   You are taken to a page that indicates whether you have a Facebook Page currently connected.

6. **Click the blue Facebook Login button.**

   A Facebook pop-up box appears that asks whether you want to allow Woobox access to your basic information.

7. **Click Allow.**

   All the Facebook Pages you are an admin of appear on the setup page.

8. **Select the radio button next to the Page you want to connect to the application and then click the Select Page button.**

   You are taken back to the Business Settings Page, where it now indicates that your Facebook Page is connected. Now you add your sweepstakes information.

9. **Click the Promotions link in the upper-right corner.**

   You are taken to Your Offers screen, which shows you don't currently have any offers.

10. **Click the blue Add an offer hyperlink.**

    You are taken to the page where you can select what type of offer to add.

11. **Click the Add Sweepstakes hyperlink.**

    You are taken to the page where you can add all the details of your sweepstakes, as shown in Figure 3-14.

Book VI Chapter 3

Using Third-Party Contest Applications

Here is more information about each of the fields on that page:

✦ **Title:** The title of your sweepstakes. The title can be a maximum of 100 characters.

✦ **Description:** You have a maximum of 255 characters to describe your offer.

✦ **Restrictions:** You may want to specify if there is one entry per person or one entry per person per day.

✦ **Start date and End date:** The start date and end date of your sweepstakes.

✦ **One per user:** This is a drop-down menu with the following selections (pick the best option for your sweepstakes):

   • *Allow User to Enter Themselves Multiple Times*

   • *One Entry Per E-Mail Address*

   • *One Entry Per Facebook User*

   • *One Entry Per Facebook User Per Day*

   • *One Entry Per Twitter User*

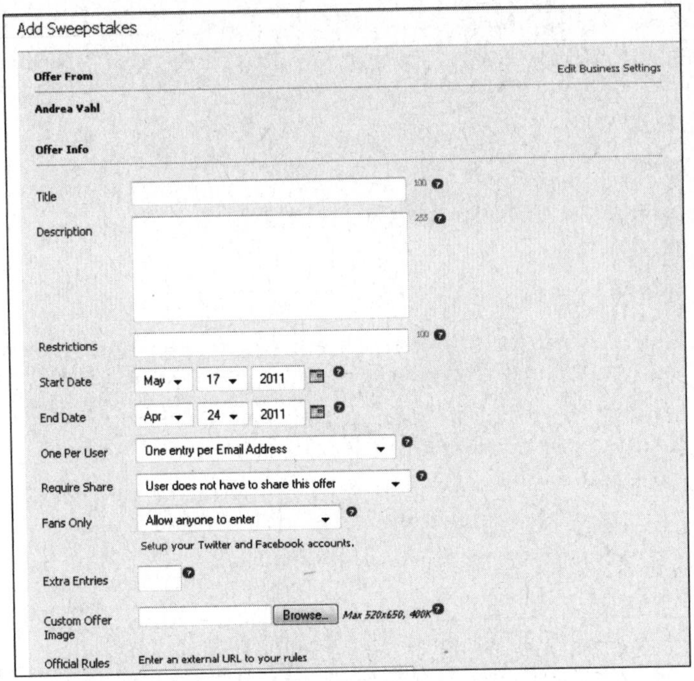

Figure 3-14:
Enter your
sweepstakes
details.

✦ **Require share:** This is a drop-down menu with the following selections:

- *User Does Not Have to Share This Offer*

- *User Must Share Offer Link on Twitter*

- *Ask User to Share Offer on Facebook (w/SKIP)*

You can facilitate more entries if you ask the user to share the offer on Facebook.

✦ **Fans only:** This is a drop-down menu with the following options:

- *Allow Anyone to Enter*

- *User Must Follow Me on Twitter (use this option if you're running your sweepstakes on Twitter)*

- *User Must Be a Fan on Facebook*

The final two options are grayed out until you enter your Twitter or Facebook accounts on Woobox. It's a good idea to let only people who Like your Page to enter the sweepstakes. Because you have linked your Facebook Page, you will be able to select User Must Be a Fan on Facebook.

✦ **Extra Entries:** You can give extra entries to people who get their friends to enter your contest. Put how many extra entries you want to give out to a person for every Friend who enters. Leave it blank if you don't want to give out extra entries.

✦ **Custom offer image:** You can upload a special image that will show on the offer page. It must be a maximum of 520 x 650 pixels tall and no more than 400K in file size.

✦ **Post entry image:** You can upload a special image that will show after the person has entered your sweepstakes. It must be a maximum of 520 x 650 pixels tall and no more than 400K in file size, but is better at 150 pixels tall because of the layout of the post entry page.

✦ **Official rules:** If you have your rules available on a Web site, enter the URL of that Web site. Or you can just type your rules in the larger box.

After you have entered all your sweepstakes information, click the Add Sweepstakes button at the bottom of the page. You are taken to the screen that shows your sweepstakes (now live and shareable if you are within the date range), as shown in Figure 3-15.

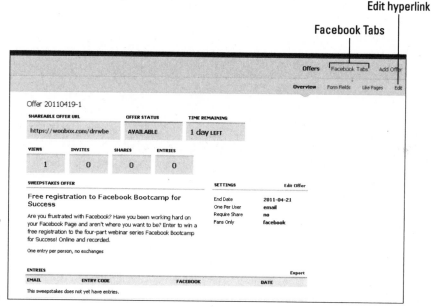

Figure 3-15: Your sweepstakes is now live.

You can edit the dates or any of the information by clicking the Edit offer hyperlink. You also want to add the contest to your Facebook Page. To add it to your Page, follow these steps:

1. **Click the Facebook Tabs link in the upper-right corner, as shown in Figure 3-15.**

You see boxes for the Coupons Page Tab for Facebook, Sweepstakes Page Tab for Facebook, and the Group Deals Page Tab for Facebook.

2. **Click the Install the Sweepstakes tab hyperlink in the Sweepstakes Page Tab for Facebook box.**

   You are taken into Facebook with a drop-down menu to indicate the Facebook Page where you want to install the Sweepstakes application.

3. **Select the Facebook Page where want to add the Sweepstakes tab and click the blue Add Sweepstakes button.**

   You are taken to your Facebook Page where the Sweepstakes app is now added, but you must specify which offer to show. You will have the message Check Back for Our Fan Offer.

4. **Click the Edit Tab Settings hyperlink.**

   You are taken into Woobox to select the offer you want to show on your tab (see Figure 3-16).

5. **Select the radio button next to your sweepstakes and click the Save App Settings button.**

Figure 3-16:
Select your
offer.

Sweepstakes App for Facebook

Non-Fan Image   Browse...   *Max 520x650, 400K*

Offer Ended   Browse...   *Max 520x650, 400K*
Image

Show Offer   **You haven't selected an offer to show on your tab.**
Select an offer to show on your tab:
○ Free registration to Facebook Bootcamp for Success (View)

Save App Settings

You can also select whether you want to have a Non-Fan Image uploaded so that you let people know that there's a sweepstakes they can enter if they click Like. You will have to design this image on your own or hire someone to design it for you. If you don't use your own image, a default one will be used. You can also have an Offer Ended image for when the contest is over, if you want. This may be a good way to show people that you do have special offers on your Page and they should watch for future offers.

You can now navigate back to your Facebook Page to see your offer showing on the Sweepstakes tab, as shown in Figure 3-17.

Figure 3-17:
Your
Sweepstakes
on Facebook.

To alert your Facebook community to your sweepstakes, you can share the link to the Sweepstakes tab and let people know to enter there. Or you can post the link to the Shareable Offer URL that is available in the Offer area (refer to Figure 3-15).

In the Offer area, you can track the entries, views, and how many people are sharing the sweepstakes with their Friends.

Unfortunately, when you're ready to select a winner, Woobox doesn't have an automated tool to help you with that process. You can download the names to an Excel spreadsheet and then use a random number generator such as that found at http://www.random.org/ to pick a number that would correspond to the row in the Excel spreadsheet.

Chapter 4: Promoting Your Contest and Analyzing the Results

In This Chapter

✔ Using a blog tour to drive traffic to a contest

✔ Publicizing a contest on a Web site or blog

✔ Allowing entries from anywhere on the Web

✔ Promoting a contest with Twitter, LinkedIn, and YouTube

✔ Handling external contests

✔ Watching the numbers

✔ Strategizing for future contests

*Y*our contest is set up and the prizes are ready; now comes the fun part — getting those entries! The success of your contest comes when you can drive more traffic to your entry site. We discuss different things to do to promote your contest in Chapter 2 of this minibook, and we go a little more in-depth in this chapter.

Then, later in the chapter, we take a look at your contest results, what they mean, and how you can improve them next time.

Setting Up a Blog Tour

A blog tour is a fantastic way to get exposure to a whole new audience, but it does take some planning and legwork. One way to kick off a blog tour is to contact bloggers and ask whether you can write a guest post or whether they can post about your contest.

Some blogs are "single-voice" blogs, meaning that only the original author writes posts, and they do not have guest posts. Other blogs welcome guest posters as it gives the blogger a short respite from pumping out content. Figuring out which type of blog you're approaching is not difficult. Just take a look through the posts and look at the author byline. If the posts never show a guest poster or author bio of someone other than the blog owner, you can safely assume that it's a single-voice blog.

When you contact bloggers to ask about promoting your contest, either through a guest post by you or by mentioning it themselves, contact them at least a month in advance so that they have plenty of time to respond.

In the following ways, you can find blogs that are a good fit for your message:

✦ **Research blogs to contact, and have a list of blogs that would be a good fit for your message.**

You can also start with bloggers you know and have relationships with. Often, they will be very receptive to a guest post. A good guideline is to approach bloggers that have complementary businesses and are not direct competitors. So, if you have a graphic design business and are giving away your services, you may want to look at blogs about business or marketing.

✦ **Perform blog searches based around keywords on the following sites:**

• `http://technorati.com`

• `http://blogsearch.google.com`

• `http://alltop.com`

✦ **Familiarize yourself with the style of the blogger.**

Make a short list (or a long one if you are ambitious) of the bloggers you want to approach about a guest post. Poke around on their blogs and get to know the style of the bloggers. You might even comment on some posts before approaching them.

✦ **Prepare an introductory e-mail about what you would like to post about and describe how it can help the bloggers' audiences.**

It's best if you can offer them valuable content that can help their readers in addition to getting them to sign up for your contest. Because everyone loves a contest, most bloggers will be receptive to having you encourage contest entries.

✦ **Schedule your blog tour so that it coincides with the time when your contest is live and you can properly promote your guest posts.**

Then you need to create the content for the blog tour. Get your guest post to the bloggers with ample time for them to review it and suggest any changes.

✦ **When the guest post is live, make sure that you are doing all you can to promote it.**

You want to help bring traffic to the blog as well as to promote your content and encourage contest entries. Tweet about the guest post, post it to your Facebook Page, update your status in LinkedIn, and send it to your e-mail list if appropriate.

Promoting Your Contest on Your Blog or Web Site

You should also have your own blog post about the contest. You may want the post to be simply an announcement, or you can have some valuable content go with the contest announcement.

If you are running the contest on Facebook, make sure that you link back to the exact link where people can enter the contest. You can find that URL by clicking the contest or sweepstakes link on the left sidebar of your Facebook Page and then cutting and pasting the URL. It will look something like this:

```
http://www.facebook.com/GrandmaMaryShow?v=app_28134323652
```

**Book VI
Chapter 4**

**Promoting Your
Contest and
Analyzing the
Results**

You may also want to post a permanent banner or widget in the sidebar of your Web site that advertises your contest so that when your blog entry is no longer as visible, you are still letting visitors know about your contest. Figure 4-1 shows Ann Taylor's recent contest for a $1,000 gift card at the bottom of its site. The link took you directly to Facebook to enter.

Figure 4-1:
Ann Taylor had a banner at the bottom of each page that linked to its Facebook contest.

Golf had a banner ad across the top area of its Web site advertising their Golf Oasis sweepstakes (see Figure 4-2).

Figure 4-2: Golfsmith's banner at the top of its Web site linking to its Facebook contest.

All it takes is a graphic and a post into a widget on your blog. If you are using the Wildfire application, Wildfire has a built-in Web-site widget that you can use. If you go to the Publish area of Wildfire and select Publish on the Web site widget, you get some code, as shown in Figure 4-3.

Figure 4-3: Code to cut and paste into a text box on your blog to give you a contest banner.

Wildfire has step-by-step instructions on how to install this code in your blog or Web site. When you are finished, the banner shows up at the bottom of every page of your site, as shown in Figure 4-4.

Figure 4-4:
A contest banner will appear on your site.

**Book VI
Chapter 4**

Promoting Your
Contest and
Analyzing the
Results

Using Facebook Open Graph to Allow Entries Anywhere on the Web

You can also use Open Graph, a Facebook protocol that integrates Web sites into Facebook, to allow entries directly on your Web site. By letting people log in with Facebook, you make it easier for them to enter and share your contest with others. Figure 4-5 shows how Blowfish Shoes is using Open Graph to enter its Shoe A Day giveaway.

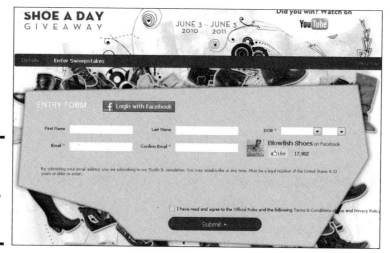

Figure 4-5:
The Blowfish Shoes entry form on its Web site.

Using Social Media to Promote Your Contest

Social media can be critical for getting the word out about your contest. Of course, you should post your Event to your Facebook Page, but how much should you emphasize it? You don't want to be obnoxious, but you want to get the word out. It can vary depending on your comfort zone, but we suggest at least two to three times per week. Vary your posts by saying things like "Have you heard we are having a contest?" or "Thanks to everyone who has entered already. Make sure that you get your entry in!" Make it light and fun.

You can also ask others to promote your contest. Either directly contact some of your Facebook Friends who would have the right audience, or just ask people to share the link with others so that they can enter.

Twitter

If you are using Twitter, you should tweet about your contest frequently. Tweet about it at different times of the day. Ask for retweets and contact some of your Twitter Friends directly in case they don't see the tweet.

Twitter also has hashtags that you can use to reach people who are tracking contests to enter. Use hashtags like #contest, #sweepstakes, #win, or #prize. Some tweets use lots of those hashtags in one, as shown in Figure 4-6.

Figure 4-6:
MyCoupons.
com uses
several
hashtags to
promote its
Facebook
contest.

Without getting too deep into Twitter, some people are monitoring certain hashtags to find tweets about that subject. You can search on the hashtag and see all the tweets with that hashtag in it. So you may get people entering your contests who are "serial contest enterers" and not really interested in your product. But you may be able to connect with these people through your posts on your Facebook Page and turn them into customers.

LinkedIn

LinkedIn can also be a good place to promote a contest. Update your status so that when your connections log in to LinkedIn, they can see it in their LinkedIn Updates area, as shown in Figure 4-7.

Figure 4-7:
Update
your status
in LinkedIn
with your
contest.

You can also create a LinkedIn Event announcing your contest. Invite your connections to the Event, and direct them to your Facebook Page to enter the contest.

Another strategy is to send out an e-mail to your LinkedIn connections, inviting them to enter your contest. But be careful about some of these strategies. Some people do not appreciate getting e-mails and feel that it constitutes spam. It's a fine line, and it is up to your comfort level on how you promote your contest.

YouTube

Another way to promote your contest is to make a YouTube video. You can show off the prize in the video or talk about what you will be providing. If you are providing some type of coaching, a video can be very beneficial so that people can get to know you a little and see your style.

Blendtec uses YouTube videos to demonstrate its blenders blending a wide variety of things while posing the question, "Will it blend?" It also uses YouTube to promote its contests, as shown in Figure 4-8. In that case, the company was giving away its blender and either an iPad or the remains of a blended iPad.

The benefit of having a video on YouTube is that you can then embed it onto a Facebook Page or onto your blog so that people can find it in multiple places. You never know how someone will stumble across your contest, and the more places on the Web you can advertise it, the better.

Figure 4-8:
Blendtec
promotes
its contests
with
YouTube
videos.

Using Facebook to Promote an External Contest

You can also use your Facebook Page to promote a contest that is being hosted on your Web site. The benefit is that you do not have to contend with all those pesky Facebook promotion rules. But make sure that you still look at Facebook's Promotion Guidelines found here:

```
www.facebook.com/promotions_guidelines.php
```

Facebook has general guidelines for when you even mention a contest or sweepstakes on the Facebook Platform, and you want to make sure that your contest adheres to those guidelines.

When you are promoting a contest on your Web site, post the link to enter frequently on your Facebook Page. Ask your community to share the link with their Friends.

You can also incorporate Facebook Connect and Open Graph on your contest site so that people can share and Like your contest entry form. That ensures that it enters the Facebook arena and gets more exposure. See Book VII for more information about how to use Facebook Connect and Open Graph.

Analyzing Your Contest Results

Tracking your results is critical in any marketing effort, and it will be very easy to see what you have gained when you have all your contest entries. But analyzing the real impact to your business may not come until later. You got a lot of entries, but did you get eventual customers and business? Have a plan in place to track later business and see where it came from.

Also, we encourage you to have some type of e-mail subscriber list that your contest entries can sign up for in addition to just Liking your Page. Contrary to some rumors, e-mail is not dead and can be an effective way to reach your customers with new offers.

Book VI
Chapter 4

Promoting Your
Contest and
Analyzing the
Results

Third-party analytics within contest applications

Third-party sweepstakes and contest applications can make tracking and analyzing the effectiveness of your contest simple. When you use the Wildfire, North Social, or Woobox applications (covered in Chapter 3 of this minibook), you will have built-in analytics. For example, Wildfire has details about visits to your contest site and entries per day, and what Web site these entries came from, as shown in Figure 4-9. Woobox and North Social track slightly different metrics.

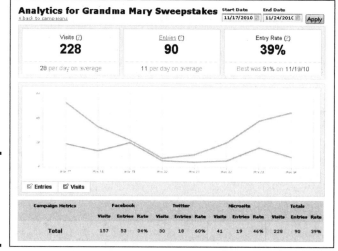

Figure 4-9: Wildfire analytics are comprehensive.

Monitoring Community Growth and Tracking Facebook Insights

Make sure that you are tracking your new Likes on your Page and comparing them to the contest or sweepstakes entries. The newest Liker will be at the top of the list. Unfortunately, you have no easy way to download your list of Likers. So, if someone enters your contest but Liked your Page a long time ago, it will be difficult to find that person.

If you're using the North Social or Woobox sweepstakes applications, you have the option of creating the contest as a Fan-only application. This means that the visitor to your Facebook Page cannot enter the contest unless he or she clicks Like. If you set your contest up this way, you won't have to track whether the person who entered your contest also clicked Like.

Track your Facebook Insights before and after the contest to see how your contest affected the interaction on your Page. For example, we looked at the Facebook Insights a month before and after we ran a contest on a Page, and we saw that the Comments and Likes to the posts more than doubled, as did the new Likes for the Page. See Book IX, Chapter 2 for more information about Facebook Insights.

Watch the trends of new comments and engagement on your Page. With luck, you'll have an influx of new people who are interested in your brand and decide to connect with you on Facebook.

Adjusting Your Strategy Based on Analytics

Analytics will be key in helping you determine where your strategy is working and where to shift your focus. We take a look at the analytics for a contest that we ran from Wildfire, shown previously in Figure 4-9.

At the bottom of Figure 4-9, notice that you can see Facebook had 157 visits with 53 entries (a 34 percent conversion rate), but Twitter had a much better return with only 30 visits but 18 entries, for a conversion rate of 60 percent. That would tell you that during the next contest, we may be well-served by focusing more efforts on Twitter.

You can also see that the entries and views went significantly down on the weekend as we did not promote the contest as heavily. We may want to try changing that in the next contest and see whether we can connect with more people who are on the Web on the weekend, looking for fun things to do, such as enter contests.

You can also compare analytics from contests if you run more than one to see what improved (or declined) in the second contest. In Figure 4-10, we ran a second contest and although we didn't get as many entries (mostly because of not promoting the contest quite as heavily), we did get a higher entry rate. The community might have seen the testimonials from the previous winners and wanted to make sure they entered the second contest.

Souplantation & Sweet Tomatoes

Souplantation & Sweet Tomatoes has had a history of good Facebook contests and promotions.

In 2010, the company had a very successful "pucker face" contest in which you would submit a photo of yourself after eating a lemon. Sweet Tomatoes ran this promotion to coincide with some of the lemon dishes it was featuring. The winner of the contest won 20 meal passes. Having a photo contest is a fun way to involve your audience, and the prize does not have to cost a lot of money. The contest was so successful that the company ran it again in 2011.

Sweet Tomatoes also ran a Refer a Friend contest through the Wildfire app, where you are entered to win ten free meals when you refer Friends to the contest.

After you enter the contest, you have the choice of publishing something about it to your Wall as well as personally inviting your Friends. These touches in your contest can really help the word spread. Then you can see some of the positive feedback users receive when they post about the winner and invite others to sign up for another round of the contest.

Book VI
Chapter 4

Promoting Your
Contest and
Analyzing the
Results

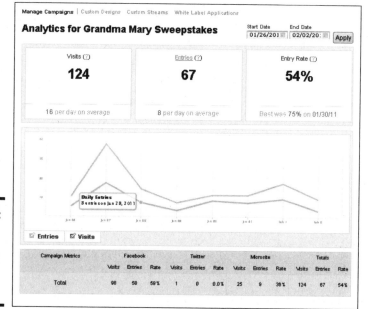

Figure 4-10:
Compare the analytics of our second contest.

Planning for Future Contests

After you have your first contest under your belt, you can start mapping out your contest schedule. When you've run one contest, you can see the benefits for your Facebook community, such as added members and more interaction. Maybe you want to run only one more contest, or perhaps three or four per year — but whatever you do, running multiple contests is a good idea for several reasons:

✦ You want to give people who entered before a second chance to win.

✦ You encourage your community to watch your Page because people like contests.

✦ It's easy to have others promote your contests because people like to win things.

✦ You can showcase some of your services and products as giveaways, which then encourage people to buy them.

✦ Contests are fun!

Plan your contests strategically so that you can promote them adequately. And, you don't want too many contests so that your community gets contest fatigue.

Cold Stone Creamery and Papa John's Pizza

Cold Stone Creamery had a Gold Cone Contest, where people could suggest their own flavor. The winners traveled to the headquarters in Arizona to perfect their winning flavors. This was reported in the Social Media Examiner on this post:

```
www.socialmediaexaminer.
com/cold-stone-transforms-
the-ice-cream-social-with-
facebook
```

Over 4,000 people entered the contest, and the Cold Stone Creamery Facebook Page saw about 66,000 new Likes to its Page over an eight-week period.

The winners are still being featured on the Contest tab of Cold Stone Creamery's Page.

Papa John's Pizza saw a similar success when it ran a Specialty Pizza Challenge contest in 2010 and received over 12,000 entries. Papa John's had a Live Stream to announce the three winners from the ten semifinalists and got a lot of buzz from the Event.

Mapping out your contests for the year

To prevent contest fatigue and to allow room on your calendar for promotion of your contests, make sure to schedule them for the year. How many contests you have and how far apart you space them can depend on the duration of the contests.

If you are running month-long contests, you may want a couple of months' buffer in between to focus on other parts of your business. So that would allow four contests per year.

How many contests you schedule may also depend on the type of contest. Are they the same, or are you giving away a different prize each week? Exodus Travels in the U.K. gave away a trip a month to each of the seven continents, so its contest lasted for seven months.

**Book VI
Chapter 4**

Promoting Your
Contest and
Analyzing the
Results

Watching for successful contest ideas

If you're planning multiple contests, you should be watching other contests that are running on Facebook so that you can get ideas for your own. It may not be easy to tell how successful a contest is, but you can watch for some clues. If the business is promoting the contest on Twitter, you can search for tweets about it to see whether many people are tweeting about the contest. If the company has a YouTube video of the contest, you can see how many views the video gets. And if you're really paying attention, you can track the new Likes on the company's Facebook Page each day, which would correlate with how many entries they might be receiving.

Searching for contests running on Facebook can be done several ways. Here is a list of ways; we go more in-depth into each of these later:

✦ Look through the Wildfire application site for contests and sweepstakes that are using the Wildfire platform.

✦ Check Votigo's Web site for its Live Showcase that highlights current contests.

✦ Look at North Social's Examples page on its Web site. North Social covers examples from many of its apps but also has a Promotions example section that covers examples of its Sweepstakes app.

✦ Watch the Facebook Ads area to see who is advertising their contests.

✦ Use the Facebook Search feature to see who is posting about contests.

✦ Use Twitter Search to search for tweets about contests.

Finding popular contests through Wildfire

You can use the Wildfire application to see what contests are being run through Wildfire. When you go to the Wildfire Application area on Facebook (http://apps.facebook.com/promotionshq/contests), you can see all its contests listed, as shown in Figure 4-11.

Figure 4-11: Wildfire contests and sweepstakes are listed and searchable in different categories.

Viewing Votigo's Live Showcase of current contests

Votigo's Web site, at www.votigo.com, has a Live Showcase of current contests that are being run through its platform, as shown in Figure 4-12. You can access the Live Showcase by selecting Clients from the top menu and then selecting Live Showcase. Not all the examples in the Live Showcase are Facebook Contests. You will need to select the Facebook Contests & Promos link under the Live Showcase heading.

Facebook Contests and Promos link

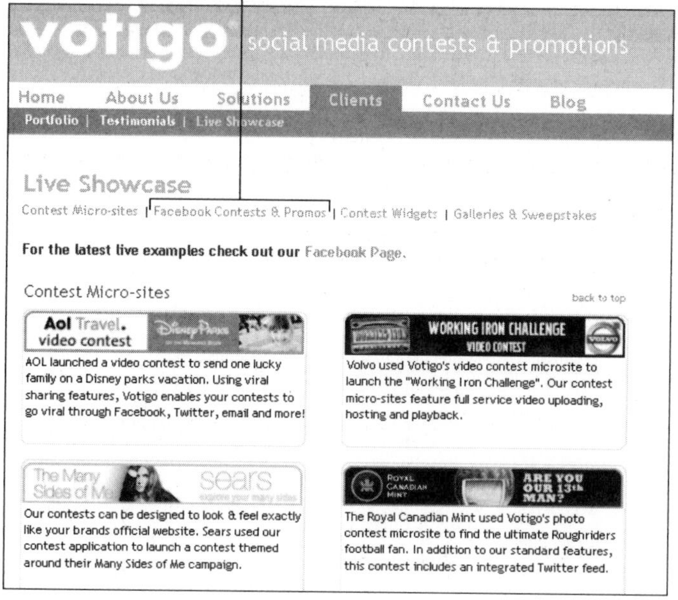

**Book VI
Chapter 4**

Promoting Your
Contest and
Analyzing the
Results

Figure 4-12:
Watch for
contests
on Votigo's
site.

Looking at North Social's Examples

North Social also has examples of the promotions using its sweepstakes application. You can see some screen shots of these at `http://northsocial.com/examples/promotions/`.

Keeping an eye on the Facebook Ad Board

Watch the Facebook Ads because they often are advertising contests. The easiest place to see all the current Ads at one time is on the Facebook Ad Board. You can access it at `http://www.facebook.com/ads/adboard`. When you go to the Ad Board, you can see all the Ads that are being served to your Profile demographic at this time. So, you need to check back at different times and possibly have different people with different demographics checking in.

Using the Facebook Search feature

Use the Facebook Search feature, at `http://www.facebook.com/search`, to search on any posts within Facebook mentioning a contest. When you go to the search area, click Posts by Everyone on the left sidebar to filter your search to posts, as shown in Figure 4-13.

Figure 4-13:
Use
Facebook
Search to
find posts
about
contests.

We actually found so many posts about the word *contest* that we added more keywords to help narrow the posts. We used "enter our contest" in the search field, as shown in Figure 4-13.

Finding contest information on Twitter

You can also use Twitter Search, at `www.search.twitter.com`, to find people tweeting about Facebook contests, as shown in Figure 4-14. You can use keywords like *enter, contest,* and *Facebook* or hashtags like `#contest`, `#win`, and `#facebook` to see who is tweeting about contests.

Book VI
Chapter 4

Promoting Your
Contest and
Analyzing the
Results

Figure 4-14:
Find people
tweeting
about
Facebook
contests.

Book VII

Advanced Facebook Marketing Tactics

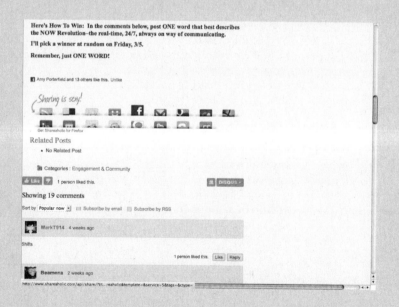

Contents at a Glance

Chapter 1: An Introduction to Advanced Facebook Marketing

Clearly, Facebook Pages are quickly becoming essential parts of most businesses' marketing strategies. But how can you find ways to stand out from the competition? You have a lot to consider as you go about developing a successful Facebook Page, but the rewards of brand exposure, loyal Fans, and increased revenue are well worth your time and effort. To fast-track your success, consider including some advanced strategies in your Facebook plan.

In this chapter, we look at some advanced marketing strategies that can take your Facebook Page from good to great.

Remembering the Nine Core Facebook Marketing Rules

Before you consider experimenting with a few advanced Facebook marketing strategies, it's important to make sure that your Facebook marketing foundation is solid. There are nine core rules to consider as you create your marketing plan. Following these rules will ensure that you stay on track and focus on the most important marketing elements as you increase your Page engagement and number of Fans, and ultimately turn your Fans into new customers. Although we also mention these rules in Book I, Chapter 2, here's a synopsis:

✦ **Give your page a human touch.** Communicate with your Fans as though you were talking to your friends, and let your personality come through in each post.

✦ **Create fresh content.** Always make sure that your content educates, entertains, and empowers your Fans to keep them engaged and coming back for more.

✦ **Cultivate engagement with two-way dialogue.** People love to talk about themselves, so craft your posts and questions around them to get them talking.

✦ **Create consistent calls to action.** To get your Fans to take action, consider offering discounts and specials or ask them to sign up for your newsletter so that you can actively communicate with them on a consistent basis.

✦ **Make word-of-mouth advocacy easy.** Make it easy for your Fans to talk about you by asking them to share your content, getting them to engage in contests, and making the experiences on your Page about them rather than you.

✦ **Encourage Fan-to-Fan conversations.** Enhance your Fans' experience by creating a community that encourages your Fans to interact with each other.

✦ **Focus on smart branding.** Treat your Facebook Page as a mini-site of your own Web site. The key is to create a Page that sparks familiarity with your brand when your existing customers visit your Page.

✦ **Be deliberate and manage expectations.** Decide why you want to have a presence on Facebook. When you understand the "why," your actions are deliberate and have purpose and your Fans clearly understand what your Page has to offer.

✦ **Monitor, measure, and track.** Make sure you have surefire methods in place that enable you to consistently track your Facebook marketing progress.

Test-Driving Some Advanced Techniques

After you've created your Page, optimized it with the essential strategies such as posting great content regularly, and built some momentum with your Fan base and ways to engage your Fans, consider taking your Facebook marketing up a notch and exploring some advanced Facebook marketing strategies. Advanced strategies take more time and effort than the basic marketing efforts, but on the plus side, they produce much bigger returns.

You don't have to reinvent the wheel when it comes to Facebook strategies. Instead, take a look at other thriving Facebook Pages and apply the same success strategies to your own Page. After you've given a new strategy enough time to gain momentum, analyze your progress. If what you're doing is working, keep doing it! After a while, if you're not happy enough with the results of your efforts, change directions and try a new tactic. (You won't know if you don't try!)

Creating a Facebook experience

Many businesses just getting started on Facebook worry that they'll be lost in the Facebook abyss. Sure, big brands such as Coca-Cola and Southwest Airlines stand out easily. But what about small to midsize companies? Many of our clients wonder if they even have a chance.

Here's the great news: There's still hope for your Page, no matter how small your company might be! You don't have to be a major brand to gain exposure and build relationships with your clients and customers on Facebook.

One way to stand out from the masses is to create *Facebook experiences* — experiences that you execute on your Facebook Page that are unique to your brand and also of great value to your Fans. No matter how big or small, these experiences can be extremely powerful.

On the Social Media Examiner Facebook Page (www.facebook.com/smexaminer), for example, we created Expert Fridays. Every other Friday, we feature a social media expert who answers our Fans' questions, directly on our Wall, for one full hour. Anyone can post their questions, and the expert will answer as many of them as he or she can in that one designated hour, as shown in Figure 1-1. These experiences have proved to be a huge hit!

Figure 1-1:
An Expert Friday session on the Social Media Examiner Facebook Page.

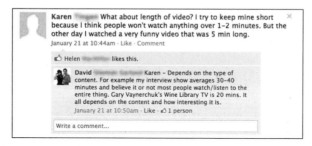

Planning the experience

If you like the concept of an experience and want to create something unique to your brand and your mission, here are four steps to get you started in the right direction:

1. **Decide on the overall vibe you want to create with your experience.**

   Do you want to add value? Perhaps you're looking to entertain? Is your desired outcome to educate, create excitement among your Fans, all of the above? Determine the kind of experience that will resonate with your Fans.

2. **Get clear on what your company does best.**

   What's your company known for? What does it do best? What do your clients tell you when they're singing your praises? Use this insight to fuel your ideas for unique experiences.

   When you're brainstorming, think of experiences you can duplicate (do multiple times). An experience you can execute consistently is key to building momentum with your Facebook community. After you create your list of ideas, choose the experience your audience will embrace the most fully (and that your team will enjoy delivering!).

3. **Map out your execution plan.**

   You want to document the process of your experience. Before we began Expert Fridays at Social Media Examiner, we followed this step. We talked about ways to find the ideal expert, the best day to announce the weekly expert, how we would post the questions and answers, and all the other specifics involved. After we talked this all out, we created a Word document that explained our process for doing Expert Friday sessions. At any time, we can refer back to our document for guidance. If we discover better ways to deliver the Expert Friday sessions, we update the document to reflect the changes. It's a work in progress.

4. **Commit to your plan.**

   For some, this is the toughest step! When you decide on your signature experience, it's crucial that you deliver. If you say you intend to do it once a week, do it. If you don't follow through, you could lose trust with your Fans, and that's something you don't want to mess with!

Optimizing the experience

After you create your experience, begin to think about how you might repurpose the content or information that comes from it. If audio is involved, perhaps you can create a podcast. Or if your experience involves video, think about using that video in an opt-in strategy for anyone who might have missed it that week. This could be a great way to build up your list.

You can also take the content from your experience and post it in new ways weeks later for those who might have missed it. Doing so allows you to continually post great content. Repurposing the content or elements of your experience creates multiple touch points throughout your marketing strategy.

Signature experiences and other "out of the box" ideas are vital to keeping your Facebook community engaged and enthusiastic about your brand. The key is to find something that you can duplicate and build on over time.

Building social proof with Sponsored Stories

Before most people make a buying decision, they want to know that their choice is a smart one. To get reassurance we look to our friends to give us their advice and recommendations. With the rise of social networks, word-of-mouth recommendations are essential for businesses in their efforts to gain popularity and expand the ranks of their clientele. Studies show that when it comes to buying recommendations, people trust friends' recommendations more than they do the actual brand. Facebook has capitalized on this behavior by creating Sponsored Stories.

Sponsored Stories take word-of-mouth recommendations from friends and promote them in Facebook Profiles as Facebook ads. This means that when you go to Starbucks, for example, and use Facebook Places to check in, that story is posted on your Wall and sent out into the News Feeds of your friends. And now, with Sponsored Stories, that post is also displayed next to the Starbucks ad (see Figure 1-2). Now Starbucks has something even better than an ad; it has social proof.

The term *social proof* refers to the psychological phenomenon of people being motivated to do things that they see other people doing. Interactions on social media sites, such as Facebook, have increased the influence and reach of social proof because now it's much easier to instantly see what your friends are doing at any time.

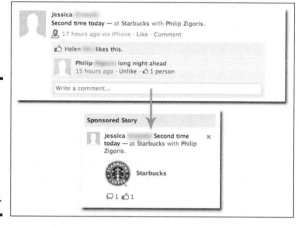

Figure 1-2:
Example
of a Fan's
Starbucks
Facebook
check-in
next to a
Starbucks ad.

The posts from the Sponsored Stories make it as though your friends are saying "I bought this!" or "I just ordered the best burger ever at Rocket Burgers!" These posts are virtual, instant recommendations and may be more powerful than a traditional Facebook ad. As Facebook put it, you have the "ability to promote your content with a user experience focus." Research from these unique ads have shown increased brand awareness, including ad recall and likeliness to recommend to a friend.

As you explore your opportunities with Facebook Ads, we encourage you to test Sponsored Stories. The word-of-mouth feature is a powerful tool to entice new users to check out your Facebook Page and your business. If you think this strategy might work for your company or product, see Book VIII, Chapter 1, where we go into more detail about setting up your own Sponsored Stories.

Experimenting with custom links

In Book III, Chapter 2, we explore custom links using iFrames. Custom links (also known as custom pages or custom tabs) in many ways are the most important piece to your Facebook marketing strategy. As you've learned, you can create multiple pages inside your Facebook Page. One powerful advanced strategy is to create a custom page to promote special products or events. Custom pages can give your product or event that extra promotion and give it the push it needs to get even greater exposure.

Event promotion

For example, if you have a physical event coming up, you might consider creating a custom page with a video from past events to showcase the experience. You can then include the Facebook comments feature from the social plugin options in order to encourage people to talk about the event. This strategy not only showcases your event via your video, but the comments section on the tab gets people talking.

When we worked with Tony Robbins, we created a special tab for his live event (see Figure 1-3). We included a video as well as features to highlight the event benefits and the pricing structure. In many ways, it's like a mini Web site.

Figure 1-3: Promoting a live event with a custom tab.

Product promotion

Another example is to use a custom tab to promote a book. You can do this for a physical book or an e-book. The secret to a successful Facebook Page that promotes a book is one that focuses on the content of the book and puts the sell of the book as a secondary goal. That way your audience will first be drawn in via your valuable content and then when they feel a part of your Facebook community, they're more likely to buy your book. Figure 1-4 shows images from Guy Kawasaki's Facebook Page to promote his book *Enchantment* (www.facebook.com/enchantment).

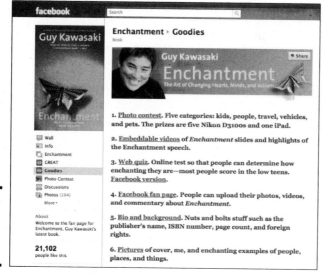

Figure 1-4:
Promoting a book with a custom tab.

Book VII Chapter 1

An Introduction to Advanced Facebook Marketing

Expanding your Page's exposure

The way to get seen on Facebook is to create multiple reasons for people to engage with your Page. Try these tips to increase the chances of your Page getting seen often:

✦ Create a custom Welcome page with a clear call to action (ask users to click the Like button!) and include a welcome video for extra impact. See Book III, Chapter 2.

✦ Set up your vanity URL for your Facebook Page (make sure that you have 25 Fans first!). See Book II, Chapter 3.

✦ Create a profile image that is the maximum size available in order to give your Page a professional, well-branded look and feel. See Book II, Chapter 2.

✦ Create a custom Fans-Only page through which you offer an incentive for those who click your Like button. This strategy will increase non-Fan curiosity and incite action in the form of non-Fans clicking the Like button. See Book III, Chapter 2.

✦ Add a Facebook app to your Page. Consider one that will increase activity and encourage more users to visit your page. See Book V, Chapter 1.

✦ Run a Facebook Ad campaign for 30 days. (For extra credit, test the new Sponsored Stories feature, described earlier in this chapter.) See Book VIII, Chapter 1.

✦ If you have a brick-and-mortar store, test Facebook Deals by creating a Fans-Only coupon and post about it on your Page. See Book 7, Chapter 4.

✦ Embed a social plugin on your Web site to drive up the number of Likes on your Page. See Book VII, Chapter 2.

Engaging with Fans

Communicating with your Fans helps keep them engaged — and coming back. Here are a few ways to keep the lines of communication wide open:

✦ Create a Facebook experience to execute on your Facebook wall. Think of what your Fans want most from you and deliver it as a Facebook experience! Discussed earlier in this chapter.

✦ Ask more questions. The more you make it about your Fans and less about you, the more your Fan base will flourish. Mix up your questions to have some related to your business and industry, some that will get people thinking in news ways, and some that entertain and keep things light. See Book IV, Chapter 2.

✦ If you have a great idea for an app, consider creating one yourself! If you can be patient as you continue to muster up some viral buzz, you might have a very successful application. See Book V, Chapter 2.

✦ Set up notifications to get continuous alerts when your Fans post on your Page. See Book II, Chapter 3.

✦ If you're having an event online or offline, consider setting up a special custom page to promote the event. (For extra credit, embed a video and a comments plug-in!) See Book III, Chapter 2.

✦ Turn your Facebook Page into a lead generator by adding a name and e-mail box to your Facebook Page. This box will help you capture the e-mail addresses of your Facebook Fans. See Book III, Chapter 2.

Getting viral exposure

Going viral isn't so great in the offline world, but it's the best of all possible worlds online. Here are a few ways to position your Page to get lots of viral exposure:

✦ Connect your other social media accounts, such as Twitter and LinkedIn, to your Facebook Page to ensure that your posts are getting even better reach and exposure. See Book III, Chapter 4.

✦ Add a PowerPoint presentation to your Facebook Page with the SlideShare app. `http://www.slideshare.net/`. A PowerPoint presentation allows you to add even more valuable content to your Page. See Book III, Chapter 4.

✦ Stream a live video on your Facebook Page using the Livestream application. `http://www.livestream.com/` Live activity will create a buzz! See Book VII, Chapter 3.

✦ Create an event using the Events feature on your Facebook Page. See Book VI, Chapter 1.

✦ Pull your blog into your Facebook Page by using the NetworkedBlogs app. When you publish a blog, it automatically gets pulled onto your Facebook Wall and into the News Feeds of your Fans. See Book III, Chapter 3.

✦ Run a contest on your Page and offer an enticing giveaway to help spread the buzz. Try the Wildfire app for contest support. See Book VI, Chapter 2.

**Book VII
Chapter 1**

**An Introduction to
Advanced Facebook
Marketing**

Chapter 2: Marketing with Facebook Social Plugins

In This Chapter

✔ Exploring social plugins

✔ Integrating Facebook with your Web site

✔ Finding the right plugins to fit your business goals

✔ Using social plugins as part of a marketing program

*A*t one time, users searched the Web independently of their peers. Today, users look at what their networks of Friends are doing, and they take their Friends' activities and recommendations very seriously. Social plugins allow you to take advantage of this new way of surveying information.

In this chapter, we cover the basics of social plugins: what they are, why they're important, and how you can use them to expand your online presence. When it comes to social plugins, you have numerous options. Therefore, we dedicate a separate section to each Facebook social plugin as well as offer suggestions for open source Facebook-friendly plugins. Open source plugins are developed outside of the Facebook platform but seamlessly integrate with Facebook and your Web site. (We get more into open source later in the chapter.) Overall, this chapter can help you decide which social plugins are the right fit for your business goals and talks about how you can integrate them with your overall marketing program.

Understanding Social Plugins

Social plugins are tools that connect your Web site with Facebook users and enable social activity among users directly on your site. With Facebook social plugins, you create an identical experience of your Facebook Page while maintaining control of your content and brand. Considering the high number of people on Facebook today, social plugins can be an extremely powerful tool. Plugins have many benefits, perhaps one of the most important being their ability to encourage your Web-site visitors to spend more time on your site.

The plugins appear as buttons and boxes on Web sites, and the content populating them comes directly from Facebook activity. If you have a plugin on your Web site, when your visitors are logged in to Facebook, they can interact with their Facebook Friends directly from your Web site. Specifically, they see their Friends' Facebook activity (such as what their Friends have Liked, shared, recommended, and posted) via the plugin on your Web site.

Here's an example of how social plugins work. Suppose that you click a link that you received in an e-mail and land on a Web site that includes a Like button. If any of your Facebook Friends have clicked that button, you see some of their names or Profile images (depending on how the site owner configured the button). Seeing that your Friends have interacted with the site makes you more likely to explore the site's content — and possibly share it with your own social networks. The Like button plugin lets this activity take place directly on your Web site rather than going through Facebook — which is exactly what marketers want. Read on to find out why.

Integrating your Web site with Facebook via plugins

Why do you want to integrate your Web site with Facebook by using social plugins? Easy answer: You gain viral visibility. You increase your exposure when you create more opportunities for users to consume your content on your Web site or blog. Also, by showing how multiple users are interacting with your content every day (ideally), the plugins create social proof and increase the credibility of your content.

The term *social proof* refers to the psychological phenomenon of people being motivated to do things that they see other people doing. Although marketers have used social proof as a fundamental principle for many years, the popularity and growth of social media has strengthened its influence and reach.

Social plugins enhance the social proof strategy because they highlight the Friends and acquaintances of the people you're directly trying to influence. In many ways, social proof acts as a "foot in the door" strategy because it takes viewers' initial interest and quickly turns that interest into acceptance. The acceptance happens when they see their peers' interactions with the information they are currently consuming. The familiarity builds trust.

Social proof is crucial in creating a successful Facebook marketing plan. The goal is to show your visitors what their peers are talking about, Liking, and posting, and in turn, your new visitors will naturally match those behaviors.

The key is to create multiple opportunities for your users to see their Friends interacting with your Web site. This activity increases traffic to your site and encourages site engagement overall. Social plugins aid in this marketing endeavor.

One example of a Web site that uses social plugins successfully is Stay N' Alive (`http://staynalive.com`; see Figure 2-1). Site owner Jesse Stay has implemented three social plugins: Like box, Activity Feed, and Recommendations. (We discuss all three in detail in this chapter.) All three plugins are optimally placed in the right column of the home page for high-traffic viewing. The plugins are not only prominently placed but also extremely active, meaning that Stay posts content to his Facebook Page and Web site consistently, keeping the social plugins updated continually.

Figure 2-1:
Social plugins used on a Web site.

**Book VII
Chapter 2**

Marketing with
Facebook Social
Plugins

Choosing the right plugins for your business

You have many options when it comes to social plugins for your Web site. To make things easy, we've separated your options into two categories. The first category consists of Facebook's own social plugins. The second category consists of open source plugins, meaning plugins that incorporate Facebook activity, but are created by third-party developers outside of the Facebook platform.

First, we look at Facebook's social plugins. Facebook offers nine social plugins, and each one has a specific function with unique benefits and multiple features.

The nine social plugins are as follows:

+ Like button

+ Send button

+ Like box

+ Login button

+ Registration

+ Recommendations

+ Activity Feed

+ Comments

+ Facepile

+ Live Stream

However, installing these Facebook plugins is not exactly simple. In most cases, if you're not familiar with programming code, installing these plugins will create some frustration for you rather quickly. If you are not familiar with code, we suggest that you turn this task over to your Webmaster. All the details needed to install the plugins can be found at `http://developers.facebook.com/docs/plugins`.

The second category of social plugins, as mentioned earlier, are the open source Facebook-friendly plugins. As we mentioned, these plugins are developed especially for your Web site and are much easier to install. (Later in this chapter, we cover how to install these plugins on your WordPress site.) However, before we get to the installation details, we first cover in detail what each social plugin can do to expand your online marketing presence by dedicating a separate section to each plugin in this chapter.

You can use just one social plugin on your Web site, or you can combine multiple plugins based on your overall marketing goals. Understanding the function of each can help you to decide what will work best for your site.

Finding Leads through the Like Button

The Like Button plugin allows anyone who's signed in to Facebook to Like the content on your Web page, such as a blog post, video, or product. When a user clicks a Like button on your Web site or blog, a short summary of the content, called a *story,* with a link back to the content on your site, is posted to the Facebook Wall of that user and also sent out into the News Feeds of all the user's Friends. This feature results in great viral visibility for you, which is why using the Like button in multiple places on your site, such as on each blog post, is a good idea.

Figure 2-2 shows a story (which is the first few lines from the article and a link back to your Web site or blog post) posted to a Facebook Wall after a user clicked a Like button on a Web site.

Figure 2-2:
Story
posted to a
Facebook
Wall by a
Like Button
plugin.

You might be wondering what the difference is between a Like button and a Like box (covered later in this chapter). You can place the Like button next to specific content on your site, such as a blog post, or even next to specific items on your site, such as a product or program you offer, whereas the Like box is associated directly with your Facebook Page and is placed on your Web site as a way to attract more Likers to your Facebook Page.

When setting up your Like button, you have the option to add a comments feature with the button. This means that users can leave a comment after they click the button. Allowing users to leave comments when they click Like can be an extremely powerful marketing strategy because Facebook weighs the comment with the link to the blog post more heavily than it would just the link. In Book IV, Chapter 2, we talk about Edge Rank and the algorithm Facebook uses to decide which posts get the most exposure in the News Feeds. When a user clicks the Like button and also leaves a comment with it, that post gets more weight than if the user decided not to leave a comment when clicking the Like button. The extra weight can increase the chances of your content getting seen by more people on Facebook. An example of the option to leave a comment after clicking the Like button can be seen in Figure 2-3.

Figure 2-3:
The option
to leave a
comment
after
clicking the
Like button.

Leave a comment here

When you set up a Like button, you have a few options for how it displays. You can choose a Like button that also displays the number of Likes next to it, or you can choose just the button with no Like count showing. If you do choose the layout with the Like count next to it, it's important to know that the Like count is the sum of the number of Likes, plus Shares, comments, and inbox messages containing a URL that can be generated from both the Like button and the Send button. In the next section, we discuss the Send button and how it can be linked to the Like button to increase your Like count and overall exposure.

Encourage your site visitors to Like your blog posts and other content on your pages as well as ask them to leave a comment. The gentle reminder will encourage more users to take action.

Share Selectively with the Send Button

The Send button is very similar to the Like button and is usually seen next to it on Web sites and blogs. However, it differs from the Like button in that the Send button is used for selective sharing, whereas the Like button has public sharing capabilities. When a user clicks the Send button next to an article or on a Web site page, a pop-up box appears with a link to the URL of the page the user is viewing, along with a title, image, and short description of the link. The user has the option to send the link to specific Facebook Friends, a Facebook Group, or a specific e-mail address. The user also has the option to add a personal message, as shown in Figure 2-4.

Like button best practices

According to Facebook, Web sites that followed the following best practices experienced three to five times greater click-through rates with the Like button:

✔ Use the version of the Like button that includes thumbnails of users' Friends.

✔ Enable users to add comments.

✔ Add the Send button alongside the Like button to increase exposure.

✔ Place the Like button at the top and bottom of articles and near visually appealing content such as videos and graphics.

Optimizing your Like button with Open Graph

With the Open Graph protocol, Facebook enables your Web site to establish a connection with your visitors and the Facebook platform. Although it may seem so at first glance, no magic is involved. Facebook uses a technical structure called a protocol to interact with other Web sites. The protocol that Facebook uses is the Open Graph. You can use the Open Graph on any Web site or blog. When you use it, the Open Graph provides Facebook with the technical tool to link information from outside Facebook with the information on the Facebook platform. By linking the information, your Web site becomes equivalent to a Facebook Page.

Why does this matter? There's tremendous value in Open Graph when you use it in conjunction with the Facebook Like button. Open Graph allows you to integrate your Web pages into what Facebook calls "The Social Graph." The Open Graph protocol can be used without Facebook, but because we're talking about Facebook marketing, we focus primarily on how it's used with Facebook.

In this chapter, we discuss the simple one-step social plugin process. For example, when a user Likes a web page using the Like button, the social plugin automates an update in the user's News Feed. It's as simple as that and it stops there. However, when you add the full Open Graph API code to your Web site, here's what happens when a user clicks a Like button on your site:

- ✔ An update is automatically published on that user's News Feed inside of Facebook.

- ✔ The updates you publish on your Facebook Page now also appear in that user's News Feed (thus giving you greater exposure).

- ✔ Your Page shows up in Facebook search results.

- ✔ You can create ads that target people who have Liked your content.

How does this work? It all starts with setting the right tags that define the content being Liked. Open graph tags are tags that you add to your Web site to describes your page's entity — what your page represents, such as a band, restaurant, or blog.

First there are tags to make the connection with Facebook. With Open Graph, you set tags for your Web pages to define them for Facebook. Using the Open Graph tags on your Web page makes your page seem as though it's on Facebook. When a reader clicks the Like button on your Web page, a connection is established between your Web page and the reader. Your page will appear on the reader's Facebook profile, just as if that reader had Liked a Facebook Page.

There are also tags to provide context of what is being Liked. With the tags, you define this information. Using the Open Graph, Facebook can collect a large amount of information about your Fans, prospects, and clients — the people you most want to connect with. You can easily imagine cross-referencing some of this information to find people with an exact match for a very specific profile you define — specifically, a profile that would likely be interested in your products and services.

The Open Graph protocol is pretty technical. If you're not familiar with code, we suggest you save yourself a lot of unnecessary stress and call your Web programmer for assistance. To learn more about Open Graph, visit the Facebook developer site: `http://developers.facebook.com/docs/opengraph/`.

Figure 2-4:
The pop-up
button that
appears
when you
click the
Send button.

Send button

In many ways, the Send button is designed to be Like's companion, meaning that you often see the two buttons side by side. Some users like to customize their messages and selectively choose whom they're sending to, whereas others like to share more openly. We recommend adding both buttons to give your users sharing options. As mentioned earlier in this chapter, the Like button count is the sum of the number of Likes, plus Shares, comments, and inbox messages containing a URL that can be generated from both the Like button and the Send button. So the two truly do work hand in hand to increase your overall exposure through social sharing from those who visit your site.

Using a Like Box to Grow Likers

A Like Box plugin brings attention to your Facebook Page while visitors are on your Web site and allows your users to interact with your Page. As mentioned in the previous section, the Like button is used to promote individual content on your site, whereas the Like box is associated directly with your Facebook Page and is placed on your Web site as a way to attract more Likers to your Page. Specifically, the Like box allows visitors to Like your Facebook Page without ever leaving your Web site or blog, something marketers see as highly advantageous.

In addition to allowing people to Like your Page with just one click, the Like box also gives you the option to add the posts from your Facebook Page, encouraging even greater social interaction on your Web site. We suggest that you use this option because it gives your visitors the opportunity to be exposed to even more of your content.

The best placement for a Like box is usually on your home page; however, you can place it on multiple pages throughout your site. You can also include thumbnails of your user's Friends to instantly indicate to your site's visitors which Friends have already Liked your Page. We recommend this option and suggest that you display at least ten Profile images because the more users you show, the greater the social-proof appeal.

 You can adjust the dimensions and number of Likers who show up in your Like box. This feature allows you to choose the size that suits your Web site design. You also have the option to include your Facebook Wall feed as well as a "Find us on Facebook" header.

Finding Out More about Your Visitors with the Login Button

The Login Button plugin allows your users to sign in to your Web site via their Facebook accounts. Take a look at Figure 2-5 to see how the *New York Times* uses this plugin on its Web site. When you install this button, you can access data such as a user's name, e-mail address, Profile picture, and list of Friends. This is valuable information to use as you communicate and market to your Facebook audience.

Facebook Login button

Figure 2-5: The Login button on the *New York Times* Web site.

When a visitor clicks the Login button on your site, he or she first sees a Request for Permission window (see Figure 2-6). Here, the user is prompted to click Allow to move forward with the login.

Figure 2-6: The Request for Permission window.

When users who have already clicked your Login button return to your Web site, if they are logged into Facebook, they are automatically logged into your site when they click the Login button and won't have to click the Allow button again. If they try to log in to your site and aren't logged into Facebook, they are prompted to log in to Facebook first.

In addition to the login feature, you also have the option to add the Profile images of the users who click the Login button. When the Login button with Faces is placed on your Web site, initially visitors will only see the Login button. After visitors click Allow (meaning that they are giving their consent to be logged in to your site via Facebook), their Facebook Profile images will appear inside the Login button box on your Web site, along with all their Friends who also have signed in to your Web site via the Login button.

You have the option to not include the Profile images with the Login button; however, you will increase your social proof appeal if you include the images of your users. This will entice Friends of the users who visit your site to also log in with the Login button.

Now you have access to review all the public Facebook information on that user, including a user's name, Profile picture, interests, list of Friends, and more. As mentioned earlier, this could be valuable information as you collect data on the demographics, Likes, and interests of the users who visit your site.

Using Recommendations for Social Proof

The Recommendations plugin is a box that shows the recent, most popular content on your Web site or blog and the number of times it has been shared. Specific content gets listed in the Recommendations box based on the number of times your viewers Like or share content from your site onto their Facebook Profiles and Pages. This means that if someone clicks the Like button attached to an article on your site, that article will be considered one recommendation. The blog posts, articles, videos, or other form of content that gets socially shared the most will be highlighted in the Recommendations box. You can see this in action in Figure 2-7.

Figure 2-7:
A Recommendations social plugin on a non-Facebook Web site.

Facebook Recommendations Plugin

Visitors on your site will see the recommended content regardless of whether they are logged in to Facebook. If they are logged in to Facebook, they will see the content their Friends have shared at the top of the Recommendations box.

The benefit of this plugin is its ability to spotlight your most popular content for new visitors to your site. When the Recommendations box pulls in your content that your users interact with most, this increases the chances that new visitors will also interact with your content and in turn learn more about your business.

Spotlighting Your Latest Content with the Activity Feed

An Activity Feed plugin allows users on your site to see what their Friends are interacting with, such as Liking or recommending the content on your site. It is very similar to the Recommendations plugin, but it highlights the person and the action the person took, such as "Amy Porterfield *Liked* 8 Ways to Improve Your Blog." Visitors can also see the number of times certain content on your Web site has been recommended.

A visitor to your site can see the recent activity on your site regardless of whether he is logged in to Facebook, but if a visitor is logged in to Facebook, the visitor will see the activity from their Friends only. However, the plugin gives you the option to include recommendations, meaning that the top half of the Activity Feed box will be activity from the user's Friends and the bottom half will be recommendations (Likes and shares) from everyone on your site. We suggest that you show the recommendations on your Activity Feed. Figure 2-8 shows an Activity Feed social plugin at work.

Figure 2-8:
The contents of the Activity Feed box.

The Activity Feed plugin is a great way to guide your visitors to the content that their Friends and peers have already shown interest in. Because people in the same networks tend to enjoy similar content, it's likely that your new visitors will also be interested in the content their Friends have recommended.

Optimizing the Comments Feature

The Facebook Comments plugin allows you to add an interactive posting and discussion feature to specific pages on your Web site. The most popular way that this plugin is used is to include it as the main way your users can add their Comments to your blog site.

Encouraging your Web site or blog readers to leave comments on your site is important because this allow users to share their thoughts and be heard and gives them an opportunity to connect with others on your site. Comments also act as social proof for your site because the perceived value of your content increases as the number of comments increases.

When using the Facebook Comments plugin, your visitors who leave a comment have a few options. They can leave a comment as their Facebook Profile or as any Page they administer. They can also choose to have their comment posted to their Facebook Wall (on their Profile or Page, depending whether they posted as their Profile or their Page). When they leave the Post to Facebook check box selected, a story publishes to the News Feeds of their Friends or Fans. This increases the visibility of content on your site because the story links back to your blog post or Web site.

What makes Facebook Comments different from other blog-commenting systems is that the comments get posted on your blog site as well as on Facebook. This allows Friends and Fans to respond to the discussion by liking or replying to the comment directly in their News Feed on Facebook or in the Comments area on your blog site. Also, threads (strings of conversations in the Comments area) from both inside of Facebook and from the Comments area on your Web site stay synced, meaning that no matter where the comment is made for the original blog post, it will always show up in your Comments box and on Facebook. The conversations are then indented, making it easy to identify separate conversations. You can see this in action in Figure 2-9. Also, all the Likes on the comments are synced in both places. The viral exposure from this plugin is extremely powerful. Figure 2-9 shows the Facebook Comments plugin at work on the TechCrunch Web site.

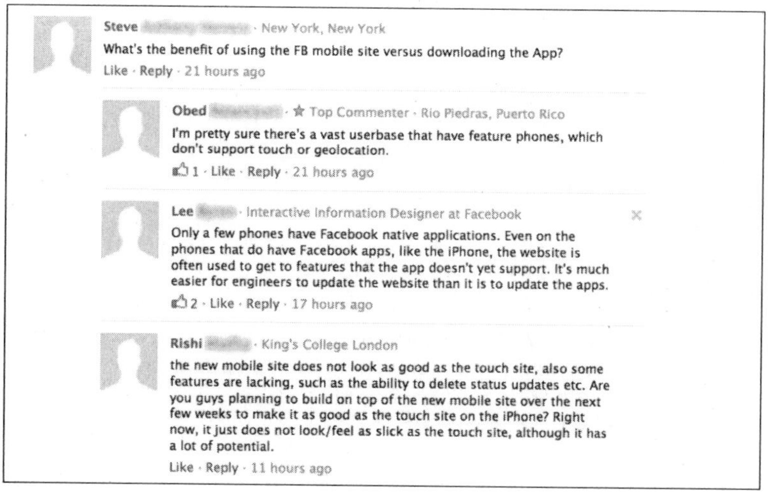

Figure 2-9:
The
Facebook
Comments
plugin at
work on the
TechCrunch
Web site.

Steve ▓▓▓ · New York, New York
What's the benefit of using the FB mobile site versus downloading the App?
Like · Reply · 21 hours ago

Obed ▓▓▓ · ★ Top Commenter · Rio Piedras, Puerto Rico
I'm pretty sure there's a vast userbase that have feature phones, which don't support touch or geolocation.
👍 1 · Like · Reply · 21 hours ago

Lee ▓▓▓ · Interactive Information Designer at Facebook   ✕
Only a few phones have Facebook native applications. Even on the phones that do have Facebook apps, like the iPhone, the website is often used to get to features that the app doesn't yet support. It's much easier for engineers to update the website than it is to update the apps.
👍 2 · Like · Reply · 17 hours ago

Rishi ▓▓▓ · King's College London
the new mobile site does not look as good as the touch site, also some features are lacking, such as the ability to delete status updates etc. Are you guys planning to build on top of the new mobile site over the next few weeks to make it as good as the touch site on the iPhone? Right now, it just does not look/feel as slick as the touch site, although it has a lot of potential.
Like · Reply · 11 hours ago

The Facebook Comments box also uses social relevance to order the blog comments. That means that each user logged in to Facebook will see what Facebook calls "relevant and interesting comments." These are the comments made by the user's Friends and Friends of Friends, as well as the most liked and active discussions, at the top of the Comments box. For example, the comments I would see at the top of a Facebook Comments box would be different from the comments you see, because we have different Friends and connections on Facebook. So the experience is personalized for everyone.

You have multiple ways to optimize the comments system on your site:

✦ Enable the Comments plugin in multiple areas on your Web site, including specific Web pages, articles, photos, and videos. This allows your users to interact with your site in more ways than one.

✦ Respond to your user's comments often and in real time when possible. This allows you to create one-on-one relationships with the visitors to your site. Refer to Figure 2-9 for an example of a Comments box on a Web site.

✦ Encourage users to post a comment by asking for their feedback about your article, video, photo, and so on, or by asking a question at the end of your post.

If your site does not already offer comment functionality, or if you're using a comment system that is getting minimal interaction, you may want to consider installing a Comments plugin. You have great potential for your online exposure to increase as users share their comments on your site.

Optimizing Your Connections with Facepile

The Facepile feature shows users the Profile images of their Friends who have signed in to your Web site or have Liked your Page (see Figure 2-10). One benefit of this feature is that it does not display if the user doesn't have Friends who have signed in to your site. Therefore, the social plugin displays only when appropriate.

Figure 2-10: The Facepile social plugin on a non-Facebook Web site.

Don't worry if you don't have a lot of Likers for your site. The Facepile plugin dynamically resizes its height, so it won't look awkward if only a few Friends are featured in the box.

You have two options when configuring the Facepile plugin:

✦ **Include a Login button:** When you include this button (refer to the preceding section), your users can sign in via the button, and then the faces of their Friends who have already signed in to your site appear in the Facepile box.

✦ **Omit a Login button:** If your Web site has a separate sign-in process not connected to a Facebook Login button, you can install the Facepile box without the Facebook Login button, and the Facepile box will display the faces of those who sign in to your site via your separate sign-in process.

Following the social-proof-appeal strategy, when you have the opportunity to display Friends' faces on your site, do it! As mentioned elsewhere, people are more likely to look to their Friends for recommendations and suggestions than they are to search independently on the Web. The Facepile plugin creates social proof by showing users which of their Facebook Friends have already signed in to a Web site or Liked your page. Depending on your preferences, you can customize your Facepile box to show just a few Profile images or multiple rows of user images.

Seeing a familiar face on a Web site can create an instant connection between the visitor, her Friends, and your site. Also, it's easier for your visitors to "know, Like, and trust you" when they see that their Friends have already embraced your site.

The more users your site attracts, the greater the chances are that your new visitors will see their Friends' Profile images in your Facepile box. If your site is brand new, you might want to wait a little while to build some momentum before you install this plugin. You will get greater impact with it if your users see many of their Friends inside the Facepile box.

Promoting a Live Event with Live Stream

The Live Stream plugin allows real-time comments on your site. It is best used when something is happening on your Web site, such as a live Webinar (which is when viewers can see the activity on your computer screen while you are talking) or a podcast. If you are hosting a live Webinar on your Web site, your users can come to your site and comment on the Webinar activity in real time. Those comments then get posted on the user's Facebook Wall (see Figure 2-11) and into their Friends' News Feeds. This gives your live event viral exposure.

Figure 2-11:
A comment generated by a Live Stream plugin.

Amy Porterfield Loved the live Facebook interview with former President George Bush today.

50 seconds ago via Facebook Live · Like · Comment

This social plugin is great for live events because it creates a buzz around the experience on your Web site. It isn't a good choice for static sites. Instead, you would want to choose a plugin specifically for blog posts, articles, and similar static content.

Capture Audience Data with the Registration Plugin

The Registration social plugin allows your audience to sign in to your Web site with their Facebook account. Non-Facebook users can also use this plugin to register for your Web site.

To use the plugin all you need to do is add a single line of code to create a registration form on your Web site. When users log into Facebook and click the Registration button on your Web site, the form will pre-populate with information from their profile, as shown in Figure 2-12.

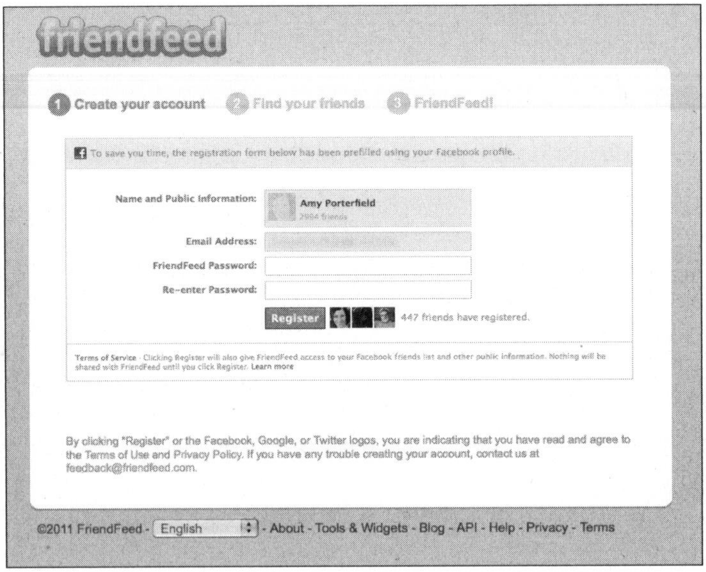

Figure 2-12:
A Registration sign-in form on a Web site.

If users are not logged into Facebook when they come to your Web site, the Register button automatically reads Login instead and prompts users to log in to their Facebook account. After they log in to Facebook, they see the prepopulated form to register for your site. *Prepopulated* means that a user's name, e-mail address, birthday, gender, and current city can automatically appear in the form, depending on how you set up the Registration plugin. This prepopulation feature in the Registration plugin reduces drop-off during registration because users obviously find filling out the remainder of the form much easier. This ease in turn increases the number of users who complete registration on your Web site.

You might be wondering how this plugin is different from the Login plugin. Think of the Registration plugin as an advanced Login button with additional features and benefits. Both buttons allow you to collect data about your users upon log in/registration; however, the Registration button also allows your users to create a username and password to log in to your site. They can then use that username and password each time they return to your site.

In addition, the form that the plugin creates allows you to add fields to ask for additional data not supplied by Facebook. When the user logs in for the first time, you can prompt users to answer questions you create. For example, you might want to ask users questions related to your niche. If you own a wine shop, you might ask users to tell you their favorite wine. Or if you're a Realtor, you might ask users to add the ZIP Code of the location in which they're looking to buy a home.

To learn more about the flow of the Registration button and to get ideas how you might use it, go to

```
http://developers.facebook.com/docs/user_registration/flows/.
```

Finding and Installing Open Source Facebook Plugins

As mentioned earlier, open source Facebook-friendly plugins incorporate Facebook activity but are created by third-party developers outside the Facebook platform. These plugins are very similar, some being almost identical, to the Facebook social plugins, but are much easier to install (meaning that no coding is involved!). It's important to note that open source plugins not only include access to Facebook activity, but many also include access to multiple social networks, which can expand your overall online reach. We explore some plugins that include multiple social networks in the section "Using share buttons for multiple social networks," later in this chapter.

Most popular open source social plugins

If you are considering adding a few open source social plugins to your Web site or blog, and you are looking for some help in choosing the best ones, we suggest starting with the following:

✦ Like button

✦ Like box

✦ Comments box

As a refresher, we suggest that you add the Like button to the top or bottom of each of your blog posts. This gives your content greater viral visibility and attracts new visitors to your site when it gets posted in the News Feeds of your visitors' Friends.

We suggest the Like box because it is a great way for visitors to become an instant Fan of your Facebook Page without ever leaving your Web site. Because the goal is to always keep visitors on your site as long as possible, the Like box is an extremely useful marketing tool. We also suggest that you choose the option in this box to show your Facebook Page activity as well. This gives your Facebook content even greater exposure on your Web site.

And finally, the Comments box is crucial for your blog. Without active commenting on your blog site, you can't gauge your audience's interest in your content. Plus, blog comments are great social proof. Although the Facebook Comments box has many useful features, we also especially like the commenting system Disqus. Although this commenting tool does not post comments directly to Facebook, it does allow easy commenting and includes the threading feature we mentioned, where you can comment directly under another's comment, keeping specific conversations synced. Also, most blog readers have Disqus accounts and are familiar with the system, making it more likely that they will leave a comment on your blog post. You can access the Disqus WordPress plugin by going to `http://wordpress.org/extend/plugins/disqus-comment-system`.

Using Share buttons for multiple social networks

Social media Share buttons are a great option if you want to combine multiple opportunities for visitors to share your content. These buttons offer your visitors choices about how they want to share your content with their social networks without ever leaving your site. You have several open source Share Button plugins to choose from; here are two of our favorites:

✦ **SexyBookmarks:** This plugin offers a row of different social bookmarks and social networks, such as Facebook, Twitter, and LinkedIn. Your reader can place his cursor over any of the icons to see it pop up on his screen. The reader can then click any of the icons and can share your content directly with that social network or bookmarking site. You can see this in action in Figure 2-13. To access the WordPress option for this plugin, go to `http://wordpress.org/extend/plugins/sexybookmarks`.

Figure 2-13:
The Sexy-Bookmarks plugin on a blog site.

✦ **Digg Digg:** This plugin provides multiple ways for your visitors to share your content on their social networks. They have two versions of this plugin: a static version and one that floats to stay in view as your reader scrolls down the length of the post. You can see this plugin as it floats in the middle of a blog post in Figure 2-14. To access the WordPress option for this plugin, go to `http://wordpress.org/extend/plugins/digg-digg`.

**Book VII
Chapter 2**

**Marketing with
Facebook Social
Plugins**

Digg-Digg Social Sharing Tool

Figure 2-14:
The Digg Digg plugin on a blog site.

Installing a WordPress plugin (the easy way!)

WordPress is the most widely used blogging platform and offers hundreds of social plugin options. Here are the universal steps to install a plugin on a WordPress platform:

1. **Log in to your WordPress dashboard.**

   In the left column of your dashboard you will see multiple categories with links under each category.

2. **Click the Plugins link.**

   You can find this link in the left column on your dashboard. After you click the Plugins link, you can see a list of plugins that are already installed on your WordPress site. Near the top of the page you will see an Add New button.

3. **Click the Add New button.**

   Now you can see a search field with a drop-down menu to the left of it. The drop-down menu has the options Term, Author, and Tags. Make sure that the drop-down menu next to the search box says Term.

4. **Type** Facebook Like Button **in the search box.**

   Multiple plugins appear in a list format. Each plugin has a short summary explaining the features for each list's plugin. You can take the time to research which plugin meets your needs, or you can do a little research in advance and quickly search for the one you already know you want. If you want a suggestion, our favorite WordPress Like button plugin is called "FaceBook Like Button Plugin for WordPress," by author Dean Peters. This plugin will likely appear when you search for "Facebook Like Button" in the plugins search field.

5. **When you find the plugin you want to install, click Install Now under the specific plugin name.**

   You then may see a page that asks you to enter your ftp username and password. This information is needed to host the plugin on your Web server. If your ftp username has been previously added, you may not be prompted for this information.

6. **Enter your ftp username and password and click Proceed. (Note: If you do not remember your credentials, you can contact the company that hosts your Web site to get this information.)**

   After you do this, you see an Installing Plugin page. The installation starts automatically. Wait a few seconds, and you will see a `Successfully installed plugin` message and an Activate Plugin link.

7. **Click Activate Plugin.**

   After you do this, you are ready to set up your plugin.

***8.* Click the Settings link to the newly activated plugin.**

You can find the Settings link of your plugin by locating the Settings category in the left column of your WordPress dashboard. After you click on your new plugin, you see a page with options to change the settings of the plugin. Each Settings page differs depending on the plugin. If you have questions, you see a link back to the official page of the plugin that you just installed. You can click that link to find out more information about your plugin and find answers to any questions you may have.

Chapter 3: Discovering Live Streaming

In This Chapter

✔ Exploring how streaming live video can enhance your business

✔ Choosing a video-streaming method

✔ Streaming from your Web site with the Live Stream plugin

✔ Streaming from Facebook with the Livestream application

✔ Marketing your streaming event

*L*ive streaming is used to stream live video for different types of events, from college football games to company announcements. It can be used for brand events and business events wherever they are. It's also a great way for musicians and all kinds of artists to connect with their fans. Live streaming gives you an additional communication platform for your event, and simultaneous live streaming chat boxes can make these video events even more interesting for everyone.

In this chapter, we first look at what live streaming can mean to you. Then we discuss both the plugin and the application and show you how to set each of them up. Finally, we tell you how to use these tools to get more out of your live events.

Understanding the Benefits of Streaming Video

Streaming adds a whole new social dimension to any event. Here are the reasons why:

✦ **Audience reactions:** You can see who is participating in the event and gain insight into how well your event is going over with your audience.

✦ **Increased traffic:** The live social stream drives more traffic to your event. Viewers post updates to their social networks and bring in more of their friends to watch the event. With a relatively small number of well-connected viewers sharing your content, you don't need to have a huge budget to create a popular event.

✦ **More social engagement:** The most important social addition is the increased engagement you can create around an event because viewers can participate. This is why you want to share your event in the first place, right?

For a glimpse of the social video experience, have a look at Facebook's official live streaming Page at http://www.facebook.com/FacebookLive.

Attracting viewers with chat

Live social streams work best when used in conjunction with a live event, broadcast through live-streaming video. This is because the stream of comments from other viewers naturally pulls others in to share their own thoughts and comments.

Combining a stream of comments with your video broadcast is a way to grow your audience organically during the broadcast itself. Facebook makes it easy to build a larger and more interactive community around your event.

Live streaming your event with a real-time Facebook chat box opens your audience to your fans and their Facebook friends. These real-time chat boxes, also called live social streams, allow you to have millions of viewers interacting at the same time. Chat boxes are powerful communication tools when they're used on the same page next to your live streaming video content. The chat box invites viewers to participate by reading other viewers' comments and sharing their own. Chat boxes also include embedded Share buttons (see Figure 3-1).

Getting closer to customers

Facebook is a social platform; it's where people come to chat with friends. In this social environment, live streaming gives businesses a tool to get closer to their audience. With a little planning for both social media and offline promotion, it's easy for businesses to cultivate interaction, create buzz (see the last section of this chapter), and expand their audience thanks to social media.

Supplementing traditional advertising

Given the size of Facebook and the viral nature of social media, live streaming through Facebook can give you as much visibility as any form of traditional media advertising. A live chat box helps you engage a large audience around your live streaming video.

Keep in mind, however, that you won't be able to control all aspects of your live-streamed marketing communication. Streaming gives your viewers a platform to share their opinions, exchange ideas with friends, and read all the other comments posted by other viewers.

Figure 3-1:
Live
streaming
video with
a chat box
and share
buttons.

Choosing Your Streaming Method

Currently, you have two main ways to use live streaming on Facebook and take your live event to a whole new dimension:

✦ **The Live Stream plugin** creates a chat box on your own blog or Web site (see Figure 3-2). If you already have your own video feed or content — meaning that you already have the setup to create and broadcast videos — the Live Stream plugin allows you to create a live stream chat box next to your live streaming video. To access this plugin, visit `http://developers.facebook.com/docs/reference/plugins/live-stream/`

For more information on Live Stream and Facebook's other social plugins, see Book VII, Chapter 2.

Figure 3-2:
A Live Stream social plugin (chat box) on a Web site.

✦ **The Livestream for Facebook application** supports both do-it-yourself video broadcasting and live stream chat boxes on your Facebook Page (see Figure 3-3). If you need a tool to broadcast your live videos inside of Facebook, the Livestream application is for you. Whereas the Live stream social plugin is the actual chat box you place on your Web site and use during live events, this application gives you an easy-to-use tool to do both: video broadcasting on your Facebook Page and a live stream chat box. To access this application, visit `http://apps.facebook.com/livestream/`.

Although there are a few options for video streaming on Facebook, we focus on Livestream for Facebook because it's widely used and is the application Facebook uses for its own live videos. We figure that what's good enough for Facebook is good enough for us!

Figure 3-3:
A
Livestream
video and
chat box
application
on a
Facebook
Page.

How do you know which to choose? Your choice depends on what you need to do:

✦ If your business needs to have your video broadcasts streamed from your own Web site, you'll want to use the Live Stream plugin to interact with your community on Facebook.

✦ If your business needs a broadcasting tool and wants to take full advantage of your Facebook community, you'll want to look at the Livestream application for publishing your videos on your Facebook Page.

Things change rapidly in this field, and other solutions might exist for you at the time you read this chapter. Other companies that you should check out for live video streaming on Facebook are Ustream (www.ustream. tv/), Justin.tv (www.justin.tv/) and Vpype (http://vpype.com/). Also, YouTube has been recently talking about a live streaming application, so don't forget to watch developments there, as well.

In the next two sections, we show you how to create a live stream with both tools.

Streaming from Your Web Site with the Live Stream PlugIn

The Live Stream plugin lets users visiting your site share comments in real time, right next to the actual video. This live stream chat box is ideal for creating an interactive experience if you're streaming a video for a webcast, live Web chat, or webinar.

Creating a live stream chat box for your blog or Web site with the Live Stream plug-in is simple. You can even embed multiple Live Stream chat boxes on one Web site simply by specifying unique URLs for each stream (see Step 2 of the following list).

To add a Live Stream plugin, follow these steps:

1. **Go to** http://developers.facebook.com/docs/reference/plugins/live-stream/.

2. **Complete the form as follows:**

Note: The App ID field, which is your Facebook application ID, is defined for you.

- **Width:** Enter the width of the plugin, in pixels.

- **Height:** Enter the height of the plugin, in pixels.

The default height setting is 500 and default width setting is 400; not all users have the same configuration on their computers as you do on yours. We recommend that you test these settings first by adding the plugin to your Web site with the default settings and adjust as needed.

- **XID:** XID stands for external ID and is a unique identifier for an object not generated by Facebook, such as your own live event. If you have multiple live events taking place, you will need multiple live stream boxes on the same page. Therefore, you need to specify a unique XID for each to ensure that each live chat box on your page is different. Facebook specifies this by adding the XID you create to the code generated for the chat box. XIDs can contain alphanumeric characters (Aa–Zz, 0–9), hyphens (–), percent signs (%), periods (.), and underscore characters (_). Create one that's easy to associate with your live stream box. An example of an XID for a live event is womens_ health_expo.

- **Via Attribution URL:** Enter the URL that users are redirected to when they click your application name in a Facebook post. Figure 3-4 shows an example of an attribution URL.

Attribution URL

Figure 3-4:
Example
of an
attribution
URL.

- **Always Post to Friends:** If you select this box, the comments your users post in your Live Stream chat box will also post automatically to their Facebook profile and in their News Feeds. Use this feature when the posts in the chat box will likely make sense to others who will see them out of the context of the live event they're posting about.

3. **Click the Get Code button.**

4. **Copy the code and remember to save it in a text file for future reference.**

5. **Open your blog or Web site.**

6. **If you're familiar with embedding code, go to the place where you want to put your Live Stream chat box.**

   The most popular places for a live stream chat box is in a blog post, next to your streaming video, or on a sidebar of your Web site.

   If you're not comfortable inserting code into your Web site or blog, this is the time to hire a programmer to help you. A programmer can likely get you set up within an hour at most.

7. **Paste the code in exactly as it is.**

   You will now have your Live Stream chat box in place.

Unfortunately, this is an area where technology does get buggy. The Live Stream plugin code occasionally has display issues when it is placed directly inside a blog post. There are many reasons why this can happen, and you may not be able to solve all display issues. If you do have an issue, test your Live Stream code by moving it to the sidebar, for example, and then test to see what's possible on your Web site and what you can work with.

Streaming from Your Facebook Page with the Livestream Application

Are you ready to try your hand at broadcasting an event directly through your Facebook Page? You can now create your own real-time broadcast and have a real-time chat box at the same time thanks to the Livestream application!

Livestream is a third-party application. To better understand third-party applications, go to Book V.

The basic Livestream package is free, but if you want your video to be advertisement free, or you need to customize it, you'll need to purchase a package. You also have to go through a simple verification process before you can have more than 50 viewers at the same time. This is a process used by Livestream to limit piracy, but after you go through this initial step, you have access to live streaming to an unlimited number of viewers.

It's important to note that the Livestream application does not work on your personal Facebook Profile. You need a Facebook Page to use this application. Your broadcast will be set up under a tab on your Page. But Facebook is known to change things, so check back in the future to see whether it becomes available on Facebook Profiles, too.

Creating a Livestream account

If you want to use the Livestream application to create and broadcast your own video through your Facebook page, you need a Livestream account. (If you want to broadcast from an existing Livestream account, whether your own or someone else's, you can skip this process.)

To set up a Livestream account, follow these steps:

1. **Go to** http://livestream.com.

2. **Click Sign Up in the top-right corner of the screen.**

   You see a screen that asks, "What would you like to do?"

3. **Click Broadcast.**

   You are now on the Livestream Account Center page.

4. **Enter a name for your channel.**

   As you type your channel name, Livestream will populate the Short Name and Channel Page fields and instantly let you know whether the name is available (if not, you need to choose a new name). See Figure 3-5.

Figure 3-5:
The
Account
Center
page.

5. **On the same page, click Launch Free Channel or Launch Premium Channel, as shown in Figure 3-6.**

   The premium channel lets you stream with no advertisements; however, it costs $350 per month. If you're okay with ads, choose the free channel.

Figure 3-6:
The two
channel
launch
options.

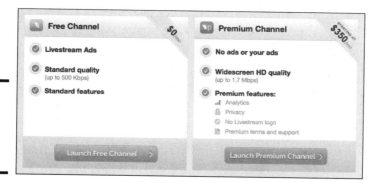

6. **Enter your sign-up information and click Sign Up in the bottom-right corner.**

   A Congratulations! screen confirms your sign up.

Installing the application

After you've established a Livestream account, you're ready to install the Livestream application, as follows:

1. **Go to** www.facebook.com **and log in to your account.**

2. **Go to** http://apps.facebook.com/livestream.

3. **Locate the Page where you intend to use the Livestream application.**

   If you already have several Facebook Pages, you will see them all listed under Pages Without Livestream. If you've created only one Page, you will see only that Page listed, as shown in Figure 3-7.

Figure 3-7:
The
Livestream
for
Facebook
application
page.

4. **Click the Add Page Tab button on the Page where you intend to use Livestream.**

   You are automatically taken to a permission request page.

5. **Click Add Livestream to accept the permission request (see Figure 3-8).**

   Livestream requires permission to access your basic information, including name, Profile picture, gender, networks, user ID, list of Friends, and any other information you have shared with everyone.

Figure 3-8:
Permission
request
for the
Livestream
application.

After you accept the permission request, you are automatically redirected to your Facebook Page.

Adding Live Stream to a tab on your Page

When you're on your Page tab, you will see the Getting Started page for Livestream. A few things are explained here, including the following: how to stream live in one click to Facebook; your channel page on livestream.com; your Web site; and mobile devices. Everything will be recorded and made available in an on-demand library on Livestream.com.

You can add Livestream to one Page at a time by following these steps:

1. **Choose the channel you want to use on your page (see Figure 3-9).**

A channel is just like a TV channel that you select from Livestream. You get to choose what you intend to broadcast. It can be your own channel or a channel that already exists on Livestream. After you select your channel option, you see the Channel Settings page.

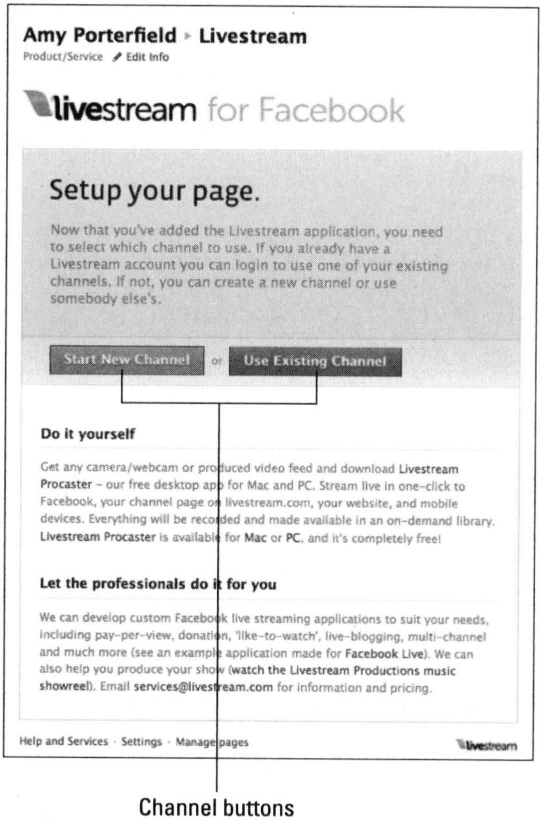

Amy Porterfield ▸ **Livestream**
Product/Service ✎ Edit Info

livestream for Facebook

Setup your page.

Now that you've added the Livestream application, you need to select which channel to use. If you already have a Livestream account you can login to use one of your existing channels. If not, you can create a new channel or use somebody else's.

[Start New Channel] or [Use Existing Channel]

Do it yourself

Get any camera/webcam or produced video feed and download **Livestream Procaster** – our free desktop app for Mac and PC. Stream live in one-click to Facebook, your channel page on livestream.com, your website, and mobile devices. Everything will be recorded and made available in an on-demand library. **Livestream Procaster** is available for **Mac** or **PC**, and it's completely free!

Let the professionals do it for you

We can develop custom Facebook live streaming applications to suit your needs, including pay-per-view, donation, 'like-to-watch', live-blogging, multi-channel and much more (see an example application made for **Facebook Live**). We can also help you produce your show (watch the Livestream Productions music showreel). Email services@livestream.com for information and pricing.

Help and Services · Settings · Manage pages   **livestream**

Figure 3-9: Channel options.

Channel buttons

2. **Click Login in the upper-right corner and enter your Livestream login details.**

   You see more options to set up your channel, including the channel name and description.

3. **Select the channel you want to show from the drop-down list.**

4. **Add the channel description.**

   Your audience will see this description, so make it good!

5. **(Optional) Upload a banner by clicking Browse and choosing a banner image from your computer.**

6. **Click Save Changes.**

   Your Livestream Page tab is created.

Congratulations! You're now done installing the application, so all you need to do now is follow the steps to broadcast your video!

To broadcast your live video on your Facebook Page, try the Livestream Procaster. You can broadcast video directly from your camera or from your webcam on your computer. You can also broadcast what you're showing on your screen, such as a Power Point presentation. For details on broadcasting with Livestream, visit `http://www.livestream.com/platform/ procaster/`.

Creating Buzz about Your Live Stream

Now that you have your live stream up and ready to run, you want to get people interested in your live stream event. And this is where your Facebook marketing skills come into play.

Posting to your Facebook Page

Prior to your live streaming event, remember to post an update on your Facebook Page to let your audience know what's coming.

- ✦ Tell them about your live streaming event.
- ✦ Tell them why they'll find it interesting.
- ✦ Tell them how they'll be able to participate.
- ✦ Ask them to tell their friends.

During your live streaming event, be sure to let your audience on your Facebook Page know what's happening live and give them the link.

You can also create a Facebook Event and promote your upcoming event there. To learn more about Facebook Events, go to Book VI, Chapter 1.

Posting to your personal Profile

Prior to your event, you can also share the updates on your Page and your Facebook Event page. Doing so gets them onto your personal Profile and published in your News Feed.

During the live streaming event, your viewers will have the option of sharing the comments they make on the live stream chat box with their friends on Facebook. Their updates are automatically published onto their personal Profile page. This means their updates are also seen in their news feed for their friends to see. And these updates have links back to your live stream, which gives you exposure to a potentially new audience.

In addition, this gives your event extra coverage and more people are likely to come and see it while the event is going on.

Sharing viewer comments with other social media

It's easy for viewers to share their comments on Twitter as well as to their Facebook Profile. There's also a Tweet button on the live stream chat box.

You want to encourage your audience to use these social buttons often to get the viral exposure necessary to draw a crowd to your video. Calls to action are extremely important during a live streaming event. Remember, the link generated when people use these social buttons sends people back to the live stream box, bringing in more viewers and facilitating even more interaction around your event.

Partnering with other events and organizers

One of the cool things about live streaming is that you don't actually need to have your own live streaming video to chat about it. You can create a live stream chat to talk about someone else's video content if you want. You just need to be able to access the live streaming video feed.

So look for interesting upcoming live streaming videos on places such as the Livestream video library. Check with event organizers for content that your audience would love to see.

If you create your own videos, find people with audiences interested in your content and partner with them. Your video broadcasts will reach wider audiences, and you'll build an interactive community experience around your event.

As you look for opportunities to bring content publishers and communities together, remember the opportunities mobile devices offer. Not only is it easy to access Facebook on all mobile devices, it's also easy to record videos on many of them. With so many possibilities, we're sure to see more live streaming events.

Keeping Facebook users interested in the stream

As with creating other experiences on Facebook, you will benefit from a communication plan to promote your live streaming event. Here are a few key tips to help you maximize your live streaming experience:

✔ Let people know about your live streaming event before, during, and after the event.

✔ Reach out to people in different ways and on different communication platforms.

✔ Share the link to your live streaming event on Facebook, Twitter, and LinkedIn, as well as on your Web site and blog. Also e-mail your prospects and clients and invite them to your live broadcast.

✔ Use a positive conversational tone in your updates.

Chapter 4: Stepping Out with Facebook Places and Facebook Deals

In This Chapter

✔ **Understanding Facebook Places**

✔ **Getting your Facebook Place up and running**

✔ **Creating incentives with Facebook Deals**

✔ **Promoting Facebook Deals**

Facebook Places and Facebook Deals have presented an exciting opportunity for businesses that have physical locations, the brick-and-mortars, across the country. The two applications combined can create a highly valuable tool for gaining new exposure and promoting your business online.

As mentioned in Book II, Chapter 1, Places is an effort by Facebook to create a community experience with your Friends while you're out and about. Facebook Deals allows you to create specialized discounts, offers and rewards for new and returning customers.

For business owners, combining Facebook Places and Facebook Deals creates word-of-mouth marketing at its best and can dramatically increase your exposure and reach.

In this chapter, we tell you how Facebook Places work, how to access Places from a smartphone, and how to claim your Place if you have a physical location. From there, we move into Facebook Deals and tell you what they are, how to create them, and what you can do to promote your Deals to gain even greater exposure and attract a larger audience.

Exploring Facebook Places

Facebook Places allows users to share their location with Friends, find out where their Friends are, and discover new places in their area. Now when Facebook users find a favorite hot spot — say, a new coffeehouse, nightclub, yoga studio or hair salon — with one click of a button they can tell all their Friends about it.

Places for consumers

Before we dive into the specifics of how your business can benefit from Facebook Places, it's important to first understand how consumers, your potential customers, will interface with this location-based feature.

When you check in to a location, your check-ins will create a story and by default appear on your Profile (see Figure 4-1), in the News Feeds (see Figure 4-2), and in the activity stream for that place (see Figure 4-3).

Figure 4-1:
A check-in story on a personal Profile.

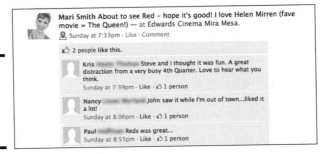

Figure 4-2:
A check-in story in a News Feed.

Places icon

Amy's post

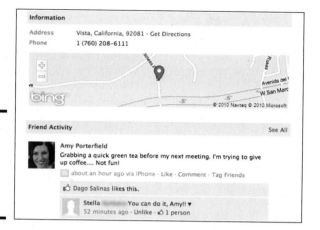

Information

| Address | Vista, California, 92081 · Get Directions |
| Phone | 1 (760) 208-6111 |

Friend Activity   See All

Amy Porterfield
Grabbing a quick green tea before my next meeting. I'm trying to give up coffee.... Not fun!

about an hour ago via iPhone · Like · Comment · Tag Friends

Dago Salinas likes this.

Stella ▓▓▓▓▓ You can do it, Amy!! ♥
52 minutes ago · Unlike · 1 person

Figure 4-3:
A check-in story in the Places activity stream.

The Facebook Places platform uses GPS to enable the Location Finder feature. You have two options for checking in to a location via a smartphone: a Facebook application or via a Web browser.

Checking in via a Facebook app on a smartphone

To check in to Facebook Places on a smartphone using a Facebook app, follow these steps:

1. **Download the Facebook application to your smartphone, if you haven't already.**

   If your smartphone has the capability to download apps, locate the apps section on your phone and search for Facebook in the apps section. After the app is downloaded, you see a screen with multiple Facebook icons, as shown in Figure 4-4, which was taken on an iPhone. If your phone has a Web browser but does not use apps, go to the section in this chapter called "Checking in via the Facebook Web site on your smartphone."

2. **Locate the Places icon on the screen and tap Places.**

3. **If you're asked whether Facebook is allowed to know your location, tap Allow.**

   You enter the Places interface.

4. **Tap the Check In button in the top-right corner.**

   You see a list of places near you.

5. **Choose your location.**

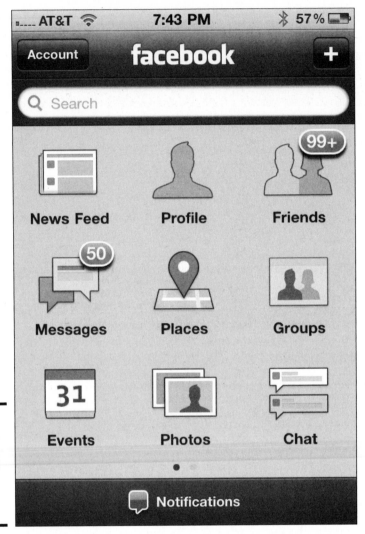

Figure 4-4:
The Facebook application home screen on an iPhone.

When your location appears, tap on that location. If you don't see your location in the list, search for it by entering the business name in the top bar that reads Find or Add a Place, as shown in Figure 4-5. If the location does not yet have a Facebook Place, you can touch Add to create it.

The Find or Add a Place field

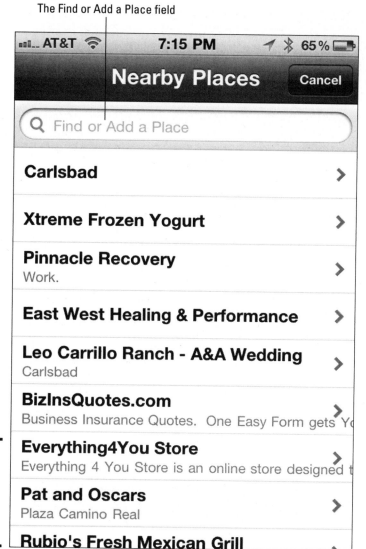

Figure 4-5:
Search
field on
the Places
smartphone
page.

6. **Tap the Check In button.**

You are taken to the screen you see in Figure 4-6.

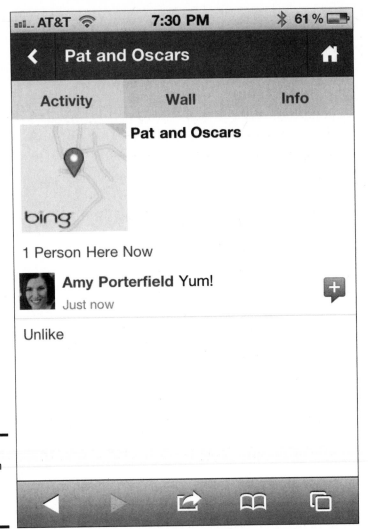

Activity   Wall   Info

Figure 4-6:
The screen you see after you check in.

Checking in via the Facebook Web site on your smartphone

You don't have to download the Facebook app to access Places. You can access Places as long as your smartphone has a browser with HTML 5 and geolocation capabilities. Here are the steps you follow:

1. **Go to** www.facebook.com **on a smartphone and log in to your Facebook account.**

2. **Tap the More tab in the top-right corner.**

   You see a drop-down menu.

3. **Tap Places in the drop-down menu.**

   You see your Facebook avatar at the top of the screen as well as a list of all your Friends who have recently checked in to Places.

4. **Tap Check-In in the top-right corner.**

   A pop-up box appears and asks whether you want to use your current location.

5. **Tap OK to use your current location.**

   You see a list of locations near you.

6. **Tap your location in the list.**

   If you don't see your location in the list, search for it by entering the business name in the Search field on this screen. If the location doesn't yet have a Facebook Place, you can touch Add to create it.

7. **Tap Check In.**

After you check in, you can tag the people you're currently with. Tagging, as discussed in Book III, Chapter 2, gives you the ability to identify and reference people in your status updates, photos, and videos. Just as you can tag a friend in a photo on Facebook, you can now tag the people who are with you at your location.

You must be Friends with someone before you can tag that person.

When you check in to a location, you also have the opportunity to tell people more about what you're doing by including a comment along with your check in. When you check in at Starbucks, for example, you can add a comment that says what you're up to.

Connecting with others at your location

Another great feature of Facebook Places is the ability to find out who else is currently at your location. Once you check in, if any of your friends are also checked in to the same location, you will see their picture under the Here Now section on your check-in screen, as shown in Figure 4-7.

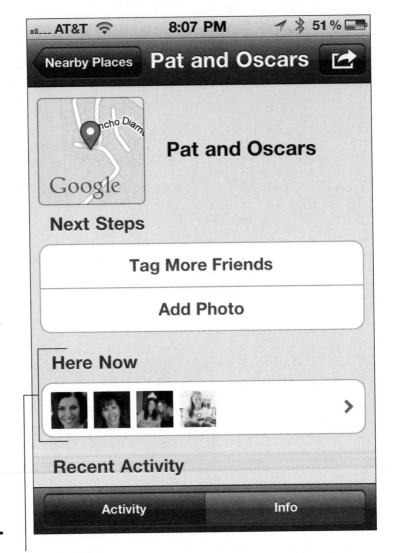

This shows who's here

This feature is visible for a limited amount of time and available only to those who have checked in, meaning that not everyone on Facebook can go to a location and see who's there. You must be checked in to get this info.

Exploring privacy options

Mark Zuckerberg, the founder of Facebook, said that Facebook Places is about finding places and sharing them with Friends, not about sharing your location with the world. You get to decide who sees your location and how much information about your location gets shared with others. You're in control of your location on Facebook.

Facebook will never share or expose your location automatically. To be clear, only Friends can tag you and check you in to a place. The first time a Friend attempts to check you in, you will be notified. At this time, you have the option to now allow the check in. (You can also go into your privacy settings and disable this feature before you begin using Facebook Places. Depending on your notification settings, if you allow Friends to check you in, you can be notified via a Facebook notification and a mobile notification.

There are three controls on the Facebook Privacy Settings page that relate to Places: Things I Share, People Here Now, and Things Others Share. While logged in to Facebook, on your Privacy Settings page, click Customize Settings to see all three sections.

✦ **Things I Share:** In this section, two areas are related to Places that you will want to review. First, you can decide who sees the places you check in to. You can customize this area by choosing only Friends, Friends of Friends, everyone on Facebook, or you can customize it and choose which people you want to share your check-ins with on Facebook.

✦ **People Here Now:** Also in the Things I Share section, you can choose whether you want to be included in the People Here Now section, meaning that after you check in, you decide whether you want your Friends and other people checked in nearby to see you on the list of those who are currently at the location.

✦ **Things Others Share:** Under the Things Others Share section, you can allow your Friends to check you in to a location. You can choose Enable or Disable for this feature.

Places for businesses

When you understand how a consumer interacts with Facebook Places, you can see the benefits of this location-based feature to a brick-and-mortar business. Your customers can tell all their Friends that they're at your location and can add comments about their experience.

This type of information exchange serves as valuable social proof. As mentioned earlier, people trust their friends' recommendations more than they trust brands and businesses, and the Places check-in functionality can serve as a powerful recommendation from your customers.

Third-party apps for Places

Facebook Places has opened data to allow developers to access areas of Places. This means that developers can now create applications that will pull in information about people, locations, and groups.

Facebook Places is rapidly evolving and has already begun to integrate third-party apps. Specifically, you can benefit from the third-party apps that you can use to track check ins.

Leader boards, also called dashboards, can help you monitor your customer check ins. To find options for leader board apps, we suggest doing a search for "leader board" or "places" inside of Facebook to find a few to choose from.

A leader board shows you the people who have checked in the most often to your location. You can create a game out of encouraging your visitors to compete for the top spot. You can offer deals or specials to the top spot customer, thus creating a fun competition among customers. This type of game can be extremely powerful in boosting sales.

Launching a Facebook Place

Getting your Facebook Place up and running involves two steps. First, your Facebook Place needs to be created, either by you or a customer. Second, you must "claim" your Facebook Place to gain control over it. The following sections describe how to do both.

Locating your Place

Your Facebook Place is created when someone is physically at your location and attempts to check in. If this is the first time a check in has been attempted, at your location, the person checking in can search for your location and tap Add via his or her mobile device, and your Place will automatically be created. After your Place has been created, you can then follow the steps to claim it as your business.

If your business name doesn't have a listing on Places yet, it's because no one has tried to check in to it on the mobile interface. You need to use the mobile interface to add your business, check in there, and then go back to the computer and claim your Places Page.

To do all this, you need to be physically at your business location. This is a geolocation program, so your phone's location will be what Facebook puts on your Places page.

To locate your Place, follow these steps:

1. **Go to** www.facebook.com **and search for your business name.**

   You can be anywhere on Facebook and use the Search bar at the top of every screen.

2. **If you don't see your Places Page, create it.**

   If your business name doesn't have a listing on Places no one has tried to check in to it on the mobile interface.

3. **Use your smartphone to search for your business.**

   You do that by going to www.facebook.com on a smartphone. You need to be signed in to your personal account.

4. **Tap the More tab in the top-right corner.**

   You see a drop-down menu.

5. **Tap Places in the drop-down menu.**

   You see your Facebook avatar at the top of the screen and a list of all your Friends who have recently checked in to Places.

6. **Tap Check In in the top-right corner.**

   A pop-up box appears, asking whether you want to use your current location.

7. **Tap OK to use your current location.**

   You see a list of locations near you.

8. **Type in the name of your business in the Search bar.**

   If you don't see your business in the list of locations near you, type the name of your business and a short description to add it.

9. **Tap Add.**

   Your Place has been created but not yet activated.

10. **Tap Check In.**

    Your Places Page is activated.

Claiming your Place

If you have a brick-and-mortar store, you need to claim your Places Page as it shows up in mobile Facebook. Then you will have the opportunity to merge your Places information with your Official Business Page on Facebook. A good process would be to create your Official Business Page first and then go and claim or create your Places Page.

To claim your Place, follow these steps:

1. **Go to** www.facebook.com **and search for your business name.**

   You don't need to be on a smartphone to do this step. Also, you can be anywhere on Facebook and use the Search bar at the top of the screen.

2. **If your business's Place already exists on Facebook, click it to visit its page.**

   You will know it's a Facebook Places Page because it will be listed under the Places header in the Search drop-down menu, as shown in Figure 4-8.

Figure 4-8:
A Places Page listed in the Facebook search menu.

3. **Click the Is This Your Business? link in the left column.**

   You see a pop-up box asking you to select a box to claim that you're an official representative of the physical location.

4. **Click the verification box and click the Proceed with Verification button.**

   You see a claiming process page.

5. **Enter your business information and click Continue.**

   To claim your business, Facebook asks you to provide the following information:

- Official name of business

- Business address

- Business phone number

- Business Web site

- Third-party listing (such as Yelp or a BBB listing)

- Your relationship to the location (for example, Owner)

6. **Verify your business by giving additional information and then click Submit.**

   You are asked to verify that you are the owner of the business either through an e-mail or document verification process.

   Your e-mail address must be a business e-mail (one that has your business name in the domain name). If you choose document verification, you will have to provide scanned images of the businesses' phone or utility bill that includes your place of business name and address.

After your claim is confirmed, you will own your Place on Facebook. Even though you already have all the information that a Places Page contains on your regular Business Page Info Tab, by claiming your Place, you can manage your Place's address, contact information, business hours, Profile picture, admins, and other settings that people will see in their Facebook Mobile application.

Now you can go back to your computer, search for your Places Page, as outlined previously, and edit and fill in more information.

Facebook may ask you whether you want to merge your Places Page with your Official Business Page. Think very carefully before you decide to "merge" them, because it will modify your Official Page and might make it impossible to direct people to a Custom landing link! As of this writing, you can't undo a merge.

A merged Page looks like Figure 4-9. Note how the number of check-ins displays in the left column on the Page. Seeing a number here is how you know the Pages have been merged.

Figure 4-9:
A merged Places and business Page.

Check-ins

Introducing Facebook Check-in Deals to Your Community

Check-in Deals (www.facebook.com/deals/checkin/) is a location-based rewards service that offers special discounts and giveaways for visitors of physical locations who check in using Facebook Places. Using Check-in Deals is a terrific way to drive traffic to your brick-and-mortar locations and bring in more customers. The opportunity to create these unique deals gives you a vested interest in claiming your Place on Facebook. When users check in to your location, they see a yellow or green ticket next to your location to let them know you're offering a deal. Deals gives you a way to entice customers with discounts and other special offers to help you build raving, loyal customers and attract new business.

You have several compelling reasons to experiment with Facebook Check-in Deals, including these:

✦ **To build customer loyalty.** Deals allows you to build valuable relation-ships with an interested audience. For the customers who are already at your store, you can create incentives for them to keep coming back by offering great deals they can't refuse.

✦ **To spread the word.** Typically, Facebook users have Friends. When someone checks into your business and finds that you're offering a deal, that person's 130+ friends potentially can be exposed to your offer. This word-of-mouth marketing is priceless!

✦ **To attract new customers.** More than 200 million people use Facebook on their mobile devices. By offering a deal when people are searching their location, you are giving them a great reason to stop by your business.

Choosing a Deal

You can offer four types of Facebook Deals:

✦ **Individual:** To create incentives that will encourage people to visit your business, you want to create a high-value, individual check-in deal.

✦ **Friend:** The Friend Deals allows you to create a deal for multiple people who come to your store together. When they check in together, they are rewarded with a special group deal. You are allowed to offer deals to up to eight people when they check in as a group. Because several people have to come in together to claim your discount, you can increase over-all exposure to your business.

Often, people in the group will be new to your business, so this deal attracts both loyal customers and new ones, too. Encourage existing customers to bring along their Friends.

✦ **Loyalty:** In the past, businesses would have to get punch cards or rewards cards printed in advance to promote a loyalty program to their customers. Now you can see this same model in a digital format and set up your loyalty program in just minutes.

You can set up a loyalty program that track those people who check into your business numerous times. Loyalty deals keep customers coming back often. A great feature of the loyalty deal is that the number of check-ins can vary. You can have your customers check in no fewer than two times and no more than 20 times.

✦ **Charity:** This deal allows you to make a donation to the charity of your choice each time someone claims your deal. You will have to mange the donation process on your own. The Charity deal allows you to incorpo-rate giving back with growing your business. It's a win-win for everyone involved.

You can run only one type of deal at a time.

Defining your offer and setting deal duration and quality

In addition to choosing the deal, you will need to write a short summary of your offer as well as define how customers can claim the offer. To make your offer easy to claim, we suggest asking your customers to show the offer via their mobile phone screens. That way your customers don't have to remember to print the offer before they visit your store.

You will also need to decide on the deal duration as well as the deal quantity. The deal duration is the length of time you want your deal to run. After you set the date and time, Facebook manages the rest.

As for the deal quantity, you can limit the number of specific deals you're giving out. This is important because if you're giving a steep discount or a physical giveaway, you will want to monitor your quantities closely. You can do this by selecting the number of people who can redeem your deal. If you don't mind how many people redeem your offer, you can choose Unlimited.

Last, you can limit the number of times a customer can redeem your offer. Currently, you have two options: once per user and no more than one every 24 hours.

Promoting a Deal

The social distribution factor of Facebook Deals is a highly attractive reason to experiment with this app. When a deal is claimed by a customer, it is then shared in the News Feed of that Facebook user, therefore allowing all their Friends to reap the same deal if they choose.

When you create a new deal, you will want to make sure you consistently promote it to your Facebook followers on your Facebook Page and Place. You can also share your offer on Twitter, LinkedIn, and your blog. The more places your customers and potential customers see your offer, the more likely they are to take you up on it!

You can also promote your deals by purchasing Facebook ads. You can be laser focused with your Facebook ads and target specific demographics and locations to attract your ideal customer. (You can learn more about Facebook ads in Book VIII.) In addition to promoting your offer on social networks and testing out Facebook ads, Facebook will also help you by promoting your deal when users are near your location. Here's how it works: Let's say I have the Facebook app loaded on my iPhone and I have opted to receive notifications from Facebook. (Notifications are similar to text messages and appear on your phone as pop-up boxes.) Facebook sends your offer as a notification to my phone when I'm near your location. If I wasn't already aware of your store, the notification of a special offer might pique my interest enough to visit your store. If I check-in to your location, the deal will appear on my Places check-in page.

Setting up a Deal on Places

There is no cost to set up a Facebook Check-in Deal. Here are the simple steps to create an active offer:

1. **Go to your business's claimed Facebook Place.**

   Deals can be created only on claimed Places, so make sure to claim your Place right away. (We discuss the process in "Claiming your Place," earlier in this chapter.)

2. **Click Edit Page in the top-right of the Page.**

   You see a page with multiple options in the left column.

3. **Click Deals from the list in the left column.**

   You're taken to the Create Deal dashboard.

4. **Click Create a Deal for This Page.**

   You see the four types of deals: individual, friend, loyalty, and charity (refer to "Choosing a Deal," earlier in this chapter).

5. **Click the deal you want to create.**

   You see two sections where you need to fill in offer details.

6. **In the Deal Summary section, enter your offer.**

   For example, you might say "25% off when you spend $50 or more." You have a 50-character limit for your summary, so choose your words wisely!

7. **In the How To Claim section, enter the instructions on how to claim the deal.**

   You have just 100 characters to do this, so keep it brief. For example, you might say, "Show this offer on your mobile device at check out to redeem your deal."

   As previously mentioned, make your offer easy to claim. We suggest asking your customers to show the offer via their mobile phone screens. That way, your customers don't have to remember to print the offer before they visit your store.

8. **Specify how many check-ins are required before the customer can claim the deal.**

   The number of check-ins applies only if you're creating a loyalty deal.

9. **Specify the duration of your deal by choosing a start and end date and time.**

10. **Choose the deal quantity.**

Make sure to choose a quantity that you will be able to fulfill, because if you don't deliver on your offer, you could have many angry customers expressing their frustration on Facebook and other social networking sites. This is not the kind of exposure you want!

11. **Decide how many times a customer can claim this deal.**

You can choose Claimable Once Per User or Claimable Once Every 24 Hours Per User.

12. **Click Save to submit your deal for review.**

All deals are subject to review within 48 hours. All low-quality deals can be rejected or pulled from Facebook at anytime.

After submitting your deal, you will receive a message that confirms your deal's start and end dates as well as information on best practices to help you prepare your business to run the deal, such as ideas for promoting your deal and making sure you have enough supplies on hand if you're doing a giveaway.

When your deal is approved, you can begin promoting it by posting a status update on your Facebook Page or Place. You can also consider running a marketplace ad on Facebook, as discussed in Book VIII.

It's important that you train your employees on all the specifics of tracking and honoring your deals. You will want to make sure that all employees have the details of the offer, including what the offer is, how many you intend to give out, and your specific terms and conditions. If your employees are well trained, your Facebook Deal strategy can be executed flawlessly.

Expanding the Reach of Your Facebook Deals

Facebook recently launched another deal program called Deals on Facebook and they are promising it to be even bigger than Check-in Deals. If you're familiar with Groupon or Living Social, you'll find that Deals on Facebook has a similar foundation. Facebook's goal with this program is to offer interesting experiences for their users to share with their Friends as well as create a place where businesses can offer great discounts while exposing Facebook users to new experiences.

Facebook has made it easy to find deals in your area by offering e-mail and notification updates when new deals are posted. And when your Friends Share, Like, or Buy a deal, you may see that deal in your News Feed. Facebook also added a Deals link in the left column on your Facebook home page, and when you click it, you see a display of all the deals in your area, as seen in Figure 4-10. When you click a deal that interests you, you're taken to a page where you can Like, Share, or Buy without ever leaving Facebook.

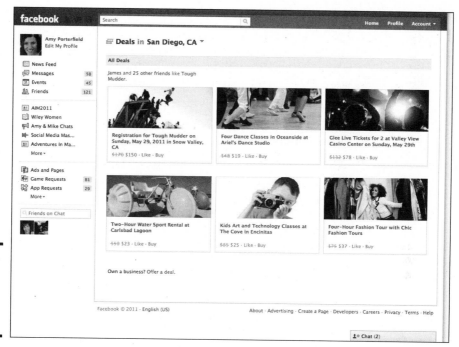

Figure 4-10:
Deals on
Facebook
shown on a
home page.

Book VII
Chapter 4

Stepping Out with
Facebook Places
and Facebook Deals

You might be wondering whether promoting with Deals on Facebook is a smart decision for your business. One of the biggest benefits to promoting special offers on Facebook is the social sharing factor. Social sharing is essentially free advertising for you. If your business is a restaurant or you're a retailer or have any type of brick-and-mortar business, Deals on Facebook can be a very useful marketing tool to increase your exposure online and drive more traffic to your business. Currently, Facebook distributes your deal in eight ways:

✦ **The Facebook Home Page:** Users who have deals in their area will have a Deals link in the left column on their home page.

✦ **The Deals Page:** This page shows your deal along with others.

✦ **Sponsored units:** Your deal will be eligible to be a Sponsored deal and will show people their Friends who have Liked or purchased your deal (providing social proof).

✦ **Personal messages and Wall posts:** With the Share button on your deal Page, people can share your deal with their Friends and add a personal message to the post.

✦ **News Feed stories:** When people interact with your deal by buying it, Liking it or sharing it, a short summary of your deal with a link to it will be posted into their News Feed and all their Friends can learn about your deal as well.

✦ **Onsite notifications:** When a user buys one of your deals, Facebook will notify that user's Friends and tell them about his or her recent purchase.

✦ **Deals tab:** Your deal is eligible to run in the column on the right side of other deal pages. You will then be seen by people already interested in finding deals.

✦ **E-mails:** Facebook will e-mail people when their Friends have Liked or bought a deal that they have also liked or purchased. Facebook will also e-mail people who have subscribed to get deals in your location.

Deals on Facebook is not free; however, there is currently no set minimum to participate, thereby making entry into the Deals program accessible to most businesses. The fee to advertise varies depending on your offer details. To get more info about Deals on Facebook, including pricing options, visit `http://www.facebook.com/deals/business/`.

Initially, Deals on Facebook is available to people in Atlanta, Austin, Dallas, San Diego, and San Francisco; however Facebook have big plans to expand quickly. By the time you're reading this, Deals on Facebook just might be in your town!

Book VIII

Facebook Advertising

The 5th Wave   By Rich Tennant

VP Sales

"It's web-based, on-demand, and customizable. Still, I think I'm going to miss our old sales incentive methods."

Contents at a Glance

Chapter 1: Advertising in Facebook

In This Chapter

✔ **Attracting new clients with Facebook advertising**

✔ **Designing your campaigns to meet your goals**

✔ **Setting your budget and timeline**

According to eMarketer (www.emarketer.com), Facebook ads brought in $1.86 billion in revenue for Facebook in 2010 and are projected to bring in $4 billion in 2011. That's a lot of money, so it shouldn't surprise anyone that Facebook makes an effort to keep that revenue stream a-flowin'. Clearly, Facebook has a vested interest in making the ads an easy and pleasant experience for both the marketer and the Facebook community.

In this chapter, you dive into the basics of Facebook advertising and find out how to start making the right decisions that will get you the results you want. You discover how to set your goals, allocate a budget, and set your timeline.

In Chapter 2 of this minibook, you get to set up your first campaign, target your ad, and start running it. By the time Chapter 3 comes around, you'll be ready to hone your advertising skills by doing some ad testing, measuring your test results and modifying your campaign if needed. Hang on — it's going to be fun!

Introducing Facebook Advertising

Placing ads on Facebook provides one of the most targeted advertising opportunities on the Internet today. You decide the exact demographic to see your ad — your choices here include age, sex, education, location, and even keywords in your target's Profile. You can even choose to advertise only to people who have a birthday that day. When you can narrow down the audience who sees your ad to that granular of a level, you can be pretty sure that whoever clicks your ad is your target customer.

Facebook structures its advertising similarly to Google Ads. You either opt for cost per click (CPC) — a model where advertisers pay their host only when their ad is clicked — or you pay based on how many thousands of people see your ad (impressions; CPM). (CPM stands for cost per thousand — okay, really *cost per mille* — and *mille* = 1,000 in French.) Facebook makes use of an auction-based system, where you bid on how much you're willing to pay for each action. (By *action* here, we mean either each time some-one clicks your ad, or each time Facebook places your ad in front of 1,000 people.) You can easily set it up so that your ad shut is off when you reach a daily limit, and you can target times of the day you advertise, along with many other variables. Find more coverage on this in Chapter 2 of this minibook.

You might want to use the CPM option when bidding on your ad so that you are paying for the views — and not paying if someone clicks your ad. Your ad testing will show you the best bidding strategy.

Facebook advertising differs from Google Ads in one important respect, though: With Facebook, you choose your audience by demographics, whereas Google Ads (also known as Google AdWords) target advertising based on keywords in searches. Because you can show your ad to a specific demographic, knowing your target demographic is critical. You might have some general thoughts about who you're trying to reach in terms of your marketing efforts, but we recommend going through your customer list — or a small sampling if your list is large — and chart the following attributes:

✦ Age

✦ Sex

✦ Location (if you have a business that isn't local)

From your Facebook Page, take a look at the Insights area — (Facebook's statistics area which shows your community demographics including gender, age, and location) to find out more about what demographic you're currently connecting with on Facebook. Here are the steps to get to that demographics info via Insights when you are logged into Facebook as your Page:

1. **Click the View Insights link, located on the upper-right side of your Page right below the Admins list, as shown in Figure 1-1.**

   You're taken into the Insights area for your Page. The first graphs show your Page Overview which includes your Users (how many people Like you) and Interactions (how many comments and Likes on your posts). Insights are covered in more detail in Book II, Chapter 2.

2. **Click the See Details link above the Users graph.**

   You see detailed information about new Likes, activity, and demograph-ics. Scroll down to the Demographics section where your demographics are broken down by age and gender, as shown in Figure 1-2. And these demographics on your Page will help you decide demographics in your ad campaign.

View Insights link

Figure 1-1:
Click the
View
Insights
link to see
your Page
statistics.

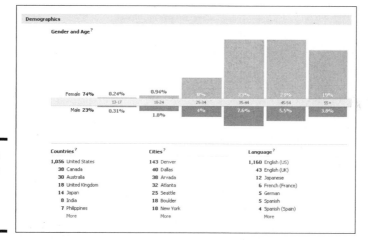

Figure 1-2:
View Page
demo-
graphics
here.

Not only do you need to decide the target demographic for your ad but
also what to advertise. You can create a Facebook ad for your Page, for a
Facebook Event, for an external Web site, and more.

So why would you want to pay to advertise your Page? The answer is to
reach out to new people who might not have another means of discovering
you and your expertise, product, or service. In essence, you're paying for
people to Like you — highly targeted people who'll see your updates every
day. (Assuming, of course, that you're in fact posting every day, and they're
watching their News Feed.) These new members of your community will

value your expertise in your field, get to know you and at some point (hopefully) buy something from you.

If you're advertising a paid event, you can probably see right off the bat the value of paying for advertising. But what if you're advertising a free event? How can that end up making money for you? Simple — by giving you a new connection. After you meet someone in person, you've made a connection with the person and have the potential to deepen your relationship to get that person to know, like, and trust you. Then, when he or she needs your goods or services, you end up being the first person who comes to mind.

Understanding How Facebook Advertising Works

We're sure you've seen Facebook ads on the right-hand column of a Facebook Page. (If you haven't, though, check out Figure 1-3.) If you've ever wondered how these ads know that you live in a certain city or are interested in this or that, precise targeting is the answer.

Figure 1-3: Ads are located on the right column.

In the Facebook model, ads always appear in the right-hand column. As many as four ads are displayed in the column at one time, depending on where you are within Facebook. One ad is displayed on your home page and is reserved for clients with an ad budget of $30,000 or more per month.

Up to four ads are typically displayed on your Profile Page or on Fan or Group pages. You can't choose whether your ad will receive the top, middle, or bottom position, but the bid you place for the ad and how many clicks your ad is receiving affects the placement. (You'll find more on bidding strategies in Chapter 2 of this minibook.)

Before we walk you through the mechanics of how to set up an ad, we want to give you a bit of background on how Facebook advertising works so that you can have a successful advertising campaign. (Think of it as our gift to you.)

Advertising on Facebook versus other platforms

Facebook ads work a little differently than a Google or Yahoo! ad or even a banner ad. (If you aren't familiar with banner ads, don't worry; we'll go into a little more detail on that topic in a bit.)

Similar to Google and Yahoo!, Facebook ads work on an *auction system*. You place a bid for ad space, essentially letting Facebook know how much you're willing to pay per click (Facebook uses the term cost per click, or CPC) or pay per thousand impressions (CPM). Depending on how many other people are bidding, you might pay less for your click— and, if you bid too low, your ad might not be shown at all.

For ads placed within the search engine platforms — the Google or Yahoo! approach, as it were — you select certain keywords entered in the searches and bid on that keyword. For example, if your business is car insurance, you could opt for "car insurance" or "car insurance quotes" or "auto insurance" as your keywords. CPC prices can range from $0.10 to a few dollars, depending on how competitive the market is for those keywords.

Banner ads are ads placed on targeted Web sites or blogs that you believe your customers will visit. These ads typically appear on at the top, bottom, or sides of the Page. You typically pay a flat rate per month to display a banner ad. A sample banner ad is shown in Figure 1-4.

When people click your banner ad, they're taken to your site. More highly trafficked sites have higher monthly rates. Banner ads are typically either placed on a Web site by purchasing space from the owner of the site directly or are placed on a number of Web sites after you purchase an advertising package from a broker who works with multiple Web sites. The click-through rate (CTR), the percentage of visitors to the site who click your ad, is typically fairly low on banner ads.

Facebook takes a different approach. Within Facebook, you're selecting the demographic viewing your ad and people within that demographic (after all) might or might not be searching for car insurance. Say that you determined that your ideal customer is a 35-year-old male, college graduate, who lives within 25 miles of your city. You can easily enter those target demographics into your ad so that only people who meet those criteria will see the ad.

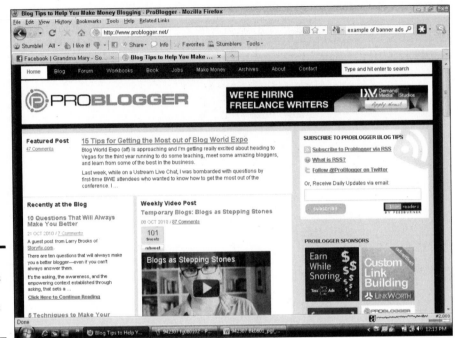

You can also enter keywords into the Likes and Interests area of the Targeting section of the ad placement page, but those are keywords within people's Profiles. This means that people have entered in their Profile that they like volleyball or yoga, or they have Liked The Beatles' Facebook Page. Figure 1-5 shows some of the interests in one of the author's Profiles that will translate into keywords. So if a vineyard ran an ad with *wine* as a keyword, that ad would potentially be shown to her on her sidebar in Facebook.

When you create a Facebook ad, as we show you how to do in Chapter 2 of this minibook, you will be able to enter the demographics and Likes and Interests into the targeting section. Figure 1-6 shows the Targeting section of Facebook ads, and you can see how specific you can be with your demographic.

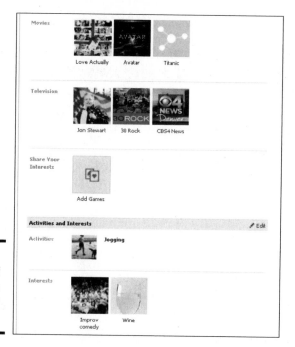

Figure 1-5:
Info area of
your Profile
shows your
keywords.

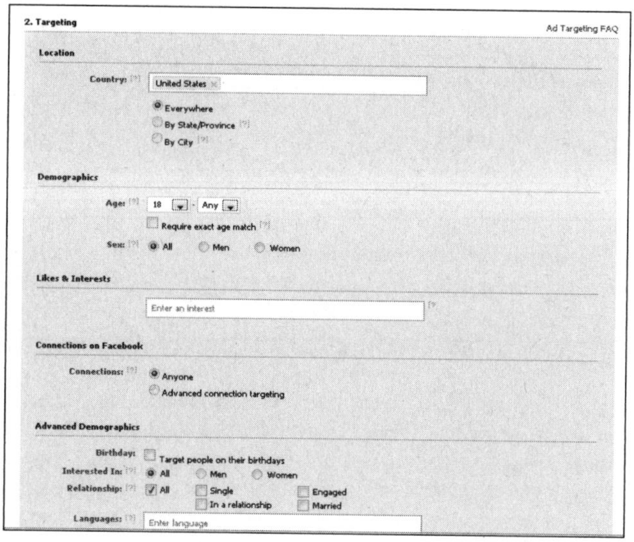

Figure 1-6:
Targeting
section of
Facebook
ads.

Be careful when using keywords in Facebook advertising because people might or might not have chosen to add those interests or keywords into their Profile. You might be excluding potential customers, which is always a risk when you narrow your target audience.

The biggest difference between Facebook ads and search engine ads is that within Facebook, the click-through rate might be lower than within the search engine advertising you'd use with Google or Yahoo! because people might not be actively searching for what you're advertising. (That's bad.) But if they do click your advertisement, you know that they are your target demographic. (And that's good.)

Defining ad types

Facebook allows you to create many different types of ads. You can advertise

+ Pages
+ Events
+ External Web sites
+ Applications
+ Sponsored Stories

When you advertise something internal to Facebook, such as your Page, Group, Event or Application, you are creating an Engagement ad. The Engagement ad allows people to respond to your ad without actually leaving the Page by clicking Like or clicking to RSVP to your event. Figure 1-7 shows some sample Engagement ads.

For example, if you're advertising your Fan Page, the Like button will be included in the ad, allowing the person to Like your Page without ever going there. Also, people can join your group or RSVP to your event in the same way. When someone clicks the Like button in the ad, they will automatically Like your Page and start getting your status updates in their News Feed. If they click the RSVP, they'll be able to RSVP right from the ad.

Engagement ads are a good thing because they make it easier for the person to Like your Page or RSVP. If you have powerful ad copy that makes people want to connect with you, you lessen the chance of them forgetting to Like you after they look at your Page. Engagement ads make it easier to get the outcome you're looking for — either someone Liking you or responding to your RSVP. This is extremely powerful and emphasizes the need for good ad copy.

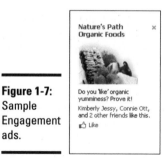

You don't need to do anything special to create an Engagement ad. Facebook automatically creates this layout for you when you indicate that you're advertising your Fan Page, Group, or Event. Read about how to create your ad in Chapter 2 of this minibook.

If someone does click the Like button or RSVPs to your event, you'll be charged for a click, though. Facebook tracks the people who click the Like button as Actions in the Stats area of your Page, as shown in Figure 1-8. Then you know how many Likes you got right from the ad versus how many clicked the ad to go to your Page. (In-depth statistical analysis of your ad performance — including info about how to work effectively with the Stats area of your Page — is covered in Chapter 3 of this minibook.)

Figure 1-8:
Facebook
ad statistics
tally actions
and clicks.

Daily stats for the week of: Sep 26 ▼

Date	Imp.	Social %	Clicks	CTR (%)	Actions	AR (%)	Avg. CPC ($)	Avg. CPM ($)	Spent ($)
10/02/2010	24,591	0.4%	22	0.09	7	0.03	0.38	0.34	8.32
10/01/2010	31,789	0.4%	20	0.06	8	0.03	0.50	0.31	10.00
09/30/2010	37,221	0.1%	17	0.05	12	0.03	0.59	0.27	10.00
Lifetime	**93,601**	**0.3%**	**59**	**0.06**	**27**	**0.03**	**0.48**	**0.30**	**28.32**

Facebook's newest type of ad is called Sponsored Stories. You can advertise activities that happen in the News Feeds such as individual posts, Likes of your Page, or check-ins with Facebook Places. The Sponsored Story is then shown to a Facebook user's Friends.

Figure 1-9 shows an example of a Sponsored Story from Starbucks where they are advertising check-ins. In this case, Jessica checked into Starbucks' Facebook Place, and Jessica's Friends will see this ad in their right sidebar. The Sponsored Story can drive increased trust to the Starbucks brand.

You can also advertise individual posts to encourage new connections. When someone Likes or comments on a post on a Facebook Page, the Sponsored Story is shown to that person's Friends. The ad could encourage comments on the post and Likes to the Page. We cover Sponsored Stories in depth in Chapter 2 of this minibook.

Figure 1-9:
Sponsored
Story ad.

Designing campaigns with ads

In the Facebook Ads Manager, you arrange your ads into campaigns. A *campaign* is a group of similar ads, with the same purpose, but that have slight variations. For example, you can run multiple ads to test what ad title, picture, or copy converts better. By *convert*, we mean attaining the outcome you desire. If you're advertising your Facebook Page, your goal is to get people to Like your Page. So if you run an ad and get 30 clicks but only 15 people Like your Page from those clicks, your conversion rate is 50 percent. If you change the copy of your ad and have 30 people click your ad and 20 people Like your Page, your conversion rate is 66 percent. The second ad is converting better and gets you more for your money.

The Ads Manager is the place where you can see all your campaigns in one place and access your reports and settings. We discuss the Ads Manager in Chapter 2 of this minibook.

You can also run campaigns around different geographic locations, different demographic targets, or different likes and interests. Figure 1-10 demonstrates the hierarchy of campaigns and the ads within them.

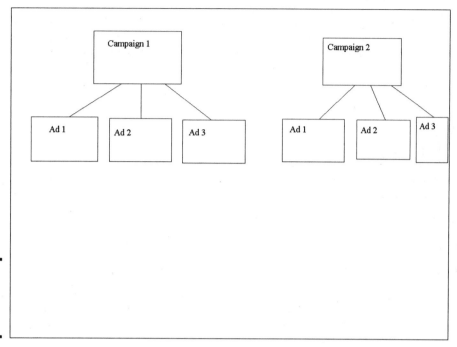

Figure 1-10:
Hierarchy
of an ad
campaign.

For every different product, service, or goal that you have, you'll want to create a new campaign. You can set daily budgets for your whole campaign and for each individual ad. You can run a single ad, but it will be placed under a campaign heading that you choose. Create a new campaign when you're advertising

✦ A particular product

✦ A particular product in a region or country

✦ An Event

✦ Your Fan Page

Within those campaigns, you'll have different ads to test the performance of your copy, your call to action, and different targeting or bidding strategies. Check out the details of two campaigns in Figure 1-11, based on different variables.

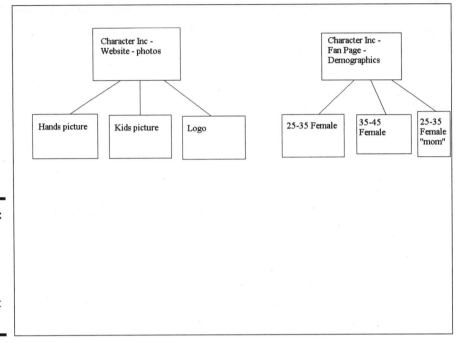

Figure 1-11:
Two campaigns with different ads based on different variables.

You might want to run two identical ads — one using the CPC model and one using CPM — to see which gives you a better return on your investment (ROI).

Typically, you'll want to run some test campaigns first with smaller budgets to find out which ad is performing the best. And lest you think this testing will break your bank, you can set a daily budget so that the ad will automatically stop running when it reaches your limit. Then, after you know which ads are performing best, you can run them for longer periods with bigger budgets.

Knowing what you can't advertise

Facebook has guidelines on what you can and can't advertise. They review each ad for appropriate language, content, and formatting. If your ad doesn't comply with their guidelines, Facebook *will* reject it. Some of the items that you can't advertise include

✦ **Work-at-home sites that promise easy money for little or no investment**

✦ **Multilevel marketing opportunities, such as Mary Kay and Avon**

✦ **Sites that have *domain forwarding*, where the URL listed forwards to another Web site**

Even if your site is innocently forwarding the domain, many places that do have domain forwarding can be doing so for shady reasons, and Facebook has drawn that line in the sand.

✦ **Landing pages that have a pop-up window**

Having a pop-up window might be an innocent way to get subscribers to your e-mail list, but many people don't like pop-ups, and sometimes you can't even close them. Facebook decided to make this one of the items that it controls for its users.

✦ **And the more obvious stuff:**

- Tobacco

- Gambling

- Pornography

Some advertisements are heavily restricted as to what language you can use in the ad and what demographic you're targeting. See the Facebook Advertising Guidelines at `http://www.facebook.com/ad_guidlines.php` if you're advertising any of the following:

✦ Dating sites

✦ Alcoholic beverages

✦ Health products

✦ Diet supplements or weight loss products

✦ Subscription services (such as ring tones)

Identifying Your Goals

Before you start spending money, have a goal in mind. What does a successful ad campaign look like? Attracting 50 more Fans? Selling 25 more widgets? Having 10 people sign up for your newsletter? Whatever goal you decide upon, write it down and come up with a way to track your progress.

Make sure you know where your baseline rests. How many Fans do you get per week through your current efforts? How many Web site hits from Facebook do you receive currently? With that info in hand, you can then assess whether it's cost effective to pay for your campaign.

Gaining connections

Advertising your Fan Page is one of the best things you can do with Facebook ads. You know that the people who click your ad are in your target market and enjoy Facebook. Connecting with new people on your Fan Page allows them to get to know you and your company.

Before you begin your ad, collect some baseline data on how your Facebook Page is performing currently. The Insights feature on your Page makes it easy. Some measurements to note are

✦ How many new Likes to your Page do you get per week on average?

✦ To what extent are your current Fans are making the extra effort to interact with you — Likes, Comments, and so forth?

✦ What is your current demographic?

We talk more about Insights in Book IX, Chapter 2, but the following step list show you how you can access the numbers for your baseline data.

1. **Log into Facebook as your Page and click the View Insights link in the upper-right corner.**

Doing so takes you into the Insights area, which has some nice graphs, as shown in Figure 1-12. You can download all your data into an Excel spreadsheet or a comma-separated value file (`.csv`). Then you can do some weekly or monthly totals of your data.

Export button

Figure 1-12: The Insights area shows graphs of Active Users and Likes.

2. **Click the Export button in the upper-right part of the Page.**

   A window pops up, asking what date range and what file format you'd prefer, as shown in Figure 1-13.

Figure 1-13:
Select the date range and the file format.

Export Insights Data

| Excel (XLS) | Comma-Seperated (CSV) |

Start Time: 2/3/2011

End Time: 3/4/2011

Learn how to sync data with Excel 2010   Download Cancel

3. **Select the format you prefer, Excel or Comma Separated, and choose the date range; then click the Download button.**

   With this file, you can get the data to graph how many Likes you are getting per week, how many Likes and comments you receive on your posts, and your demographics.

Write down all these measurements or save them in a file so you can compare them against your Insights after you run the campaign to make sure you're reaching people on Facebook who will interact and be part of your community.

If your current Facebook community isn't too large, go through and see whether you can determine how many of your Fans are actual customers and how much money they have spent with you over time. With that information in hand, you'll have a more accurate picture of the impact your Facebook community has on your bottom line. That's not to say that having a community is not of value in itself, but you are a business, after all, and your advertising dollars need to be well spent.

Facebook's Engagement ads make it easy for people to Like your Page right in the ad and potentially giving you greater return on your ad. But if people are going to click over to your Page to see what you are about first, consider a special "Welcome" tab as mentioned in Book II so that if someone does click your ad, they are not just sent to the Wall.

The Welcome tab should tell more about your business and give them a compelling reason to join your community. Figure 1-14 shows the REI Welcome tab that tells you to click the Like button and gives you some special tabs within the Page to learn more about the company.

**Book VIII
Chapter 1**

Advertising in Facebook

Figure 1-14:
REI has
a call to
action to
Like its
Page and
gives you
information
about its
non-profit
partnerships.

Acquiring leads

Acquiring leads for your business with Facebook ads could be your goal.
Maybe you'd like your potential leads to sign up for your newsletter or for a
free half-hour consultation or a free quote. In this case, you've probably set
up your ad so that clicking it sends users to a Web site outside Facebook.
When you do this, make sure the site that you send them to — a site often
referred to as a "landing page" — correlates directly with the Facebook ad.

You might want a special landing page designed so that your call to action is
very clear. If you send visitors to your general Web site, they might not see
the small box where they need to request your newsletter, or they might be
distracted by all the other nice things on your Web site and forget to request
a quote. It's okay if the landing page is a part of your Web site, but just make
sure that the call to action is very clear. An example of a good landing page
is shown in Figure 1-15. The only thing you can do on this page is "Try it for
Free" (people always like free) or give the company a call. There is no menu
to start clicking, nor are there distracting ads on the side.

Figure 1-15:
This landing page doesn't distract from the call to action.

If your goal is to simply drive awareness of your brand rather than acquire leads, you might want to have your phone number or store address in the ad so someone doesn't necessarily have to click to contact you. If you're having a grand opening or open house, put as many details as you can fit in the 135 characters you have available in the body of the ad. See Chapter 2 of this minibook for more information on creating your ad.

Making Your Initial Decisions

Map out your strategy before you start. How long you run your ad, how much you want to spend and how often you change things around are all decisions that need to be made.

Allocating a budget

Allocate a budget and time for the initial testing as well as the longer term Facebook ad. You don't want to be spending money on an ad week after week that isn't converting as well as it could be.

Your initial testing budget should be about one-tenth at most of your entire ad budget. Run each variation of your ad for a short time. Even with just 20 clicks, you can start to see whether one is out-performing another significantly.

In allocating a budget, knowing what your clicks are worth to your bottom line is critical. How your product is priced and how many conversions you need to be profitable are both factors when setting your budget. Think of it this way: If you need 100 people to visit your site before you get a sale and your product has a net profit of $20, it doesn't make sense to spend more than $0.20 per click.

Rotating your ad

Plan on rotating your ad every couple of days to keep things fresh, especially if you're advertising to a small demographic. Again, this isn't a "set it and forget it" campaign. Hopefully, after you finish your testing, you'll have zeroed in on a couple of ads that perform well. Facebook makes it easy to run one ad for a couple days, and then automatically turn it off and have the next ad start running for a couple days. (For more on how to rotate your ads, check out Chapter 2 in this minibook.) Figure 1-16 shows a series of ads that all performed well for a client. These ads have eye-catching pictures and engaging headlines. The ad campaign targeted moms who responded well to the ads by clicking them.

Figure 1-16:
Series of ads that convert.

You can always go back to an earlier ad, but plan on rotating ads regularly.

 If you aren't getting as many clicks as you'd like, try adjusting your demographics to a slightly wider range by adding more keywords, a larger age range, more cities, or cities included within 50 miles if you previously chose 25, for example.

Setting a timeline

How long should you run your ads? This question is intimately tied with your budget and how effectively your ad is converting. Make sure to allocate time to do your testing. Testing might take a few weeks, depending on how many campaigns you're testing and how many ad variations you have.

 Allow time for your ads to be approved. Ads are manually reviewed by Facebook and can take anywhere from a couple hours to a full day for approval. After the ad is approved, it starts running automatically. The ad approval process is covered in Chapter 2 of this minibook.

Chapter 2: Creating a Facebook Ad

You will find many places to start an ad because Facebook wants to make spending money with Facebook easy. In this chapter, we show you one of the many places to start a Facebook ad. Keep in mind, though, that you may see links in other areas of Facebook, such as in your sidebar of your personal Profile or on your Fan Page, that will lead you to the area where you can create your Facebook ad. All the links essentially end up at the same place — that is, to the area where you can start your Facebook advertising campaign.

In Chapter 1 of this minibook, we cover the basics of Facebook advertising: how to identify your goals and set your budget. This chapter will be Facebook's favorite because you discover how to give Facebook some of your money by creating an advertising campaign.

Designing a Click-Worthy Ad

What makes an ad click-worthy? A good headline? An eye-catching picture? Or some really enticing copy within the ad? The answer is most likely a combination of all three. This section tells you some of the keys to creating an engaging and click-worthy ad.

The following sections cover advertising an external Web site, as well as advertising something internal to Facebook, such as a Fan Page, App, or Event. The main difference between these two types of ads is that Facebook fills in some of the information for you if you're advertising something internal to Facebook.

As mentioned in Chapter 1 of this minibook, when you create an ad for something internal to Facebook, you create what's called an *Engagement* ad, which lets users Like your Page or RSVP to your Event right from the ad itself. You should keep this feature in mind as you consider what types of ads you want to create.

Advertising an external Web page

Advertising an external Web site differs slightly from advertising something internal to Facebook in that you choose your own title — *and* you need to upload a picture.

Take the following steps to get started:

1. **Log into your Facebook account by going to** www.Facebook.com **and filling in your e-mail and password in the top-right boxes.**

Your personal Home page appears.

2. **Go to** www.facebook.com/advertising.

You can either just type this in to the browser after you have logged in, or open a new window and go to this Web site. You're then taken to the Facebook Ads Overview and Case Studies area, shown in Figure 2-1.

Figure 2-1:
Use the
Facebook
Ads
Overview
and Case
Studies
section to
help you
with your ad
campaign.

3. **Click the green Create an Ad button in the upper-right corner of the Facebook Ads Overview screen.**

The area where you design your ad shown appears, as shown in Figure 2-2. The destination defaults to advertise something within Facebook where you are an admin (such as a Facebook Page, Event, or App).

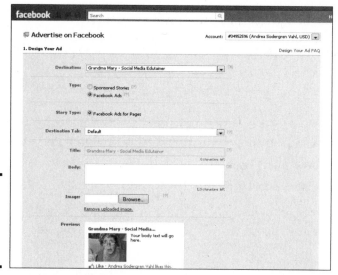

Figure 2-2:
Designing
your ad
begins with
this screen.

4. **Next to the Destination field, click the arrow next to the drop-down menu and select External URL, which is the choice at the top of the list.**

   A URL field appears.

5. **Enter the Destination URL.**

   The destination URL is the full Web site name where you would like to send your advertising traffic, such as `http://www.socialmedia examiner.com`.

   If you have a question about the fields, click the question mark symbol to the right of the field for more explanation about what to enter.

   After you enter the destination URL, the Suggest an Ad button, shown in Figure 2-2, will become active, which means that it isn't grayed out any longer and you can now click it . . . But wait! It would be better not to, because you probably don't want to use the ad it suggests for you, for the following reasons:

   - The suggested ad copy is pulled from the information in your Web site description, which may be too general.

   - The picture placed in the suggested ad could be from anywhere on your Web site and may not be relevant.

   Your ad will be more effective if you craft your own message — with your own title, text, and an appropriate picture.

Writing a title

The title appears above the picture and should be interesting! You have to make it interesting *and* concise, though, because you get to use only 25 characters.

Check out the following examples (which are all fewer than 25 characters):

Do Your Have Teeth Stains?	(Poses a question)
Try Our Free Samples	(Offers something for free)
No More Aching Back	(Solves a problem)
Attend Our One-day Sale	(Sends out a call to action)

In your ad title, you are allowed to have capital letters at the beginning of each word, in contrast to the body of the ad, which does not allow for excessive capitalization. The authors have seen ads with entire words capitalized, but Facebook typically doesn't let you do that. See the "Minding Facebook Terms and Conditions" section, later in this chapter, for more grammar and capitalization rules.

TIP

To see many more examples of what other people are currently advertising perhaps garner ideas for titles, take a look at Facebook's Ad Board. The Ad Board consists of all the current ads that could be shown to your Profile based on the ad's target demographics. So when advertisers set up their ad to be shown only to women aged 45–55, if you're a woman in that age range, you can see that ad in the Ad Board area. Go to `http://www.facebook.com/ads/adboard` to see them.

Crafting your message

You have 135 characters to work with in the Body text box as shown in Figure 2-2, so you want to make them count! Start by considering the keywords you want to have in the ad that in order to attract attention.

Make sure that you emphasize the benefit that your offer provides to your ad's readers. What problem do you solve for the customer? Starting your text with a question or two can work well to engage the reader and give him or her something to relate to. Then follow the question by identifying the benefit that will solve the problem. Here are some examples:

> Are you always short on time? Use our home cleaning service to gain time *and* have a clean home to enjoy!

> Would you like to earn your degree? You can in just 6 months with our online program.

Take a look at the sample ads in Figure 2-3 for some examples of good ad copy.

Figure 2-3:
Examples of compelling ads.

Make sure to include a strong "call to action" at the end of the body text. Tell your audience what you want them to do. "Click here to find the best shoes," "Click to access the free report," and "Click to get your free quote" are all good calls to action.

As mentioned in Chapter 1 of this book, make sure that your Web page or "landing" page matches the call to action in the ad. If you're asking your ad audience to sign up for your newsletter, direct them to a place on your Web site where they can easily enter their information to get it. (If you make it the least bit inconvenient or confusing, you'll lose ad responders in a flash.)

Choosing an image

Images make your ad more eye-catching, and Facebook now requires them, anyway. Your image can be a logo, photo, or icon and should relate to the title and body text of the ad.

The photo should be clear and not too "busy"; it'll be only 110 pixels wide by 80 pixels tall. To upload your image, following these steps:

1. **Click the Browse button next to the Image field.**

   A pop-up box appears with the files on your computer.

2. **Navigate to your image by first finding the correct folder that the image is in and then click the image you want to use in your ad.**

   The filename of the image appears in the File Name field in the bottom of the pop-up window.

3. **Click the Open button next to the File Name field.**

   The pop-up box will close and you see the image showing in the preview window of the ad, as shown in Figure 2-4. Uploads must be less than 5MB.

Figure 2-4:
Your ad is
shown in
the preview
window
while you
write it.

Engagement ads: Advertising a Facebook Page, App, or Event

As mentioned in the beginning of the chapter, there are a few differences between creating an Engagement ad — something you have on Facebook, such as a Page, App, or Event — and creating an ad for an external Web site. The process that you use for an ad for an external Web site begins with the same steps that you use for an Engagement ad, but when you create the external site ad, the title and image are automatically filled in for you. Facebook uses the title and picture from your Fan Page, App, or Event. Cool, huh?

An advantage of an Engagement ad is that people can Join, Like, or RSVP right from the ad itself, without even going to your Page. If you're advertising an app that you created, the ad shows names of friends of the person viewing the ad who has used the app.

Another nice thing about Engagement ads is that you have given users the ability to Like your Page (the desired outcome, of course) with one click, and the more convenient you make things for the user, the better. You don't want users to have to click your ad and have to be transported to the Facebook Page — they might forget to Like it! That would mean that you got charged for a click without getting the Fan.

Yet another compelling aspect of Engagement ads is that they show the Friends who have already Liked your Fan Page (see Figure 2-5), or who are attending your Event or using your app, depending on what you are advertising Social "proof" is a powerful tool; when people see that their friends like something, they are much more to become fans themselves. Social proof is the idea that if your Friends like it, you might like it, too.

Figure 2-5:
Social proof in Engagement ads. You can see which Friends are already Fans of the Page.

When users click the title, image, or body of the ad, they are taken to the Facebook Page. When users click Like, they will Like the Page and not be taken to the Page. You will be charged for a click in both instances. See Chapter 1 of this minibook for more information on cost per click advertising.

To begin creating an Engagement ad, follow these steps:

1. **Log into your Facebook account by going to www.Facebook.com and filling in your e-mail and password in the top right boxes.**

   You are taken to your personal Home page.

2. **Go to** www.facebook.com/advertising.

   You can either just type this in to the browser after you have logged in, or open a new window and go to this Web site. You will be taken to Facebook Ads Overview and Case Studies area.

3. **Click the green Create an Ad button in the upper-right corner of the Facebook Ads Overview screen.**

   You are then taken to the Design Your Ad screen.

4. **Click the down arrow next to the Destination field.**

   A drop-down menu appears in which you can select your Facebook Content. The menu shows any Facebook Pages for which you are an administrator; it also lists any upcoming Events that you have created or are attending and you see any Apps that you have created.

5. Select what you want to advertise.

You can also easily start an ad for your Fan Page by going to your Page and, in the right sidebar of your Page, clicking the Promote with an Ad link, as shown in Figure 2-6. If you do click the link, you're prompted that you're using Facebook as your Page, and you'll need to switch to your personal Profile.

Promote with an Ad link

Figure 2-6:
Create your
ad right
from your
Facebook
Page.

Title matters

When you advertise something internal to Facebook, the title of the ad is automatically filled in with the title of your Fan Page, App, or Event — and you can't change the title, so we hope that you like it! Take a look at the pre-view window to see how your title appears.

If you have a long title for your Event, Fan Page or App, Facebook will cut the title short because of the space it fits into. Unfortunately, you can't do anything about that, either, but you can compose the body text in such a way as to make your advertisement clear.

Using the body text to encourage engagement

The body text of your ad allows for only 135 characters, so you have to make your body text very compelling. Be sure to compose it with your desired outcome in mind, whether that is to get your readers to Like your Page, RSVP to your Event, or use your App.

If you are advertising your Page, include in the ad what the reward is for Liking your Page. Give people a reason to click the Like button right away rather than have to look at your Fan Page first. For example, what do you offer on your Fan page? Tips, tricks, discounts, free things? Work the benefits of becoming a fan into your body text.

If you are advertising an event, what is the benefit of attending your event? Community, knowledge, networking? Always work to answer the question that's on the mind of the customer: "What's in it for me?"

Make sure that you provide a very clear call to action in your body text. If you are advertising your Page, for example, tell people to "Click the Like button." Or if you are advertising your Event, tell them to "RSVP now."

Choosing an image

Although the ad you're creating will automatically be populated with the image from your Event, Page, or App if you have an image loaded there (and you should!), you are able to change the image file. For the purpose of promoting your brand, it's better to keep the image consistent in all your ads and pages, but if you have a compelling reason to change it, just follow these steps to place a new one:

1. **Click the Browse button next to the Image field.**

   A pop-up box will appear with the files on your computer.

2. **Navigate to your image by first finding the correct folder that the image is in and then click the image you want to use in your ad.**

   The file name of the image appears in the File name field in the bottom of the pop-up window.

3. **Click the Open button next to the File name field.**

   The pop-up box closes and you see the image showing in the preview window of the ad. Uploads must be less than 5MB.

Meeting Facebook's terms and conditions

As you are crafting your ad, be aware of Facebook's terms and conditions (found at `www.facebook.com/ad_guidelines.php`) so that your ad isn't rejected, thereby resulting in the waste of your precious time. In Chapter 1 of this minibook, we cover some of the sites and products that you are not allowed to advertise. Facebook also has many rules concerning the grammar, punctuation, and capitalization within the ad. Here are the grammar rules:

+ **Grammar:** The ad body must be grammatically correct with complete sentences and correct spelling. The ad can't contain excessive repetition, such as "buy, buy, buy." (You don't want to sound like a used-car salesperson, anyway!)

+ **Capitalization:** Ads must use proper, grammatically correct capitalization. You may not capitalize the first letter of every word or an entire word, such as "BUY NOW." Acronyms can, however, be capitalized.

+ **Punctuation:** Use logical, grammatically correct punctuation with no unnecessary punctuation such as multiple exclamation points, as in "Buy now!!!" Also, you can't use exclamation points in the title of the ad.

✦ **Symbols:** Symbols must be used according to their true meaning and can't be repeated unnecessarily. You also cannot substitute a symbol for a word, such as use an ampersand (&) for "and," the dollar sign ($) for "money," or the at sign (@) for "at." You may use the $ symbol if it is paired with a dollar amount, as in "$100."

Facebook ads are reviewed by a group of individuals who sometimes have different standards for what meets the Facebook guidelines. You may find that some ads are approved that violate the rules. But it's best to try and play by the rules. It's Facebook's sandbox.

Sponsored Stories

Facebook's newest type of ad is called Sponsored Stories. You can advertise activities that happen in the News Feeds such as individual posts, Likes of your Page, or check-ins with Facebook Places. The Sponsored Story is then shown to a Facebook user's Friends. Sponsored Stories are currently not widely used and some debate exists over their effectiveness.

You can use them for Facebook Pages, apps, and to advertise when someone checks into your Place. The idea behind the ads is that they show when someone is Liking your Page, using your app, or checking into your Place — giving you that social proof we mention earlier in this chapter and throughout the book. But people are questioning whether that social proof is enough to move someone to act without the call to action in the copy. The ads look different because there is no copy, as shown in Figure 2-7, and above the ad are the words "Sponsored Story."

Figure 2-7:
Sponsored
Story ad.

To use the Sponsored Stories feature, follow these steps:

1. **Log into Facebook as your personal Profile.**

2. **Go directly to the ad creation screen by going to** `www.facebook.com/ads/create`.

   You can just type this into the browser after you have logged in or open a new window and go to this Web site. You see the Design Your Ad section.

3. **Click the down arrow next to the Destination field.**

   A drop-down menu appears in which you can select your Facebook content.

4. **Select the Page or app that you want to advertise.**

5. **Select the radio button next to Sponsored Story, as shown in Figure 2-8.**

   You see the preview of the ad.

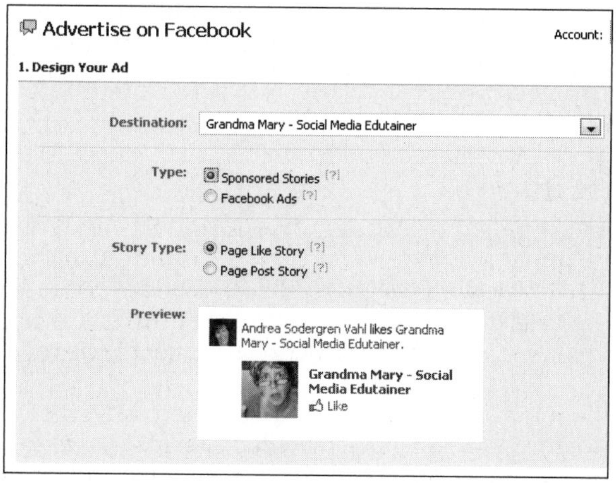

Figure 2-8: Select Sponsored Story.

> **Advertise on Facebook**   Account:
>
> **1. Design Your Ad**
>
> Destination: Grandma Mary - Social Media Edutainer ▼
>
> Type: ⦿ Sponsored Stories [?]
> ○ Facebook Ads [?]
>
> Story Type: ⦿ Page Like Story [?]
> ○ Page Post Story [?]
>
> Preview: Andrea Sodergren Vahl likes Grandma Mary - Social Media Edutainer.
>
> **Grandma Mary - Social Media Edutainer**
> 👍 Like

6. **Choose Page Like story or Page Post story.**

   The Page Like story shows the ad to a Friend of someone who Likes your Page along with the information that that Friend Likes your Page. The Page Post story shows the ad to a Friend of a person who Likes your Page, but it shows a random Wall post that you posted recently. You cannot choose which Wall story is shown.

   If you selected App, you have only a choice of an App Share Story in Step 7. An App Share story is shown when someone shares your App on Facebook.

   You can select more targeting for your ad if you choose, which we cover in the next section. By default, your Sponsored Story is being shown to Friends of people who Like your Page or, if it's your app, Friends of people who use your app.

   We recommend the Page Like story over the Page Post story. Sometimes the Page Posts can be confusing and seem disconnected when they appear in an advertisement. The idea behind them might be to show users a flavor of the type of stories you post, but the fact that you can't choose which stories are posted makes this feature less desirable.

Using Laser Targeting

Now the fun part of designing your ad begins: targeting your audience! When you add different demographics, you can see exactly how many people your ad is potentially reaching. We think that this is the most interesting part of the ad process because as you tweak and change your targeting fields, you see how many people may be in your market. The targeting fields include location, age, sex, education, Likes, interests, and more. The better you know your customer, the easier this section is to work with.

Here's a review of the steps to get to the Advertise on Facebook page where you design your ad:

1. **Log into Facebook as your personal Profile.**

2. **Go directly to the ad creation screen by going to** `www.facebook.com/ads/create.`

   You can just type this in to the browser after you have logged in or open a new window and go to this Web site. You see the Design Your Ad section.

If you haven't done so already, use the previous sections of this chapter to complete the Design Your Ad section based on what you're advertising: an External URL or something within Facebook, either as a standard Facebook ad or as a Sponsored Story.

There is no way in Facebook ads to save your partially completed ad as a draft to complete later. You have to complete all the steps at one time and place your order for the ad.

When you have completed filling in the Design Your Ad section, scroll down the page to the second section titled Targeting, shown in Figure 2-9.

Location

The first way to narrow down your audience is by the location of your business. If the product you're selling is useful to a strictly local audience, then entering a location in the Targeting area, as shown earlier in Figure 2-9 is especially beneficial to you. If, for example, you have a dry cleaning store in Des Moines, you have no reason to show that ad to people in San Francisco.

To enter a location, follow these steps:

1. **In the Location section of the Targeting area as shown earlier in Figure 2-9, enter the country your business is in.**

   The default country is the one you live in (as set in your personal Profile). You must have one country in this field at the minimum. If your business is global, you can add up to 25 countries per advertisement. To add another country, start typing the country into the Country field and a drop-down menu appears with the countries you can select.

2. **Select one of the following radio buttons: Everywhere; By State/Province; or By City.**

   If you select By State/Province, you can enter multiple states in the box that appears.

If you select By City, you can also choose multiple cities and cities within a range of miles — 10, 25, or 50 mile range — of the specified city.

As you narrow your target audience who will see your ad, you will notice that the Estimated Reach counter, on the right side of the page, changes. The Estimated Reach is the number of people who could be shown your ad based on the information in their Profile.

Demographics

Targeting by demographics is a great way to reach your ideal client. If you know, for example, that your most responsive audience consists of females between the age of 35 and 50, you can enter that in this section (refer to Figure 2-9).

Facebook gives you the option to require an exact match within an age range if you select the Require Exact Age Match box. This means that if a user turned 51 yesterday, that user will not be shown the ad for which you selected the age range of 25 to 50. However, it's better not to require an exact match because Facebook will give you a "discounted bid" for people who click your ad who are slightly outside the range (although Facebook does not provide an exact idea of "slightly" and it doesn't specify its definition of "discounted bid").

Interests

A great way to reach your perfect customer is by using the Interests field. The Interests area is a powerful targeting tool that you can use to focus on likely customers. When you aim for grabbing the attention of a specific niche, your ad will be more powerful. Imagine if you have that you like Yoga in your personal Profile how much more likely you would be to click on an ad for a new Yoga studio in your area.

You want to enter keywords that will match users' interests based on what they've entered in their Profiles and what Facebook Pages they have Liked.

So, for example, if you are selling running shoes, some good keywords to enter are "running" and "jogging," as shown in Figure 2-10.

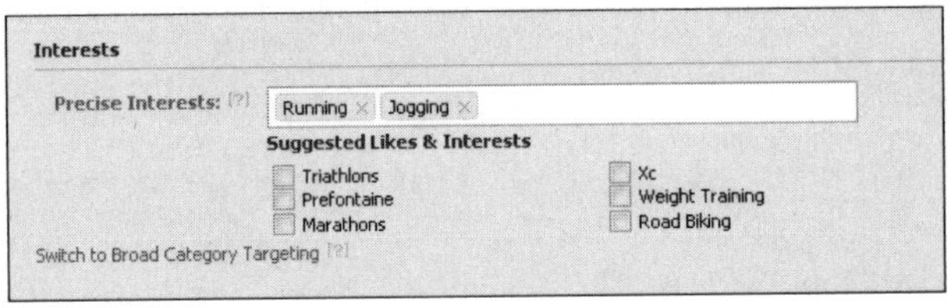

Figure 2-10:
Entering
Interests.

> **Interests**
>
> Precise Interests: [?]   Running ×   Jogging ×
> **Suggested Likes & Interests**
> ☐ Triathlons   ☐ Xc
> ☐ Prefontaine   ☐ Weight Training
> ☐ Marathons   ☐ Road Biking
> Switch to Broad Category Targeting [?]

As you start typing a word in this field, a drop-down menu appears, listing with possible matches to your word. These matches can be helpful in finding similar Likes and Interests keywords that you hadn't thought of.

If an Interests keyword you enter doesn't appear in the Interests field, Facebook didn't find a match for that keyword.

Click the Switch to Broad Category Targeting link to use a broader range of general terms to target, such as "Outdoor Fitness Activities."

In the example shown in Figure 2-11, "Accountant" is a match but "Accountant Department" is not.

Figure 2-11:
Make
sure your
keyword is
in the small
gray box
shown.

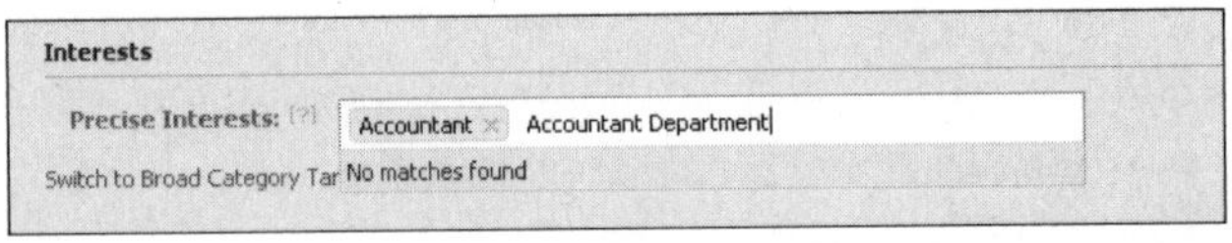

> **Interests**
>
> Precise Interests: [?]   Accountant ×   Accountant Department|
> Switch to Broad Category Tar No matches found

Depending on the keywords you enter, Facebook may (or may not) offer some Suggested Likes and Interests, as shown in earlier in Figure 2-10. If you decide that the suggested keywords are also a good fit, select the boxes to have those keywords appear in your ad.

All the keywords you enter use Boolean operator "or", not "and". This means that every keyword you enter should give your ad a wider reach by targeting people who have that keyword in their Profile. For example, if you enter the keywords "cats" and "dogs," your ad is shown to anyone who has either "cats" or "dogs" (or both) in their Profile, rather than being shown to only those who have both terms in their Profile or Fan Page.

Target fans of your competition. One of the most effective ways to use the Likes and Interests area is to target fans of a particular Page — specifically, fans of your competition. If you're business is a large chain of fast-food restaurants, for example, you can target the fans of another large chain. Powerful stuff! And it's all kosher within the Facebook advertising terms. Just type the name of the Page in the Likes and Interests section (making sure that it appears in the gray box that signifies a match).

You may even decide to mention the competition in your ad. Be careful of trademark infringement, of course, and definitely don't use the other company's logo.

Here's another, similarly powerful angle: Say that you're in a musical group that's trying to make a name for itself. Pick a famous band whose music is similar to yours and create an ad that targets the fans of that band. The body text of your ad might say something like this: "Hey, [Famous Band] fans, if you like [Famous Band], then you'll love us." An ad like that receives many more clicks because it lures people who already have a strong interest in a particular style of music.

The more clicks you receive, the lower your cost per click.

Connections on Facebook

The next area in the Targeting section is called connections on Facebook, This area offers five types of connections:

✦ **Anyone:** Default selection — no connection restriction.

✦ **Only People Who Are Not Fans of Your Page:** A good selection to make so that you're not paying to advertise to someone who already Likes you.

✦ **Only People Who Are Fans of Your Page:** Possibly use if you are trying to get the word out about a new product or service (although with any luck, people will see your Page updates).

✦ **Advanced Connection Targeting:** You can use this to advertise to Fans of a Page you administer.

✦ **Friends of Connections:** Show your ad to the Friends of people who Like your Page.

With this feature, you can target people connected to Pages, Events, or App that you are an administrator of. But why pay for an ad targeting these people when you can connect with them for free through your Page, Event, or App? Therefore, we don't recommend using the Connections feature to find targets for your ad.

The only section that you may want to use is the last one where you can target your ad to Friends of the connections to your Page or Event. This may be beneficial in that your Fans might have similar friends who would also Like your Page or come to your Event. In any case, it's interesting to see your second level of influence by entering your Fan Page and seeing how many friends your Fans have collectively.

Advanced Demographics

You use the Advanced Demographics area of the Advertise on Facebook ad creation page to target people in very specific ways. For example, if your business is a restaurant, you might target people on their birthday by creating an ad that says "Happy Birthday! Come in for a free dessert this week and mention that you saw this ad." Or you could offer something special for the birthday boy or girl.

Other possibilities for advanced targeting are to single people, married people, people who speak a particular language — the possibilities are endless.

When your ad speaks to a particular niche of a wider audience, it has a better chance of being noticed.

Education and Work

You can use the Education and Work area to target college graduates, people who attended a specific college or majored in a specific subject, or people who work at a specific company. Many Facebook users don't enter this information in their Profiles, though, so we suggest that you leave this area blank unless you have a very good reason to target these niche audiences.

Narrowing your reach too much may result in fewer clicks. It's a balancing act between finding your perfect target and making sure you get enough clicks. If you aren't getting as many clicks as you want, you may have to widen your restrictions and use a broader target audience. You don't have to use all the targeting options that are available.

Setting Your Bidding and Pricing Goals

You have your ad designed and your niche targeted. Now it's time to pay the piper. How much are you willing to spend for your ad? After you've completed the Targeting section (covered in the previous section of this chapter), scroll down and find Section 3, which is Campaigns, Pricing and Scheduling. This is the last section you have to complete before placing the order for your ad.

If you have never created an ad or campaign before, you will see the screen shown in Figure 2-12. If you have created an ad before, you will have a drop-down menu with your past campaign names and you won't have to enter the Account Currency and Time Zone fields because you already entered that information with your previous campaign.

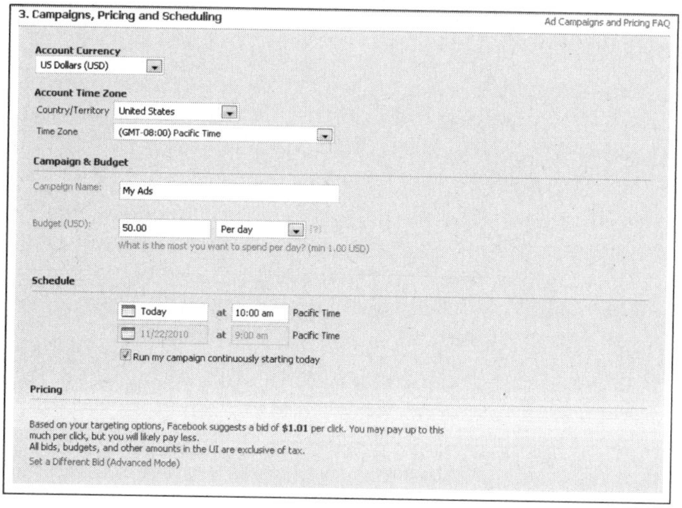

Figure 2-12: Campaigns, Pricing and Scheduling.

To complete the Campaigns, Pricing and Scheduling section, use the following steps

1. **Set your Account currency from the drop-down list, the currency you will use to pay for the ad.**

2. **Set the Account Time Zone so that Facebook knows when to run the ad if you select specific times.**

3. **In the Campaign Name field, enter your Campaign Name.**

   The default name is My Ads, but you should make it something more descriptive. In Chapter 1 of this book, we describe designing your campaign; refer to that chapter for ideas of how to structure your campaign names to reflect the different types of ads within that campaign. You can always edit the campaign name after it is running if you decide you would like the name to be more descriptive. See Chapter 3 of this mini-book to see how to change the name.

4. **In the Budget field, set your Daily Budget.**

   When you reach the limit of your budget, Facebook shuts off your ad automatically. No need to worry about spending more than you thought or forgetting to turn your ads in the campaign off. If you're running test ads first, keep this daily budget low.

5. **If you want your campaign to run during specific dates, deselect the box next to Run My Campaign Continuously Starting Today and then enter the start date and end dates by click the respective calendars as shown in Figure 2-12 in the Schedule section.**

   These settings are handy if you want to run your ad for only five days, for example and then have it automatically turned off. If you leave the default selection checked indicating to Run my campaign continuously starting today, then you will have to remember to turn your campaign off.

   Facebook suggests a bid for you. (You need to look hard or you may miss it; the suggested bid is at the very bottom of the Campaigns, Pricing and Scheduling section.) The bid suggestion defaults to a Cost per Click bidding style.

   If you want to stick with the bid, Facebook suggests, click the Review Ad button at the bottom of the page. You are taken to a page that shows you how your ad looks and reviews your targeting information. If your ad looks good, click the Place Order button. But if you need to edit the ad, you can click Edit Ad.

   If you would rather choose a different bid, or try CPM, click the Set a Different Bid (Advanced Mode) link.

   If you choose the Advanced Mode, you now have the option to select Pay for Impressions and change your bid, as shown in Figure 2-13.

Figure 2-13:
Advanced
Mode
bidding
options.

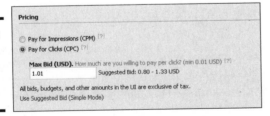

At the start of your campaign, it's hard to tell whether you should pay for clicks or pay for impressions, so determining which is the best route to take will require some experimentation.

When you select CPM, you pay for a certain number of people to be shown your ad (which doesn't mean that they will all actually *see* your ad). If you pay $0.60 for 1,000 people to be shown your ad and only 100 people actually click it, you still pay $0.60.

When you select CPC, you pay for each click. So if you bid $0.60 per click and 500,000 people are shown your ad and 100 people click, you will pay $60.00. In this case, it's better to go with the CPM option because both methods produced only 100 clicks but the CPM option cost only $0.60.

The general school of thought is that CPM is better for raising general awareness because you're paying for the people who are shown the ad. CPC is more effective when you want a specific click or response. But at the end of the day, you're trying to make money — not spend more. So test which one is cheaper for you to run, and run it that way. We covered this topic in more detail in Chapter 3 of this minibook.

After you have selected your desired bid in the Advanced Bidding mode, click Review Ad and make sure the ad is correct. Then click Place Order.

You cannot save your ad as a draft. So make sure that you click Place Order for your ad before navigating away from the Advertise on Facebook ad setup page.

After you place your order for the ad, the Facebook ad team will review your ad to make sure it complies with Facebook terms. Depending on the time of day and level of activity with Facebook ads, this can take anywhere from a few minutes to a few hours. Your ad status shows Pending Review while your ad is being reviewed. You receive an e-mail when the ad has been reviewed; the e-mail states whether your ad was approved and is running or whether your ad was rejected. If your ad was rejected, Facebook doesn't tell you exactly why. The e-mail sends you the link to its terms and conditions and lets you figure it out on your own.

Getting Help: From the Facebook Ad Team

The Facebook Ads Help section is one of the most complete areas within Facebook Help. You can find step-by-step instructions for setting up your ad, case studies, and use a glossary. Also, whenever you see a question mark (?) next to a term or box, you can click it to get an explanation in a pop-up box.

Facebook has a very comprehensive Guide to Advertising here: `http://www.facebook.com/adsmarketing`. Also, within the Facebook Help section, you can find answers to Facebook ads questions: `http://www.facebook.com/help/?page=409`.

Chapter 3: Testing, Measuring, and Modifying Your Ad

In This Chapter

✔ **Becoming familiar with the Ads Manager**

✔ **Exploring split testing**

✔ **Making sense of the reports**

✔ **Optimizing your campaign**

*T*esting, measuring, and modifying your ad is one of the most important things you can do to ensure that you're getting the most for your dollar. Unfortunately, testing is one of the most overlooked aspects of the Facebook advertising experience because it can be overwhelming.

Because of the many variables to test and tweak, you might feel daunted at first, but if you approach it systematically, you can come away with an ad that has a high click-through rate at a low cost.

In this chapter, you begin by familiarizing yourself with the Ads Manager, where all your ad campaigns are displayed. Then you discover how to begin your split testing, view the Facebook ad reports, and optimize your campaign.

Now it's time to ratchet up your Facebook advertising expertise!

Understanding the Ads Manager

The Ads Manager is your Facebook ads dashboard. Here you see an overall picture of each campaign, the campaign status, and how much you are spending. From the Ads Manager, you can drill down into each campaign and get the campaign statistics.

After you have created your first ad, as you did in Chapter 2 of this minibook, you are taken to the Ads Manager whenever you click the Ads and Pages link on the left sidebar of your Facebook Home Page on your personal Profile.

The Ads Manager shows you all your ad campaigns in one place, as shown in Figure 3-1.

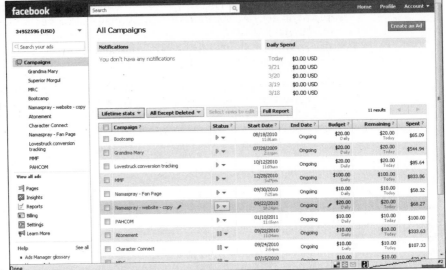

Figure 3-1:
The Ads Manager page shows you an overview of all your Facebook ad campaigns.

You can also get to the Ads Manager directly at http://www.facebook.com/ads/manage.

At the top of the screen, you see your Notifications and Daily Spend. Notifications include updates such as whether your ad was approved or declined or your credit card was charged. Daily Spend is a running total of how much you have spent each day across all campaigns.

Below the Notifications and Daily Spend areas are four boxes (refer to Figure 3-1) as follows:

✦ **Lifetime Stats:** When you click this box, you see a drop-down menu as shown in Figure 3-2. You can adjust the range of dates for the Ads Manager to Today, Yesterday, Last Week, or Custom. If you select Custom, you see a date range that you can input manually. Selecting any of the other options changes the Ads Manager table to only those selected dates.

Figure 3-2:
The drop-down menu lets you adjust your range of dates for the Ads Manager.

+ **All Except Deleted:** This drop-down menu allows you to select which campaigns are displayed in the Ads Manager. You can choose to view the default All Except Deleted, Active, Scheduled, Paused and Completed, or Deleted. When you choose any of the selections, the Ads Manager changes to reflect your selection.

+ **Select Rows to Edit:** This button is grayed out until you select a box next to one or more of the campaigns, as shown in Figure 3-3. You can then edit the titles or budgets of the campaigns if you click the button again. In case of Figure 3-3, the button text switched to Edit 2 rows because we selected 2 campaigns. We don't find this feature particularly useful unless you have a large number of campaigns for which you need to change the budgets.

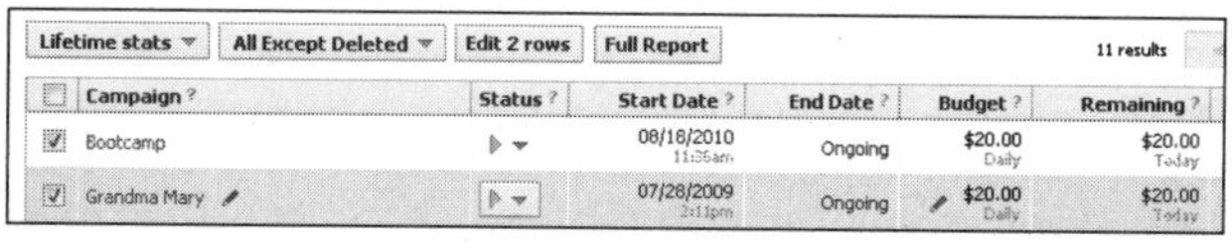

Figure 3-3:
Select rows
to edit.

+ **Full Report:** Click this button to get your overall Advertising Report. This report shows in-depth statistics from all your campaigns in one place. We cover this report later in this chapter.

Just under the buttons, you see a chart with different columns. You see the overall picture of what campaigns are running, how much you have spent on each campaign, and when campaigns started and ended, as follows:

+ **Campaign:** The name of each campaign. A campaign may have several ads within it.

+ **Status:** Each campaign will be running, paused, completed, or deleted. The status will be indicated by different symbols:

  • *Running:* Green arrow symbol (see Figure 3-1),

  • *Paused:* Pause symbol (two lines similar to the pause symbol on a CD Player).

  • *Completed:* Check mark. An ad campaign is completed if you run an ad for a set amount of time.

  • *Deleted:* Red *x*.

+ **Start date:** The start date of the campaign.

+ **End date:** The end date of the campaign. You may choose to run a campaign for a specific length of time or stop the campaign manually.

+ **Budget:** The maximum amount you're willing to spend on a campaign per day or during the life of the campaign. Each ad can have its own budget, and the campaign can have an overall budget.

+ **Remaining:** The amount still available in the campaign's daily or lifetime budget.

+ **Spent:** The total amount you have spent on the campaign.

On the left sidebar of the Ads Manager, you see a number of links that let you navigate to different areas, as shown in Figure 3-4.

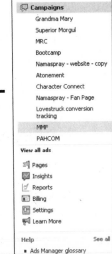

Figure 3-4: You can access different areas with the left sidebar on the Ads Manager page.

Most of these links are directly related to Facebook ads, but you can also access your Pages and Facebook Page Insights from the sidebar. Here's the scoop on each of the sidebar items:

+ **Search Your Ads box:** Use this search box to search through your ads or campaigns. The search will find an ad or campaign with keywords you enter in this box. The search will occur only by ad title or campaign name, not on the text in the ad.

+ **Campaigns:** All your campaigns are listed. Click any campaign name to navigate to that campaign.

✦ **View All Ads:** Clicking this link displays all your ads from every campaign on the right side of the screen. You see more stats and information similar to the Full Report button on the Ads Manager.

✦ **Pages:** Clicking this link takes you to a listing of all the Facebook Pages you administer.

✦ **Insights:** Clicking this link gives you a snapshot of all the Insights of your Pages on the right side of the page.

✦ **Reports:** This link takes you into the Reports area of Facebook Ads, which we cover later in this chapter.

✦ **Billing:** Click this link to change your billing method and track how much you spend each day.

✦ **Settings:** From here you can change your Facebook Ads account information, add permissions so that other users can access your Facebook ads account or the Reports, and change the notifications you receive. We cover more about this area shortly.

✦ **Learn More:** Clicking this link takes you to the Facebook ads help section.

Adding an Admin to Your Facebook Ads Account

You can add an admin to your Facebook Ads account so that someone else can have access to the ad campaigns or access to the Ad Reports alone. This can be helpful if you want someone else to be able to change your ads, manage your campaign, or just view the reports. To add an admin, follow these steps:

1. **Log into your Facebook account.**

You see the home page of your personal Profile.

2. **Click the Ads and Pages link on the left sidebar.**

You are taken to the Ads Manager.

3. **Click the Settings link on the left sidebar (refer to Figure 3-4).**

You see the Settings area of the Facebook Ads.

4. **Scroll down to the Permissions section as shown in Figure 3-5 and click the Add a User button on the right side.**

A pop-up box appears in which you can add a user and select the access the user has to your Facebook Ads, as shown in Figure 3-6.

Figure 3-5:
Add an
admin
to your
Facebook
Ads account
in the
Permissions
section.

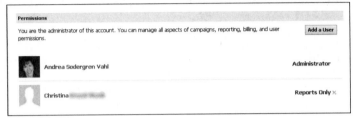

Figure 3-6:
Add the
user and
select
General
User or
Reports
Only.

5. **Enter the name of the user you want to add in the box if you're Friends with that person on Facebook.**

   If you're Friends with that person on Facebook, enter the person's Facebook e-mail login to add him or her to your account.

6. **Select General User or Reports Only from the drop-down menu and then click Add.**

   The person you're adding now appears in the Permissions area.

Now that you understand the navigation of the Facebook Ads Manager, you're ready to drill down into the Facebook campaigns and test your ads. (Refer to Chapter 1 of this minibook to see how to set up campaigns.)

Testing Your Ad

With any type of Facebook ad that you create, you want to test a number of different variations to find out which one performs the best. Ads that are performing well have a higher number of clicks and will be rewarded with a lower cost from Facebook. Refer to Chapter 2 of this minibook for more information on how the bidding and cost per click works.

Your bid price is not the same as what you will actually pay but rather what you are willing to pay. Facebook adjusts the actual cost per click based on what other advertisers are bidding.

To create these variations, Facebook makes it easy to copy an existing ad that you've created and change the copy, image, targeting, Web site, or bidding. For any major change, though, we suggest creating a new ad instead of just changing the existing ad. That way, you'll have a record of the ad performance to compare.

For each campaign that you run, rest assured that you don't have to change each and every variable. That would be exhausting and time consuming. Instead, map out two or three changes to test. For example, maybe select two different titles but keep the copy, image, and targeting the same. Or, keep the body text the same but change the title and the image. You get the idea.

This approach is called *multivariate testing, A/B testing,* or *split testing.* As we mention, you typically want to change only one or two things at the most at a time and keep the other variables the same. Just changing one thing at a time is the best if you have the budget and the patience because then you know that any difference between the two ads is solely attributable to the one thing that you changed. Choose what variables you want to test for each campaign and map out your plan so that it's systematic. Maybe you run an ad for one day with one call to action, and then run a different ad the next day with a different call to action — and then compare the two.

Make sure you have enough data to make a valid conclusion. We recommend having least 20 clicks and to have the ad run for at least two days for a sound comparison. You don't need to have the exact same number of clicks to compare two ads because many of the variables can be different, such as the bid price and market. You can use a more relative number to compare the ads, such as click-through rate (CTR) or click per thousand (CPM), because these are percentages and not absolute numbers.

Your main goal is to get a high *CTR,* which is the number of clicks your ad receives divided by the number of the number of times your ad is shown on Facebook *(impressions).* After all, Facebook judges your ad on how many people click it, and Facebook rewards ads with higher CTR by showing them more and giving them a lower cost per click (CPC).

You will be running through a cycle similar to these steps:

1. Create a new ad.

2. Run the ad for a period of time to gather statistics.

3. Analyze the results of the ad (CTR, demographics, action taken).

4. Decide which variables to split-test.

5. Repeat.

Split-testing your three ad variables: Copy, image, and targeting

The easiest way to do split-testing is to copy all the information from a previous ad to a new ad. That way, you can tweak the one thing you want to change and keep everything else the same. To create a new ad from an existing ad that you've created (as shown in Chapter 2 of this minibook), take the following steps:

1. **Log into Facebook.**

   You will be on your home page.

2. **Click Ads and Pages link on the left column.**

   You're taken to the Ads Manager page.

3. **Click the name of the Campaign that your ad is in.**

   You see a screen with the ads within that campaign and the various statistics they each have. Assuming that you're just starting, you'll see just the one ad that you created.

4. **Click the ad name.**

   You're taken to the stats area for that exact ad, and you see the Preview of the ad as it would look within Facebook.

5. **Click the Create a Similar Ad button, below the Preview on the right side of the page, as shown in Figure 3-7.**

   You are taken to the design section of Facebook ads. All the information from the previous ad is automatically filled in, and you can now change the copy, the image, the title, and the demographics for your split-test.

Figure 3-7:
Start here to do ad split testing.

You cannot save a draft of the ad, but you can set it to run at a certain time. Begin the editing process only when you're ready to place the order for the ad.

Copy

Your *copy* includes the ad title and body. If you're advertising something within Facebook, such as your Fan Page or a Group or an Event, you won't be able to change the title of the ad. And if you have a longish name for your Page or Group or Event, it will get truncated to fit the 25-character title. Unfortunately, you can't do anything about that.

If you're advertising a Web site outside Facebook, you can change the title, though. Try two different titles and see which encourages more clicks. Figure 3-8 shows two titles that were split-tested. The one on the right performed better. Sometimes you won't know exactly why a certain title or copy performs better; this is why you split-test. In this case, the idea of creating leadership resonated better with people than boosting confidence.

Figure 3-8: Split-test ad titles.

Also make sure to test the text in the body of the ad. Test different language and calls to action.

To get ideas on different copy, take a look at the Facebook Ad Board at `www.facebook.com/ads/adboard`.

Image

Your ad image can be very important when catching people's eye. Try split-testing your ad between your logo and a picture of your product, for example. If you're advertising something within Facebook, we recommend keeping the image the same so that when someone goes to the Event or Fan Page or Group, the image is consistent.

The maximum image file size is 5MB but the image will display at only 110 pixels wide by 80 pixels tall in the ad. Make sure that the picture is clear and not too intricate.

Targeting

After you've run an ad, you can take a look at the clicks on your ad and break it down by demographics. That data is found in the Responder Demographics report, which we discuss later in this chapter in the "Responder Demographics" section.

To change the targeting, scroll down to the Targeting section, adjust the location, age range, Likes & Interests, and others that you might want. To delete Likes & Interests that you had previously entered, click the x next to Likes & Interests, shown in Figure 3-9. You can also add Likes & Interests by typing them in the box.

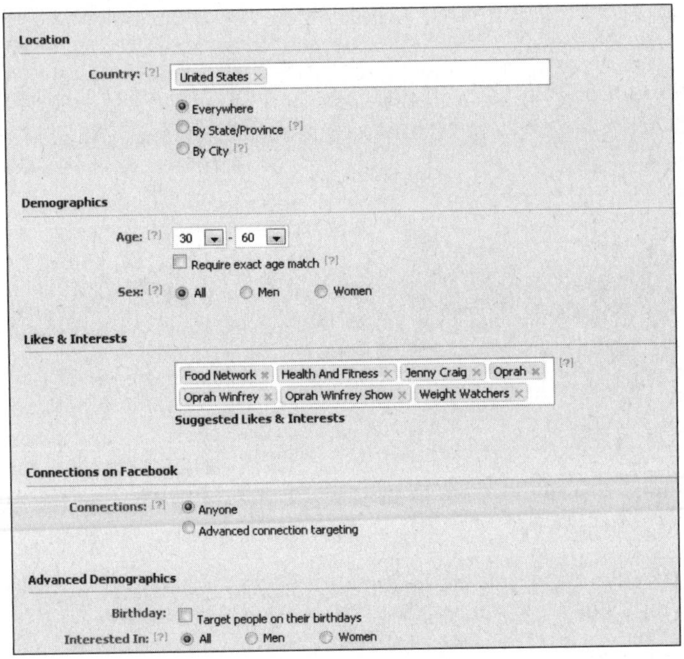

Figure 3-9: Adjust your targeting.

After you make one or two changes to your ad, click Place Order at the bottom of the screen to go to the Facebook Ads Team for approval. You have created a new Ad, and it must go through the approval process even if you have made only a slight change to the ad.

Testing your landing page

If you're advertising a Web site outside Facebook. you want to make sure that your Web site is optimized for what you're advertising. For example, if you'd like someone to sign up for your newsletter, send that viewer to a Web page that shows the benefits of the newsletter, a box for them to enter their name and e-mail, and not much else. Or, if you're advertising a sale, send those viewers to the direct page where you talk about the sale. Don't make the user hunt through your Web site to find the relevant content.

That being said, you can also split-test your landing pages. Design two similar pages and see which one gets better results when you send traffic to it. In this case, you do want to keep the actual ad copy the same so you can really measure the difference.

Split-testing landing pages doesn't have to be too hard. If you have created a page about your product along the lines of www.*yourwebsite.com/product name*, you would create another page on your site such as www.*yourwebsite. com/productname2*. The two pages would be almost identical except for the different copy or layout or images that you wanted to test. Send traffic to each of these pages with your Facebook ad and see whether one page converts the visitors into buyers better. Make sure that you have some analytics program installed on your Web site to measure the traffic, and watch when people are purchasing your product from one landing page or the other landing page.

Viewing Facebook Reports

Facebook Reports— are a goldmine of data. Sometimes sifting through that goldmine can be a bit tedious and confusing, but you can always find some good nuggets. Facebook Reports is the area in the Ads Manager where all your data on your ads is available, such as impressions, clicks, actions, actual cost per click, and more. The two most helpful reports are Advertising Performance and Responder Demographics.

The reports can be accessed a few different ways. The easiest way to drill down into data for a specific ad is to follow these steps:

1. **Click the Ads and Pages link on the left side of your home page in Facebook.**

   You will be taken to the Ads Manager page.

2. **Click the Reports link on the left side, as shown in Figure 3-10.**

   You're taken to the Ad Reports area, where you can drill into each campaign's reports and each ad's individual reports.

Figure 3-10:
The Reports link on the left side will take you to the Ad Reports area.

The Ad Reports area has drop-down menus from which you can select the type of report that you'd like, and you can filter the reports by campaign or ad. If you have multiple Facebook Ad accounts, you will also have the option to filter your reports by account. You would have multiple accounts if you have been added as an admin to other ad accounts, as mentioned earlier in this chapter. Figure 3-11 shows the Ads Reports area.

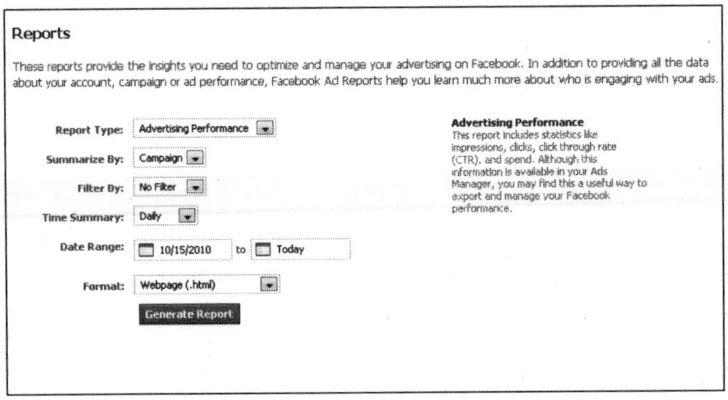

Figure 3-11:
Select what type of report you'd like.

The first report on the drop-down menu is the Advertising Performance Report. This report includes statistics such as Clicks, Impressions, Click Through Rate, and Spend. Similar information is available in the Ads Manager, but the report goes a step further and will tell you conversions and cost per conversions if you're advertising a Fan page.

To get your Advertising Performance Report, follow these steps:

1. **Select Advertising Performance from the Report Type drop-down menu (selected by default).**

2. **Select Ad from the Summarize By drop-down menu.**

3. **Select Campaign from the Filter By drop-down menu.**

Now all your campaigns are available. You can select one or multiple campaigns to have in the report.

4. **Select the Time Summary you'd like (the next drop-down menu).**

You can select Daily, Weekly, or Monthly. The report in Figure 3-12 shows Weekly.

5. **Select the appropriate date range (the Date Range fields).**

6. **Select what format you would like your report presented (the Format field).**

You can select Webpage (.html), (which will then display on a Web page after you click it), Excel .csv, or Multilanguage Excel .csv. More on downloading your report into Excel shortly.

7. **Click the blue Generate Report button at the bottom.**

Figure 3-12 shows a sample Advertising Performance report for one campaign.

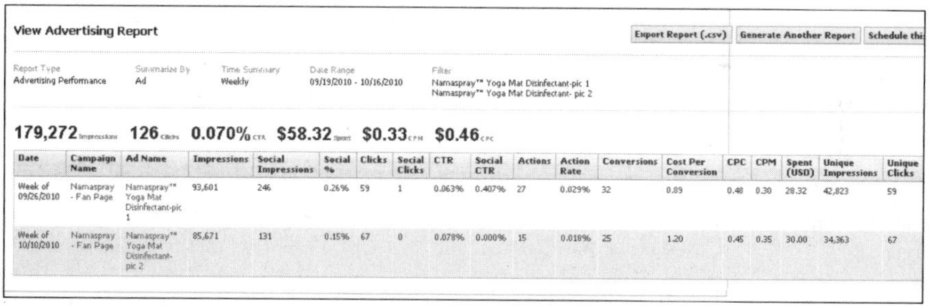

Figure 3-12:
Compare all the ads from one campaigns in an Advertising Performance report.

Book VIII
Chapter 3

Testing, Measuring, and Modifying Your Ad

Reading the Advertising Performance report

If you haven't run ads before on Google or other Web platforms, some of the terms on the Advertising Performance report can look like Greek. Here are the definitions of the terms in the Advertising Performance report shown in Figure 3-6:

✦ **Impressions:** How many times the ad has been shown to a Facebook user.

✦ **Social Impressions:** How many times the ad was shown to a Facebook user and also had one of their personal friends showing as "Liking" the Page or attending the Event. This is valid only for advertising things within Facebook, such as Fan Pages, Events, or Groups.

✦ **Social %:** Shows what percentage of the total Impressions were Social Impressions.

✦ **Clicks:** The actual number of clicks on the ad. This can also include a click if someone Liked your Fan Page right from the ad itself.

✦ **Social Clicks:** Shows how many clicks you received from an ad that was showing that a personal friend Liked your Fan Page or had responded to an Event RSVP. Again, this is only valid only when you advertise Fan Pages, Groups, or Events.

✦ **CTR:** How many times your ad was clicked, divided by the number of times your ad was shown (impressions).

✦ **Social CTR:** This is the Social Clicks divided by the social impressions. Theoretically, this number should be higher than the CTR because the ad included a personal friend who Liked the Page, and thus "social" proof. But that's the theory.

✦ **Actions:** The number of people who took the action desired from the ad itself, such as Liking your Fan Page or responding to your eEvent.

✦ **Action Rate:** The number of actions divided by the number of impressions.

✦ **Conversions:** Measurement of How many people total responded to your call to action. This counts actions from the ad itself and includes when someone goes to your Fan Page and then clicks Like.

✦ **Cost Per Conversion:** Automatically calculates for you your cost per Fan, or cost per RSVP, or cost per person who joins your Group.

✦ **CPC:** How much it actually cost you for each click you received. This number is calculated even if you didn't bid on the cost per click model, which is helpful for comparison. It will take how many clicks you received (even if you're paying by impression) and calculate how much it cost you for each click.

✦ **CPM:** Cost per thousand impressions. Even if you did not bid with the CPM model when you placed your ad, Facebook Reports will calculate it for your reference. This is helpful if you do decide to switch to the CPM bidding model so that you can compare how your ads are performing between the different bidding models.

✦ **Spent:** The amount you spent for that time summary you chose in the report: Daily, Weekly, or Monthly.

✦ **Unique Impressions:** How many times your ad was shown to a unique person. Compare this against Impressions to see how many times your ad was shown to the same person.

✦ **Unique Clicks:** How many different clicks you received. This data is helpful to know if the same person happened to be shown your ad twice and clicked it both times because the second click wouldn't be a unique click.

✦ **Unique CTR:** Unique Clicks divided by Unique Impressions. Again, in relation to the unique clicks and the unique impressions, you want to know whether new people are clicking through to your ad or if it is one person clicking on your ad over and over. It's best to have your Unique CTR come close to your CTR, but there is nothing you can do to control who is clicking on your ad.

When comparing campaigns, make sure to compare the numbers like the CTR or CPC to get "fairer" comparisons. If you're going to compare two ads, try and run them with similar bids and similar times of the day to get a true picture of which ad performed better. You can set the ads to run at certain times of the day when you create the ads.

Responder Demographics report

Another report that you can run is the Responder Demographics report. This report gives you great information about the types of Facebook users who are viewing or clicking your ads. To run this report, follow the following steps:

1. **Start from on the Ads Manager page, as described earlier in this chapter.**

You can also go there directly at `www.facebook.com/ads/manage`.

2. **Click Reports, in the left column.**

3. **From the Report Type drop-down menu, select Responder Demographics.**

4. **Select Ad from the Summarize By drop-down menu.**

5. **Select Campaign from the Filter By drop-down menu to see a list of your Campaigns.**

6. **Check the box next to the desired Ad Campaign.**

7. **Select the Time Summary and Date Range you would like to see.**

8. **Click the blue Generate Report button.**

From this report, you can see who actually clicked your ad in certain age ranges; see an example in Figure 3-13. You might think that your target demographic is the 45–54 range, but there are a larger percentage of people in the 55–64 range who click the ad. With this information in hand, you might want to adjust your ad to target only that age range in your ad Targeting section to get more clicks and more traffic.

**Book VIII
Chapter 3**

Testing, Measuring, and Modifying Your Ad

Date	Campaign	Ad Name	Demographic	Bucket 1	Bucket 2	% of Impressions	% of Clickers	CTR
Dec 2010	Grandma Mary	Grandma Mary - Social Media Edutainer 2	country	US		100.000%	100.000%	0.072%
Dec 2010	Grandma Mary	Grandma Mary - Social Media Edutainer 2	gender_age	F	25-34	0.206%	0.000%	0.000%
Dec 2010	Grandma Mary	Grandma Mary - Social Media Edutainer 2	gender_age	F	35-44	33.511%	20.642%	0.044%
Dec 2010	Grandma Mary	Grandma Mary - Social Media Edutainer 2	gender_age	F	45-54	36.653%	31.193%	0.061%
Dec 2010	Grandma Mary	Grandma Mary - Social Media Edutainer 2	gender_age	F	55-64	21.800%	38.532%	0.127%
Dec 2010	Grandma Mary	Grandma Mary - Social Media Edutainer 2	gender_age	F	65-100	6.158%	7.339%	0.086%
Dec 2010	Grandma Mary	Grandma Mary - Social Media Edutainer 2	gender_age	F	Unknown	1.672%	2.294%	0.099%
Dec 2010	Grandma Mary	Grandma Mary - Social Media Edutainer 2	region	Unknown		0.935%	0.000%	0.000%
Dec 2010	Grandma Mary	Grandma Mary - Social Media Edutainer 2	region	us	Alabama	1.734%	0.000%	0.000%
Dec 2010	Grandma Mary	Grandma Mary - Social Media Edutainer 2	region	us	Arizona	1.738%	0.000%	0.000%

Figure 3-13: This report breaks down who saw your ad and who clicked your ad by age range.

The Responder Demographics report will also show you the percentage of users who saw your ad by region. The columns in this report might be blank if there were an insufficient number of impressions or users who clicked your ad within that demographic group, but that doesn't necessarily mean that the number is zero.

We have seen that the Responder Demographics report doesn't always show the % of Clickers and CTR columns. So be aware that these numbers may or may not be available.

Exporting to a CSV file

To analyze the data in your ad reports more fully, consider exporting your reports to a CSV file, which you can use in Excel or similar programs. You may want to export the data to give yourself a visual graph of the different numbers or to compare the numbers side by side of one campaign to another. You can export your data from a few different areas:

✦ **Ad Manager itself:** See all the campaigns that you've ever run and then export the statistics.

✦ **Campaign:** Within each Campaign, you can export the overall statistics.

✦ **Reports:** Within the Reports area, you can get more refined data.

To export the data within the Ad Manager, first click the Full Report button above the data. You then see all your data for all your campaigns, as shown in Figure 3-14. Then click the Export Report (.csv) button at the top of the screen.

Also note that you can change the contents of the table from the drop-down menus. You can change the date range using the Date Range box.

Figure 3-14:
Export your
data from
the Ads
Manager to
a CSV file.

View Advertising Report

Export Report (.csv) | Generate Another Report | Schedule this Report

Report Type: Advertising Performance
Summarize By: Campaign
Time Summary: Custom
Date Range: Lifetime

9,731,730 Impressions **3,490** Clicks **0.036%** CTR **$2,522.28** Spent **$0.26** CPM **$0.72** CPC

Date Range ?	Campaign ?	Impressions ?	Social Impressions ?	Social % ?	Clicks ?	Social Clicks ?	CTR ?	Social CTR ?	Actions ?	Action rate ?	CPC ?	CPM ?	Spent ?
Lifetime	Grandma Mary	1,714,826	833,439	48.60%	879	465	0.051%	0.056%	193	0.011%	0.62	0.32	544.94
Lifetime	Superior Morgui	1,654,402	18,449	1.12%	557	15	0.034%	0.081%	0	0.000%	0.55	0.18	304.57
Lifetime	MRC	35,637	0	0.00%	36	0	0.101%	0.000%	17	0.048%	0.57	0.58	20.63
Lifetime	Bootcamp	212,632	5,733	2.70%	74	10	0.035%	0.174%	7	0.003%	0.88	0.31	65.09
Lifetime	Namaspray - website - copy	192,417	32	0.02%	134	1	0.070%	3.125%	0	0.000%	0.51	0.35	68.27
Lifetime	Atonement	1,623,437	0	0.00%	335	0	0.021%	0.000%	0	0.000%	1.00	0.21	333.63
Lifetime	Character Connect	411,299	12	0.00%	108	0	0.026%	0.000%	0	0.000%	0.99	0.26	107.33

To export the statistics from a report that you run, follow the steps as outlined in the earlier section on viewing Facebook reports but select Excel .csv in Step 6.

Adapting your campaign

After you have the data, what do you do with it? For starters, always make sure that you're digging into the reports deeply enough — the data can be tricky! For example, say you have two ads that ran with exactly the same copy and only the picture changed. From the data in Figure 3-15, you might infer that the ad with "pic 2" performed better. After all, it received more clicks, has a better CTR, and boasts a better CPC.

Figure 3-15:
Comparing
initial data
on two ads.

Lifetime stats ▾ | All Except Deleted ▾ | Select rows to edit | Full Report | 2 results

	Ad Name ?	Status ?	Bid ?	Type ?	Impressions ?	Social % ?	Clicks ?	CTR ?	CPC ?	CPM ?	Spent ?
	Namaspray™ Yoga Mat Disinfectant- pic 2	‖	$1.51	CPC	85,671	0.2%	67	0.078%	$0.45	$0.35	$30.00
	Namaspray™ Yoga Mat Disinfectant-pic 1	‖	$1.51	CPC	93,601	0.3%	59	0.063%	$0.48	$0.30	$28.32
	Totals				179,272	0.2%	126	0.070%	$0.46	$0.33	$58.32

TIP

You can access the Advertising Performance Report quickly within a campaign by clicking on the Full Report button (refer to Figure 3-15).

However, when you dig into the Advertising Performance report, as shown in Figure 3-16, the ad with "pic 1" had more Actions, which means that more people ended up Liking the Fan Page — almost twice as many, in fact. So, the ad with "pic 1" is the one that should be run more.

**Book VIII
Chapter 3**

Testing, Measuring,
and Modifying
Your Ad

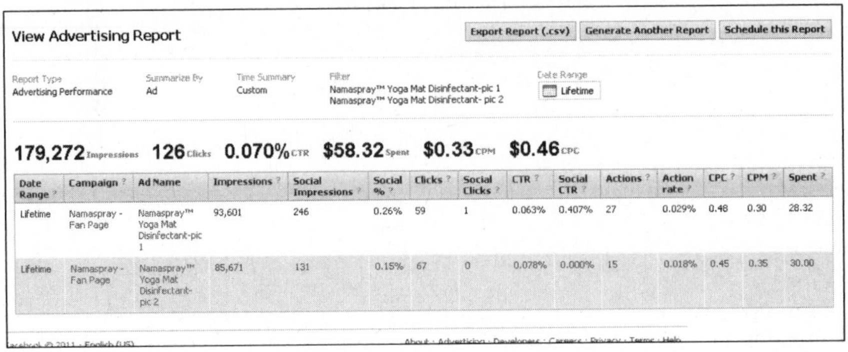

Figure 3-16:
Dig deeper
into the
data to
compare the
conversions.

| View Advertising Report | | | | | | | | | Export Report (.csv) | Generate Another Report | Schedule this Report |

Report Type: Advertising Performance   Summarize By: Ad   Time Summary: Custom   Filter: Namaspray™ Yoga Mat Disinfectant-pic 1 / Namaspray™ Yoga Mat Disinfectant- pic 2   Date Range: Lifetime

179,272 Impressions **126** Clicks **0.070%** CTR **$58.32** Spent **$0.33** CPM **$0.46** CPC

Date Range	Campaign	Ad Name	Impressions	Social Impressions	Social %	Clicks	Social Clicks	CTR	Social CTR	Actions	Action rate	CPC	CPM	Spent
Lifetime	Namaspray - Fan Page	Namaspray™ Yoga Mat Disinfectant-pic 1	93,601	246	0.26%	59	1	0.063%	0.407%	27	0.029%	0.48	0.30	28.32
Lifetime	Namaspray - Fan Page	Namaspray™ Yoga Mat Disinfectant-pic 2	85,671	131	0.15%	67	0	0.078%	0.000%	15	0.018%	0.45	0.35	30.00

Facebook © 2011 · English (US)   About · Advertising · Developers · Careers · Privacy · Terms · Help

Also, as noted in Figure 3-13, take a look at the demographics responding to your ad. If you're getting a higher response from a certain age range, look at removing the underperforming age ranges from your ad targeting and just focusing your ad toward the responsive age ranges for a better CTR.

Rotate your ads every few days to keep them fresh. If you're targeting a narrower range of people, they will potentially see the ad multiple times, and the ad won't be as effective.

Testing and tracking your Facebook ad may take some practice. There are lots of things that you can vary to see what gives you the best CTR or the highest conversion rate. Don't get discouraged if it seems hard at first. After a while, you'll really see a difference in the performance of your ads, and you'll get a lot more for your hard-earned advertising dollar.

Book IX

Measuring, Monitoring, and Analyzing

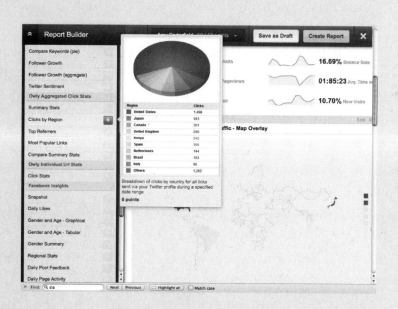

Contents at a Glance

Chapter 1: Setting Realistic Targets to Identify Success

In This Chapter

✔ Understanding the difference between social monitoring and social measuring

✔ Knowing the benefits of real-time engagement

✔ Determining the best social metrics for your business

✔ Identifying the optimal times to reach your ideal audience

Gone are the days that businesses can operate behind closed doors. The popularity (or should we say "massive explosion") of social networking has busted open those doors and there's no turning back.

Your customers are now all *social customers*. They love to share, chat, post, Like, and comment, and when they have something important to say (good, bad, or worse), they are quick to share it on their social networks. Their comments run the gamut from the best raves to the worst rants.

This chapter first examines the importance of social monitoring and describes ways that you can take advantage of the social conversations related to your niche and your business. From there, we explore strategies related to social measuring and discuss how you can best measure your prospects' and customers' social activities, and in turn use this information in your marketing messages to get your Fans to take action.

Your customers and prospects are going to "be social" with or without you, so it behooves you to pay attention, take notes, and get in the conversations at just the right times. This chapter will help you do just that!

Exploring Social Monitoring and Measuring

If you're just dipping your toe into the ever-changing Facebook waters, the idea of taking on social data tracking may be a bit daunting. You might be thinking, "Where do I start?" And when you do collect the data, you then might ask, "What the heck do I do with it?" We address both of those questions and many more throughout this section.

The purpose of tracking online activity is to identify the overall impact of your efforts. The data you collect can help you support your customers, promote your brand, and grow your business. And although we have been exploring Facebook marketing throughout this book, it's important to note your monitoring and measuring of social media activity should take a holistic approach, meaning that you want to include all social activity that is important to you, no matter whether it's coming from Facebook, Twitter, YouTube, or a different social network. All sites that matter to your clients should matter to you.

In addition to listening to your Fans, you should also do a reality check and find out whether all your social media marketing efforts are worth your time and effort. Is what you're doing really working? When exploring monitoring and measuring strategies, you first want to set your key performance indicators. Ask yourself these questions:

✦ What do I want to achieve?

✦ What does success look like? What are the indicators of my success?

✦ By what date will I complete this goal?

Although you find some overlap in the data, monitoring and measuring are two different processes. Both involve similar data. However, when it comes to taking action, that data is analyzed and used differently. This chapter closely examines both processes to better understand what overall tracking can do for your business.

The Importance of Social Media Monitoring

Monitoring is a bit like having the ability to eavesdrop while pressing your big digital ear up against the computer screen. You get to listen to all the chatter about you and your company as well as hear what's being said about your competitors and industry. In this section, we explore what it means to monitor social media activity and, after you collect the data, what you can do with it to improve your overall marketing initiatives.

First, monitoring involves identifying a set of keywords that are relevant to your business and brand. Knowing what words your prospects and customers are using online to research your niche or business is paramount to overall marketing success.

After you identify your keywords, you plug the keywords and information regarding your social media accounts into a monitoring tool. (We review your options for monitoring tools in depth in Chapter 3 of this minibook).

The monitoring tool then tracks the communications that are most important to your niche and business and organizes the data for you in a way that is easy to digest, such as comprehensive charts, tables, and lists. Overall, monitoring allows you to know who's talking about a topic (specific keywords you identified) and what they're saying about it.

To put a successful social-monitoring plan in place, you must first understand why monitoring is important to your business and then look closely at what you can do with the information you collect.

Why monitoring online conversations is important

Monitoring is all about listening to online conversations with the intent to learn, engage, and support. The benefit of social media monitoring is the opportunity to join the conversations that matter most to your business and the relationships with your Fans.

When it's working in your favor, Facebook can function as a word-of-mouth machine, broadcasting every customer rave that hits the Facebook airwaves. When you're engaged with your Fans and firing on all cylinders, Facebook can be your best friend.

But at some point, all best friends have spats. Sooner or later, someone will use Facebook to tell the world that your product is "lacking" or that your delivery department is "slow" or that your call center response time is "horrendous." It's bound to happen.

In both cases — that is, the "singing your praises" scenario and the "lackluster results" scenario — your goal is to be prepared to engage. You want to respond to both types of posts as quickly as possible. That's why monitoring is a crucial component of your overall social media marketing strategy.

In the case of the raving, happy Fans, catching them in the moment will only elevate their appreciation and admiration of you. They will feel heard and appreciated. See Figure 1-1 for an example of a positive exchange on Facebook.

Figure 1-1:
Admins
from the
Facebook
Page Social
Media
Examiner
are quick
to respond
to Fans'
appreciation.

In the case of the ranting, frustrated customer, keep in mind two main reasons that responding quickly is crucial. First, you want to take care of your customer. If someone's upset, you want to genuinely meet his or her needs and put the fire out quickly.

Second, you want the rest of your online audience to see that you take care of your customer. What you say and do for one client or customer directly affects all viewers' perceptions of you, so this is your chance to make lemonade out of lemons and shine a good light on yourself.

Situations like these give you the opportunity to protect your brand. One aspect of an effective monitoring strategy is to guard your brand's reputation and keep it polished at all times. Plus, as a brand, you can increase your social proof by engaging in these important, in-the-moment, two-way dialogues. They increase Fan trust and admiration.

Understanding the importance of real-time engagement

Monitoring online conversations is important if you want to stay in the loop with conversations related to your niche and your business overall. With that said, the optimal outcome of social media monitoring is to take full advantage of the opportunity of real-time response. The goal is to get in on the conversations that matter most at just the right time. In this section, we give you a few examples to illustrate just how important real-time response is for your business.

Say that you're the owner of an online store that sells wine, and your goal is to increase your overall sales. Monitoring for phrases such as "wine pairing," "the best wine that goes with," or "wine recommendations" can help you help others. Knowing when people are talking about your area of specialty gives you an "online icebreaker" — it allows you to join the conversation at just the right time and even do a little consultative selling. And best of all, because you're monitoring in real time, you're joining the conversation at a time when people are open to suggestions and in need of help. In essence, they're raising a digital hand and saying, "Hey, I need your expertise over here!"

Overall, the element of real-time monitoring is crucial when you want to make an impact online. To help you grasp the magnitude of this, we want to tell you about a post that was shared on Twitter and Facebook. Tim Ferriss, the best-selling author of *4-Hour Work Week* and *4-Hour Body* (published by Crown Publishers), was trying to give a $100,000 donation to St. Jude's Hospital. Not too shabby, right? Although he tried to contact the hospital multiple times, his calls were never returned. So, out of frustration, Tim took to the social media airwaves, as shown in Figure 1-2.

Figure 1-2:
Tim Ferriss
posted
these status
updates on
Facebook
and Twitter.

Imagine that you were St. Jude's Hospital and saw Tim's post online, in real time. You'd be sure to reach out immediately, right? If a Fan posts something negative about you, or perhaps asks advice of you, and you're delayed in your response, someone outside your company will likely step in to diffuse the situation or offer a better solution. That "someone" just might be your biggest competitor coming to the rescue.

Tim had almost 200 people respond to his post with different nonprofit suggestions for his donation. (*Note:* St. Jude's did reach out to Tim quickly, and he posted that he was talking with the hospital about his possible donation, as shown in Figure 1-2.) Now do you see why real-time response is so crucial?

Monitoring the right way

Social media monitoring is not just about identifying and responding to your online detractors. To develop a clear picture of what's being discussed online, you should monitor more than just your customers' and prospects' conversations about you. In this section, we take a look at additional ways to use these monitoring strategies to take your marketing initiatives to the next level.

An additional way to use monitoring strategies is to follow the conversations of industry thought leaders, your top competitors, and your partners. The goal is to cover all the bases. Also, consider monitoring keywords that are associated with products or services that may be complementary to your own. The conversations might give you insights and ideas into possible partnership opportunities or brand extensions.

Monitoring is keyword based, so the right words are crucial. Here are some suggested keyword ideas that you can monitor:

✦ The names of key people in your company

✦ Your company name

✦ All brand names associated with your company

✦ Product names

✦ Names of your services

✦ The top three competitors' names

✦ Names of industry thought leaders

✦ Names of businesses that you partner with

✦ Competitive product names and services

✦ Industry or niche keywords

Clearly, when it comes to monitoring, you have a lot of information to pull from. You can monitor all the public conversations that are taking place online at any given time. To get you started in the right direction, the communication that is posted on Facebook as status updates, @tagging, comments to Facebook posts, Twitter updates, direct messages, and comments on blogs should be monitored.

Setting up a listening station is the most important piece of social monitoring. While listening, observe with the intent to genuinely understand group dynamics and behaviors. Look out for the influencers and leaders, because these are the people who can spread the word about your business. Notice how people interact with each other, and pay close attention to the community norms. Overall, make sure that you understand the rules of engagement before you begin to interact and add value.

To review, here are some of the most important benefits of social monitoring:

✦ You're more responsive to your Fans' needs when you can help them in their time of frustration or confusion.

✦ By jumping into the conversations online at just the right time, you stay relevant and at the top of your Fans' minds.

✦ By monitoring regularly, you begin to fully understand the voice of your customer.

✦ Monitoring online communication allows you to see others sing your praises. When your Fans post compliments, rave reviews, and praise, this is great social proof. Take screen shots of these posts to use in your marketing materials. (The term *social proof* refers to the psychological phenomenon of people being motivated to do things that they see other people doing.)

✦ Monitoring allows you to spot trends, keeping you on the edge of your industry.

✦ When you understand what your Fans are talking about when it comes to your brand, you can better deliver the features and benefits that your audience is asking for.

The Importance of Social Media Measuring

In comparison to monitoring, measuring is more statistical and occurs over a period of time versus in real time. In the following sections, we explore how measuring your social activity can allow you to evaluate the success of your social media efforts as well as better understand the behaviors and habits of your customers and prospects. We also examine what data is best for you to measure depending on your marketing outcomes. With all the data on the Web today, the last thing you want to do is to get bogged down with too much information! When you know what to measure, you can streamline your efforts and save yourself a lot of time and stress.

Why measuring online activity is important

The benefit of measuring activity that relates to your brand, company, and industry on Facebook and other social networks is to spot trends, behaviors, and reactions early. The goal is to analyze the data quickly and act on it to get your biggest bang for your time and efforts. Constant benchmarking is crucial to ascertaining whether things are working in your favor.

To begin measuring, first you identify a combination of keywords that reflect your business and brand. To help research and identify the best keywords for your niche or market, some useful keyword tools include Google's keyword tool (`http://googlekeywordtool.com`), Scribe SEO (`http://scribeseo.com`), and Google Alerts (`http://www.google.com/alerts`).

Keyword tools make it easy to find out what people are searching for online. For example, with Google's keyword tool, you can enter a word or phrase and the tool will give you multiple suggestions of other popular keyword phrases that are also searched for online, as shown in Figure 1-3. You can then do some research to find out what words are searched for the most and determine the words that best fit your brand.

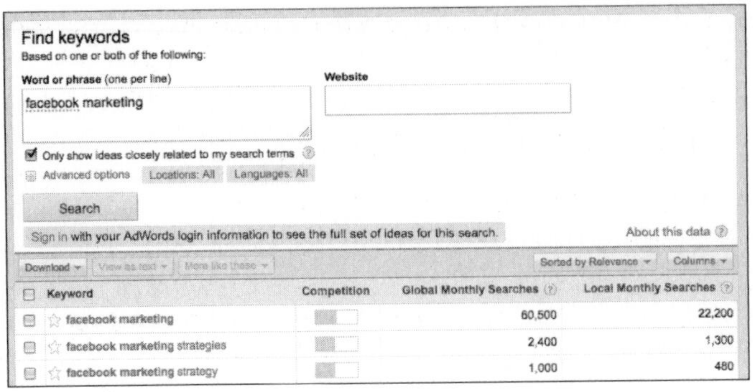

Figure 1-3:
Keyword suggestions from Google's keyword tool.

Next, you plug your keywords into a monitoring tool. (Again, we review monitoring tools in depth in Book IX, Chapter 3).

The monitoring tool can then scan the Internet; grab all blog posts, online articles, videos, and so on with those keywords; and disseminate the information in different data combinations to build patterns that tell a story about the social activity collected. For example, the tool might tell you the specific keywords that were mentioned on specific social media channels and how many times they were mentioned. This type of data is useful to find out what people are talking about online and where they are talking.

After the tool grabs the information, the measuring starts. Monitoring tools allow you to analyze the data, to splice it and dice it in different ways to gather a full understanding of its meaning. One of the major benefits of measuring the data is that it keeps you accountable. When you see what's working and what's not, you then take action to do more of what's working and tweak where you're falling short.

Understanding what social measuring can do for your business

Before you can strategically decide which social indicators are best to measure, you must first be clear on why you want to track the data and what you'll do with it after it's collected.

Here are a few reasons that you might want to take advantage of measuring social activity. See whether you can identify with any of the following examples:

✦ **Spy on the competition:** What are they doing online? What do their customers say about them?

✦ **Understand your ideal client:** What does she want? What does she need? What makes her tick? What words does she use when talking about your brands and services?

✦ **Participation:** You want to join in on the real-time conversations that matter most to your business. When people online are talking about your industry (niche, topics, and so on), you want to get in on the conversations to generate exposure for your company. You can offer advice or just share your thoughts and insights.

✦ **Market intelligence:** You want to listen to what people are saying in your industry so that you can create better products and services.

✦ **Reputation management:** You want to know what your customers are saying about you. You want to know in real-time the good and the bad comments so that you can address both quickly.

✦ **Set up a listening portal:** You want to set up a support team to monitor your clients' needs and concerns and address issues quickly. (We talk about setting up a successful social media team in detail in Book I, Chapter 2.)

Determining what you should measure for your return on investment (ROI)

When it comes to tracking and measuring online data, you have numerous options. Therefore, in addition to knowing why you want to track and measure the data, you also want to identify which metric indicators are most important to you. For example, if you post content with links to your blog, it's important to track which links get the most clicks from your Fans using a link tracking tool, such a bit.ly (`http://bit.ly/`). bit.ly is a free tool that allows users to shorten, share, and track links (URLs). You copy and paste a long URL into bit.ly's portal, and the tool automatically generates a shorter link that can be used on social networks or anywhere on the Web. These shorter links are then trackable, meaning that bit.ly will tell you how many times that link has been clicked and on what social sites it has been shared, as shown in Figure 1-4. Over time, this data can help you see which content your Fans interact with the most.

Figure 1-4:
Click
metrics
from a bit.ly
dashboard.

Or, if you're looking to increase the comments on your Facebook Page, you might want to track which posts are getting the most comments using Facebook Insights. Insights is Facebook's built-in analytics dashboard. You can use it to look at trends in the activity on your Page, including how many comments you're getting from your posts. We talk in detail about Facebook Insights in Chapter 2 of this minibook. This, too, can paint a picture of what types of posts your Fans respond to best — the most favorably and frequently.

This is, after all, one of the ultimate benefits (and goals) of monitoring and measuring: Uncovering information that allows you to increase the impact of your social media posts. For example, tracking the time of day you generate the most activity on your Page, such as clicks and comments, can help you decide the best time of day to post a call to action.

Say that you own a store for runners and you're currently having a special on running shoes for men. By analyzing your data, focusing especially on how many men are engaging with your content, the time of day they're most active on your Page, and what content they're engaging in, you can find out the best time of day to post your promotion and how you craft your post around this data.

By measuring these behaviors at this depth, you can reach more of your targeted audience with each post and turn your Fans into loyal, paying customers.

Read on for specific ideas on what to measure based on your business outcomes and goals.

Turning social activity into key metric indicators

When it comes to social media activity, you can track and measure numerous indicators. Here are the most important areas to consider:

✦ Engagement

✦ Brand awareness

✦ Influence

✦ Sentiment

✦ New Likes/unsubscribes

✦ Click activity

✦ Financial return

✦ Volume

To better understand how each of these indicators can support your marketing efforts, we dive in a little deeper to explore the benefits of each. To help you decide which indicators are a good fit for your business, remember to keep your marketing goals in mind as you read through the options.

Engagement

Engagement refers to the relevance of the Facebook Page to users and the actions they take when they visit the Page. You can measure engagement by taking a look at the types of activities users engage in, for example, becoming a Fan, writing on your Wall, Liking and commenting on an update, uploading a photo or video, or mentioning your Page in their status updates. You can monitor this information through the weekly and monthly stats of your Facebook Insights (see Book IX, Chapter 2 for more details on using Insights) and by spending time on your Page on a daily basis.

You can also monitor and measure all the words and phrases being used by your Fans and prospects when they talk about your brand. Are they what you expected? Are they the same words that you're using to explain your programs and services? These words and phrases are key to understanding how people are talking about your business! In addition, when you know the words your Fans use online, you can build rapport more quickly because using the same words creates a connection.

Brand awareness

Brand awareness speaks to how much your company is talked about on the social Web and, even more important, why people are talking about you. Is it in relation to a product announcement, a press release, or some company news you've played a role in? Or did someone write a review or mention your company in a blog post? Regardless of where the awareness comes from, you don't want to be the last one to hear about it.

You may want to add a reference point to your social mention tracking and see how many times your company and products are mentioned along with your competitors' over a 30-day period. This type of monitoring is often called *share of voice* , and the information needed to monitor share of voice can be accessed through third-party monitoring tools. You add up all the mentions of you and your competitors and divide your mentions by the total to arrive at your "share of voice."

Influence

Influence refers to how much your company is referenced and respected on Facebook. If suddenly a company whose Facebook Page had 10,000 Fans were to post a link to your new video on YouTube, and your video went viral overnight as a result, you'd be able to attribute your success to being discovered on that company's Facebook Page. You would be able to monitor the activity on one of the social listening tools, such as Netvibes (`http://www.netvibes.com`), as shown in Figure 1-5, and you would want to send a shout-out to the company for helping to make your video a success. In the future, when you launch a new video, you'll probably want to add that company to a list of companies to alert.

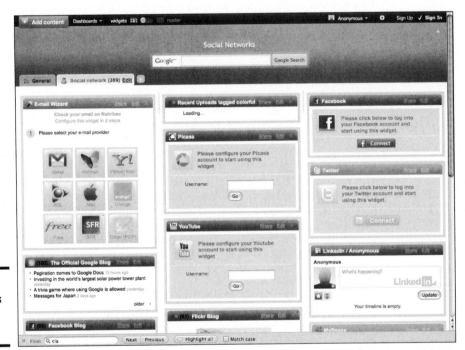

Figure 1-5:
A Netvibes listening station.

Sentiment

Sentiment comprises both positive and negative reactions to your brand on Facebook. Perhaps someone ordered a product from you and was dissatisfied with the color or the overall quality. Perhaps that person goes to your Facebook Page and writes that he'll never order another product from you again. But what if your customer service reps were monitoring the page in real time and offered to take the product back, refund the customer's money, and send him a new model? You could nip the situation in the bud and not only undo the negative sentiment but also turn it around significantly.

New Likers/unsubscribes

It's important to measure how many new Likers can be attributed to individual updates and your collective activity on Facebook. If people respond favorably by Liking your Page, and especially if they respond to a specific update, you can gain a good sense of how your users feel about that type of content. For example, if videos get more attention than other links, you'll want to post more videos for your Fans.

On the other hand, if users unsubscribe in reaction to a particular update, that will give you invaluable information, too. Perhaps users don't want to see that type of content from you. Or maybe you've overloaded your users with too many updates. Although ascertaining why you lose one Fan here and there might be hard, on the other hand, a major exodus will be very revealing. You can monitor the number of new Likers and unsubscribes on Facebook Insights.

Click activity

Click activity refers to the times when a person clicks your Facebook Ad and is taken to your Web site or a tab on your Facebook Page. The click activity is important to measure to know how effective your ad campaign is and whether you'd want to run it again or tweak it to make it different for the next time around. You can monitor information on the Facebook Ad reports (see Book XIII, Chapter 3 for more about these reports). Clicks are also tracked for Page Likes and event RSVPs. You'll want to know whether your event is drawing people in on Facebook; if not, you might need to change the description or the date. Will you have enough interest to run it? You can see information about Likes and RSVPs on the Facebook Insights reports. (See Chapter 2 in this minibook for more on Facebook Insights.)

Financial return

What are you getting in return for the time that you spend on your Facebook marketing efforts? Have you increased your number of Fans? Sold an online or in-person event via Facebook promotions? Brought more people to your Web page and in turn sold them into your programs or services? Had people download a white paper or report that, in addition to adding value, also promoted a product or service? Brought more people to a special offer through a Facebook-specific promo code?

To see a real financial return on your social media activity, think in terms of conversion. The goal is to convert an interested potential customer into an actual paying customer. Social media allows you to add value and create engagement, trust, and affinity with your Fans. After you have captured your Fans' trust, it's time to sell them your programs and services.

Tracking tools can show you how much traffic is generated, what content is of interest to your Fans, and how often they are engaging with you. To see a financial return on your social media activity, use the data from these metrics to help you generate activity and create and sell products, programs, and services for your ideal audience.

Volume

Volume looks at how frequently people search for your company on search engines. Facebook Pages come up in search engine results for your company name, so someone who is looking for your Web site might also decide to check out your Facebook Page. Your Google Analytics will show what Facebook tabs on your Page sent traffic to your Web site, which is all the more reason why you want to make sure to have your Web URL prominently displayed in the About box on your Facebook Wall and on the Info tab.

Demographics

Commonly used, *demographics* include age, race, gender, language, location, and household income level. For example, tracking tools such as HootSuite (www.hootsuite.com) can incorporate Google Analytics to show you a breakdown of visitors by region (as shown in Figure 1-6) and Facebook Insights can show the breakdown by gender, as well as by countries, cities, and languages, as shown in Figure 1-7. You may already know the demographics that are most associated with your products and services, but if you suddenly discovered, through monitoring your Facebook Insights reports, that you had a significantly different group coming to your Facebook Page, it could potentially affect not only your social media marketing efforts but also perhaps demonstrate that your company is connecting to a different demographic than you realized! You may want to adjust your products and services accordingly.

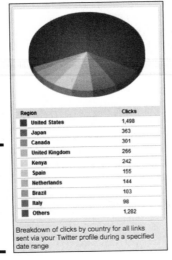

Figure 1-6: Regions data generated by HootSuite.

Region	Clicks
United States	1,498
Japan	363
Canada	301
United Kingdom	266
Kenya	242
Spain	155
Netherlands	144
Brazil	103
Italy	98
Others	1,282

Breakdown of clicks by country for all links sent via your Twitter profile during a specified date range

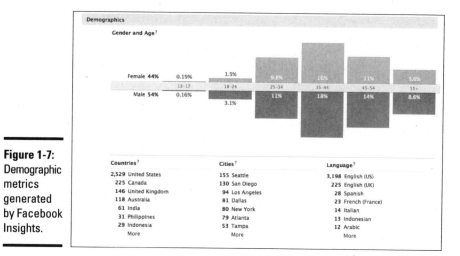

Figure 1-7:
Demographic
metrics
generated
by Facebook
Insights.

Chapter 2: Exploring Facebook Insights

In This Chapter

✔ Using Facebook's built-in monitoring tool

✔ Making sense of Insights' tracking details

✔ Determining the most important data to track

✔ Knowing how to use the data to create a thriving Facebook Page

Insights is Facebook's built-in analytics dashboard, which you use to look at trends revealed by the activity on your Page. Insights helps you get a feel for who is using your Page and how those users are interacting with it. In this chapter, we dive into the data and explore ways to better understand your Facebook user's behaviors in relation to the content you share. The key is to find out which of your marketing strategies are working and to replicate those efforts, and conversely to understand what isn't working so that you can create more productive and meaningful interactions. Now who doesn't like to do more of the good stuff and less of the bad stuff, right? And don't worry: we've set up this chapter so that exploring the analytical data of your Facebook Page will not be painful, we promise!

In this chapter, we look at how to interpret the myriad graphs and charts that Facebook Insights offers as well as how to use the data to generate a positive impact on your social media strategy.

Making Sense of Insights Information

Think of Insights as your personal road map to Facebook success. That may sound a bit cheesy, but Insights truly can help you navigate your way to a thriving Facebook Page. You will get a better understanding of how to interpret your unique Page information, and you can make informed decisions about the direction to take your content and ultimately how to bring more users to your Page.

Understanding analytics is a crucial component for creating, implementing, and maintaining an effective strategy. By moving beyond clicks, Likes, and posts, you can begin to understand what your audience expects to gain from its interactions with you as a brand, and be in a position to fulfill your audience's expectations.

Understandably, marketers want to ensure that their Facebook marketing efforts produce a return on investment, but without taking the time to review Facebook Insights information, it's like shooting in the dark. Fortunately, no matter what goals you have for your campaign, you can use the metrics to guide your next steps.

You must have at least 30 people Like your Page before the Insights dashboard becomes available for viewing.

Exploring User and Interaction Insights data

In this section, we examine the two types of data that Insights collects: User data and Interactions data. By diving into each one, you can better understand the demographics of your Fans, their behaviors, and what they like most about your Page.

There are two main ways to access Insights for your Page. On your Page, in the top-right admin section, click the View Insights link. Or, click the Edit Page button and then click the Insights link on the left navigation menu. Both links will take you to the Insights dashboard.

After you're inside the dashboard, you see three options in the left column: Page Overview, Users, and Interactions. The following sections take these page by page to give you a solid understanding of each one.

Page Overview

Page Overview, the screen you land on when you first enter the Insights dashboard, gives you combined data on users and interactions. Users are the people who have Liked your Page and interacted with or viewed your Page or its posts. Interactions can be viewed in 1-, 7-, and 30-day counts. The term *interactions* refers to the number of times that people (both Fans and non-Fans) have viewed a News Feed story. Figure 2-1 shows you the Insights Page Overview.

There are several things you can do on the Page Overview page. On the top-right corner of the page, you see where you can change the date range by week, month, or custom date range. You also have a button to export the data, as shown in Figure 2-2.

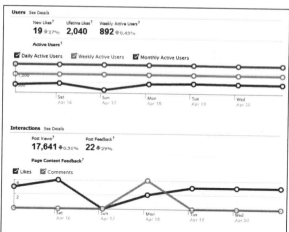

Figure 2-1:
There are
two main
areas on
the Page
Overview:
Users and
Interactions.

Page Overview gives you date range options

Figure 2-2:
You can
toggle the
date range
and export
data on the
Overview
page.

Here's how you export data from the Insights dashboard:

1. **Click the Export button at the top-right corner of the dashboard.**

The Export Insights Data dialog box appears.

2. **Select a file format (Excel or CSV).**

3. **Select a date range.**

4. **Click the Download button.**

This data file will go to your Downloads file or to where downloads are configured to go on your computer.

There is a hidden set of icons on the right top of the overview graphs and on all the graphs in the User and Interaction sections, as shown in Figure 2-3.

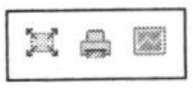

Figure 2-3:
A hidden set of icons lives on all the Insights pages.

These icons are as follows:

✦ Full Screen toggle

✦ Print

✦ Save Image

These icons can be very useful if you need to present the information in another document or want to share them.

After you've downloaded your data file, you have a very rich file to analyze (it contains seven pages of data):

✦ **Key Metrics:** Includes the following: the number of daily, weekly, and monthly active users; daily and lifetime Likes and Unlikes; daily Page views from users logged in to Facebook; your potential to be seen in the News Feeds; and specifics about your Page activity from your Fans.

✦ **Lifetime Country:** Shows the countries where your Fans reside.

✦ **Lifetime Gender and Age:** Shows the age ranges and gender of your Fans.

✦ **Lifetime City:** Shows the cities where your Fans reside.

✦ **Lifetime Language:** Shows which languages your Fans use.

✦ **Daily Internal Referrers:** Shows the top places inside Facebook that referred visitors to your Page.

✦ **Daily External Referrers:** Shows the top places outside Facebook that referred visitors to your Page.

All the data described in the preceding list may or may not be of use to you, depending on your overall marketing goals. You likely will find the key metrics most useful because they tell you a great deal about the activity on your Page. However, if you're a brick-and-mortar business, the city data will be of great interest to you as well. It all depends on your type of business and your goals for your Page.

Later in this chapter, we discuss how to determine the most important data to track as well as how you can use the Insights data to reach your ideal audience. But before we jump into examining the data, it's important to drill down into the Insights data to see what information you can access. Still looking at the Page Overview, you can see there are two main areas: Users and Interactions. This Page Overview provides a quick snapshot of what you can find out when you go deeper into the analytics. You have two ways to go deeper: by clicking the See Details link for each section or by clicking the User and Interaction links on the left menu.

The interactive graph lets you select and deselect data on the graph. The User section has New Likes, Lifetime Likes, and Monthly (or Weekly, if selected) Active Users. The Interactions graph has Likes and Comments. Each dot on the graph has information that comes up when you hover over it.

Both the Users and Interactions sections on the Page Overview have two parts: a row of numbers and an interactive graph.

The row of numbers have little green and red arrows and percentages next to each set of numbers, as shown in Figure 2-4, to show you the difference from the previous week or month, depending on what date range you have selected.

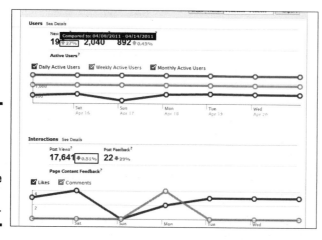

Figure 2-4:
You can get a quick idea of activity by looking at the arrows and percentages.

Users data

You can find out more about your users by drilling down to the second screen of the Insights dashboard, where you can view more details about your Fans' activities and demographics. From the first page of the Insights dashboard, click Users in the left column to get to this screen.

When you're there, you can see that the top line tells you the number of New Likes, Lifetime Likes, and Active Users:

✦ **New Likes:** The number of people who have Liked your Page by 1-day or 30-day periods.

✦ **Lifetime Likes:** The total number of people who have Liked your Page.

✦ **Active Users:** The number of people who have interacted with or viewed your Page or its posts. This data includes interactions from Fans and non-Fans by 1-week or 30-day periods.

An example of Users graphs is shown in Figure 2-5.

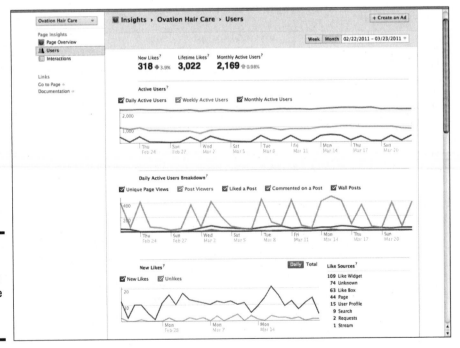

Figure 2-5:
Users graphs that show active users and new Likes.

The following list of the six Users graphs explains what each graph represents:

✦ Active Users looks at 1-, 7-, and 30-day counts of people who have interacted with or viewed your Page or its posts.

✦ Daily Active Users Breakdown is the 1-day counts of people who have interacted with or viewed your Page or its posts.

✦ New and Total Likes are the number of people who have Liked your Page, Unliked your Page, sorted by unique Page views, post viewers, Liked a post, commented on a post, and Wall posts.

There's an important number to look for in the New and Total Likes graph. First, toggle the view to Daily; then, deselect the Total Likes check box. You are now left with the daily Unlikes. You can see how many people have Unliked your Page, as shown in Figure 2-6. If you find that people are Unliking your Page, you need to look at what you're sending and make sure it matches what people thought they were Liking in the first place.

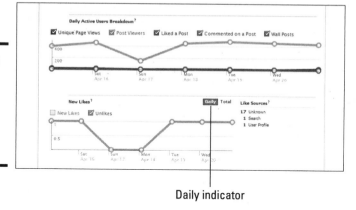

Figure 2-6:
Find out here whether anyone is Unliking your Page.

Daily indicator

✦ Demographics refers to the aggregated demographic data about the people who Like your Page based on the information they provided in their user Profiles regarding age (13–17, 18–24, 25–34, 35–44, 45–54, and 55+) and gender, country and city where they live, and the default language setting selected when they accessed Facebook. Figure 2-7 shows a graph that identifies the country they live in and the language they speak.

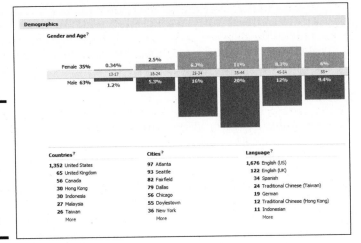

Figure 2-7:
Find the demo-graphics for your business Page community.

✦ Activity Graphs looks at Page views, the total number of hits to your Facebook Page by logged-in Page views and unique Page views; these include interactions from Fans and non-Fans. Underneath the Page view data, you can discover more about which tabs were viewed when logged-in users visited your Page, and external referrers info, the top external domains sending traffic to your Page. There is also a number for the external referrers to your Page. You might find that people are coming from your Web site or from someone else's site to your Page, as shown in Figure 2-8.

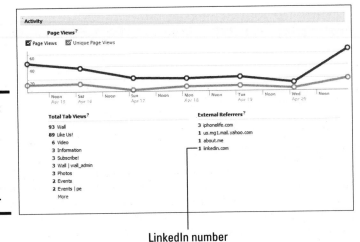

Figure 2-8:
Keep tabs on which sites are sending people to your Page.

LinkedIn number

Tracking which external sites are sending traffic to your Facebook Page is important because it can give you clues about your audience. Pay attention to the content on the external sites that are referring traffic to your Page. This is likely the content that attracts your ideal audience. We discuss referrer sites in more detail later in this chapter when we look at tracking activity outside Facebook.

✦ The last graph on the Users page is Media Consumption, where you can find out how many users clicked to watch a video, view a photo, or listen to an audio clip.

The Users data can provide valuable information about the ways users are interacting with your Page and no doubt can help you strategize the next steps for enhancing the content you share on Facebook. We explore these together later in this chapter when we discuss evaluating the impact of your content.

Interactions data

You can find out details about how users are interacting with your Page by drilling down to the third screen of the Insights dashboard. Click Interactions in the left column to get to this screen.

When you're there, you can view more information about Interactions. The top line gives you details on post views. The view can be toggled by week or month, or by a custom date range. Here you can see the Post Views and Post Feedback.

✦ Post Views reports the number of people (Fans and non-Fans) that have seen a News Feed story posted by your Page.

✦ Post Feedback reports the number of people who have commented on or Liked your posts in their News Feeds.

An example of Interactions graphs appears in Figure 2-9.

The following list explains the two Interactions graphs:

✦ Daily Story Feedback looks at how people engaged with your posts and reports the numbers for Likes, Comments, and Unsubscribes.

In addition, you can see more information about the Page Posts, such as the number of impressions your posts are getting and the percentage of Likes and comments. The message you posted is also visible below this graph. As we explore later, this too can shed light on how a post ranked by taking a look at the words and language you used.

✦ Page Activity shows the number of Mentions, Discussion posts, Reviews, Wall Posts, and Videos posted.

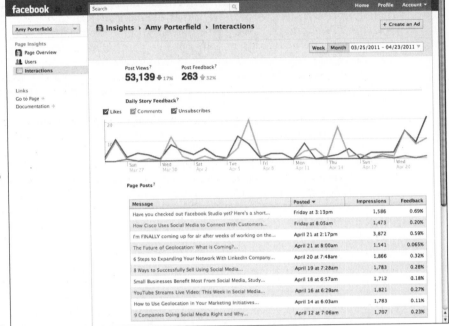

Figure 2-9:
Interactions graphs showing daily story feedback and activity data from Page posts.

Determining the Most Important Data to Track

In this section, we explore your Facebook tracking options. Here we determine what activities are the most important to track, based on your overall Facebook goals and business strategies. Specifically, we look at your Like activity, the impact of your content, Facebook comments, and unsubscribes. Also, we explore ways to reach your ideal audience and take a look at your Facebook Page activity that occurs outside the Facebook platform. So put your analytical hat on and let's dive in!

Tracking your Like activity

Users can tell you specifically what they think about your Facebook Page every step of the way, from the initial Like (which gives them the ability to engage with your Page via writing on your Wall and sharing posts, photos, links, and videos) to every item they post or leave a comment to one of your posts. From this data, you can start to see a clear pattern that explains what your Fans think about the content you post.

Content is king! If you're constantly producing content that your Fans enjoy and find valuable, they will keep coming back for more. That's why evaluating what content gets your users' attention most often is so important.

Perhaps every day for three days you posted a link with a message about a new post published on your blog. One of those posts receives 21 Likes, another receives 11 Likes, and the third receives 5 Likes. What types of things should you be looking at? Well, you might be curious to see the day and time of day the posts were made. So consider that the post that received 21 Likes occurred on a Tuesday at 3 p.m., the post that received 11 Likes was made on a Monday at 4 p.m., and the 5-Like post was made on a Friday at 9 a.m.

Over a period of time, you can see whether a pattern emerges. For example, are more people engaging with your Page on Tuesdays versus Fridays? Or are your users more inclined to be on your Page later in the day than earlier? You also want to take a look at the topic of the posts. Was the post that received 21 Likes about a topic your users are more interested in? Was there something about the way you posted your message? In the 21-Like post, perhaps you started your message with a catchy question or added some humor. You want to evaluate all these variables to see whether you can detect a trend to take advantage of.

Also, not every post you make on your Facebook Page is related to a blog post, obviously. Consider that you simply post a question to try to get your users engaged in a conversation. One question you post is about weekend plans and receives 2 Likes; another question asks who will be attending the South by Southwest (SXSW) Music and Media conference this spring and receives 18 Likes. What can you tell about the differences in the questions? Perhaps your users don't really care about what others on your Page are doing on the weekend but really connect to the SXSW conference. Of course, you can't make sweeping statements based on only a couple of reactions, but if you make a point to review which questions and conversations generate the most Likes, you'll start to see what is most important and relevant to your users.

Evaluating the impact of your content

What is the impact of your content, and who are you currently reaching? Evaluating the impact of your content can help you decide whether you're on the right track or whether you need to make adjustments to your content strategy. In the following sections, we explore ways to evaluate your content strategy as it relates to the data you collect from Insights.

Setting goals for your content

To begin with, your Facebook content will have very limited impact if no one is seeing it. One of the first numbers you should look at and keep in your mind's eye is how many lifetime Likers your Page has. Perhaps your Page has a total of 500 people who have liked the Page. You might set goals for increasing the numbers each month. For that, you'll need to be thinking in more detail about the activities you're doing outside Facebook to bring people to your Page. We get into the ins and outs about your activity outside Facebook a little further along in this chapter, but for now, keep that in the back of your mind.

At this point, you want to pay attention to whether increasing the number of posts you do each week will create more Likers; the only way to find that out is by experimenting. So, for a few months, you might want to shift around how you've previously been doing things. You can do this by adding more posts, alternating the day and time, paying attention to the messages of your posts (for example, begin by asking a question), using keyword-rich language, adding humor, or making posts shorter.

When you look at your Insights graphs, you want to see whether you have an increase in number of lifetime Likers and what your monthly and weekly numbers look like after altering your posts. It's important to note that by adjusting the date ranges on the right side of the Insights dashboard, you can compare the number of Active Users by day and month.

Consider that you've posted similarly for the first quarter of the year and your number of Active Users is significantly lower in the month of January than for February and March. What can you surmise about the dip in numbers?

You may want to look at a number of other variables, such as what topics predominated in January's posts versus those of February and March. Perhaps you did a series of posts about predictions for the new year, and those didn't resonate with your users as much as your posts about how-tos for Facebook and LinkedIn did.

Or, maybe your users weren't spending as much time on Facebook in January after getting back to work following the holiday season. Or maybe the decrease had nothing to do with your content but more about your users' schedules. We can have an impact on some things when it comes to the content we post, but we can't influence everything. A good rule of thumb is to try to replicate to the best of your ability what's working and to omit the actions that aren't generating good results.

Delivering content that people Like

Although the rules of content aren't etched in stone and certainly don't produce the same types of results on every Facebook Page, three types of content are known to be favored by Facebook users: video, audio, and photos. This may explain why Facebook has built a specific graph to measure Media Consumption into Facebook Insights. As you embark on the process of evaluating your content, take a look at past months to see how media has been received on your Page. If media hasn't been a regular part of your content strategy, this may be a good time to explore using it.

Large brands can teach us a few things about Facebook. For example, Coca-Cola, which has the most number of Fans for a worldwide brand, with more than 23 million (at the time of this writing), has posted 44 videos and 193 photos to its Page. Fans have followed suit by adding their own videos and photos to the Page. Starbucks, which is the second-highest-ranking world-wide brand Facebook Page, with more than 20 million Fans, has posted 31 videos and 135 photos to its Page. Starbucks Fans have also added videos and photos about Starbucks to the Page. Although your business isn't Coca-Cola or Starbucks, who can argue with the strategy of a brand that has more than 23 million Fans?

The relationship of landing Pages to content

You hear a lot of talk about landing Pages on Facebook — and rightfully so. A Facebook administrator can set the Page where a person lands when he or she is new to a Facebook Page. If you create a Page with a call to action (for example, by asking users to Like your Page), provide a contact form, or add a video describing your business, you can see in the Users Activity graph how many users navigated to your Wall after arriving on the landing Page. This number can tell you a good deal about the landing Page and whether it's serving its intended purpose. If this strategy seems to in some way alienate the user (such as by seeming to be too pushy and sales-like), users may click away from your Page. However, if something caught their attention and made a favorable impression, you will see that reflected in the numbers because users will navigate from the landing Page to the Wall.

Likes, comments, and unsubscribes — Oh, my!

The Daily Story Feedback graph is a good storyteller, and the stories come from facts, not imagination. The graph can tell you what days your posts received Likes, comments, and — heaven forbid — unsubscribes. No one wants to see unsubscribes on his Page, but in the event you do, you'll definitely want to take note. What happened that day on your Page? Were comments posted that may have been off-putting to the user? Had you increased your number of posts and the users were getting tired of seeing your updates in their News Feeds? You won't have any sure way to tell.

The best you can do is to ask yourself a few questions to see whether you can find any explanations on your side. You will always have people coming and going on Facebook Pages and you can't take it personally, but while you're taking a look at the impact of your content, it's worth thinking about. Of course, if you see a mass exodus — well then, that's another thing!

You also want to see which days generate the most Likes and comments to see whether you're reaching your users with content that they can relate to.

Perhaps one of the most interesting stories the Daily Story Feedback graph can tell you is about Page posts — messages you posted, the date and time they were posted, and the number of impressions and percentage of feedback they received. Keep in mind here that *impressions* refers to the number of times the post was seen in the News Feed or on the Page Wall.

What posts received the highest number of impressions? How can we explain why some are viewed more times than others? Is it the topic? Is it the wording of your post? For example, one post about Mashable's 2010 awards might receive more than 450 impressions, and a post about Quora might receive 100. We can assume by these findings that your users have taken note of a high-profile name such as Mashable, and they're interested in reading about the awards. Maybe they are less interested in Quora at the moment.

You can experiment with this hypothesis and post other links related to Mashable. Do they, too, receive a high number of impressions? Does Quora continue to score lower? Should you write about Quora or post links to other blog posts written about it? Maybe not. Again, this is where experimentation can pay off.

You built it, but did they come?

Assessing the impact of your content in relation to the Page Activity graph can be compared to the notion that a picture is worth a thousand words. If your Page is receiving a high number of mentions and people are writing on your Wall, adding new discussions, and uploading videos, suffice to say that your content is inviting. You have the kind of Page that people want to hang out on and be affiliated with.

It's not a given that a Page with even the best intentions will generate that type of activity. The difference might come down to whether the Page fosters community or is filled only with its own updates. "Why do some Pages and brands attract more users than others?" may be the million-dollar Facebook question, but our hunch is that engaging, informative, and unique content plays a big role.

Reaching Your Ideal Audience

You have to love demographics; they can be so revealing at times! By taking a look at the Users Demographics graph, you can tell a lot about your Page and who it's attracting and keeping. In the following sections, we examine the most important analytics to track so that you can determine the best way to attract and communicate with your ideal audience.

Who's been viewing your Facebook Page?

By knowing who's visiting your Page and interacting with your posts, you can take your Page to an entirely new level of success. Knowing more about your Fans and viewers allows you to deliver exactly what they want to continue to build their trust with you.

What's the gender and age of your users? What cities and countries do they come from? What languages do they speak? Do the numbers reveal what you expected?

Say that you're introducing a new product line for men between the ages of 35 and 44. Sixty percent of your overall users are women, and 30 percent of them are currently between the ages of 35 and 44. As part of your social media marketing strategy, you might want to attract your target audience to your Facebook Page. This may suggest that you should think about the content you're posting so that it has greater likelihood of appealing to 35–44-year-old men. Consider, too, that your product will more likely be used by men in a warm climate, it's January, and the majority of your users are from the Northeast region of the United States. You may need to adapt the types of posts that would reach users in other regions.

Using Insights to target your marketing message

Now that you understand your Insights Dashboard and you know who's been viewing your Page, how do you use it to target your message to a sub-group of your Fans? First, navigate to your business Page and then follow these steps:

1. **Click the Edit Page link.**

   Your administrative dashboard appears.

2. **Click the Marketing link from the left side navigation.**

3. **Click the Send an Update link.**

   The Send an Update Page appears.

4. **Check the Target this Update box.**

   The Target this Update box allows you to target the message to your community based on location, gender, and age.

5. **Select the location, gender, and age you want to target your message to.**

   This message goes only to the people who fit the target.

6. **Type the subject and message in the appropriate text boxes.**

   You can also attach or record a video or post a link.

7. **Click the Send button.**

Think of the possibilities! If you have branch offices, you can target messages with discounts or special deals to people who live in those cities. If you have an event that is location specific and is most appropriate for young women, you can craft a message and send only to women aged 20–40 who have Liked your Page. Check out Figure 2-10 for an example of a targeted message.

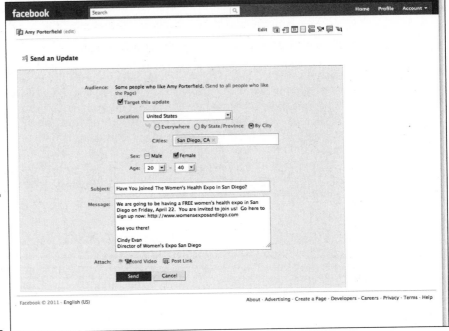

Figure 2-10:
Target
marketing
message
based on
location,
gender and
age.

By paying very close attention to your Insights, you can see which groups of people you can target with your messages.

Evaluating activity outside Facebook

When it comes to evaluating activity outside Facebook, you want to be sure to monitor one graph on a regular basis. That's the Activity graph on the Users screen of the Insights dashboard, where you'll see two very important words: *external referrers*. Like all activity on the Web, the number of external referrers can make or break a Web site. You may have experienced the good fortune of having someone write about your Facebook Page, without any involvement on your part, on a hugely popular blog and suddenly see a surge in activity on your Page. However, as we said, that would be good fortune (or perhaps a little more like magical thinking). That being said, chances are good that the external domains that refer traffic to your Facebook Page have had something to do with the actions you have taken outside of Facebook.

What kind of actions are we talking about? We mean things like the following:

✦ Putting social icons on your Web site and blog

✦ Adding your Facebook URL on your LinkedIn profile

✦ Integrating your Twitter and Facebook updates

✦ Promoting your Facebook Page URL on other sites you comment on

✦ Adding your Facebook Page URL when you write a guest blog post

✦ Adding the URL to your e-mail newsletter signature

In other words, promote, promote, promote!

You want to know which sites generate the most referrals to your Page so that you can think strategically about when and how to promote your Facebook Page.

Chapter 3: Using Third-Party Monitoring Tools and Analyzing Results

In This Chapter

✓ **Knowing what to look for in a social tracking tool**

✓ **Finding out how to choose the tool that is best for your business**

✓ **Viewing quick summaries of popular third-party tools**

*N*ow that you understand the power of monitoring and measuring your social activity, it's time to talk about third-party monitoring and measuring tools. After all, you shouldn't take this on alone. The torrent of data at your fingertips just might make your head spin!

The great news is that numerous third-party tracking tools have been designed to streamline the tracking process. These tools scan, grab, and organize your data for easy digestion. And here's the great news: Many of these tools are free or inexpensive.

In this chapter, we look at the key factors you should consider when choosing a tracking tool for your business. In addition, we examine the core features of multiple different third-party tracking tools to help you make a well-informed decision for your monitoring and measuring needs.

How to Choose the Tool That's Best for Your Business

When you first begin to monitor your social media activity, keep it simple and streamlined. Just because a tool might have 20 different features doesn't mean that you should try them all from the get-go. To save yourself some frustration and stress, first get comfortable with the basic features of the tool and move forward to the more advanced features only after you've mastered the basics.

When choosing a tracking tool, you need to be clear about what's important to you and your team. For example, the price of a tool might be your number-one deciding factor, whereas another company might be more concerned with a tool's reporting features. It all just depends on your personal preferences and needs. The following sections describe some key factors to consider when researching third-party monitoring tools.

User flexibility

Although you may start out with just one person in your company who is monitoring your social media activity, you may later decide to add multiple people to your tracking strategy. You want to make sure that you're satisfied with the way the tool allows multiple users to interact at any given time. Not all tools are user friendly in this area.

Ease of setup

If you select a good tool that meets your needs, the most time-consuming task will be the setup. After you have taken care of this step, the rest will be easy — and, in many cases, automatic. But before you get to the automation, you first must enter all the data you want to measure. When selecting a tool to fit your needs, make sure that you have compiled a list of all the login details for your social sites as well as a list of your needs, including the types of filters (demographics, regions, languages, and so on) and all the keywords you want to track. This data, when compiled before you start to search for a tool, can help you determine which tool has the features that best fit your needs.

Ease of use

You must feel comfortable using the user interface, or you will quickly abandon the tool. User-friendly dashboards are essential. In many ways, this is a personal preference, and you'll benefit from taking a little time to test the navigation of a few tools before you make a final decision. Many of the tools have guided tours that you can explore before signing up. A tour is a great way to get a sense of the how you navigate the tool.

Ease of reporting

Each tool has a different depth of analysis ability; therefore, you want to determine just how much reporting you need. If you want to keep it simple, you might decide to track just a few metrics, including weekly click rates, the number of comments on a post, and the number of Likes on your Facebook Page. If that's the case, you wouldn't need a tool that promises depths of analysis and extensive reporting templates. Be careful not to pay for what you don't need.

Cost

If you're just starting out and aren't yet confident that your tracking outcomes are on target with your business goals, taking baby steps might be wise. We encourage you to choose one of the tools that offers a free version and then upgrade to a paid version when you're certain that the tool will work for you. Also, when looking at cost, consider how important your monitoring needs are and how much time you can dedicate to monitoring.

Training and support

Many of the tools, both free and premium, offer great guided tours to review before you make your decision. Take advantage of these tours. In addition, before you choose a tool, find out whether the tool comes with training videos to help you get started quickly. Tutorials and training videos that walk you through the different features and benefits of the tool are extremely useful and allow you to get up and running quickly. They also allow you to get a good sense of where to start and what you might want to build up to when you feel more comfortable.

Tracking Tools: Your Third-Party Options

After you're clear about the factors that are most important to you when choosing a tracking tool, it's time to get down to business and choose a tool. In this section, we look at just a few of the many third-party tools that are on the market today.

Each of the following tools differs in its approach, metrics, depth of analysis, channels measured, reporting ability, and user interface. If your goal is to keep costs down, you may find that a combination of free tools works best for you. Or, if you're willing to pay a premium, just one tool may be all you need to cover everything you want to do. The key is to identify your tracking needs first and then research which tool, or combination of tools, best meets your needs.

Many of the tools discussed offer multiple levels of membership. When you find a tool that best fits your needs, make sure to research it closely to find the level of membership (if applicable) that best fits what you're looking for in the tool's features and functionality.

bit.ly

http://bit.ly

bit.ly is a free tool that allows users to shorten, share, and track links (URLs). You copy and paste a long URL into its portal, and bit.ly automatically generates a shorter link that can be used on social networks or anywhere on the Web. You don't need to set up an account to shorten a link. bit.ly makes it easy by allowing you to cut and paste your URL into its tool right from its home page, as shown in Figure 3-1.

However, if you create an account with bit.ly, you can view real-time traffic and referrer data, as well as location and metadata related to your click activity for all your links. It's useful to track where your link is getting the most activity, along with the date and time people are clicking your link the most frequently. See Figure 3-2 to view the bit.ly user interface.

Figure 3-1:
The bit.ly home page allows you to shorten a link without an account.

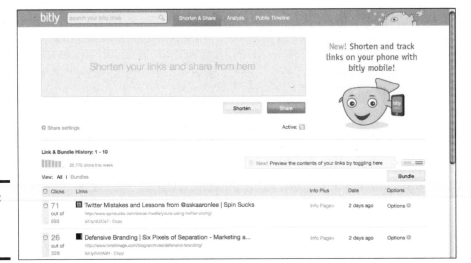

Figure 3-2:
The bit.ly user interface.

Google Alerts

www.google.com/alerts

Google Alerts is a free service that includes e-mail updates of Google results that users set up based on the choice of query or topic. You can specify what you like to receive by update types, frequency, and volume. To take full advantage of this free tool, we recommend that you set up multiple alerts, including keywords and phrases related to your niche. Provide your name and your company name, as well as the names of your competitors and their

products and services. Also, if you're involved in an Event, track the Event name before and after the Event to find out what people are saying about it. Figure 3-3 shows the Google Alerts user interface.

Figure 3-3:
The Google
Alerts user
interface.

Google alerts
beta

Search terms: _____ Preview results

Type: Everything
How often: once a day
Volume: Only the best results
Deliver to: amycporterfield@gmail.com

Create Alert

Google Analytics

www.google.com/analytics

Google Analytics is a free tool that provides insights into Web-site traffic and marketing effectiveness, allowing users to see and analyze traffic data. To set up Google Analytics, you need to copy and paste a few lines of code into your Web site to get the tool to start tracking the activity on your site. One of the many great features of this tool is its ability to uncover trends in your visitor activity — meaning that it gives you visual representation of how your users are interacting with your site over specific periods of time. This data can help you identify what your visitors are responding to most on your site. See Figure 3-4 to view the Google Analytics user interface.

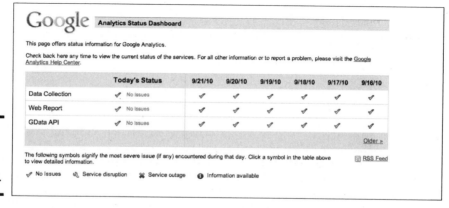

Figure 3-4:
The Google
Analytics
status page.

Google Analytics Status Dashboard

This page offers status information for Google Analytics.

Check back here any time to view the current status of the services. For all other information or to report a problem, please visit the Google Analytics Help Center.

	Today's Status	9/21/10	9/20/10	9/19/10	9/18/10	9/17/10	9/16/10
Data Collection	✓ No Issues	✓	✓	✓	✓	✓	✓
Web Report	✓ No Issues	✓	✓	✓	✓	✓	✓
GData API	✓ No Issues	✓	✓	✓	✓	✓	✓

Older »

The following symbols signify the most severe issue (if any) encountered during that day. Click a symbol in the table above to view detailed information.

RSS Feed

✓ No Issues   Service disruption   Service outage   Information available

HootSuite

http://hootsuite.com

HootSuite's social media dashboard helps organizations identify and grow social media audiences by tracking campaign results and industry trends in real time. HootSuite has a Web-based dashboard, so you don't have to download any software to use it and you can access your data online from anywhere. One of the best features of HootSuite is a tool called Hootlet. Hootlet is a button that you place on your browser's toolbar. When you come across an article or blog post you want to share with your social networks, you can schedule a post to multiple social networks simultaneously with a click of a button. The Hootlet makes it easy to share great content with your Fans and customers.

In addition, the multiple-panel user interface makes managing multiple channels easy. See Figure 3-5 to view the HootSuite user interface. Notice how the different tabs make it easy to manage multiple social sites from one dashboard.

Multiple accounts can be listed on the same screen

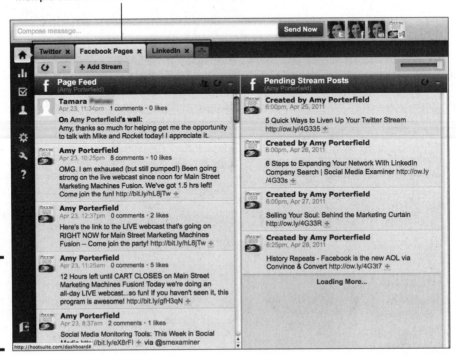

Figure 3-5: The HootSuite user interface.

Radian6

www.radian6.com

Radian6 offers multiple comprehensive tools that gather online discussions and gives businesses the ability to communicate, analyze, manage, track, and report on their social media monitoring and engagement efforts. As does HootSuite, Radian6 has a Web-based dashboard option that allows you to monitor in real time. The Radian6 dashboard, one of this company's many tools, has a workflow management feature that allows you to assign specific social tasks to team members, making your tracking plan a streamlined effort. The cost of the Radian6 tools is higher than most tools mentioned here, so it tends to be more attractive to mid- to large-sized companies that need to track data across multiple channels, products, and departments. See Figure 3-6 to view the Radian6 user interface.

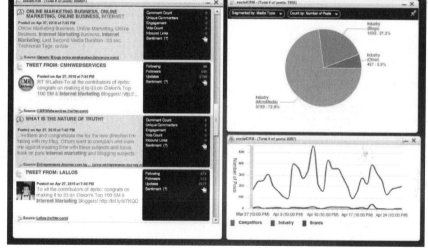

Figure 3-6:
The Radian6 user interface.

Lithium Social Media Monitoring

http://www.lithium.com/what-we-offer/social-customer-suite/
    social-media-monitoring

Lithium Social Media Monitoring provides real-time social media brand monitoring and management through tracking brands, company mentions, and ranking content sources. As is Radian6, this tool is more costly than the others listed here and tends to be more attractive to mid- to large-sized businesses. In case you're in the market for an all-encompassing monitoring and measuring solution, this company also offers the Lithium Social Customer Suite, which is a complete set of social tracking apps. We like to think of it as social media monitoring and measuring on steroids. See Figure 3-7 to view its user interface.

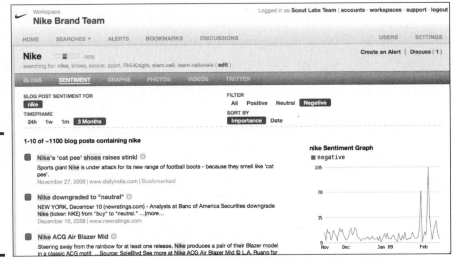

Figure 3-7:
The Lithium
Social
Media
Monitoring
user
interface.

Social Mention
www.socialmention.com

Social Mention is a free service that is very similar to Google Alerts, except that it specifically tracks data from over 80 social media networks. Its real-time, social media, search-and-analysis platform allows you to track and measure what people are saying on Facebook and other social media properties about your company and products. The service can send you daily e-mail alerts of the keywords you want to track. One unique feature of this tool is its analysis service, which reports on the likelihood that your brand is being discussed online, the ratio of positive to negative mentions, the likelihood that people talking about your brand will do so repeatedly, and the number of unique mentions of your brand online. This data is extremely valuable to identify how people feel about your programs and services. See Figure 3-8 to view the Social Mention user interface.

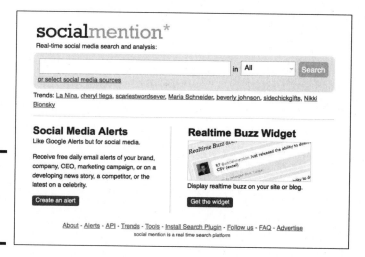

Figure 3-8:
The Social
Mention
user
interface.

Sprout Social

http://sproutsocial.com

Sprout Social monitors key metrics, discussions, and connections with users, and helps businesses to increase brand awareness across demographic groups. A great feature of this tool is the engagement and influence scores. These scores are determined by your engagement activity, as well as by your Fan growth and interest level over time. The tool shows you how your scores compare to the average user as well as gives you advice to help you increase your overall scores. See Figure 3-9 to view the Sprout Social user interface.

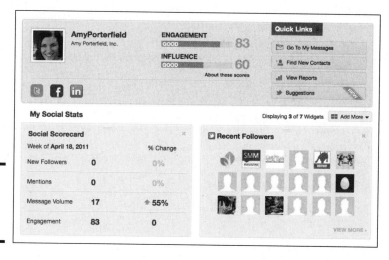

Figure 3-9:
The Sprout
Social user
interface.

SWIX

http://swixhq.com

SWIX helps users compare clicks, costs, and the conversion rates of social marketing efforts so that they can see the return on investment (ROI) of their shares on Facebook. They currently offer two tools, Campaign Manager and Analytics. In a nutshell, the Campaign Manager tracks social media traffic to any Web site, and Analytics is similar to Google Analytics except that it tracks social media metrics. SWIX has a monthly fee structure and offers different fee levels, making it easy for almost everyone to use its tools. One great feature with SWIX is that it allows you to create a scoreboard of all your most important social media metrics. This at-a-glance setup makes tracking your activity and progress over time easy. See Figure 3-10 to view the SWIX user interface.

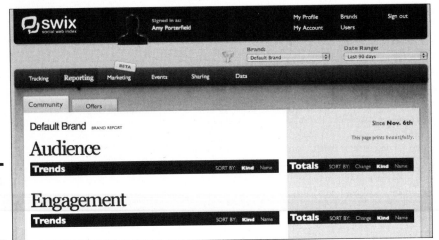

Figure 3-10: The SWIX user interface.

Topsy

http://topsy.com

Topsy is a free, real-time search engine that indexes and ranks search results based upon influential conversations people are having about specific terms, topics, pages, or domains queried. What makes this search engine different than traditional search tools is that it tracks what people are actually talking about, meaning that you see what people think and feel about the topics that are discussed. Understanding the sentiment, the human side of the online conversations, gives you a better understanding of your potential audience. See Figure 3-11 to view the Topsy user interface.

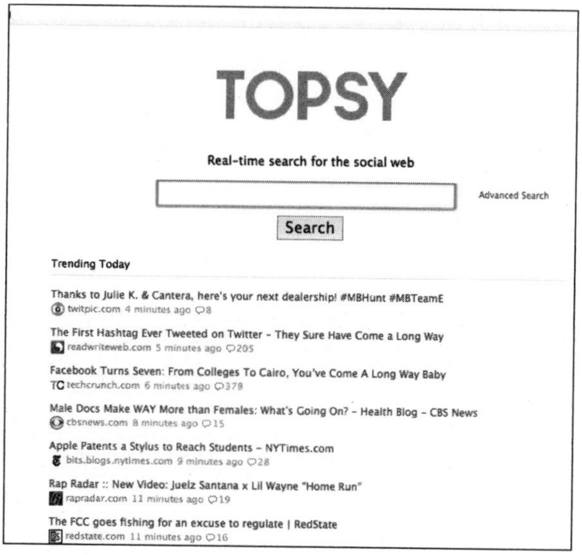

Figure 3-11:
The Topsy
user
interface.

Klout

http://klout.com

Klout is a free influence-tracking tool. It gauges the influence level of any social media user by combining several data points (followers, comments, clicks on links, retweets, and so on). You can use it to identify your most influential customers with the intention to communicate with them, to see who's most influential in your industry, and to find out where you fall into the influence mix as well. After you know your own influence score, you can monitor it to see whether it increases or decreases based on your social activity. This is a great indicator to find out what's working for you. See Figure 3-12 to view the Klout user interface.

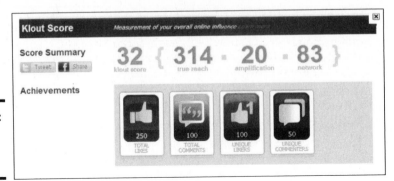

Figure 3-12:
The Klout user interface.

Finding the Biggest Payoff with Your Tracking Efforts

After you are clear about the data you want to collect, you may decide that you need to grab data from Facebook Insights, Google Alerts, and HootSuite. Managing multiple tools takes some organization, no doubt, but if combining tools meets your needs, you should do that.

Specifically, Facebook limits what information third-party developers can access and monitor. That is why it's important to use the data from Insights if you cannot get the data you need from other tools. But as you know, Facebook Insights monitors only activity related to Facebook. Therefore, you need to research third-party tools to expand your monitoring beyond Facebook.

It all comes down to your tracking goals, resources, time, and money. Only you can determine what's best for your business. Here's a tip: The more actions you can link to the results you obtain from your tracking data, the bigger the payoff. If the data you collect helps you streamline your support team, correct a flaw in your product, ignite a new idea for a partnership, and/or solidify new relationships with potential clients, your tracking strategy can then become a vehicle for growing your sales. You can increase the ROI on your time, money, and efforts when you use the data to see real results in your business.

Analyzing Results and Taking Action

One of the ultimate goals of Facebook marketing is to move your Fans to action. To do this, you must try different strategies to discover what works best for your team. That is why monitoring and measuring is key to your success. By analyzing this data, you can strategically decide what your next steps should be.

In this section, we explore how you can create a plan that will help you take the data that is most crucial to your business and put it to action to see real results. In addition, we touch on the importance of eliminating time wasters and being as flexible as possible to make changes to your strategies when challenges arise. In social media marketing, your ability to be able to quickly course correct is critical to your success!

Creating a tracking guide

In Book IX, Chapter 1, we discuss the importance of monitoring and measuring and why it's crucial to the success of your social media plan. Here we show you how to create an overall tracking plan. To streamline your monitoring and measuring process, the key is to create a quick guide for easy reference. The payoff for this extra step is big and worth the time! After you put a plan of action in place (in the form of a tracking guide), the data becomes manageable and you can more easily understand how to use it to your advantage. The result: Having growing numbers of Fans and increasing engagement will not feel like work but instead be an enjoyable experience. What a concept!

Create a monitoring schedule

Inside your company, identify your front line listening and response teams — specifically, who will monitor the data and who will be assigned to respond to the conversations in real-time. These people will be the faces of your company, so choose them wisely! In addition, behind the scenes, who will analyze the data? Look at your team and assign tasks as needed.

When you're putting your monitoring schedule together, remember that quick response is the goal. Therefore, make sure to cover all bases. For example, what is your plan for nights and weekends? If you're not a 24/7 company, one option here is an alerting system. Some third-party tools will send you a text message when a post has been made. Although you don't want this to happen all the time if you have active accounts, when you can't be around a computer, this might be a smart solution. When you're choosing your monitoring tools, be sure to look into alerting features.

In addition, depending on how often you and your team will evaluate the data, decide ahead of time how often you should run reports. We suggest starting with just one report a week to track your progress. As you expand your social media activity overall, and start seeing more engagement, you might want to track biweekly. Also, decide which reports you will run so that they become a weekly automatic task.

Map out an internal and external communication plan with your team

When it comes to your communication plan, you have two paths to explore. First, create an internal path within your company. For your internal path, look at your data and ask, "Who needs to know?" Many small to mid-sized companies have different departments whose staff follow different metrics. We suggest that you meet with your team in advance to clarify what information needs to be sent to specific teams. You should consider the following teams when you create your internal communication plan:

+ Sales

+ Marketing

+ Customer Service

+ Human Resources

+ Research and Development

+ Management and Executives

In addition to looking at your internal team, you should also consider how you will be communicating with your customers and Fans — your *external* path of communication. As you monitor the online conversations, different situations will arise, and you want to be ready for them. Specifically:

+ **How will you respond to people posting questions about your products or services?** And how will you respond when you find someone asking about something related to your area of expertise? Will you offer your support (and, in the process, take advantage of consultative selling)? Plan this strategy in advance to be prepared!

+ **What is your plan for when a crisis arises?** You need to document this plan in advance and identify who on your team should be responding and what responses should be used for specific situations. For example, if you sell products on your Web site and your site goes down, you may have many frustrated customers posting on social networks that your site is not working. A crisis plan for this situation might be to designate one person on your team to always communicate on your social networks when your company is having challenges with your Web site. By informing your Fans and customers right away, you eliminate the potential of negative chatter before it starts.

+ **How will you respond to negative and positive posts?** Make it a goal to respond to all comments about you, good or bad. For example, how will you respond to an angry blogger who posts negative feedback about your #1 product? You want to have your plan in place and your team trained in advance.

✦ **How will you respond to posts on your Wall that are not aligned with the goals that you have set out for your Facebook community?** For example, it's common for some Fans to post promotional details about their products and services to your Wall. This tends to clutter the Page and detracts from the conversations your Fans are having. Define which posts are not acceptable on your Page and how you will address them in advance so that your team will be ready to handle any situation that comes your way.

Allocating manpower and resources from analysis

Once you have been collecting your data consistently, you will begin to see patterns and areas you could tweak for improvement. When you get a clear picture of what you need to do, you'll also need to decide whether additional staff or other resources are needed. As always, focus on the growth of your business, and when making a decision to possibly take on more work or to change what you've been doing, weigh the financial, time, and manpower implications against the overall business goal.

Identifying the time wasters

When considering whether to pursue a particular goal or strategy, ask yourself: Are you doing it because you truly believe that you should or just because everyone else is doing it? With the popularity of social media, this is a common mistake. We hear all the hype over a tool or a strategy and jump on it, thinking that we'll be left behind if we don't use it. The real question you need to ask is, "Does this make sense for my business?" Stay focused on expanding your business and take on only the projects that you expect to produce valuable results.

Making adjustments on the fly

Whether you're a new user of social media marketing or have been doing it for a while, you're likely to stumble at times. Don't get bogged down by these events: The goal is to fail fast and move on. With a tracking system in place, you can identify issues quickly and rectify them before too much damage is done.

Social media moves fast. The good news is that when you do have challenges, if you respond to them quickly, they are more easily forgotten. Remember that the media is always changing, especially Facebook! So if you stay in the know and are aware of trends and behaviors early on, you will have a huge competitive advantage.

Building on your success

As you continue to build momentum with your social media strategy, pay close attention to your own best practices. What strategies are working for you on Facebook? Does a pattern emerge regarding the strategies that are working? Your Fans are likely to respond well to certain things while other engagement attempts of yours will fall flat. As long as you monitor your success and continue to make adjustments on the fly, some clear best practices will surface over time. (Remember what we said earlier: If it ain't broke, don't fix it.) When you find a strategy that is producing good results, continue with it and build on it. Add in more of what is working and abort the strategies that aren't showing you the results you're after.

Index

Q

R

S

Notes

Notes

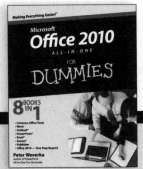
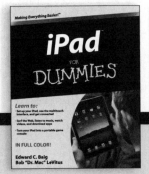

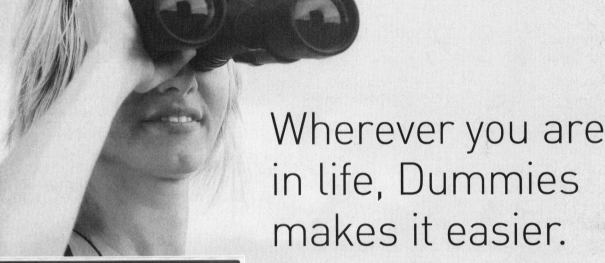

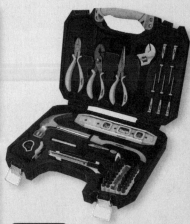